HOMELAND SECURITY
OPERATIONAL ANALYSIS CENTER

The Risk-Mitigation Value of the Transportation Worker Identification Credential

A Comprehensive Security Assessment of the TWIC Program

HEATHER J. WILLIAMS, KRISTIN VAN ABEL, DAVID METZ, JAMES V. MARRONE, EDWARD W. CHAN, KATHERINE COSTELLO, RYAN MICHAEL BAUER, DEVON HILL, SIMON VÉRONNEAU, JOSEPH C. CHANG, IAN MITCH, JOSHUA LAWRENCE TRAUB, SARAH SOLIMAN, ZACHARY HALDEMAN, KELLY KLIMA, DOUGLAS C. LIGOR

Published in 2020

Preface

This report responds to congressionally mandated requirements to conduct a comprehensive security assessment of the Transportation Worker Identification Credential (TWIC®) program. The U.S. Department of Homeland Security (DHS) commissioned the Homeland Security Operational Analysis Center (HSOAC) to conduct this study to address the requirements laid out in Public Law 114-278, Section 1(b), Comprehensive Security Assessment of the Transportation Security Card Program.

The TWIC program includes a security threat assessment to determine whether someone poses a national security, transportation security, or terrorism threat. It also provides for a card credential and requirements for its use at maritime facilities that are regulated by the Maritime Transportation Security Act.[1] Anyone with unescorted access to a secure area at a regulated maritime facility or vessel is required to possess a valid TWIC card.

For this report, HSOAC researchers sought to address TWIC's risk-mitigation value in the maritime environment and analyze the costs and benefits of regulation that would require high-risk facilities to use TWIC in conjunction with an electronic biometric reader. Other issues discussed include the use of TWIC at facilities, the appropriateness of vetting standards, whether the fee structure is appropriate for the current costs of vetting, the time required for TWIC's issuance, and the program's duplication or redundancy with other federal and state credentialing programs.

TWIC's risk-mitigation value lies in its ability to deter attacks against maritime facilities and reduce facilities' vulnerabilities by giving them a means of identifying unauthorized people. TWIC's strength is in preventing people known to be higher risk from gaining persistent access to the maritime environment. However, TWIC is just one component of a multilayered access control solution, so it is not possible to determine the security value of TWIC alone. TWIC can help *detect* threats other than high-risk people gaining access, but, generally, other components of an access control system *prevent* those threats. Also complicating the risk-mitigation assessment is that TWIC's use at ports varies significantly, and many facilities have adopted more-robust access control measures than the bare minimum that regulations require.

In terms of the costs and benefits of the pending regulation for high-risk facilities, the study team found that the specifics of those requirements for TWIC readers could affect many more facilities and cost around 50 percent more than initially estimated. Observations from visits to several ports suggest that there are likely more cost-effective methods of reducing the risk to maritime facilities than requiring everyone to use an electronic biometric reader at every entry

---

[1] Public Law 107-56, Uniting and Strengthening America by Providing Appropriate Tools Required to Intercept and Obstruct Terrorism Act of 2001, October 26, 2001.

into a facility's secure area. Rather than attempting to isolate the risk-mitigation value of TWIC, taking a system approach could determine how to best mitigate security vulnerabilities and where security benefits will have the best return on investment.

This research was sponsored by the Research and Development Partnerships Group in the DHS Science and Technology Directorate and conducted within the Strategy, Policy, and Operations Program of the HSOAC federally funded research and development center (FFRDC).

About the Homeland Security Operational Analysis Center

The Homeland Security Act of 2002 (Section 305 of Public Law 107-296, as codified at 6 U.S.C. § 185), authorizes the Secretary of Homeland Security, acting through the Under Secretary for Science and Technology, to establish one or more FFRDCs to provide independent analysis of homeland security issues. The RAND Corporation operates HSOAC as an FFRDC for DHS under contract HSHQDC-16-D-00007.

The HSOAC FFRDC provides the government with independent and objective analyses and advice in core areas important to the department in support of policy development, decisionmaking, alternative approaches, and new ideas on issues of significance. The HSOAC FFRDC also works with and supports other federal, state, local, tribal, and public- and private-sector organizations that make up the homeland security enterprise. The HSOAC FFRDC's research is undertaken by mutual consent with DHS and is organized as a set of discrete tasks. This report presents the results of research and analysis conducted under task order 70RSATR0000029, Assessing the Risk-Mitigation Value of TWIC® at Maritime Facilities.

The results presented in this report do not necessarily reflect official DHS opinion or policy.

For more information on HSOAC, see www.rand.org/hsoac. For more information on this publication, see www.rand.org/t/RR3096.

Contents

Figures

Tables

Summary

The Transportation Worker Identification Credential (TWIC®) is one of multiple measures introduced by the Maritime Transportation Security Act (MTSA) to enhance security at U.S. ports. Anyone with unescorted access to a secure area at a MTSA-regulated facility,[2] vessel, or outer continental shelf (OCS) facility must have a TWIC card.[3] Congress established TWIC to help prevent a transportation security incident—a security incident that results in a significant loss of life, environment damage, or transportation system or economic disruption. TWIC's primary function is to establish that a Transportation Security Administration (TSA) security threat assessment (STA) is conducted; the TWIC card can also serve as an identification document. Each facility must maintain an access control program at its secure areas and verify three things at every access point: (1) each person's identity, (2) that the person holds a valid TWIC card, and (3) whether the person has a business purpose at that facility. Currently, facilities are required only to conduct visual verification of the TWIC card, either at each time of entry or at time of enrollment into a facility physical access control system (PACS). A pending regulation, "Transportation Worker Identification Credential (TWIC)–Reader Requirements,"[4] which we call the TWIC-reader rule, would require that any facility that the U.S. Coast Guard (USCG) has determined to be of high risk electronically inspect the card and, using biometrics, match it to the holder.[5]

U.S. Government Accountability Office (GAO) reports have criticized the U.S. Department of Homeland Security (DHS) for failing to demonstrate that the TWIC program is effective at reducing risk and improving maritime security.[6] Public Law 114-278, Section 1(b), calls for a comprehensive security assessment on the TWIC program and its value in mitigating risk at ports. Some assessment questions in the law pertain to program administration and whether the vetting standards are appropriate for determining whether someone presents a security risk,

---

[2] By *facility* through this report, we are specifying a MTSA-regulated facility and generally refer only to its regulated secure area where TWIC is required. (Many facilities are defined as secure in their entirety.) We use the terms *facility*, *maritime facility*, and *MTSA-regulated facility* interchangeably throughout this report.

[3] MTSA affects approximately 13,825 vessels, 3,270 facilities, and 56 OCS facilities. Throughout this report, we generally refer to only facilities, given that this is where TWIC is in greatest use, but we include MTSA-regulated facilities, OCS facilities, and vessels as appropriate.

[4] U.S. Coast Guard (USCG), "Transportation Worker Identification Credential (TWIC)–Reader Requirements," *Federal Register*, Vol. 81, No. 163, August 23, 2016, pp. 57652–57713.

[5] The TWIC-reader rule would also require facilities to maintain access logs and check cards against a list of canceled cards.

[6] GAO, *Transportation Worker Identification Credential: Internal Control Weaknesses Need to Be Corrected to Help Achieve Security Objectives*, Washington, D.C., GAO-11-657, May 10, 2011a; GAO, *Transportation Worker Identification Credential: Card Reader Pilot Results Are Unreliable; Security Benefits Need to Be Reassessed*, Washington, D.C., GAO-13-198, May 8, 2013a.

whether the fee structure is appropriate for the current costs of vetting, the time required for TWIC issuance, and whether there might be unnecessary duplication or redundancy with other federal and state credentialing programs. Other assessment questions in the law relate to the way TWIC is used at facilities: whether requiring use of biometric readers at high-risk facilities would yield a benefit greater than their cost; what alternatives exist to biometrics; and what technology, business process, and operational impacts TWIC and electronic readers have on facilities.

Efforts to provide a straightforward answer to the question of TWIC's risk-mitigation value are complicated by the fact that TWIC cannot be separated empirically from the access control programs into which it is integrated. It is important to acknowledge that TWIC cannot mitigate all risks in the maritime environment. Instead, it can influence risk only where gaining physical access to the facility through an entry point is necessary. Yet TWIC is only *one component* of facilities' access control programs, which might also consist of such elements as fencing, security guards, and security cameras. Therefore, TWIC's ability to mitigate the threat of those seeking to gain physical access is directly related to the quality of the access control program as a whole: These security measures work in tandem to deter and deny threats. Furthermore, facilities face many threats that do not require physical access through entry points. For example, attacks in the cyber realm, attacks launched from the water, or attacks using a drone would not necessarily require physical access through a gate or other entry control point. No matter how stringent the STA standards or how robust the inspection methods used at entry points, TWIC cannot reduce the risk presented by threats not requiring physical access.

To understand TWIC's risk-mitigation value as required by Public Law 114-278, Section 1(b), DHS commissioned the Homeland Security Operational Analysis Center to complete this comprehensive assessment. To do so, we collected data from TSA, the USCG, DHS, previous research, and public sources and conducted an extensive site survey of maritime facilities, visiting 45 port areas and conducting 200 interviews. In this report, we establish factors that increase or decrease TWIC's security value, and, in the case of the TWIC-reader rule, we can determine what TWIC's value would need to be to offset the costs of establishing further access control requirements for facilities. Table S.1 lists the sections of the public law and the chapters of this report in which we discuss these issues in more detail.

Table S.1. Crosswalk from Public Law 114-278 to Chapters in This Report

Public Law Paragraph	Focus	Report Chapter
1(b)(3)(A)(i)	Vetting standards	5
1(b)(3)(A)(ii)	Fee structure	5
1(b)(3)(A)(iii)	Redundancy with other credentials	9
1(b)(3)(A)(iv)	Variation among federal and state threat assessments	9
1(b)(3)(B)	The application process	5
1(b)(3)(C)(i)	Known or likely risks at ports	4–7
1(b)(3)(C)(ii)	Nonbiometric alternatives	9
1(b)(3)(C)(iii)	The effects of TWIC and TWIC readers	6–8
1(b)(3)(C)(iv)	Program costs and benefits	5–8
1(b)(3)(C)(v)	Reports by GAO and by the DHS Office of Inspector General	3
1(b)(5)	The final report	All

Findings About the TWIC Vetting Standards and Process

The STA vetting standards are intended to identify people who pose a national security, transportation security, or terrorism risk and to reduce such individuals' ability to access the maritime environment. Although 46 U.S.C. § 70105(c) is titled "Determination of *Terrorism Security Risk*" (emphasis ours), TSA is required to—and does—consider a broader set of risks to national security and transportation security. In addition, 46 U.S.C. § 70105 is broadly written to include a variety of criminal disqualifications, most of which have no specific nexus to terrorism. Questions about the TWIC vetting standards appear to stem often from the security risk that the program is intended to mitigate. One of our interviewees, in raising whether TWIC was an antiterrorism or anticrime program, asked about the purpose of the disqualifying criminal offenses: "Is there a nexus to terrorism?" Facility operators we interviewed often had the expectation that TWIC would enhance general security and therefore reduce the risk that an employee would harm other people at the facility, damage material at the facility, or steal from the facility. For some of these respondents, the STA's standards did too little to protect them from these types of risks.[7] Facility operators do have the authority to determine who is authorized for access and could—and frequently do—perform additional background checks in addition to the STA.

We found the terrorism threat in the maritime environment to be low, given the rare occurrence of terrorist incidents in the maritime sector in the past and the decreased threat of

---

[7] About half of risk group A facilities and about one-third of non–risk group A facilities in our sample suggested that the STA standards were not stringent enough for all types of employees at their facilities.

Risk group A facility is the USCG term for a high-risk facility. Although there were initially risk groups B and C as well, these categories have since been phased out, so a facility is now either a risk group A facility or a non–risk group A facility.

sophisticated terrorist attacks inside the United States since 9/11, which is consistent with the Federal Bureau of Investigation's threat assessment in the maritime sector. MTSA also states that federal crime, such as trafficking and smuggling, was a concern at U.S. ports. An interagency commission in 2000 found that seaports were frequent conduits for this type of crime; but, given the lack of consolidated information on seaport crime data statistics, we cannot ascertain the degree to which these problems persist.

Appropriateness is ultimately a decision based on congressional intent for the TWIC program. The STA would detect known or suspected terrorists who seek to legally gain persistent access to the maritime environment through its check of the terrorist watch list. Specifically when considering threats of terrorism, our review of the literature suggests that past criminality and incarceration are not strong predictors of future terrorism.[8] If the TWIC program's purpose is to prevent only threats to national security, threats to transportation security, and terrorism risk, the vetting standards likely initially disqualify a significant number of people who do not present that level of threat, given that the number of people who present such a threat is very small. A TWIC applicant who meets the disqualification standards but can demonstrate that they do not present a risk to national security or transportation security or of terrorism may apply for a waiver. Criminal background checks can also contribute to the general security of the maritime environment, so the vetting standards are not wholly inappropriate in that they might have utility in reducing crime. Determining whether standards are appropriate requires a clear understanding of what TWIC is—and is not—intended to achieve. The federal government and industry might have different objectives in determining risk, with the federal government focused on risks to national security and transportation sector and of terrorism, and with industry also concerned about profits and worker safety. This means that there might be inherent tension between (1) how stringent the criminal-history standards are and (2) how satisfied stakeholders are with the TWIC program. Overall, TWIC standards and the redress process attempt to strike a balance between the two camps. This balance trends toward a higher risk tolerance given that a single vetting standard must apply to the entire population working in the maritime sector—a population of more than 2 million people—and that management for a facility may choose to adopt additional criteria beyond TWIC vetting standards to satisfy its specific security needs.

---

[8] The National Consortium for the Study of Terrorism and Responses to Terrorism, the University of Massachusetts Lowell, Indiana State University, and Paul Gill et al. have looked at criminal history as one of a combination of risk factors related to terrorism. In these studies, researchers have found that criminal history, among other risk factors, can suggest a slightly higher likelihood of engaging in terrorism. Crimes were wide ranging and of a variety levels of severity. Literature evaluating the performance of risk-assessment tools—which use a multitude of risk factors rather than simply prior criminal history—suggests that such tools are better than relying on chance but not by much. Many of the tools rely on the structured professional judgment of clinicians or analysts about the importance of different risk factors on a case-by-case basis and are not intended to provide reliable results for screening a population en masse.

Some of those we interviewed brought up historical concerns about the rollout and early administration of the TWIC program, such as the length of the processes for TWIC issuance and resolution of waivers. These were also areas of historical concern noted in reports by GAO and the DHS Office of Inspector General. TSA has improved the process significantly, and, when queried during our interviews, many respondents felt that TWIC cards were now being issued promptly. Around half of TWIC applicants receive their TWIC cards within a week of application, and more than 99 percent of applicants receive initial adjudication of their applications in less than 30 days. For people who seek redress, the average processing time in 2018 (as of October 1, 2018) was 26 days for an appeal request and 47 days for a waiver request.[9]

In terms of costs, the STA is actually comparable to or more cost-efficient than private background checks, considering that it includes continuous monitoring of holders and a high-quality card credential. However, not all interviewees perceived this value because (1) they might have been unaware that there is continuous monitoring for TWIC holders and saw TWIC as a one-time background check; (2) they had not chosen to use TSA's list of canceled cards, so the TWIC screening essentially *was* a one-time background check; (3) they were not aware of the differences between a private company's terrorism check and the government's or the interviewees' companies were not concerned about a terrorism threat; or (4) they felt that the TWIC standards were too low to be effective.

Findings About TWIC Use at Ports and the Value of TWIC Readers

As indicated above, risk tolerances varied greatly among facilities. This is perhaps not surprising, given dramatic differences in facility features, such as size, type of industry, proximity to population centers, and number of people needing access. These differences affect a facility's vulnerabilities, as well as the possible consequence of a terrorist event or other catastrophic attack, which therefore affects risk.

Our review of past attacks in the U.S. maritime environment suggests that the threat of a highly damaging incident in the maritime environment is low. Crime, including organized crime, is a concern at ports, although criminals generally do not seek to disrupt commerce the way a transportation security incident would. Facility interviewees were in general agreement that identity assurance and background checks are beneficial security measures to mitigate risk, though they were considering a wide range of risks to their business and profitability. Some specifically credited TWIC with improving the general security environment at their facilities and had little to no identity assurance or access control measures prior to TWIC's introduction.

---

[9] TSA, *Transportation Worker Identification Credential Appeal Timelines Fiscal Year 2019 Report to Congress*, February 1, 2019.

Others felt that TWIC's standards were equal to or less than security measures they were already implementing at their facilities.

In particular, facility interviewees' opinions differed about whether having federal authorities conduct background checks directly was efficient. In the past ten years, many facilities have integrated TWIC into their security procedures; if federal authorities no longer conducted STAs, management of those facilities would need to significantly reconfigure their procedures in a way that could be disruptive and costly. Although many of the people we interviewed were critical of or frustrated by TWIC, few actively advocated for its abolition. The pending TWIC-reader rule requires the use of electronic biometric readers and seeks to eliminate possible human error in the inspection of TWIC holders at higher-risk facilities. Respondents we interviewed at those high-risk facilities often strongly objected to the need to perform biometric identity assurance as a matter of risk mitigation.[10] They did not perceive that the government had presented sufficient evidence to prove the security value (essentially, that the benefits outweigh the costs) in using biometrics for access control in the maritime environment. We conducted a revised break-even analysis, consistent with the USCG's regulatory analysis related to the TWIC-reader rule, and our updated results suggest that the costs of electronic biometric card readers (under the parameters set by the pending rule) likely exceed the benefit to industry. This is because readers are ultimately costly and mitigate only certain types of threats, forcing facilities to prioritize a source of vulnerability that might not be the most jeopardizing in their specific circumstances. The uncertainty about whether readers will be required and, if so, for which facilities—now undetermined for 18 years[11]—creates market instability that drives up costs of readers and might deter facilities from acting unilaterally to adopt the use of electronic readers (because they do not want to make investments that might not comply with future regulations).

This is not to say that readers do not enhance security, and readers might be a beneficial and worthwhile investment for facilities (and vessels). Many facilities already do more than the minimum required for access control. Many use PACSs and proximity card readers, which provide electronic verification that credentials (whether TWIC or a facility-specific badge) are authentic, valid, and not expired. A few have adopted other means of screening that increase their confidence in the reliability of authorized people; some chemical facilities conduct drug tests, and many offshore platforms screen all personnel for weapons. Some have even found that the use of electronic biometric readers can be both cost saving and security enhancing, given that they can automate gates and therefore reassign security and law-enforcement officers to other

---

[10] The USCG initially designated three risk groups—A, B, and C—however, on August 23, 2016, the USCG decided to collapse the designation between risk groups B and C. Therefore, high-risk facilities are often called risk group A facilities, with other facilities called non–risk group A facilities. Facilities that handle vessels carrying more than 1,000 passengers, U.S.-flagged vessels carrying more than 1,000 passengers with more than 20 crew members, and facilities handling CDC fall into risk group A. U.S.-flagged vessels carrying more than 1,000 passengers with fewer than 20 crew members are technically also in risk group A, but they are exempt from the TWIC-reader rule.

[11] MTSA was initially implemented in 2002 and envisioned that TWIC cards would be used in conjunction with TWIC readers. The first proposed rulemaking to introduce TWIC readers was issued in 2006.

security functions. The TWIC card allows for a variety of modes, such that facilities can adopt additional measures that bring greater assurances of card authenticity and identity verification, short of all the requirements of electronic inspection required in the TWIC-reader rule. Interviewees from quite a few facilities told us that they appreciated electronic readers for other reasons, such as a better accountability for personnel at the facility in case of an emergency. Given these benefits, industry might, over time, adopt security-enhancing measures, such as electronic readers, without such measures being mandated.

Findings About TWIC's Security Value

The maritime sector faces a variety of risks, with different threat actors, methods, and objectives. The TWIC program is strongest in reducing the risk presented by a known or suspected terrorist who seeks to attack a maritime facility that would require persistent insider access via possession of a TWIC. The STA process would detect these people, presumably denying them a TWIC (or deterring the person from applying), and such a person would have difficulty maintaining continual access to a facility without a valid TWIC card. The TWIC card is similarly effective in reducing the risk from someone with a disqualifying criminal history who would have been willing to engage in illicit activity at the facility, such as smuggling, that might aid a terrorist group.

TWIC's STA prevents such a person from becoming a trusted insider at a facility. Although readers would reduce the human error in detecting a counterfeit TWIC or a TWIC being used by someone other than the person to whom it was issued, a competent security guard conducting the appropriate visual inspection of a TWIC should detect someone seeking to gain entry over an extended period. The major exception to this case would be someone who had initially passed the STA; had been issued a valid TWIC; and had been found, prior to the TWIC's expiration, to have possible terrorist ties. In circumstances in which such a person's TWIC card is revoked but cannot be recovered by law-enforcement officials, use of an electronic card reader in conjunction with the Canceled Card List would dramatically increase the chances of detection.

The TWIC program is less effective at stopping threats for which an attacker (or attackers) seeks one-time access to a facility to conduct an attack and is not easily deterred in gaining entry. Such an attacker would have a variety of attack paths from which to choose in conducting an attack, some of which do not require legally gaining authorized access. The TWIC program might provide some additional ability to detect these threats. A TWIC card reader could increase the likelihood that invalid TWIC cards are detected, and biometrics provide a robust mechanism for identity verification. The value of detection in mitigating risk, however, is still dependent on the capacity for prevention. The ability to prevent such a threat is determined by other mechanisms at the entry point, such as the guard, PACS, or deployable physical barriers. An attacker could also choose an attack path that circumvents entry points entirely, such as via the waterside or online.

Our review of reported breaches of security at facilities over a five-year period suggests that people more often gain unauthorized access to facilities via other means (e.g., climbing over a fence, entering from the water, sneaking past an unattended gate, hiding in a vehicle) than by using an invalid TWIC. The most damaging maritime attack against a U.S. facility in recent history was in the cyber realm and required no physical facility access—the NotPetya cyberattack, which temporarily halted U.S.-based terminal operations of container shipper Maersk.[12] Our analysis of the threats to the maritime environment suggests that the threats that TWIC is best intended to mitigate are present but not the most pressing. But even if low probability, these threats could be high impact. Policymakers will need to determine whether such a trade-off is appropriate in relation to the TWIC program as currently implemented.

The pending TWIC-reader rule would require additional identity assurance and credential authentication mechanisms in the program's requirements. These requirements would increase the potential for threats to be detected, but, in our interviews with experts, detection did not appear to be the primary problem for facilities. For example, TWIC readers were identified in the regulatory analysis supporting the TWIC-reader rule as beneficial in reducing the threat of truck bombs. However, facilities are not required to have bollards or physical barriers at the facility that could be deployed quickly to prevent a truck bomb from entering the facility if identified.

The current requirements of the TWIC-reader rule could also be adjusted to reduce costs, thereby making it more favorably balanced in relation to commensurate benefit. The USCG could reduce the affected population, by refining the definition of *high-risk facility*, to bring a more favorable cost–benefit estimate for TWIC readers, or make adjustments to the requirements for electronic inspection, such as requiring them only intermittently. It could also reexamine secure areas to refine the locations where a TWIC card is required. However, our study does not prove that further investment in TWIC is the most efficient security investment for facilities, and our observations during the port visits suggest that there are likely more cost-effective methods of reducing the risk that maritime facilities face. In addition, there might be lower-cost options to bring greater security value from the TWIC program as currently implemented. For example, TSA is developing a mobile application that allows facilities using only visual inspection to check the Canceled Card List at essentially zero cost. To better serve maritime security, rather than attempting to isolate TWIC's risk-mitigation value, the federal government, by taking a system approach, could determine how to best mitigate security vulnerabilities and where security benefits will have the greatest return on investment.

---

[12] Kim S. Nash, Sara Castellanos, and Adam Janofsky, "One Year After NotPetya Cyberattack, Firms Wrestle with Recovery Costs," *Wall Street Journal*, June 27, 2018.

Acknowledgments

This research involved the dedicated and contributions of multiple colleagues to whom we are extremely grateful. Debra Knopman served as a senior adviser for our effort initially and stepped into a larger capacity assisting our team when a need arose. Anu Narayanan also assisted in developing our risk analysis methods and was always available as a sounding board for ideas. Jason Michel Etchegaray advised our interview team, providing insights on best practices for interview structure, coding methods, and qualitative research. Jonathan William Welburn helped shape our thinking of questions about risk and adaptive adversaries and assisted with our study of biometrics. Keith Gierlack and Brodi Kotila provided assistance in the regulatory history of the Transportation Worker Identification Credential (TWIC®). John Plumb led our trip to San Francisco and participated in other site surveys. Katherine F. Tiongson allowed us to tap into her wealth of wisdom and expertise built from a USCG career. Abbie Tingstad played a key role in our risk and operational analysis early in the study and always remained an interested and supporting party. David Richardson provided consummate administrative support.

Many other colleagues at RAND assisted with critical questions and expert input. We thank Karen Sudkamp for assisting with research on the possible nexus between criminality and terrorism and on criminality at ports. Bryce Downing carefully reviewed reports from the U.S. Government Accountability Office and the U.S. Department of Homeland Security Office of Inspector General. Victoria A. Greenfield provided welcome advice and feedback on our break-even analysis. Michelle Grisé lent legal assistance on TWIC standards and alternative models. Mark Toukan provided useful information on deterrence theory and access control systems. Colin P. Clarke helped advise and guide our terrorism threat analysis. Our colleagues Jennifer Lamping Lewis, Douglas C. Ligor, Sheng Tao Li, Norah Griffin, Sean McKenna, Patricia K. Tong, Thomas Light, Brian Briscombe, Barbara Bicksler, and Anne Stickells conducted and provided the analysis on TWIC fees. We thank Melissa Bauman for her review and advice on the structure and flow of our final report. Our quality assurance reviewers, Brian A. Jackson, Andrew R. Morral, Philip S. Anton, Ryan Consaul, and Charlene Downey, provided invaluable advice, critique, expertise, and support. Thanks also to Lara Schmidt, the Strategy, Policy, and Operations Program leadership team, and the Homeland Security Operational Analysis Center operations team.

We are also extremely grateful to everyone who participated in our study or otherwise provided assistance. This includes facility operators and security officers who allowed us to visit their facilities and participated in interviews. We benefited from incredible hospitality and transparency during those conversations. We would like to also thank personnel from vendor and trade organizations who patiently answered our questions and flagged useful information for us. A debt of gratitude also exists to USCG sector personnel who assisted us in selecting and contacting facilities and in providing their own insights and guidance to us during our site surveys. The Federal Emergency Management Agency also provided extremely useful information on its Port Security Grant Program and answered our multiple rounds of follow-up questions. And, last but by no means least, we give an incredible thanks to our project sponsors at the U.S. Department of Homeland Security, the Transportation Security Administration, and the USCG for enabling us to do this research and their support throughout.

Abbreviations

ACS	American Community Survey
ATSA	Aviation and Transportation Security Act
CCL	Canceled Card List
CDC	certain dangerous cargo
CHRC	criminal-history record check
CIN	credential identification number
CMS	card management system
CRA	consumer reporting agency
CSOC	Colorado Springs Operations Center
DHS	U.S. Department of Homeland Security
DOB	date of birth
DOJ	U.S. Department of Justice
DOJ	U.S. Department of Transportation
EED	Extended Expiration Date
FBI	Federal Bureau of Investigation
FEMA	Federal Emergency Management Agency
FFRDC	federally funded research and development center
FSO	facility security officer
FSP	facility security plan
FY	fiscal year
GAO	U.S. Government Accountability Office
GDP	gross domestic product
GPA	Georgia Ports Authority
GPO	U.S. Government Publishing Office
GTD	Global Terrorism Database
hazmat	hazardous material
HME	Hazardous Materials Endorsement
HSOAC	Homeland Security Operational Analysis Center
HVE	homegrown violent extremist
I&A	Office of Intelligence and Analysis (U.S. Department of Homeland Security)
IBIA	International Biometrics and Identity Association
ID	identification
IDENT	Automated Biometric Identification System
IED	improvised explosive device
ILA	International Longshoremen's Association
ILWU	International Longshore and Warehouse Union
ISIS	Islamic State of Iraq and Syria
IT	information technology
LPR	lawful permanent resident
MARSEC	Maritime Security (U.S. Coast Guard system)
MISLE	Marine Information for Safety and Law Enforcement
MPI	Migration Policy Institute

MSRAM	Maritime Security Risk Analysis Model
MRSP	manufacturer's suggested retail price
MTSA	Maritime Transportation Security Act
N/A	not applicable
NCIC	National Crime Information Center
NCTC	National Counterterrorism Center
NDC	Navigation and Civil Works Decision Support Center
NIJ	National Institute of Justice
NIST	National Institute of Standards and Technology
NPRM	notice of proposed rulemaking
NVIC	navigation and vessel inspection circular
OCS	outer continental shelf
OFAC	Office of Foreign Assets Control
OIG	Office of Inspector General (U.S. Department of Homeland Security)
OMB	Office of Management and Budget
OPM	U.S. Office of Personnel Management
PACS	physical access control system
PDI	preliminary determination of ineligibility
PII	personally identifying information
PIN	personal identification number
PSS	port security specialist
QTL	Qualified Technology List
RIN	risk index number
RORO	roll on/roll off
SAFE Port Act	Security and Accountability for Every Port Act of 2006
SAVE	Systematic Alien Verification for Entitlements
SIDA	Security Identification Display Area
SME	subject-matter expert
SPOP	Strategy, Policy, and Operations Program
S&T	Science and Technology Directorate (U.S. Department of Homeland Security)
STA	security threat assessment
START	National Consortium for the Study of Terrorism and Responses to Terrorism
TEU	20-foot-equivalent unit
TIDE	Terrorist Identities Datamart Environment
TIM	Technology Infrastructure Modernization
TSA	Transportation Security Administration
TSDB	Terrorist Screening Database
TSI	transportation security incident
TVS	Transportation Vetting System
TWIC	Transportation Worker Identification Credential
UES	Universal Enrollment Services
USA PATRIOT	Uniting and Strengthening America by Providing Appropriate Tools Required to Intercept and Obstruct Terrorism
USCG	U.S. Coast Guard
VSL	value of a statistical life

1. Introduction

The U.S. Department of Homeland Security (DHS) asked the Homeland Security Operational Analysis Center (HSOAC), a federally funded research and development center operated by the RAND Corporation, to conduct a comprehensive security assessment of the Transportation Worker Identification Credential (TWIC®) program, as required by Public Law 114-278, 2016. The study reported here fulfills the requirements in Section 1(b) and complements earlier HSOAC work related to Section 1(a) on improving the Transportation Security Administration's (TSA) credentialing process for vetting TWIC applicants.

Background on TWIC

TWIC is a biometric credential that is required for unescorted entry to secure areas of vessels, outer continental shelf (OCS) facilities, and port facilities regulated by the Maritime Transportation Security Act (MTSA) of 2002,[13] as well as for credentialed merchant mariners.[14] The TWIC program has two core components. The first is the security threat assessment (STA) that TSA performs to determine whether someone presents a security risk. If an applicant passes this STA, TSA issues the applicant a biometric-enabled card credential—a TWIC card. Almost 2.3 million people nationwide currently hold the credential, which is valid for five years.[15]

Administered jointly by TSA and the U.S. Coast Guard (USCG), the program is part of a layered approach to security intended to deter and prevent a transportation security incident (TSI) in the maritime realm. The Maritime Transportation Security Act (MTSA) defines a TSI as "a security incident resulting in a significant loss of life, environmental damage, transportation

---

[13] Public Law 107-295, Maritime Transportation Security Act of 2002, November 25, 2002. MTSA regulates "approximately 13,825 vessels, 3,270 facilities, and 56 Outer Continental Shelf (OCS) facilities" (USCG, "Transportation Worker Identification Credential (TWIC)–Reader Requirements," *Federal Register*, Vol. 81, No. 163, August 23, 2016, p. 57654). If a vessel, port facility, or OCS facility has a secure area, it is subject to TWIC requirements (USCG, "Transportation Worker Identification Credential (TWIC) Implementation in the Maritime Sector; Hazardous Materials Endorsement for a Commercial Driver's License," final rule and request for comments, *Federal Register*, Vol. 72, No. 16, January 25, 2007, p. 3492; USCG, 2016, p. 57654). Throughout this report, we generally refer to only facilities, given that they are where TWIC is in greatest use, but this includes MTSA-regulated facilities, OCS facilities, and vessels as appropriate.

The term *secure area* is defined as "the area over which the owner/operator has implemented security measures for access control in accordance with [its] security plan" (Commandant, U.S. Coast Guard [USCG], *Guidance for the Implementation of the Transportation Worker Identification Credential [TWIC] Program in the Maritime Sector*, Washington, D.C., Navigation and Vessel Inspection Circular 03-07, July 2, 2007, p. 4).

[14] A merchant mariner credential is required for all crew members of U.S. ships with a gross register tonnage higher than 100 and for all vessels that are required to operate with a licensed master, regardless of size.

[15] TSA, *Transportation Worker Identification Credential Appeal Timelines Fiscal Year 2019 Report to Congress*, February 1, 2019.

system disruption, or economic disruption in a particular area."[16] The TWIC program's purpose is to

> enhance the security of ports by requiring such security threat assessments of persons in secure areas and by improving access control measures to prevent those who may pose a security threat from gaining unescorted access to secure areas of ports.[17]

As we discuss in greater depth in Chapter 5, the statute provides a definition of *transportation security incident* but no standard or threshold of what constitutes a significant loss of life or a security threat. Although the definition of *TSI* does not include the word *terrorism*, terrorism was a core driver in the establishment of MTSA, the Security and Accountability for Every Port Act of 2006 (SAFE Port Act), and the TWIC program.[18] Terrorism has been the primary purpose referenced in discussions of TWIC program objectives documented in the congressional record. MTSA, however, identifies that greater identity assurance can bring benefits in deterring and preventing port cargo crimes and smuggling, as well as terrorist actions.[19] The disqualifying offenses included in the STA (as directed by Congress) suggest that it is also not intended to be an encompassing crime-reducing program at ports. For example, although smuggling and racketeering are disqualifying offenses for TWIC holders, theft—a major cause of crime at ports—is not. Even if TWIC were capable of bringing benefits in reducing local or petty crime, those alone would not be sufficient justification for government intervention in a largely private industry.[20]

A TWIC does not give the holder the right to enter a maritime facility. Operators of MTSA-regulated facilities determine who is authorized to have access to those facilities' secure areas. A facility must ensure that every unescorted person in its secure areas has passed an STA, validate their identity, and verify that they have a business purpose. Possession of a valid TWIC indicates that the holder has passed an STA and is one way of validating identity, but it does not verify

---

[16] Pub. L. 107-295, 2002. This definition is codified at U.S. Code, Title 46, Shipping; Subtitle VII, Security and Drug Enforcement; Chapter 701, Port Security; Subchapter I, General; Section 70101, Definitions.

[17] USCG, 2007, p. 3492.

[18] The SAFE Port Act is Public Law 109-347, Security and Accountability for Every Port Act of 2006, or the SAFE Port Act, October 13, 2006. According to Code of Federal Regulations, Title 49, Transportation; Subtitle B, Other Regulations Relating to Transportation (Continued); Chapter XII, Transportation Security Administration, Department of Homeland Security; Subchapter D, Maritime and Land Transportation Security; Part 1570, General Rules, and Code of Federal Regulations, Title 49, Transportation; Subtitle B, Other Regulations Relating to Transportation (Continued); Chapter XII, Transportation Security Administration, Department of Homeland Security; Subchapter D, Maritime and Land Transportation Security; Part 1572, Credentialing and Security Threat Assessments, which relate specifically to TWIC's STA, the purpose of the STA is to identify those who present a security threat. *Security threat* is defined in 49 C.F.R. § 1570.3 as "an individual whom TSA determines or suspects of posing a threat to national security; to transportation security; or of terrorism."

[19] Pub. L. 107-295, 2002.

[20] As we discuss in greater depth in Chapter 2, maritime facilities operate under a variety of structures. Common ones are state and county port authorities that lease facilities to private operators. Another example would be a wholly private operator on private land.

that the holder has a business purpose. Currently, the USCG requires that only visual inspection be used to authenticate and validate cards. But—as we discuss extensively later in this report—a recent rulemaking, which is currently delayed, would require that the card be used in conjunction with electronic biometric card readers as an access control measure for validating the authenticity of a TWIC card and verifying the identity of the TWIC cardholder.

Assessment Questions Raised in Public Law 114-278

Public Law 114-278 Section 1(b) poses a wide range of questions about the TWIC program to be addressed in our research study.[21] The primary question is whether the program is effective at "enhancing security" and "reducing security risks for [MTSA-regulated] facilities."[22] This question of effectiveness, which ties into other aspects of the law, as noted later, is not simply whether TWIC has risk-mitigation value but also whether that risk-mitigation value offsets the costs that the law imposes.

Sections 1(b)(3)(A) and 1(b)(3)(B) call for a review of the credentialing process, including the vetting standards used in the TSA process, to determine whether it is appropriate. The law calls for this study to examine the card's fee; the length of time required to review applications, appeal, and waiver requests; and whether the TWIC card is redundant or duplicative of other federal- or state-issued transportation security credentials or access control programs.

Section 1(b)(3)(C) expands on questions about TWIC's security value: (1) To what extent does TWIC, as currently implemented, address known or likely security risks in the maritime and port environments? (2) Is a nonbiometric credential alternative possible? (3) What are the

---

[21] Public Law 114-278, an act to require the Secretary of Homeland Security to prepare a comprehensive security assessment of the transportation security card program and for other purposes, December 16, 2016. The exact language of Section 1(b) that is relevant to the contents of this study is as follows:

> (b) COMPREHENSIVE SECURITY ASSESSMENT OF THE TRANSPORTATION SECURITY CARD PROGRAM.—(3) CONTENTS.—The assessment commissioned under paragraph (1) shall—(A) review the credentialing process by determining—(i) the appropriateness of vetting standards; (ii) whether the fee structure adequately reflects the current costs of vetting; (iii) whether there is unnecessary redundancy or duplication with other Federal- or State-issued transportation security credentials; and (iv) the appropriateness of having varied Federal and State threat assessments and access controls; (B) review the process for renewing applications for Transportation Worker Identification Credentials, including the number of days it takes to review application, appeal, and waiver requests for additional information; and (C) review the security value of the Program by—(i) evaluating the extent to which the Program, as implemented, addresses known or likely security risks in the maritime and port environments; (ii) evaluating the potential for a non-biometric credential alternative; (iii) identifying the technology, business process, and operational impacts of the use of the transportation security card and transportation security card readers in the maritime and port environments; (iv) assessing the costs and benefits of the Program, as implemented; and (v) evaluating the extent to which the Secretary of Homeland Security has addressed the deficiencies in the Program identified by the Government Accountability Office and the Inspector General of the Department of Homeland Security before the date of enactment of this Act.

[22] Pub. L. 114-278, 2016, § 1(b)(1).

technology, business process, and operational impacts of card readers and the credential itself? (4) What are the costs and benefits of TWIC as currently implemented?

Many of these questions raised in Public Law 114-278 highlight issues identified in the U.S. Government Accountability Office (GAO) and DHS Office of Inspector General (OIG) inquiries into TWIC. Section 1(b)(3)(C) specifically calls for our research study to evaluate the extent to which these previous program deficiencies have been addressed.

Data Sources and Our Approach to the Research Questions

This is the first comprehensive security assessment of the TWIC program, and we collected information from a variety of sources to better understand maritime facilities and answer the many research questions posed by Public Law 114-278. We conducted an extensive literature review, including material about access control programs and deterrence—particularly in the context of counterterrorism, the terrorist threat in the maritime environment, the possible nexus between crime and terrorism, and background check programs. We thoroughly examined material related to the TWIC program, including GAO and OIG studies on the TWIC program and regulations relevant to TWIC. We also reviewed information in USCG and TSA policy documents related to TWIC, which includes TSA's TWIC technical advisories, the USCG's navigation and vessel inspection circulars (NVICs), policy letters from the USCG's TWIC/MTSA Policy Advisory Council, and TWIC-specific documents produced by the TSA Office of Intelligence and Analysis's (I&A's) Maritime Branch and the USCG's Office of Port and Facility Compliance. The USCG's regulatory analysis in 2015, *Transportation Worker Identification Credential (TWIC)–Reader Requirements: Final Rule—Regulatory Analysis and Final Regulatory Flexibility Analysis* specifically discusses the costs and benefits of TWIC readers,[23] and we used this as the foundation for our own analysis on the topic.

We also utilized data from two USCG databases. The first, the Marine Information for Safety and Law Enforcement (MISLE) system, provides information about significant events and USCG actions in the maritime environment nationwide. The USCG uses MISLE "to schedule and record operational activities such as vessel boardings, facility inspections, marine casualty investigations, pollution response actions, breaches of security, law enforcement actions, and search and rescue operations."[24] USCG personnel enter information directly into MISLE, or information is drawn from documents submitted to or collected by the USCG. In essence, MISLE is the activity log for the regulated maritime environment. Specifically, we used data that

---

[23] Office of Standards Evaluation and Development, Standards Evaluation and Analysis Division, U.S. Coast Guard, *Transportation Worker Identification Credential (TWIC)–Reader Requirements: Final Rule—Regulatory Analysis and Final Regulatory Flexibility Analysis*, Washington, D.C., USCG-2007-28915, November 2015.

[24] USCG, "Privacy Impact Assessment for the Marine Information for Safety and Law Enforcement (MISLE)," DHS/USCG/PIA-008, September 3, 2009.

facilities reported to the USCG on attempted and successful breaches of security at their locations, as well as TWIC inspection–related data.

The second, the Maritime Security Risk Analysis Model (MSRAM), is a USCG-developed tool and database for understanding risk for a variety of maritime targets, including facilities. USCG port security specialists (PSSs), using their subject-matter expertise and inputs from facilities, enter data that are then used to calculate a vulnerability score and estimate of consequence under the assumption of one of several potential threat scenarios. The USCG's 2015 regulatory analysis on the TWIC-reader rule used information from MSRAM to estimate the benefits of enhancing access control and security measures at U.S. maritime facilities and on U.S.-flagged vessels. To do so, the USCG estimated the consequence of three types of attacks in which TWIC was seen to play a threat-mitigating role—truck bombs, terrorist assault teams, and passenger or passerby explosives and improvised explosive devices (IEDs). To calculate the potential consequence of terrorist attacks, including the number of affected facilities, we drew on the USCG's previous analysis of MSRAM and present our own analysis in Chapter 8. For more information about MSRAM, see Appendix C.

Last, to understand how TWIC is used in practice and the security environment at MTSA-regulated facilities, we conducted an extensive study of the port environment. We conducted 200 interviews with facility operators, security professionals, industry representatives, and labor representatives, covering 164 facilities in 45 port areas. Our goal in these visits was to provide an inclusive look at ports and facilities by observing a sample of ports and facilities that might best represent typical and relevant atypical TWIC operations. Given the timeline and scope of this assessment, we were not able to develop a representative sample of the TWIC population. We developed an initial sampling method, gathered input from TSA and the USCG, and augmented this list with referral sampling from our visits. Most of our interviews were with facility security officers (FSOs). By law, an FSO is required to have knowledge of the facility's security organization, security systems and their operational limitations, and current security threats. Interviews were confidential, and we used a semistructured interview protocol to ask questions on TWIC and security-related themes. This means that we did not ask the same set of questions to all respondents but tailored our interviews given time constraints, the respondent's knowledge of the topic, and each question's applicability to the facility or port. We designed our interview structure to elicit fact and expert opinion on facility operations, access control vulnerabilities, access control policy and procedures, and past threats and security incidents at facilities. Interview data provided critical inputs in understanding the maritime environment, especially given the dearth of concrete quantitative data about risk in the maritime environment and the variance between facilities (as discussed in more detail in Chapter 2). We formally coded and analyzed our interview content. In evaluating our data, we considered representativeness and concurrence, which is consistent with recognized qualitative research practices.[25] For a complete description of the method we used to determine which ports to visit and whom to interview, see Appendix A.

We elected to use a semistructured interview approach rather than conduct a structured data call in the form of a survey on the TWIC program for several reasons. First, using an interview protocol allowed us to elicit more-comprehensive, -nuanced, and -detailed answers on the TWIC program, which were necessary to answer the questions in Public Law 114-278. Second, semistructured interviews provided flexibility, given the complexities of the port environment, to adjust interviews to solicit the most-relevant information depending on the interviewee's responsibilities and the nature of the facility. Third, interviews allowed us to clarify respondent answers, whereas a survey would typically lend itself to closed-ended questions. Fourth, in-person visits allowed our team to see firsthand the various configurations and operations of facilities—something that is not easily communicated through a data call. Finally, we did not have adequate time in the schedule to develop and test a survey instrument and approach that would (1) yield meaningful results initially, given the complexity of the space and the assessment time frame and (2) allow for appropriate follow-up with survey respondents to support interpretation of the results.[26] Ensuring adequate response rates for surveys is always challenging, particularly when respondents are unsure about surveyors' intentions. Our interview approach also allowed to us to build confidence with respondents that our data-collection effort was independent from the government and confidential. One implication of our approach is that, although it allowed our team to identify a range of possible concerns and issues related to TWIC, our results might not be generalizable to the full MTSA-regulated facility population. In other words, we cannot concretely say that a concern is held or problem is experienced among a specific percentage of facilities or TWIC holders. A structured data call might be able to provide such insights, provided that a sample could be representative. (It is difficult to even determine what a representative sample would be, given challenges with information about ports, facilities, and TWIC stakeholders, as discussed in greater detail in Appendix A.) A structured data call could also be more useful for collecting factual information, such as physical attributes about facilities (e.g., size, number of access control points, current modes of access control programs, the number of readers in use at a facility). A structured data call would be useful to conduct if

---

[25] Greg Guest, Arwen Bunce, and Laura Johnson, "How Many Interviews Are Enough? An Experiment with Data Saturation and Variability," *Field Methods*, Vol. 18, No. 1, February 2006, pp. 59–82; Anton J. Kuzel, "Sampling in Qualitative Inquiry," in Benjamin F. Crabtree and William L. Miller, ed., *Doing Qualitative Research*, Newbury Park, Calif.: Sage Publications, 1992, pp. 31–44; A. Kimball Romney, Susan C. Weller, and William H. Batchelder, "Culture as Consensus: A Theory of Culture and Informant Accuracy," *American Anthropologist*, Vol. 88, No. 2, June 1986, pp. 313–338.

[26] Even if we had determined that we had enough time to field a survey, we could not identify, early in the project, a comprehensive list of current FSOs or other security managers who would be most appropriate to complete a data call. (We discovered that facility personnel change frequently enough that this is a challenge for the USCG.)

Congress were considering major changes to the TWIC program and would like to identify their potential operational effects on facilities.

These various sources of data that we were able to collect helped us bound the risk space within the maritime environment, TWIC's orientation toward those risks, and the practical experience of maritime facilities in employing TWIC as one measure of security infrastructure. We also considered a variety of modeling and structured approaches to evaluating TWIC's risk-mitigation role, but the diversity of how TWIC is integrated into other security measures at facilities and of risk among those facilities themselves severely limits the utility of a simplified model. Therefore, we built our analysis of risk-mitigation value—particularly of the reader rule—on the USCG's risk analysis model. We found data limitations in almost every area of the TWIC program. The USCG made basic information available about facilities' function and contacts, but it was not always current, accurate, or complete.[27] Information about facility security measures is detailed in facility security plans (FSPs), but these are not accessible online or in a format in which they can be combined or compared across the industry. USCG data in MSRAM on facilities' risk has classification restrictions. Information about TWIC holders is self-reported and not necessarily updated, such that we cannot identify job positions across the TWIC population or where their TWIC cards are employed. These are only some examples. These data limitations have led us to make largely qualitative, rather than quantitative, judgments about TWIC's risk-mitigation impact. Other questions in Public Law 114-278 necessarily lend themselves to qualitative judgments. Because many of its questions ask about the appropriateness or adequacy of functions, we have laid out the objectives of these functions and the details of their operation. We have either presented a conclusion on appropriateness or adequacy—if warranted by the information—or set up the trade space for decisionmakers in making determinations about the program.

The Structure of This Report

In Chapter 2 of this report, we provide further information on how TWIC fits into access control programs at maritime facilities, TWIC's purpose and function, and implementation of the TWIC program, including the pending rulemaking on electronic biometric readers. We also explain why understanding risk in the maritime environment is difficult and complex. In Chapter 3, we address whether concerns raised in past GAO and OIG reports about the TWIC program have been resolved. In Chapter 4, we lay out the threat environment for the maritime industry, discussing the terrorism threat and broader security risks that maritime facilities face. In Chapter 5, we address the effectiveness of the STA process in identifying people who might present a threat to facilities. In Chapter 6, we examine how TWIC is used at facilities as part of

---

[27] Not only does this information change over time—for example, a facility might change ownership or business focus—information is gathered from facilities' self-reporting and might not have been gathered accurately initially.

their access control programs. In Chapter 7, we discuss the limitations of TWIC's risk-mitigation potential and the reasons that TWIC has no inherent risk-mitigation value. In Chapter 8, we consider the pending rulemaking to require high-risk facilities to have higher standards of TWIC verification by providing an analysis of the costs and benefits of the TWIC-reader rule.[28] In Chapter 9, we consider alternatives to the TWIC model and other transportation-related credentials. In Chapter 10, we present our conclusions, responding specifically to each question in Public Law 114-278. Table 1.1 provides a crosswalk between the sections of Public Law 114-278 and where in this report we discuss those issues.

Table 1.1. Crosswalk from Public Law 114-278 to Our Study Findings

Paragraph	Focus	Report Chapter
1(b)(3)(A)(i)	Vetting standards	5
1(b)(3)(A)(ii)	The fee structure	5
1(b)(3)(A)(iii)	Redundancy with other credentials	9
1(b)(3)(A)(iv)	Other federal and state threat assessments	9
1(b)(3)(B)	The application process	5
1(b)(3)(C)(i)	Known or likely risks at ports	4–7
1(b)(3)(C)(ii)	Nonbiometric alternatives	9
1(b)(3)(C)(iii)	The effects of TWIC and readers	6–8
1(b)(3)(C)(iv)	Costs and benefits of the program	5–8
1(b)(3)(C)(v)	Previous GAO and OIG reports	3
1(b)(5)	The final report	All

We also provide supporting appendixes. In Appendix A, we provide more information about our port visits, including the method we used to ensure that we had an inclusive understanding of the port environment. In Appendix B, we provide the full list of standards that can disqualify someone for a TWIC card on a criminal basis. In Appendix C, we provide background on MSRAM and how the USCG has used it to inform a regulatory analysis on TWIC. In Appendix D, we provide additional background on the GAO and OIG reports on the TWIC program. In Appendix E, we provide a detailed analysis of TWIC's fee structure. In Appendixes F and G, we provide supporting details relevant to our break-even analysis presented in Chapter 8.

---

[28] USCG, 2016.

2. Background on the TWIC Program and Maritime Facilities

A primary function of MTSA is to require access control programs at regulated maritime facilities—physical barriers, FSPs, and enhanced identification (ID) measures for personnel—which responds to Congress's concerns about the criticality of ports to U.S. commerce. In this chapter, we discuss the role of an access control program at a facility in mitigating risk (in general terms) and how the TWIC program is a component of access control programs. We provide further background on the purpose and implementation of the TWIC program, including a history of the program, the division of responsibilities between TSA and the USCG, and methods available to facilities in using TWIC as part of their security programs. We also discuss the importance of ports as a component of the country's critical infrastructure and the complexity of the maritime environment. Last, we clarify the difference between maritime facilities and ports and explain why we used facilities as our unit of analysis in this study.

The Role of Access Control Programs

The National Institute of Standards and Technology (NIST) provides standard terminology for information security programs that can be applied to physical security programs as well. Using its terms, *physical access control* can be defined as "the process of granting or denying specific requests to . . . enter specific physical facilities."[29] *Access control mechanism* refers to a "security [safeguard] . . . designed to detect and deny unauthorized access and permit authorized access."[30] Any access control program has certain canonical components to establish proper access control:

- identification, providing identifying information for a user
- authentication, verifying the identity of that user through a mechanism, such as a personal ID number (PIN) or biometrics
- authorization, granting access privileges to the user.

MTSA requires a facility to identify, authenticate, and authorize anyone who has unescorted access to its secure area. The TWIC card serves to fulfill some, but not all, of these purposes. The TWIC card provides identifying information (a holder's name). It also provides three possible means for authenticating a user's identity—a visible photo printed on the card and a unique PIN and fingerprints stored on the integrated chip. The card itself can also be authenticated using a digital signature stored on the card or use a challenge–response

---

[29] Richard Kissel, ed., *Glossary of Key Information Security Terms*, Washington, D.C.: National Institute of Standards and Technology, U.S. Department of Commerce, NISTIR 7298, revision 2, May 2013, p. 2.

[30] Kissel, 2013, p. 2.

authentication of a stored key. Each facility is responsible for using its own standard to determine whether someone is authorized for access; a TWIC card does not entitle someone to gain access to a facility. Later in this chapter, we discuss in more detail the methods by which a facility can conduct authentication and authorization.

Access control programs can reduce security risk at facilities in multiple ways. Before we discuss this potential security risk mitigation, let us first define what we mean by *risk*. The standard DHS definition of *risk* is the potential for an outcome that is unwanted, as determined by its likelihood and consequences.[31] We can further break out *likelihood*, using DHS's lexicon, as the probability of an attack being attempted (i.e., the threat) and the probability of it being successful (i.e., the vulnerabilities). Therefore, an extended definition of *risk* is the potential for an adverse outcome as a function of threat, vulnerability, and consequence. *Threat* is the "capabilities, intentions, and attack methods of adversaries."[32] *Vulnerability* encompasses the physical features or operational attributes, such as location or security posture, that make the entity (in this case, the maritime facility) susceptible to an attack.[33] *Consequence* is the effect of the adverse outcome, which is typically measured in terms of human, economic, mission, or psychological effects.[34]

The steps necessary to penetrate the secure area of a facility (because of access control measures) could deter someone who presented a threat from pursuing their attack. In the specific case of TWIC, a would-be attacker could be deterred by the prospect of undergoing an STA, which requires providing biometric and biographic information to the federal government for the purpose of a background check. If the STA deters the would-be attacker, they would therefore be unable to become a properly authorized, *unescorted* person at a facility (because this requires a TWIC card). Someone without a TWIC could also be deterred from attacking a facility if they see the access control measures in use as a challenging or insurmountable security measure. Access control programs can also reduce the vulnerabilities at facilities. The STA process might prevent a known or suspected threat actor from being granted a TWIC card, which might reduce that actor's ability to gain access to the facility and conduct an attack. Someone without a TWIC card might be unsuccessful in an attempted attack because they could not gain access to the facility. Figure 2.1 depicts these concepts visually. Of course, access control programs cannot mitigate all types of threats, and facilities still have other points of vulnerability, as we discuss in greater detail in Chapter 7.

---

[31] DHS, *DHS Lexicon Terms and Definitions*, Instruction Manual 262-12-001-01, October 16, 2017, p. 563.

[32] DHS, 2017, p. 661.

[33] DHS, 2017, p. 705.

[34] DHS, 2017, p. 111.

Figure 2.1. Methods by Which Access Control Programs Reduce Risk

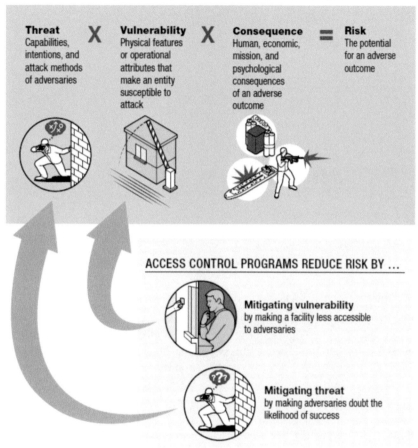

SOURCE: Definitions from DHS, 2017.

Background and Purpose of the TWIC Program

On November 25, 2002, MTSA was signed into law. The law cites two major security concerns at U.S. ports. One is that "ports often are a major locus of Federal crime, including drug trafficking, cargo theft, and smuggling of contraband and aliens."[35] The other is that ports are "susceptible to large scale acts of terrorism that could cause a large loss of life or economic disruption."[36] MTSA called for a range of port security measures, including greater requirements for identity assurance: "Biometric identification procedures for individuals having access to secure areas in port facilities are important tools to deter and prevent port cargo crimes,

---

[35] Pub. L. 107-295, 2002, Section 101(6).

[36] Pub. L. 107-295, 2002, Section 101(7).

smuggling, and terrorist actions."[37] It requires the Secretary of Homeland Security to issue biometric transportation security cards to applicants not deemed a security risk who need unescorted access to secure areas of MTSA-regulated facilities and vessels.[38]

Although the terms *transportation security card program* and *TWIC* often are used interchangeably, they are not synonymous. MTSA and the SAFE Port Act, signed into law on October 13, 2006, set the parameters for background checks and identity assurance for access control, and TWIC is the current government framework for meeting those requirements.[39]

The TWIC program actually predated MTSA. TWIC originated from efforts to improve airport security after the September 11, 2001, terrorist attacks.[40] President George W. Bush signed the Aviation and Transportation Security Act (ATSA) into law on November 19, 2001, in an effort to fundamentally change how the United States "approaches the task of ensuring the safety and security of the civil air transportation system."[41] ATSA established TSA and, among other things, permitted TSA to require background checks for people with access to secure areas of airports and to consider using biometric and other emerging technologies to verify the identities of people entering such areas.[42] TSA established the TWIC program in December

---

[37] Pub. L. 107-295, 2002, Section 101(11).

[38] Pub. L. 107-295, 2002, Section 102. Section 102 amends Title 46 of the U.S. Code (Shipping) to require that the Secretary "issue a biometric transportation security card to an individual . . . unless the Secretary decides that the individual poses a security risk under subsection (c) warranting denial of the card." MTSA does not set a deadline for implementation of the transportation security card requirements.

[39] Pub. L. 109-347, 2006, §§ 104(c), 106. The SAFE Port Act also specifies an implementation schedule that requires the Secretary to establish a priority for each U.S. port based on risk and assessed vulnerabilities and to implement the program at the ten highest-priority ports by July 1, 2007, and at all other U.S. ports by January 1, 2009 (Pub. L. 109-347, 2006, § 104[a]). Per Section 104, the regulations implementing the transportation security card program

> shall include a background check process to enable newly hired workers to begin working unless the Secretary makes an initial determination that the worker poses a security risk. Such process shall include a check against the consolidated and integrated terrorist watch list maintained by the Federal Government. (Pub. L. 109-347, § 104[c])

Section 106 identifies a range of crimes, including treason, espionage, and sedition, that are disqualifying for the purpose of the transportation security card program.

Finally, Section 125 provides for a "threat assessment screening, including name-based checks against terrorist watch lists and immigration status check, for all port truck drivers with access to a secure area of a port . . . ." (The Section 125 requirement is not connected to the transportation security card program.)

[40] GAO, *Transportation Security: DHS Should Address Key Challenges Before Implementing the Transportation Worker Identification Credential Program*, Washington, D.C., GAO-06-982, September 29, 2006, p. 9.

[41] U.S. House of Representatives, *Aviation and Transportation Security Act*, Washington, D.C., House Report 107-296, November 16, 2001.

[42] ATSA added to Title 49 of the U.S. Code a new section providing that the head of the newly created TSA to "require background checks for airport security screening personnel, individuals with access to secure areas of airports, and other transportation security personnel" (Public Law 107-71, Aviation and Transportation Security Act, November 19, 2001, § 101) and providing for improved airport perimeter access screening, authorizing TSA to use "biometric or other technology [to] positively verif[y] the identity of each employee and law enforcement officer who enters a secure area of an airport" (Pub. L. 107-71, 2001, § 106[a]). With ATSA, legislators also sought to

2001. The credential was intended "to be a universally recognized identification card accepted across all modes of the national transportation system, including airports, seaports, and railroad terminals, for transportation workers requiring unescorted physical access to secure areas in this system."[43] In practice, the maritime sector is the only transportation sector in which TWIC is the required credential.

A History of Implementation of the TWIC Program and the Pending Status of the Reader Rule

As initially conceived, the TWIC program would require the use of biometrically enabled credentials and electronic biometric card readers. The 2006 notice of proposed rulemaking (NPRM) for the TWIC program included both components,[44] but, in response to comments received on the proposed rule, DHS decided to implement the TWIC program in two phases. The first rulemaking (2007) revised 49 C.F.R. Part 1572, set forth a process for issuing TWICs, and required MTSA-regulated vessels and port facilities to "use . . . TWIC as an access control measure . . . ."[45] The 2007 rule did not prescribe a particular method of inspecting or validating TWIC; it provided only that any owner or operator of a MTSA-regulated facility or vessel "change their existing access control procedures to ensure that merchant mariners and any other individual seeking unescorted access to a secure area of their vessel or facility has a TWIC."[46] NVIC 03-07, issued on July 2, 2007, states that facility screeners should compare the holder's facial features to the photo imprinted on the card, check the expiration date, and examine the unique identifying surface features of the card for signs of tampering. This use of the card as a "flash pass" would satisfy the initial requirements for visual inspection. Alternatively, the NVIC permits a facility to integrate TWIC into existing physical access control systems (PACSs). A facility with a PACS could elect to use another ID card as its access credential—such as company or facility ID—but the NVIC requires that each individual still have a TWIC in their possession or readily available.

---

improve access control in secure areas, directing that TSA "consider the deployment of biometric or similar technologies that identify individuals based on unique personal characteristics" and

> establish pilot programs in no fewer than 20 airports to test and evaluate new and emerging technology for providing access control and other security protections for closed or secure areas of the airports. Such technology may include biometric or other technology that ensures only authorized access to secure areas. (Pub. L. 107-71, §§ 106[c]–[d])

[43] GAO, *Port Security: Better Planning Needed to Develop and Operate Maritime Worker Identification Card Program*, Washington, D.C., GAO-05-106, December 10, 2004, p. 5.

[44] TSA and USCG, "Transportation Worker Identification Credential (TWIC) Implementation in the Maritime Sector; Hazardous Materials Endorsement for a Commercial Driver's License," *Federal Register*, Vol. 71, No. 98, May 22, 2006, p. 29395–29462.

[45] USCG, 2007, p. 3492. DHS issued the final rule implementing TWIC as a transportation security card program on January 25, 2007. The electronic TWIC-reader requirements were carved out of this 2007 final rule.

[46] USCG, 2007, pp. 3492, 3495.

NVIC 03-07 required that vessels and facilities comply with TWIC regulations by September 25, 2008, but this deadline was extended to April 15, 2009,[47] because of difficulties enrolling TWIC users. The USCG ultimately adopted a phased compliance schedule, a temporary TWIC equivalency, and other strategies to help facilities meet compliance deadlines.[48] In 2014, in light of an anticipated surge when the five-year credential expired, TSA made a one-time concession that any TWIC holder could extend their card for three years for a reduced fee.

The second phase of TWIC is still ongoing. In March 2013, the USCG published an NPRM for a rule that would require owners and operators of certain MTSA-regulated facilities and vessels to use electronic readers designed to work with TWIC as an additional access control measure.[49] Informed by comments provided to this NPRM, a pilot program conducted at some maritime facilities using electronic readers, and an economic regulatory analysis, the USCG issued its TWIC-reader requirements in 2016.[50] This second rulemaking, often referred to as the TWIC-reader final rule, focused on the requirements for verification and authentication of TWIC cards. Rather than applying it to all MTSA-regulated facilities as initially envisioned, the USCG determined that the requirement for electronic biometric readers would be limited to vessels and facilities deemed at "high risk" for potential TSIs.[51]

Facilities Subject to the Reader Rule

The USCG used data from MSRAM to determine which criteria would make a facility high risk. The USCG assessed port facilities and vessels according to three risk factors: (1) maximum possible direct consequences to the vessel or facility resulting from a terrorist attack;[52] (2) the potential impact of the loss of the vessel or facility (including effects on health, the economy, and security) beyond the direct consequences; and (3) how effective TWIC might be in reducing the vessel or facility's vulnerability to a terrorist attack, including an examination of whether

---

[47] USCG and TSA, "Transportation Worker Identification Credential (TWIC) Implementation in the Maritime Sector; Hazardous Materials Endorsement for a Commercial Driver's License," *Federal Register*, Vol. 73, No. 89, May 7, 2008, pp. 25562–25566.

[48] GAO, *Transportation Worker Identification Credential: Progress Made in Enrolling Workers and Activating Credentials but Evaluation Plan Needed to Help Inform the Implementation of Card Readers*, Washington, D.C., GAO-10-43, November 18, 2009.

[49] USCG, "Transportation Worker Identification Credential (TWIC)–Reader Requirements," *Federal Register*, Vol. 78, No. 56, March 22, 2013, pp. 17781–17833.

[50] USCG, 2016.

[51] The USCG initially designated three risk groups—A, B, and C—however, on August 23, 2016, the USCG decided to collapse the designation between risk groups B and C. Therefore, high-risk facilities are often called risk group A facilities, with other facilities called non–risk group A facilities. For more information, see the TWIC final rule (USCG, 2016, pp. 57653, 57679).

[52] This portion of the analysis included an examination of potential "(1) Death and serious injuries; (2) direct property damage and the costs of business interruptions; (3) environmental consequences; (4) and national security consequences; and (5) secondary economic consequences, such as damage done to the supply chain" (USCG, 2016, p. 57660).

electronic TWIC inspection would substantially reduce the effect or likelihood of an attack.[53] Aggregating the results of this analysis, the USCG developed a total score that combined the severity of an attack with the effectiveness of the TWIC program in countering that attack, then used this ranking to determine risk groups.

The USCG analysis found two groups of facilities to be high risk and therefore subject to the final reader rule. The first group was facilities handling passenger vessels carrying more than 1,000 passengers (i.e., large cruise ships and very large passenger ferries). The second group was facilities that handle certain dangerous cargoes (CDCs)—specified explosive, flammable, or noxious materials. These two groups are often referred to as *large–passenger vessel facilities* and *CDC facilities*. The USCG also found three groups of vessels themselves to be high risk: (1) vessels that carry CDCs in bulk, (2) vessels certified to carry more than 1,000 passengers, and (3) towing vessels engaged in towing barges that are subject to (1) or (2). However, the USCG limited the regulated population to vessels with crew sizes exceeding 20. Thus, only one vessel meets these criteria.[54]

The final reader rule, as currently articulated, would require any high-risk facility or vessel to use an electronic biometric reader to authenticate each credential, validate the credential against an up-to-date Canceled Card List provided by TSA, and use biometrics to confirm the cardholder's identity. Each facility would also need to maintain a record of people who have unescorted facility access.[55] This rule would essentially require that a facility have a PACS or portable reader capable of meeting the rule's recordkeeping requirements. A facility would still be able to use a locally issued credential, provided that some form of biometrics were used to verify identity. This rulemaking remains unimplemented. Although the reader rule was scheduled to go into effect on August 23, 2018, Public Law 115-230 prohibited the USCG from implementing the rule until DHS submits an assessment of the TWIC program to Congress.[56]

Confusion About the Definition of *CDC Facility*

The number of facilities that the TWIC-reader rule would affect is still unclear. The initial USCG regulatory analysis estimated that 525 facilities and vessels (at the time of the analysis) would meet the risk group A criteria. However, this analysis was based on registration forms on file with the USCG in which facilities describes their main functions. In the USCG analysis, facilities that described themselves primarily as CDC facilities included chemical facilities, petroleum refineries, and hazardous fertilizer handlers, but other types of facilities might

---

[53] USCG, 2016, pp. 57659–57660.

[54] The only vessel meeting these criteria is the *Pride of America*, a U.S.-flagged cruise ship with capacity for roughly 3,000 people that operates in the Hawaiian Islands. Although multiple other cruise ships meet the criteria in terms of passenger volume, they are not U.S. flagged and therefore not subject to MTSA requirements.

[55] USCG, 2016, p. 57653.

[56] Public Law 115-230, Transportation Worker Identification Credential Accountability Act of 2018, August 2, 2018.

ultimately meet this criterion given the breadth of the definition of *CDC*.[57] Industry also initially believed that facilities would be subject to the final rule only if the facility handled the transfer of CDC materials directly to or from vessels. The USCG later clarified that any facility with CDC material would be subject to the reader rule.[58] As we discuss in greater depth in Chapter 8, this could mean that many more facilities are subject to the TWIC-reader rule than originally estimated.

---

[57] *CDC* is defined in Code of Federal Regulations, Title 33, Navigation and Navigable Waters; Chapter I, Coast Guard, Department of Homeland Security (Continued); Subchapter P, Ports and Waterways Safety; Part 160, Ports and Waterways Safety—General; Subpart C, Notification of Arrival, Hazardous Conditions, and Certain Dangerous Cargoes; Section 160.202, Definitions; however, this regulation makes further reference to other regulations—Code of Federal Regulations, Title 46, Shipping; Chapter I, Coast Guard, Department of Homeland Security (Continued); Subchapter O, Certain Bulk Dangerous Cargoes; Part 151, Barges Carrying Bulk Liquid Hazardous Material Cargoes; Subpart 151.50, Special Requirements; Section 151.50-31, Chlorine; Code of Federal Regulations, Title 46, Shipping; Chapter I, Coast Guard, Department of Homeland Security (Continued); Subchapter O, Certain Bulk Dangerous Cargoes; Part 154, Safety Standards for Self-Propelled Vessels Carrying Bulk Liquefied Gases; Subpart A, General; Section 154.7, Definitions, Acronyms, and Terms; Code of Federal Regulations, Title 49, Transportation; Subtitle B, Other Regulations Relating to Transportation (Continued); Chapter I, Pipeline and Hazardous Materials Safety Administration, Department of Transportation; Subchapter C, Hazardous Materials Regulations; Part 171, General Information, Regulations, and Definitions; Subpart A, Applicability, General Requirements, and North American Shipments; Section 171.8, Definitions and Abbreviations; Code of Federal Regulations, Title 49, Transportation; Subtitle B, Other Regulations Relating to Transportation (Continued); Chapter I, Pipeline and Hazardous Materials Safety Administration, Department of Transportation; Subchapter C, Hazardous Materials Regulations; Part 172, Hazardous Materials Table, Special Provisions, Hazardous Materials Communications, Emergency Response Information, Training Requirements, and Security Plans; Subpart B, Table of Hazardous Materials and Special Provisions; Section 172.101, Purpose and Use of Hazardous Materials Table; Code of Federal Regulations, Title 49, Transportation, Subtitle B, Other Regulations Relating to Transportation (Continued); Chapter I, Pipeline and Hazardous Materials Safety Administration, Department of Transportation; Subchapter C, Hazardous Materials Regulations; Part 173, Shippers: General Requirements for Shipments and Packagings; Subpart C, Definitions, Classification and Packaging for Class 1; Section 173.50, Class 1: Definitions; Code of Federal Regulations, Title 49, Transportation; Subtitle B, Other Regulations Relating to Transportation (Continued); Chapter I, Pipeline and Hazardous Materials Safety Administration, Department of Transportation; Subchapter C, Hazardous Materials Regulations; Part 173, Shippers: General Requirements for Shipments and Packagings; Subpart I, Class 7 (Radioactive) Materials; Section 173.403, Definitions; and Code of Federal Regulations, Title 49, Transportation; Subtitle B, Other Regulations Pertaining to Transportation (Continued); Chapter I, Pipeline and Hazardous Materials Safety Administration, Department of Transportation; Subchapter C, Hazardous Materials Regulations; Part 176, Carriage by Vessel; Subpart J, Detailed Requirements for Class 4 (Flammable Solids), Class 5 (Oxidizers and Organic Peroxides), and Division 1.5 Materials; Section 176.415, Permit Requirements for Division 1.5, Ammonium Nitrates, and Certain Ammonium Nitrate Fertilizers—with possible CDC materials. In some cases, any amount of a material constitutes a CDC; in others, the concentration, quantity, or material condition (or combination of any of these) determines whether it constitutes a CDC. In total, more than 3,000 materials could constitute CDCs.

[58] In June 2018, the USCG postponed implementation of the TWIC-reader rule for facilities that possess CDCs but do not transfer them to or from vessels. In addition, a July 24, 2018, court order from the Eastern District Court of Virginia indefinitely delays the implementation of the TWIC-reader final rule at CDC transfer and nontransfer facilities, in response to a lawsuit brought by industry groups (Amy Midgett, "Latest Developments Regarding TWIC Reader Final Rule," *Coast Guard Maritime Commons: The Coast Guard Blog for Maritime Professionals*, August 3, 2018; USCG, "TWIC-Reader Requirements; Delay of Effective Date," *Federal Register*, Vol. 23, No. 121, June 22, 2018b, pp. 29067–29081).

Division of Responsibilities for the TWIC Program

As noted in Chapter 1, TWIC is jointly administered by TSA and the USCG. TSA is responsible for enrolling applicants, adjudicating the STA, and producing and issuing the TWIC card. The USCG works with facility and vessel owners and operators to implement and maintain compliance with TWIC program regulations.[59]

Enrollment, STAs, and Credential Issuance

An applicant applies for a TWIC card at an enrollment center at one of the hundreds of locations nationwide, each of which is operated by an authorized service provider contracted to TSA. To minimize the costs of their employees traveling to enrollment centers, some companies also contract for mobile or on-site enrollment support. At enrollment, the applicant provides personally identifying information (PII), biometric information (fingerprints), and a photograph. The applicant also provides documents that establish identity and citizenship, and the center collects the $125.25 (nonrefundable[60]) enrollment fee.

An applicant's information is checked against multiple sources to determine whether they pose a security threat per the standards delineated in 49 C.F.R. § 1572.5. The center contractor transmits applicant fingerprints to the Federal Bureau of Investigation's (FBI's) Criminal Justice Information Services for a criminal-history record check (CHRC). TSA's National Transportation Vetting Center checks biographic information from the applicant against multiple databases, including data from the Terrorist Screening Database (TSDB), the terrorist "watch list." The center checks applicant information against the U.S. Citizenship and Immigration Services Systematic Alien Verification for Entitlements (SAVE) database to determine immigration status. It also checks the information against the Automated Biometric Identification System (IDENT), which performs "fingerprint-based records checks against various criminal, immigration, and terrorist watch lists maintained by the DHS Office of Biometric Identity Management."[61] Because many of IDENT's data sources are also checked directly as part of the STA, IDENT's results provide a secondary check to catch possible derogatory information that other database queries might have missed. Checks of these databases are automated; an applicant who triggers no possible matches in any of these systems is automatically issued a TWIC in a matter of days. If an applicant's provided biometric or biographic information returns a possible match from any of these data sets, TSA manually adjudicates the results to determine an

---

[59] Commandant, USCG, 2007, Enc. 4, § 4.1.

[60] TSA does refund the enrollment fee in some unusual circumstances, such as an administrative error that might require an applicant to reapply or an applicant not having been properly informed of disqualifying criteria at the time of the application.

[61] TSA, Transportation Worker Identification Credential program brief, October 31, 2016c; TSA, "Transportation Worker Identification Credential (TWIC® Program)," briefing to the Delaware Bay Joint Area Committee/Area Maritime Security Committee, February 15, 2017a.

applicant's eligibility.[62] Depending on the results of the initial adjudication, the applicant is either approved for a TWIC card or sent a preliminary determination of ineligibility (PDI).[63] Roughly half the applicants are automatically adjudicated in two days, and TSA is required to complete the initial adjudication process within 30 days.[64]

An applicant who receives a PDI may seek redress by either appealing TSA's determination or seeking a waiver of certain standards. Reasons that an applicant might seek an appeal include a criminal conviction overturned on appeal or inaccurate immigration records. An applicant seeking a waiver acknowledges meeting the disqualifying standards but provides TSA with grounds that they do not present a security risk. When considering a waiver request, TSA considers such factors as the circumstances of the disqualifying offense, restitution, and mitigation remedies.[65] In around two-thirds of cases, applicants provide no response to the PDI or an insufficient response for the redress process to begin.[66] If, after 60 days, the applicant has made no effort to begin the redress process, the PDI becomes a final denial. Figure 2.2 provides enrollment numbers for January 1, 2015, through October 1, 2018.

---

[62] Adjudication could be required because of a case of mistaken identity (e.g., someone with a similar name or other biographic detail was returned as a possible match) or because of a true match to a record. A true match does not necessarily meet the criteria for disqualification.

[63] 49 C.F.R. § 1572.21(d); USCG, 2007, p. 3510.

[64] U.S. Code, Title 46, Shipping; Subtitle VII, Security and Drug Enforcement; Chapter 701, Port Security; Subchapter I, General; Section 70105, Transportation Security Cards; Paragraph (p), Processing Time.

[65] In adjudicating a waiver request, TSA uses the procedures delineated in Code of Federal Regulations, Title 49, Transportation; Subtitle B, Other Regulations Pertaining to Transportation (Continued); Chapter XII, Transportation Security Administration, Department of Homeland Security; Subchapter A, Administrative and Procedural Rules; Part 1515, Appeal and Waiver Procedures for Security Threat Assessments for Individuals; Section 1515.7, Procedures for Waiver of Criminal Offenses, Immigration Status, or Mental Capacity Standards; Paragraph (c)(2).

[66] We calculated this based on TSA, 2019, as confirmed by TSA.

Figure 2.2. Enrollment Numbers for the TWIC Program, January 1, 2015, to October 1, 2018

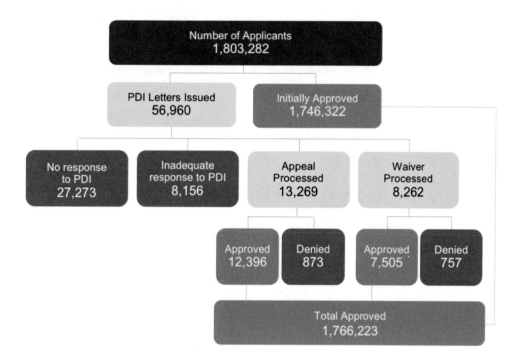

SOURCE: TSA, 2019, as confirmed by TSA.

If TSA deems the applicant to be qualified—either in the initial STA process or through the redress process—it produces a credential.[67] When the program began, someone could pick up an issued TWIC card only from an enrollment center, but they can now also choose to have the card shipped to a personal address.[68] If the card is sent to a personal address, an automatically generated PIN is sent separately; if the card is picked up from an enrollment center, the holder chooses a PIN at that time. Credential holders can change their PINs at enrollment centers at any time. A TWIC card physically displays the holder's full name, the expiration date, a photo, and credential ID number (CIN).[69] The card's chip contains a digital photo, two fingerprints, the PIN, private keys with digital certificates, and a Federal Agency Smart Credential Number (FASC-N).[70]

TSA continuously monitors the terrorist watch list and receives new, potentially derogatory information from IDENT. If a credential holder is found to no longer meet TWIC's eligibility standards, TSA revokes the credential and, in some cases, takes action to try to recover the person's TWIC card. TSA maintains a list of cards that have been canceled because they have

---

[67] USCG, 2007, p. 3510.

[68] TSA, "TWIC®," undated.

[69] The CIN is physically printed on the back of the card and can be used for visual inspection.

[70] USCG, 2016. The FASC-N is a unique number stored on the card's integrated circuit chip and can be integrated into a facility's PACS or made accessible to a mobile reader.

been lost, stolen, or revoked for a loss of eligibility. This list, the Canceled Card List (CCL), is available online for public use and updated daily.[71] TSA now posts two lists: one of canceled cards' FASC-Ns and the other, a visual CCL, of their CINs.[72] Because TSA does not have awareness of where TWIC cards are used, it does not push information to facilities about who has been added to the CCL. Instead, a facility would need to pull this information and integrate it into local access control systems and programs. This practice is similar to that used for digital security, whereby a certificate authority maintains a list of certificates it has revoked, and a third party can use that list to verify that a certificate remains trusted by the issuer.

Verification of the TWIC

Facility operators ultimately have day-to-day responsibility for ensuring that TWIC cards are verified and for managing access control programs. The USCG requires the owner or operator of a MTSA-regulated vessel or facility to maintain an FSP or vessel security plan that lays out all the vessel or facility's security measures, including an articulation of TWIC policies and procedures.[73] Among other things, "[t]he vessel or facility must conduct a positive verification of the TWIC before allowing unescorted access to a secure area . . . ."[74] This verification could happen at the time of each entry, or authorized people can be enrolled in a PACS and TWIC cards can be verified at the time of enrollment. Anyone inside the security area must still have a TWIC card on their person or easily accessible at all times, and facilities can be found liable if this is not the case. Although possession of a TWIC is required for someone to be eligible for unescorted access to secure areas of regulated ports and vessels, a TWIC does not entitle that person to access a maritime facility or its secure area.[75] Port facility and vessel operators make the final determination of whether to grant someone access to secured areas.[76] Authorized access

---

[71] Universal Enroll, "TWIC Canceled Card Lists," undated b, is maintained by UES, the enrollment service provider for TSA's STA programs.

[72] The FASC-N is a unique number stored on the card's integrated circuit chip and potentially integrated into a facility's PACS or accessible using a mobile reader.

[73] Code of Federal Regulations, Title 33, Navigation and Navigable Waters; Chapter I, Coast Guard, Department of Homeland Security (Continued); Subchapter H, Maritime Security; Part 104, Maritime Security: Vessels; Subpart D, Vessel Security Plan (VSP); Section 104.405, Format of the Vessel Security Plan (VSP); Code of Federal Regulations, Title 33, Navigation and Navigable Waters; Chapter I, Coast Guard, Department of Homeland Security (Continued); Subchapter H, Maritime Security; Part 105, Maritime Security: Facilities; Subpart D, Facility Security Plan (FSP); Section 105.405, Format and Content of the Facility Security Plan (FSP); Commandant, USCG, 2007.

[74] Commandant, USCG, 2007, Enc. 3, § 3.3.

[75] Commandant, USCG, 2007, p. 4.

[76] 33 C.F.R. § 105.405; Code of Federal Regulations, Title 33, Navigation and Navigable Waters; Chapter I, Coast Guard, Department of Homeland Security (Continued); Subchapter H, Maritime Security; Part 105, Maritime Security: Facilities; Subpart D, Facility Security Plan (FSP); Section 105.410, Submission and Approval; Code of Federal Regulations, Title 33, Navigation and Navigable Waters; Chapter I, Coast Guard, Department of Homeland Security; Subchapter K, Security of Vessels; Part 120, Security of Passenger Vessels; Subpart C, Plans and Procedures for Vessel Security; Section 120.300, What Is Required to Be in a Vessel Security Plan? Code of Federal Regulations, Title 33, Navigation and Navigable Waters; Chapter I, Coast Guard, Department of Homeland

thus requires three functions to be performed: Verify that the person has undergone an STA, establish the person's identity, and establish their business purpose. The next section presents the three methods facilities can use in meeting these requirements.

Permissible Methods of Verifying Access Requirements at Access Control Points

Visual Inspection

The simplest yet least secure method of meeting the requirements of 33 C.F.R. Part 105 is to verify the TWIC card visually (i.e., use the TWIC card as a flash pass). In this case, the TWIC card itself meets two requirements of the access control system: establishing identity and verifying that the holder underwent an STA. The person must establish business purpose through other means. For example, a truck driver might do this through a bill of lading—a shipping document verifying the transfer of goods or a scheduled container drop-off or pickup appointment; a laborer might do this by showing their labor union card and dispatch order; a facility might use issuance of a company, facility, or port credential and registration in its system as verification of business purpose. Figure 2.3 depicts this process. A guard performing visual inspection could also authenticate the TWIC card by checking the security features on the card itself—including holograms, color-shifting ink, microtext, and reflective text.[77]

Figure 2.3. Visual Verification for Access Control

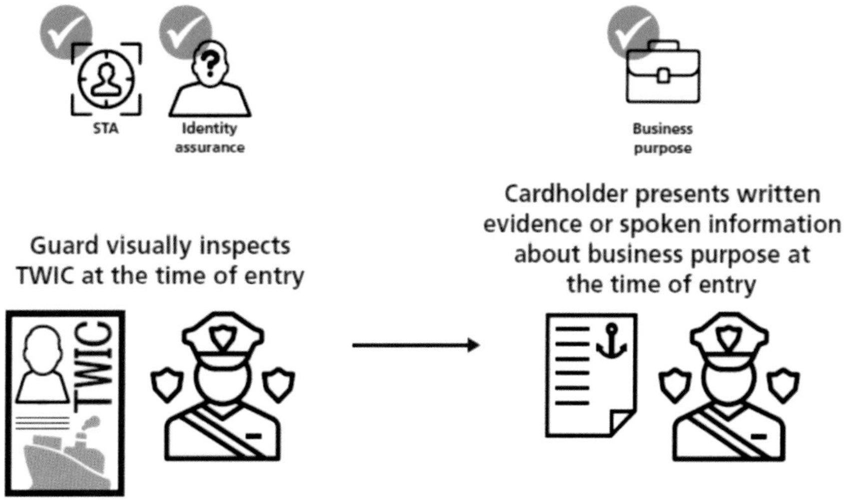

STA Identity assurance

Business purpose

Guard visually inspects TWIC at the time of entry

Cardholder presents written evidence or spoken information about business purpose at the time of entry

---

Security; Subchapter K, Security of Vessels; Part 120, Security of Passenger Vessels; Subpart C, Plans and Procedures for Vessel Security; Section 120.305, What Is the Procedure for Examination? USCG, 2007, p. 3495.

[77] The TWIC NexGen card also includes raised text.

Electronic Inspection Without a PACS

A facility can also conduct electronic inspection using a portable reader to authenticate TWIC cards without the use of an electronic PACS. Figure 2.4 depicts this process. Under current TWIC requirements, a facility can verify someone's identity by matching the person's fingerprint to the fingerprint stored on the card chip or by performing visual inspection of the card, as illustrated in Figure 2.3. (Most facilities doing electronic inspection without PACSs opt for the latter.) A facility operating without a PACS cannot operate unmanned access points with biometric readers because there is no means of verifying business purpose. TSA is also beta-testing a mobile application called Advanced Digital Visual Inspection Solution for Revocation (ADVISR™), which allows a facility to use a smartphone to check whether a card is valid and authentic. ADVISR scans the barcode printed on the reverse side of the card or allows the user to manual entry of eight digits of the card's unique CIN.

Figure 2.4. Electronic Verification Without a PACS

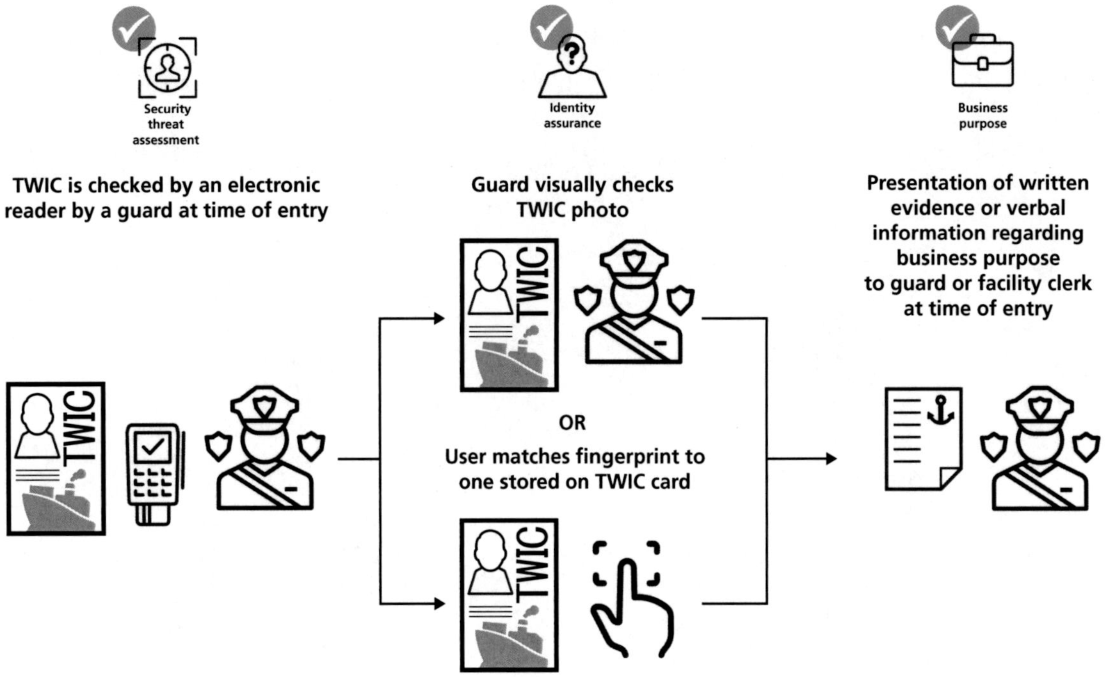

Security threat assessment

TWIC is checked by an electronic reader by a guard at time of entry

Identity assurance

Guard visually checks TWIC photo

OR

User matches fingerprint to one stored on TWIC card

Business purpose

Presentation of written evidence or verbal information regarding business purpose to guard or facility clerk at time of entry

Electronic Inspection with a PACS

A facility is also permitted to integrate the TWIC into a PACS. Figure 2.5 depicts this process. Under this requirement, the facility enrolls individuals into a PACS, verifying the TWIC when the person asks to be added to the facility's list of authorized personnel. The facility verifies the user's biometrics at that time as well, and it might require the user to verify the card's PIN. The facility also establishes business purpose through the PACS, granting access permission to an individual for a set period of time, typically not to exceed the expiration date of the TWIC. Facility management can terminate access permission if a business purpose no longer exists (or for any reason of its choosing and at any time). Upon entering the facility, the person would still need to present an identity verification document or establish identity using biometric means. We found that some facilities used TWICs for this purpose and others issued facility-specific documents.

Figure 2.5. Electronic Inspection With a PACS

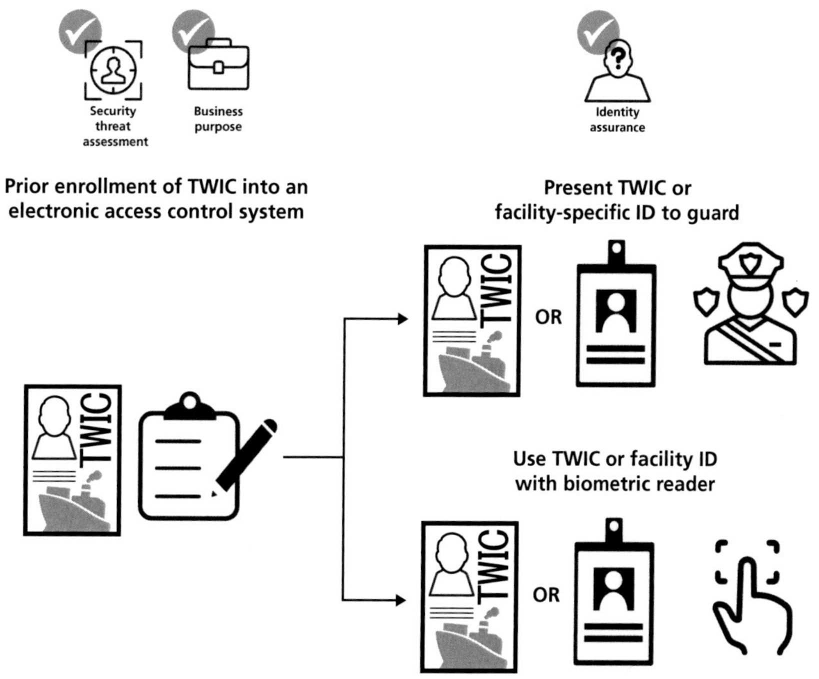

Within these three broad frameworks of establishing whether someone is authorized for access, we found numerous variations in facilities' practices. Practices also vary between access points or at different times at the same facility. Facility practices also vary at different Maritime Security (MARSEC) levels. The USCG has three MARSEC levels, which can be adjusted to reflect periods of increased risk to the maritime environment.[78]

Enforcement of TWIC

The USCG verifies compliance with TWIC requirements as part of its vessel and facility inspection processes, in accordance with the SAFE Port Act. Per statute, the USCG must include TWIC verification in one announced MTSA compliance examination annually. In addition, the

---

[78] For more information on MARSEC levels, see USCG, "U.S. Coast Guard Maritime Security (MARSEC) Levels," undated.

USCG must conduct one unannounced security spot check and additional spot checks when a facility's history of security violations warrants doing so.[79]

In addition, TSA surface transportation security inspectors also play a role in TWIC enforcement. These inspectors, either in conjunction with USCG facility inspectors or on their own, routinely travel to maritime facilities to check TWIC cards. Although a USCG facility inspector can check for multiple security compliance issues during a visit, a surface-transportation security inspector's purpose is only to verify the validity of TWIC cards.

Complexities of Characterizing the Port Environment

Collectively, U.S. ports are a critical component of U.S. infrastructure. According to the Bureau of Transportation Statistics, maritime transportation carries more goods than any other mode of transport does, accounting for 40 percent of aggregate imports and exports in 2016 (Figure 2.6).[80]

Figure 2.6. U.S.–International Merchandise Trade Value, by Transportation Mode, 2016

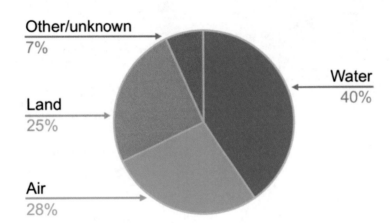

SOURCE: Bureau of Transportation Statistics, "Freight Facts and Figures 2017, Chapter 2: Freight Moved in Domestic and International Trade," updated November 5, 2017.

Ports are integral to the U.S. economy: Every day, an average of $10.3 billion of goods travels into or out of U.S. ports.[81] In a nationwide economic impact study, researchers found that U.S. coastal seaports in 2014 supported 23 million jobs and yielded $4.6 trillion in total

---

[79] Commandant, USCG, *CH-2 to 03-03, Implementation Guidance for the Regulations Mandated by the Maritime Transportation Security Act of 2002 (MTSA) for Facilities*, Washington, D.C., Commandant Publication P16700.4, Navigation and Vessel Inspection Circular 03-03, Change 2, February 28, 2009.

[80] *Maritime transportation* accounts for 45 percent of imports and 35 percent of exports. In terms of weight, maritime trade dominates all other modes combined, accounting for 72 percent of exports and 67 percent of imports.

[81] U.S. Census Bureau, "Foreign Trade," last revised June 11, 2019.

economic value, or about 26 percent of total gross domestic product (GDP).[82] Most of these effects come from goods or services that are a result of port activity, not from activities the ports conduct themselves. Ports' economic value is primarily value added—that is, the value created at each stage in the supply chain before an export exits a port or after an import enters it. As a result of their integral role in the supply chain, U.S. ports affect virtually every industry and every local economy.

The distribution of these aggregate impacts is uneven across ports. For example, the San Pedro Bay Port Complex, which consists of the Port of Los Angeles and the Port of Long Beach, estimates that it is connected to one in every nine jobs in southern California.[83] It facilitates the transport an average of $1 billion in goods each day.[84] In comparison, the Port of Hueneme, just up the coast, handles $26.5 million worth of goods each day.[85] Figure 2.7 shows the distribution of ports in terms of the average annual value of imports plus exports. The figure groups ports by orders of magnitude, so ports in each subsequent bin are approximately ten times larger than ports in the previous bin. To the far right are seven ports that move more than $100 billion in goods each year; to the far left are seven ports that move less than $100,000.

Figure 2.7. U.S. Ports, by Average Annual Total Imports Plus Exports in 2015–2017

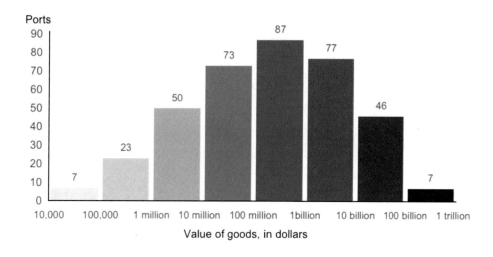

SOURCE: U.S. Census Bureau, 2019.

These vast differences in size make regulation strikingly complex, and maritime facilities vary dramatically on a wide range of other factors as well. The most apparent difference is the

---

[82] Martin Associates, "The 2014 National Economic Impact of the U.S. Coastal Port System," prepared for the American Association of Port Authorities, Lancaster, Pa., March 2015.

[83] U.S. Census Bureau, 2019.

[84] U.S. Census Bureau, 2019.

[85] HSOAC calculation from U.S. Census Bureau, 2019.

type of port operations. MTSA-regulated facilities are typically either cargo-oriented or passenger-oriented. Cargo facilities can handle containers; roll-on/roll-off (RORO) cargo, such as cars or construction or farm equipment; break-bulk cargo that is unitized, such as barrels, steel coils, or mechanical components; bulk cargo that cannot be unitized, such as sand, grain, or ore; and liquid bulk cargo, such as oil or liquid fertilizer. Some cargo facilities handle primarily material that meets the USCG's criteria for CDCs, a prime example being chemical manufacturing facilities. Passenger facilities are typically for cruise ships, other large pleasure craft, or ferries. Some facilities do not easily fit into these categories, such as the Port of Hueneme, which handles containers, break-bulk, liquid bulk, and RORO operations.

Cargo facilities also vary dramatically by volume or tonnage of cargo. Physical acreage affects the distance a facility can maintain between any dangerous material and the perimeter fencing. Some facilities are in major cities, while others are miles from population centers. Facilities also differ significantly in the extent to which they are maritime-oriented, and the maritime component might be incidental to a facility's function. Many MTSA-regulated facilities maintain ports as one of multiple modes for shipping goods, perhaps also being on a rail line, pipeline, or major highway. Airports, in contrast, rarely house operations unrelated to their primary purpose of transporting people or materials on planes. A facility could be subject to MTSA if it moves material from federally controlled waters to the material's first point of rest, not because it is adjacent to water. This means an oil refinery operating next to a river but without an operational dock would not be MTSA-regulated, but a refinery located a mile inland that receives material via an underground pipe connected to a dock would fall under MTSA's purview.

Public and passenger access varies dramatically by type and location of facility. Facilities that handle passenger vessels by their nature are open to passengers, and a facility's layout can complicate its ability to put barriers and standoff distance between secure and nonsecure areas. Such a facility also necessarily opens itself to possible loss of life in the event of an attack—it can do only so much to limit the number of people at the facility given that passengers are an essential nature of its business. Other facilities abut public use areas, limiting their ability to restrict access, or are in proximity to populated areas, limiting their ability to minimize collateral damage. On the other end of the spectrum, some facilities are transitioning to completely automated operation. Security features related to vetting people have little relevance where no one is physically at the facility.

Maritime facilities also have different ownership structures. Some facilities are completely privatized, but their ports are operated by state or local public authorities as public-benefit corporations. The port authority might directly manage port operations or might operate as a landlord—owning the infrastructure but leasing it to a private company that manages port operations, including security and MTSA compliance. We found that some ports use a hybrid model—leasing some facilities and directly operating others. These differences in ownership structure and operating model can affect a facility's access to capital, access to law-enforcement databases on criminal history, and ability to employ armed law-enforcement officers on-site.

Other important differences relate to geography, the role of unions, and seasonality. In terms of geography, for example, a facility's proximity to population centers could make a potential terrorist attack more deadly or damaging. Access control measures also correlate to geography. Although maritime facilities are usually thought of as coastal, MTSA-regulated facilities are also along the Mississippi River and other inland waterways. Some of these MTSA-regulated facilities are not directly conducting transnational operations. Coastal ports, in contrast, often do host seafaring ships that typically have foreign crews—crew members who would not be eligible for TWIC. Coastal facilities, therefore, must manage those crew members' movements to and from their vessels because they are often not allowed unescorted access to the facilities.

Unions are a critical component of port operations, especially on the West Coast, with the International Longshore and Warehouse Union (ILWU) representing all or almost all longshoremen there. The International Longshoremen's Association (ILA) represents East Coast workers, but it faces greater competition from nonunion workers, particularly in the Gulf region, than the ILWU has on the West Coast.[86] The ILWU has been more resistant to enhanced ID systems than the ILA has, and it has been critical of the TWIC program specifically.[87]

Seasonality also affects many industries, particularly cruise and liquid bulk facilities. Cruise facilities are busy during periods of optimal weather in their locations. Facilities dealing primarily in liquid fertilizer experience a large spike in the spring planting season and a lesser one in the fall, and facilities dealing in heating oil and gas have higher demands in winter.

The Facility as the Unit of Analysis

Throughout this report, we refer to maritime facilities rather than ports. *Facility* is defined in 33 C.F.R. § 101.105 as

> any structure or facility of any kind located in, on, or adjacent to any waters subject to the jurisdiction of the U.S. and used, operated, or maintained by a public or private entity, including any contiguous or adjoining property under common ownership or operation.

We use the maritime facility as our unit of analysis. A facility operates under an FSP,[88] which dictates the specific access control requirements and security measures in place at that facility.

---

[86] Kristen Monaco and Lindy Olsson, *Labor at the Ports: A Comparison of the ILA and ILWU*, 2005.

[87] "Port Security: TWIC Cards Aren't the Answer," *The Dispatcher*, Vol. 67, No. 5, May 2009, pp. 7–8; "TWIC Flunks Latest Test," *The Dispatcher*, Vol. 71, No. 6, June 2013, pp. 1, 6.

[88] Every MTSA-regulated facility is required to maintain an FSP. Per 33 C.F.R. § 105.405, an FSP must include information about the security procedures in place at the facility, methods for responding to changes in the MARSEC level, methods of securely interfacing with vessels, and information about security vulnerabilities. The facility develops its FSP, often with the assistance of a privately contracted provider, and submits it to the USCG every five years or when the FSP is amended. Each facility must have its own FSP, and it is not uncommon for a port to host multiple facilities operating under independent FSPs.

Ports or port complexes frequently consist of multiple facilities that are operated by various entities (public and private), which are often governed by separate FSPs, and FSOs or security managers might choose to implement access control measures differently at each facility. These port complexes also might not be in contiguous or consolidated operating areas. For example, the Port of South Louisiana stretches 54 miles along the Mississippi River,[89] and the Port of Houston complex stretches along the 52-mile Houston ship channel, consisting of public and privately operated facilities.[90] In other cases, although a facility might be associated with a port or port district for the purposes of the USCG characterization and grouping, there might be no actual relationship between a port authority and a maritime facility. The facility might own waterside property and operate an independent dock. Although this circumstance is uncommon where maritime traffic is consolidated in a large coastal harbor, it is very typical for MTSA-regulated facilities on inland waterways. Second, because ports are complex and vary across many dimensions (e.g., location, facility types, configuration, operations), security risks related to access control should be evaluated for each facility, rather than at the port level.[91]

Summary

TWIC, established by TSA in December 2001, is the current government framework for meeting the parameters set by MTSA in 2002 and the SAFE Port Act in 2006 for background checks and identity assurance for access control at regulated facilities. These enhanced personnel surety measures are intended to reduce the risk of terrorist attacks at ports and to reduce crime, such as cargo crimes and smuggling. TWIC is a part of the access control programs at facilities that seek to both deter and deny prospective attacks and thus reduce risk by mitigating both threat and vulnerability.

TWIC is jointly administered by TSA and the USCG. TSA is responsible for enrolling applicants, adjudicating the STA, and producing and issuing the TWIC card. TSA maintains a list of canceled cards, by FASC-N and CIN, that can be used to verify whether a TWIC card is active. For its part, the USCG works with facility operators and vessel owners and operators to implement and maintain compliance with TWIC program regulations. Facilities are ultimately responsible for identifying, authenticating, and authorizing people who have unescorted access to their secure areas. They have flexibility in how to do that. Current permissible methods of verifying authorization at access control points are (1) visual inspection of the TWIC card and verification of business purpose, (2) electronic inspection of the TWIC card (without a PACS) and verification of business purpose, and (3) electronic inspection of the TWIC card as part of a

---

[89] Port of South Louisiana, "Overview," undated.

[90] Port Houston, about page, undated.

[91] An exception to this might be a smaller port at which all facilities fall within the same fence line and everyone seeking access to any facility at the port goes through the same access control point. In this case, it might be appropriate to consider access control security risks at the port level, rather than the individual facility level.

PACS. Within these three frameworks, we found numerous variations in facilities' practices during our facility visits. The variance in facilities' practices, in addition to the variance between facilities in their levels of risk, makes for a complicated problem to analyze.

In addition to congressional questions about the TWIC program as currently implemented, many questions relate to the TWIC-reader final rule, issued in 2016, which remains unimplemented. This rule primarily affects two kinds of entities: (1) a facility or single vessel handling a large number of passengers and (2) a CDC facility. However, there is confusion about the definition of *CDC facility*, such that the total number of facilities that the TWIC-reader rule would affect is still unclear. This further complicates analysis on the impact and costs of TWIC readers.

3. Previous GAO and OIG Concerns About the TWIC Program

As part of our study, and in response to Section 1(b)(3)(C)(v) of Public Law 114-278, we reviewed multiple GAO and OIG reports on the TWIC program and previously identified deficiencies in the program. Table 3.1 outlines the GAO and OIG reports we reviewed as part of this assessment.

Table 3.1. GAO and OIG Reports Reviewed

Title	Date	Number
Port Security: Better Planning Needed to Develop and Operate Maritime Worker Identification Card Program	December 2004	GAO-05-106[a]
Transportation Security: DHS Should Address Key Challenges Before Implementing the Transportation Worker Identification Credential Program	September 2006	GAO-06-982[b]
Transportation Security: DHS Efforts to Eliminate Redundant Background Check Investigations	April 2007	GAO-07-756[c]
Transportation Worker Identification Credential: Progress Made in Enrolling Workers and Activating Credentials but Evaluation Plan Needed to Help Inform the Implementation of Card Readers	November 2009	GAO-10-43[d]
Transportation Worker Identification Credential: Internal Control Weaknesses Need to Be Corrected to Help Achieve Security Objectives	May 2011	GAO-11-657[e]
Transportation Security: Actions Needed to Address Limitations in TSA's Transportation Worker Security Threat Assessments and Growing Workload	December 2011	GAO-12-60[f]
Transportation Worker Identification Credential: Card Reader Pilot Results Are Unreliable; Security Benefits Need to Be Reassessed	May 2013	GAO-13-198[g]
Transportation Security: Action Needed to Strengthen TSA's Security Threat Assessment Process	July 2013	GAO-13-629[h]
TWIC Background Checks Are Not as Reliable as They Could Be	September 2016	OIG-16-128[i]

NOTE: Public Law 114-278 specifies that our study look at GAO and OIG reports produced prior to its enactment; therefore, we did not include OIG, *Review of Coast Guard's Oversight of the TWIC Program*, OIG-18-88, September 28, 2018a, or OIG, *DHS' and TSA's Compliance with Public Law 114-278, Transportation Security Card Program Assessment*, OIG-19-16, December 14, 2018b. In addition, because GAO, 2007, is only tangential to TWIC-related issues, we did not include it in this table.
[a] GAO, 2004.
[b] GAO, 2006.
[c] GAO, *Transportation Security: DHS Efforts to Eliminate Redundant Background Check Investigations*, Washington, D.C., GAO-07-756, April 26, 2007.
[d] GAO, 2009.
[e] GAO, *Transportation Worker Identification Credential: Internal Control Weaknesses Need to Be Corrected to Help Achieve Security Objectives*, Washington, D.C., GAO-11-657, May 10, 2011a.
[f] GAO, *Transportation Security: Actions Needed to Address Limitations in TSA's Transportation Worker Security Threat Assessments and Growing Workload*, Washington, D.C., GAO-12-60, December 8, 2011b.
[g] GAO, *Transportation Worker Identification Credential: Card Reader Pilot Results Are Unreliable; Security Benefits Need to Be Reassessed*, Washington, D.C., GAO-13-198, May 8, 2013a.
[h] GAO, *Transportation Security: Action Needed to Strengthen TSA's Security Threat Assessment Process*, Washington, D.C., GAO-13-629, July 19, 2013b.
[i] OIG, *TWIC Background Checks Are Not as Reliable as They Could Be*, OIG-16-128, September 1, 2016.

Themes from Previous GAO and OIG Reports

Several aspects of the TWIC program have been challenged during its lifetime. Table 3.2 highlights consistent themes raised in past GAO and OIG reports, which we then break out in further detail. Some of these reports are rather dated at this point, and some concerns raised by

GAO and OIG have either been overtaken by events or addressed by changes to the program. Most of GAO's and OIG's recommendations have been closed as implemented, although a handful were closed not implemented or remain open. A specific accounting of each is available in Appendix D. We have also excluded issues that are clearly in the past and not relevant to the operation of the TWIC program today, such as identified problems with some of TSA's initial contracts for the TWIC program, which relate to functions that have since been recompeted or are no longer contracted.

Table 3.2. Themes from Prior GAO and OIG Reports on the TWIC Program

Themes	GAO-05-106 (GAO, 2004)	GAO-06-982 (GAO, 2006)	GAO-07-756 (GAO, 2007)	GAO-10-43 (GAO, 2009)	GAO-11-657 (GAO, 2011a)	GAO-12-60 (GAO, 2011b)	GAO-13-198 (GAO, 2013a)	GAO-13-629 (GAO, 2013b)	OIG-16-128 (OIG, 2016)
Failure to assess TWIC's effectiveness in reducing risk					x		x		
Lack of adherence to management best practices (e.g., internal controls, planning)	x	x		x	x		x	x	x
Lack of communication between the federal government and industry	x	x					x		
Lack of identity assurance in the TWIC enrollment process					x				x
Excessive length of time for TWIC enrollment or issuance		x		x				x	
Appropriateness of eligibility standards for TWIC cardholders	x	x	x			x			
Inability to continuously vet TWIC holders' criminal histories					x	x			
Weaknesses in the TWIC-reader pilot				x		x	x		
Lack of full calculations of reader costs		x					x		
Reliability of TWIC-reader technology		x					x		
Possible value of alternative credentialing models			x			x	x		
Possible redundancies of TWIC			x			x			

Failure to Assess TWIC's Effectiveness in Reducing Risk

Although DHS officials informed Congress in June 2012 that TWIC readers would "provide an additional layer of security by reducing the risk that an unauthorized individual could gain access to a secure area," GAO found that the purpose of the pilot was not to assess TWIC's security benefits, nor were data collected that could confirm or deny whether it enhanced security.[92] Prior to the reader pilot, GAO expressed concerns about the impact that a lack of internal controls might have on TSA's ability to provide reasonable assurances that TWIC cards were issued to qualified people.[93] Moreover, DHS had neither assessed TWIC's effectiveness in improving security at maritime ports nor demonstrated that the program was more effective than previous methods at reducing risk.[94]

Lack of Adherence to Management Best Practices

Multiple GAO reports have raised concerns that the TWIC program has not implemented GAO-recommended best practices, particularly those in GAO's *Standards for Internal Control in the Federal Government* (commonly called the Green Book).[95] GAO recommended that TSA assess its existing internal controls and identify opportunities for new controls.[96] In 2017, TSA commissioned HSOAC to perform this study.

Lack of Communication Between the Federal Government and Industry

Since the initial pilots of TWIC, communication between TSA and the maritime industry has not always been direct or clear, according to GAO reports. GAO recommended that DHS and TSA follow industry-established best practices for project planning and management, including implementing a risk-mitigation plan on engaging key stakeholders.[97]

Lack of Identity Assurance in the TWIC Enrollment Process

GAO raised specific concerns that lack of internal controls could allow someone to gain a TWIC card using a false identity. In 2011, GAO investigators were able to obtain TWIC cards during covert tests of the enrollment process.[98] A 2016 OIG report raised concerns that TSA was

---

[92] GAO, 2013a, p. 35.

[93] GAO, 2011a, p. 15.

[94] GAO, 2011a, pp. 31–32.

[95] GAO, *Standards for Internal Control in the Federal Government*, Washington, D.C., GAO-14-704G, September 10, 2014.

[96] GAO, 2011a.

[97] GAO, 2004.

[98] GAO, 2011a, p. 17.

not fully using fraud detection techniques.[99] HSOAC analysts reviewed these processes as part of its separately commissioned study on TSA's internal control process for the STA and found that TSA had strengthened or was in the process of strengthening methods of electronically validating identity documents and reviewed notes from trusted agents identifying possible fraudulent documents.[100]

Excessive Length of Time for TWIC Enrollment or Issuance

GAO has repeatedly recognized concerns with the length of time between someone's application for a TWIC card and its issuance. Initially, these related to the need to initially enroll maritime workers before the program became mandatory for use at regulated facilities. GAO's 2010 report on TWIC found that lack of access to enrollment databases, inability to locate enrollment records, and lack of information technology (IT) contingency plans—coupled with incomplete applications and incorrectly denied applications—all increased the length of time between enrollment and issuance of TWIC cards, sometimes by up to seven months.[101]

Appropriateness of Eligibility Standards for TWIC Cardholders

The maritime industry and additional stakeholders have repeatedly raised questions about the standards that TWIC cardholders must meet, often stating that the standards should be related specifically to terrorism risk. GAO-06-982 highlights stakeholder concerns that including certain disqualifying offenses (e.g., lesser felonies, such as fraud), without consideration of when the person committed the offense, makes the standards too stringent and could cause people to lose their jobs.[102] Other stakeholders expressed concerns that the standards might be too low. GAO-12-60 highlights several ports and state port authorities that, at the time, issued additional worker credentials that required more-stringent background checks; GAO found instances in which workers had been denied local or state credentials but possessed valid TWICs.[103]

Inability to Continuously Vet TWIC Holders for Criminal Histories

GAO raised concerns that, because of a lack of internal controls, TSA could not make reasonable assurances that, once it issued someone a TWIC card, the person maintained

---

[99] OIG, 2016.

[100] Unpublished research.

[101] GAO, 2009, pp. 17–18, 21.

[102] GAO, 2006.

[103] GAO, 2011b.

eligibility during the card's five-year life span.[104] GAO raised this point particularly in regard to the ability to conduct continuous vetting TWIC holders for criminal histories.[105]

Weaknesses in the TWIC-Reader Pilot

DHS conducted a pilot program to test the viability of TWIC card readers in the maritime environment and the technical aspects of connecting TWIC readers to access control points. GAO raised multiple concerns about the pilot's results. According to GAO, TSA lacked defined performance standards to assess the pilot's performance; data collection was not consistent enough to ensure the collection of accurate, complete, comparable, and reliable data; and inadequate testing existed to ensure that piloted readers and TWIC cards worked as intended.[106]

Lack of Full Calculations of Reader Costs

GAO-06-982 discusses competing estimates and ambiguity regarding the cost of installing biometric reader systems at terminals.[107] In 2013, GAO found that reader cost estimates generated by the TWIC pilot were too low.[108] As we discuss in further detail in Chapter 8, we similarly found that USCG's estimates in its final reader rule analysis on the cost of installing readers at facilities were low for the costs of these technologies.

Reliability of TWIC-Reader Technology

Industry stakeholders expressed concerns to GAO in 2006 about a lack of compatibility between TWIC and existing access control systems, and GAO determined that sufficient testing had not been conducted on the TWIC program at that time.[109] Further, during the 2012 TWIC-reader pilot, not all readers withstood environmental conditions, nor could they accurately collect data required to assess the success or failure of the pilot,[110] which raised concerns about the reliability of reader technology.

Possible Value of Alternative Credentialing Models

MTSA's specifications for a "transportation security card program" do not specifically require that this program be national and directly managed by the federal government. GAO has raised questions about the analysis of alternatives that was conducted in determining that TWIC

---

[104] GAO, 2011a.

[105] GAO, 2011a.

[106] GAO, 2013a, pp. 18–19.

[107] GAO, 2006.

[108] GAO, 2013a.

[109] GAO, 2006, p. 22.

[110] GAO, 2013a, pp. 16, 20.

should be a federally managed program, particularly given some of the program's past problems. GAO called for a comprehensive comparison of alternative credentialing approaches, which might include a more decentralized approach, in achieving TWIC goals.[111]

Possible Redundancies of TWIC

GAO also raised concerns about background check program redundancies among six different programs under the purview of multiple DHS agencies and found that, at the time, DHS did not have the ability or a plan to determine efficiencies or best practices.[112] In an attempt to gain efficiencies, GAO recommended, DHS should at least coordinate STAs across programs and consider harmonizing programs that require the same background check, such as TWIC and the Hazardous Materials Endorsement (HME). Some policies existed at the time to allow holders of one credential to pay reduced application fees, but programs were not consistent in providing reciprocal benefits.[113]

Open GAO and OIG Recommendations

All but three of the recommendations from GAO and OIG reports on the TWIC program referenced in Public Law 114-278 have been formally closed. The three remaining open recommendations relate to GAO's 2011 study.[114] These open recommendations relate specifically to the requirements for a comprehensive security assessment, which we conducted as this study. The first of these relates to the need for DHS to perform an internal control assessment of the TWIC program, which is also called for in Public Law 114-278 Section 1(a). GAO found that previous HSOAC research for TSA partly addressed this recommendation, with outstanding issues related to the need to evaluate "the use of TWIC, including the Coast Guard's role in TWIC enforcement."[115] GAO, however, called for a further "internal control assessment inclusive of TWIC use and the interrelationship between acquiring a TWIC and using it in the maritime environment."[116] GAO further stated that this assessment should "assess information systems controls and related risks for reasonably assuring that use of TWIC with readers and associated systems used for access control decisions are reliable and not surreptitiously altered by cyber intrusions or attack."[117] This report provides a broader assessment of TWIC's use in the maritime environment. In this report, however, we do not address the cyber vulnerabilities of

---

[111] GAO, 2013a.

[112] GAO, 2007.

[113] GAO, 2007, pp. 5–6, 27–29.

[114] GAO, 2011a.

[115] GAO publishes recommendation status on the "Recommendations" tab of the webpage for GAO, 2011a.

[116] Webpage for GAO, 2011a.

[117] Webpage for GAO, 2011a.

access control systems. Initially, HSOAC and DHS agreed that cyber vulnerabilities in the maritime environment were outside the scope our study, and cyber vulnerabilities were not a key theme of past GAO reports. Access control systems are proprietary systems of facilities or their contract providers.

The second open recommendation pertains to similar concerns about the need for

> an effectiveness assessment that includes addressing internal control weaknesses and, at a minimum, evaluates whether use of TWIC in its present form and planned use with readers would enhance the posture of security beyond efforts already in place given costs and program risks. (product page for GAO, 2011a, recommendation 2 comments)

Chapter 6 and 7 address the general value of the TWIC program, and Chapter 8 provides our analysis of the costs and benefits of using TWIC readers. It further calls for this assessment to review

> the federally managed single credential approach in contrast to federally regulated decentralized options, such as the SIDA [Security Identification Display Area] airport credentialing model, the Hazardous Materials endorsement for truck drivers (wherein an endorsement is added to a driver's license), the federal government's own agency-specific credentialing model which relies on organizational sponsorship and credentials with agency-specific security features, or any combination thereof.

Chapter 9 provides information on alternative models.

The last open recommendation relates to the cost and benefit of readers, which we address in Chapter 8. GAO recommended that DHS use the TWIC assessments as

> the basis for evaluating the costs, benefits, security risks, and corrective actions needed to implement the TWIC program in a manner that will meet stated mission needs and mitigate existing security risks as part of conducting the regulatory analysis on implementing a new regulation on the use of TWIC with biometric card readers. (product page for GAO, 2011a, recommendation 3)

4. Security Threats to the Maritime Environment

Public Law 114-278 Section 1(b)(3)(C)(i) calls for this assessment to determine the extent to which the TWIC program, as implemented, addresses known or likely security risks. To do so, we needed to first establish the risks presented in the maritime environment. In this chapter, we first present a strategic overview of threats in the maritime environment, including terrorism, cybercrime, organized crime, and other nefarious acts. We start by discussing past attacks against the transportation sector and against the maritime environment specifically. We follow this with a broader discussion of the terrorism threat facing the United States, given that countering terrorism is a—if not the—primary purpose of the TWIC program, and what these changes might mean for vetting programs. Last, we turn to a discussion of the criminal security risks present in the maritime environment, recognizing that the dearth of detailed data about the U.S. port environment inhibits our ability to draw broad conclusions. The material in this chapter and the next is also informative background in answering Public Law 114-278's questions regarding the appropriateness of vetting standards (Section 1[b][3][A][i]).

Attacks Specific to the Transportation Sector

There have been few past terrorist attacks in the U.S. maritime sector, and none in the post-9/11 context. The FBI views the threat of terrorism in the maritime area as low, according to a recent U.S. Department of Justice (DOJ) report, although the bureau has been criticized for potentially having an incomplete picture of the threat.[118] Separate from terrorism, there have been detrimental attacks against the maritime sector in the past few years, although they do not appear to have exploited vulnerabilities related to PACSs. These have come in the form of cyberattacks against maritime facilities or companies committed by state-supported actors or unknown perpetrators. In the case of the NotPetya attack, which disrupted Maersk's cargo operations, there was significant economic damage. The maritime sector has also been the target of attacks abroad connected to terrorism or piracy (and sometimes both). When considering the value of access control programs in managing such threats, we highlight that these attacks have often come from individuals using waterside craft or passenger baggage to exploit maritime vulnerabilities. In the rest of this section, we provide further information about those instances.

Terrorist Attacks Against the U.S. Maritime Sector

A useful resource in understanding attacks is the Global Terrorism Database (GTD), a public-use repository of information on terrorist events around the world from 1970 through

---

[118] Office of the Inspector General, 2019.

2017. Maintained at the University of Maryland, the GTD is a well-respected public resource but counts more events as acts of terrorism than the U.S. government does. Although the GTD's stated criteria for what constitutes terrorism appear similar to the U.S. government's—a violent act intended to achieve a political, economic, religious, or social goal through fear, coercion, or intimidation—the GTD includes many events for which the perpetrator's intent is unknown or that the government has specifically found not to be acts of terrorism.[119] Given this expansive definition, the GTD might inflate the frequency of terrorism events but is less likely than other research data sources are to exclude events.

For terrorist events since 9/11, the GTD shows no attacks inside the United States in the maritime environment.[120] The only maritime-related attack in the past 40 years was in Escanaba, Michigan, in 1999, when animal rights activists destroyed fishing boats owned by a retired mink rancher.[121] Prior to that, a series of events in the 1970s were connected to extremist groups from Cuba or from San Juan, Puerto Rico. The majority of terrorist events in the transportation arena have been against aviation-related targets, both before and after 9/11. Figure 4.1 shows U.S. terrorist attacks, by transportation sector, from 1970 through 2018, based on GTD data.

---

[119] For example, the deadliest event during this period is Stephen Paddock's mass shooting in Las Vegas, which neither the FBI nor the Las Vegas Metropolitan Police Department considers an act of terrorism but is included in the GTD. The GTD also includes events with unknown perpetrators, which, because the perpetrator's intent is unknown, does not meet the government's criterion of political intent (FBI, "Key Findings of the Behavioral Analysis Unit's Las Vegas Review Panel (LVRP)," undated a; Las Vegas Metropolitan Police Department, *LVMPD Criminal Investigative Report of the 1 October Mass Casualty Shooting*, August 3, 2018).

[120] This result is based on an advanced search of the GTD limiting the country to the United States and the target type to maritime. We additionally ran a search of target type as transportation and reviewed the results for any maritime-related incident (finding one).

[121] This event is GTD ID 199908070005.

Figure 4.1. Terrorist Attacks Against U.S. Targets, by Transportation Sector

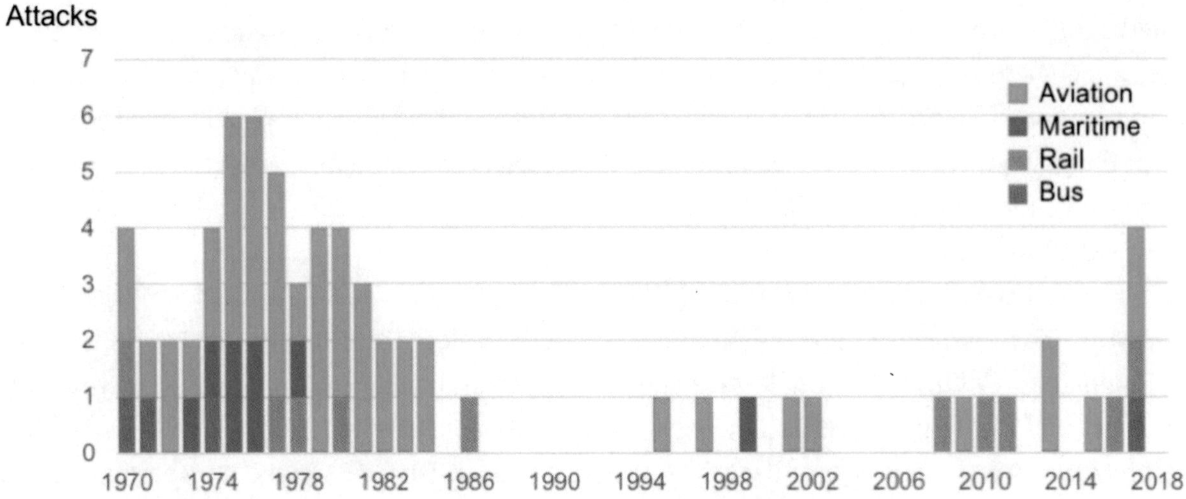

SOURCE: GTD data.

The motivations for and perpetrators of attacks against transportation-related targets in the United States have varied. Particularly after 9/11, attacks have generally been directed by al Qaeda and related groups or by homegrown violent extremists (HVEs) sympathetic to their cause. Prior to 9/11, there was a spate of plane hijackings, usually in the name of one of various political causes. There were also incidents of single-issue extremists, such as environmental activists. Of attacks in the past 40 years, the 9/11 attacks are striking in the large number of people killed or injured. No other attack related to transportation has killed more than five in the United States.

Cyberattacks Against the U.S. Maritime Sector

The most notable attack against a U.S. maritime facility was the June 2017 NotPetya cyberattack, which the White House described as "the most destructive and costly cyberattack in history."[122] NotPetya disrupted cargo operations at all of Maersk's U.S.-based facilities (in Mobile, Alabama; Miami, Florida; Newark, New Jersey; Tacoma, Washington; and Los Angeles, California).[123] The malicious code that affected Maersk's computer networks permanently disabled 45,000 computers and caused the loss of critical information about the contents of cargo holds.[124] As a result, Maersk and its customers were unable to determine where to load and

---

[122] Press Secretary, White House, "Statement from the Press Secretary," February 16, 2008.

[123] Jonathan Saul, "Global Shipping Feels Fallout from Maersk Cyber Attack," Reuters, June 29, 2017; "Maersk's Cargo Operations Hit Hard by Cyberattack," *Maritime Executive*, June 28, 2017.

[124] Andy Greenberg, "The Untold Story of NotPetya, the Most Devastating Cyberattack in History," *Wired*, August 22, 2018.

unload tens of thousands of containers. At Port Newark–Elizabeth Marine Terminal, for instance, hundreds of cargo trucks were backed up awaiting instructions. Operations at 17 of Maersk's 76 terminals worldwide were halted or severely disrupted for more than a week, costing the company an estimated $300 million.[125]

Because NotPetya spread to diverse systems across the globe, it was not immediately apparent that Maersk or the maritime transportation sector was intentionally targeted. NotPetya was later attributed to Russian state actors, and the attack might have been intended, in part, to threaten or punish multinational corporations that do business in Ukraine. As Cisco cybersecurity researcher Craig Williams said, "This was a piece of malware designed to send a political message: If you do business in Ukraine, bad things are going to happen to you."[126] Although U.S. port operations were not specifically targeted, they were very likely to be affected given that Maersk was one of several intended victims and operates several terminals in the United States. NotPetya illustrated that cyberattacks can cause physical damage that necessitates replacing infrastructure—not just repairing it or restoring information. Further, ports can be vulnerable indirectly via targeted nations, companies, individuals, or software, even if the port itself is not specifically targeted.

Both the Port of Long Beach and the Port of San Diego have been victims of ransomware attacks, although the attacks were not economically disruptive. The China Ocean Shipping Company Terminal at the Port of Long Beach reported that an attack on July 24, 2018, disrupted its communication network.[127] The Port of San Diego announced on September 27, 2018, that a cyberattack had disrupted its IT systems.[128]

Attacks Against Maritime Facilities and Vessels Abroad

Although U.S. maritime facilities have not been subjected to physical attacks that have caused a loss of life or other damage, there is at least one recent example of a port being the target of physical attack. The attack happened in Israel in March 2004, when two suicide bombers who were smuggled into the Port of Ashdod killed ten people and injured 16. The attackers avoided detection at a security checkpoint by hiding behind a false panel in a shipping container.[129]

Attacks have occurred more frequently against passenger ships than against ports. These attacks have generally, however, exploited vulnerabilities from the waterside to small boats or

---

[125] Kim S. Nash, Sara Castellanos, and Adam Janofsky, "One Year After NotPetya Cyberattack, Firms Wrestle with Recovery Costs," *Wall Street Journal*, June 27, 2018.

[126] Greenberg, 2018.

[127] Mark Edward Nero, "Long Beach Port Terminal Hit by Ransomware Attack," *Press-Telegram* (Long Beach, Calif.), July 24, 2018.

[128] Port of San Diego, "Port of San Diego Releases Additional Information on Cybersecurity Incident," press release, September 27, 2018.

[129] Andrew Beadle, "Ashdod Attack a Wake-Up Call for U.S. Ports, Says ILWU Official," *JOC*, March 29, 2004.

weaknesses in passenger screening. In 1985, four men from the Palestine Liberation Front hijacked the Italian cruise ship the MS *Achille Lauro* off the coast of Egypt. The hijackers shot and killed a 69-year old Jewish American during their attack. The *Achille Lauro* had a special symbolic importance in that it raised concerns that terrorist threats were expanding to the maritime environment.[130] Assessments at the time raised concerns that the increasing frequency of terrorist attacks, combined with the potential novel appeal of attacks in the maritime environment, might increase the frequency of attacks in the maritime sector.[131] Although there has arguably not been a surge of terrorist attacks in the maritime environment, attacks continue to be persistent against passenger, commercial, and military vessels. The Abu Nidal Organization, a Palestinian militant group, is suspected of attacking the Greek cruise ship *City of Poros* in 1988. Following a failed attempt in which the ship did not arrive at port at the expected time and a car bomb detonated prematurely , a gunman who boarded as a ticketed passenger subsequently carried out an attack, resulting in a total of 11 deaths (including the gunman).[132] The only known bombing of a passenger ship since then was the *Superferry 14* attack in February 2004—conducted by the Philippine terrorist organization, the Abu Sayyaf Group. In the *Superferry* attack, a ticketed passenger planted a bomb in his lodging and departed the ship before a timing device detonated the explosive, sinking the ship and resulting in 116 deaths.[133]

In October 2000, al Qaeda operatives attacked the USS *Cole*, detonating high explosives on a small boat that maneuvered alongside the ship's hull while it was refueling, killing 17 U.S. Navy sailors. Earlier that year, al Qaeda had made a similar attempt on the USS *The Sullivans*, but the attackers' boat sank under the weight of the explosives.

Al Qaeda carried out another successful small-boat bombing in November 2002 against the commercial oil tanker MV *Limburg*,[134] killing one crew member, causing an oil spill, and leading to a short-term collapse of international shipping business in the Persian Gulf.[135] In October 2016, unknown assailants attempted to deliver "a significant amount" of high explosives in an attack on a liquefied-natural-gas tanker in the Bab el Mandeb strait off Yemen, but the boat's explosives detonated prematurely.[136] Despite the fact that military and commercial

---

[130] Jeffrey Simon, *The Implications of the Achille Lauro Hijacking for the Maritime Community*, Santa Monica, Calif.: RAND Corporation, P-7250, 1986.

[131] Simon, 1986, p. 5.

[132] "Greece: 1988 Overview," MIPT Terrorism Knowledge Base, last updated October 31, 2005.

[133] Kit Collier and John Sifton, *Lives Destroyed: Attacks Against Civilians in the Philippines*, Washington, D.C.: Human Rights Watch, July 2007.

[134] James Jay Carafano, "Small Boats, Big Worries: Thwarting Terrorist Attacks from the Sea," Washington, D.C.: Heritage Foundation, Backgrounder 2041, June 11, 2007.

[135] National Memorial Institute for the Prevention of Terrorism, *The MIPT Terrorism Annual: 2006*, Oklahoma City, 2006, p. 26.

[136] Jonathan Saul, "Boat That Attacked Gas Tanker Off Yemen Carried Explosives: Shipowner," Reuters, November 3, 2016.

organizations use armed escorts, as well as reinforced and double hulls, these targets remain vulnerable because the challenge of threat detection makes it difficult to prevent or interdict small-boat attacks. DHS's *Small Vessel Security Strategy* raises concerns about the risks associated with the potential for "terrorists, smugglers of weapons of mass destruction (WMDs), narcotics, aliens, other contraband, and other criminals"[137] to exploit small boats.

Piracy is also pervasive in Africa and Asia. Small boats have typically been pirates' weapon of choice. In east Africa, Somali piracy peaked in 2010 and 2011, with yearly totals of more than 100 attacks and more than 1,000 people taken hostage.[138] A drastic decline to fewer than ten successful attacks per year since 2012 has been attributed primarily to the use of armed guards and situational awareness measures.[139] Nevertheless, a resurgence in piracy occurred in 2017 and 2018, including Somali pirates' first successful capture of a commercial vessel since 2012—an oil tanker made vulnerable by a low freeboard and lack of armed guards and razor wire. Complacency, in the form of poor adherence to security best practices and a failure to arm the majority of ships, is cited as a major factor in the rise in attacks, along with the sustained intent and capability of the pirates themselves.[140]

In west Africa, despite efforts to establish "secure zones" in which ships can anchor or conduct cargo transfers, the Gulf of Guinea has experienced a trend of at-anchor robberies at major ports, where pirates using small boats speed in and out before a response can be mounted. Maisie Pigeon and colleagues explained,

> As port traffic has increased, ships are spending longer at anchor waiting for a berth, making them more vulnerable to attack. These recent attacks show that pirates are following the merchant traffic and moving their operations to where easy targets can be found.[141]

However, many of the factors that make ports in the Gulf of Guinea vulnerable, including the lack of strong national coast guards, are not prevalent in the United States.[142]

---

[137] DHS, *Small Vessel Security Strategy*, DHS 20080307, revision 1.4, April 2008.

[138] European Union External Action, homepage, undated.

[139] Peter Apps, "Have Hired Guns Finally Scuppered Somali Pirates?" Reuters, February 23, 2013; Dan Harris and Dan Lieberman, "Pirate Attacks Down as Private Maritime Security Business Booms," ABC News, September 27, 2012; Dan De Luce, "Why Is It So Hard to Stop West Africa's Vicious Pirates?" *Foreign Policy*, September 23, 2016.

[140] Kieron Monks, "Piracy Threat Returns to African Waters," CNN, January 3, 2018; Kevin Sieff, "Everyone Thought the Somali Pirate Threat Had Ended. Then a Tanker Was Attacked," *Washington Post*, March 15, 2017; De Luce, 2016.

[141] Maisie Pigeon, Emina Sadic, Sean Duncan, Chuck Ridgway, and Kelsey Soeth, *The State of Maritime Piracy 2017: Assessing the Economic and Human Cost*, Broomfield, Colo.: One Earth Future, May 23, 2018.

[142] De Luce, 2016; Max Bearak, "Falling Oil Prices Spark a Rise in Kidnappings by West African Pirates," *Washington Post*, May 10, 2016.

The Threat of Terrorism in the United States Today

In this section, we discuss the evolution of terrorist threats against the United States and what this could suggest for risks to the maritime environment. The terrorist threat to the United States is still generally assessed to come from groups or individuals espousing Islamic extremism; although, as we discuss later in this section, many counterterrorism experts are concerned about the increasing threat of domestic terrorism. The foreign versus domestic character of the terrorist threat to the United States is important context, however, in considering the effectiveness of security measures, such as personnel vetting. The State Department maintains a list of foreign terrorist organizations, of which there are currently 67, but there is no official mechanism for designating domestic terrorist groups. DOJ and the FBI identify domestic terrorist "threats" (e.g., ecoterrorists, anarchists, white supremacists), but they do not officially designate domestic terrorist groups or individuals.[143] An individual can be charged with an act of terrorism under 18 U.S.C. § 2332b if their terrorist act has some foreign connection, but domestic terrorism is not itself a federal crime. Although there are means to watch-list and vet people who are tied to domestic terrorism, these mechanisms are most robust for known or suspected terrorism that has some association with a foreign terrorist organization.

Literature on the severity of the terrorism threat to the United States today presents a mixed picture, partly because the studies often do not distinguish between the threat to the United States abroad and at home. Many authors point to the continued resilience of Salafi-jihadist groups and their persistent threat to the United States. Bruce Hoffman, for example, assessed in late 2016 that the Trump administration would be "confronted with arguably the most parlous international security environment since the period immediately following the September 11, 2001, attacks—with serious threats emanating from not one but two terrorist movements and a counterterrorism strategy and approach that [have] failed."[144] Later, Hoffman also pointed out that, despite the U.S. preoccupation with the Islamic State of Iraq and Syria (ISIS), al Qaeda has "been quietly rebuilding."[145] Similarly, Jami Forbes saw al Qaeda's renewed communication efforts as a sign that the group "is attempting to reintroduce its movement to the world, and possibly rebrand its long-term strategy."[146] Forbes pointed to the group's continued focus on the West and the United States in particular. Jason Burke argued that a new jihadist threat was emerging under the

---

[143] Jerome P. Bjelopera, *Domestic Terrorism: An Overview*, Washington, D.C.: Congressional Research Service, R44921, August 21, 2017, p. 2.

[144] Bruce Hoffman, "The Global Terror Threat and Counterterrorism Challenges Facing the Next Administration," *CTC Sentinel*, Vol. 9, No. 11, November–December 2016, p. 1.

[145] Bruce Hoffman, "Al-Qaeda's Resurrection," Council on Foreign Relations, expert brief, March 6, 2018.

[146] Jami Forbes, "Does al-Qa'ida's Increasing Media Outreach Signal Revitalization?" *CTC Sentinel*, Vol. 12, No. 1, January 2019, p. 25.

al Qaeda label, "a coalition of loosely connected local groups united only by nominal allegiance to a weak central leadership."[147]

Notwithstanding the persistent threat from terrorist groups, such as al Qaeda and ISIS, to U.S. interests abroad, senior U.S. counterterrorism officials have generally described a decreased terrorist threat inside the U.S. homeland. In particular, in 2017, outgoing National Counterterrorism Center (NCTC) director Nicholas J. Rasmussen stated that it was "safe to say that we are at far less risk today of a large-scale, mass-casualty, catastrophic attack here in the homeland than certainly we were at the time of 9/11 and the aftermath of 9/11."[148] In the 2019 threat assessment, the director of national intelligence described HVEs as the most acute Sunni terrorist threat to the United States and said that the United States was still "a generally inhospitable operating environment" for HVEs, compared with many other industrialized countries.[149] He further assessed that the "frequency of attacks most likely will be very low compared to most other forms of criminal violence."[150] As early as 2011, then–attorney general Eric Holder, Secretary of Homeland Security Janet Napolitano, and director of national intelligence James Clapper authored an op-ed stating that "we have accomplished much to minimize the risk that a successful terror attack like 9/11 will ever occur on American soil," citing the ways in which the United Sates has "created a much stronger framework for managing threats to our nation."[151]

The Shifting Threat to Small-Scale Terrorist Attacks

Islamist-oriented attackers have previously come to the United States from abroad to conduct terrorist attacks—often with multiple players and against high-value targets. Although 9/11 is a vivid example of success, al Qaeda unsuccessfully planned a series of terrorist attacks to occur around the turn of the millennium, including one by Ahmed Ressam against Los Angeles International Airport. Today, instead of planning sophisticated, high-consequence attacks (that might be of the scale of a TSI), terrorist groups have encouraged people sympathetic to their cause to conduct small-scale attacks with greater likelihood of success. Jihadist terrorist propaganda often encourages self-radicalized people—HVEs—to conduct small-scale attacks on their own initiative that have high probabilities of success, even if the targets are not symbolic

---

[147] Jason Burke, "The Age of Selfie Jihad: How Evolving Media Technology Is Changing Terrorism," *CTC Sentinel*, Vol. 9, No. 11, November–December 2016, p. 21.

[148] Paul Cruickshank, "A View from the CT Foxhole: Nicholas Rasmussen, Former Director, National Counterterrorism Center," *CTC Sentinel*, Vol. 11, No. 1, January 2018.

[149] Daniel R. Coats, director of national intelligence, *Statement for the Record: Worldwide Threat Assessment of the US Intelligence Community, Office of the Director of National Intelligence*, submitted to the U.S. Senate Select Committee on Intelligence, January 29, 2019, p. 12.

[150] Coats, 2019, p. 12.

[151] Eric Holder, Janet Napolitano, and James Clapper, "We're Safer Post-9/11," *USA Today*, op-ed, September 8, 2011.

and the casualties are few. In late 2017, then–NCTC director Nick Rasmussen testified before Congress about this growing emphasis on simple attacks:

> What we have seen over time is that HVEs—either lone actors or small insular groups—tend to gravitate toward soft targets and simple tactics of opportunity that do not require advanced skills or outside training. We expect that most HVEs will continue to focus on soft targets, while still considering traditional targets, such as military personnel, law enforcement, and other symbols of the U.S. government.[152]

In their English-language propaganda, al Qaeda and its affiliates have encouraged supporters to conduct unsophisticated attacks, and ISIS in particular has instructed supporters to conduct less-sophisticated attacks against soft targets in the West—a call to action that likely contributed to a rise of such operations since 2014. In one vivid example, ISIS spokesperson Abu Muhammad al-`Adnani al-Shami called on supporters to launch a series of operations in the West, regardless of their sophistication:

> If you are not able to find an IED or a bullet, then single out the disbelieving American, Frenchman, or any of their allies. Smash his head with a rock, or slaughter him with a knife, or run him over with your car, or throw him down from a high place, or choke him, or poison him . . . If you are unable to do so, then burn his home, car, or business. Or destroy his crops. If you are unable to do so, then spit in his face . . .[153]

The group echoed this sentiment in subsequent editions of its propaganda—*Dābiq*, *Rumiyyah*, and other official ISIS publications—and praised so-called "soldiers of the Caliphate" who carried out less-sophisticated attacks in the West.[154] The message from ISIS is clear: Supporters should attack any type of target, civilian or otherwise, with any means available.

Following Adnani's call for "do-it-yourself terror," a review of attacks conducted in the United States by supporters of jihadist groups suggests a clear trend toward less-sophisticated tactics against accessible and unprotected targets. Of the 16 jihadist-associated attacks in the United States between September 2014 and June 2017, unprotected civilians were targeted on 11 occasions, and law-enforcement officers or military personnel were targeted on six occasions.[155] The tactics used in each attack likewise trended toward easier-to-acquire weapons, including fixed blades (seven) and small arms (eight), while homemade explosives were used in just one attack.

---

[152] Nicholas J. Rasmussen, director, National Counterterrorism Center, Office of the Director of National Intelligence, "World Wide Threats: Keeping America Secure in the New Age of Terror," testimony before the U.S. House of Representatives Committee on Homeland Security, November 30, 2017.

[153] Abu Muhammad al-`Adnani al-Shami, spokesperson, Islamic State of Iraq and Syria, "Indeed Your Lord Is Ever Watchful," statement, September 9, 2014.

[154] "They Plot and Allah Plots," *Dābiq*, No. 9, May 2015, p. 3; "The Rāfidah: From Ibn Saba' to the Dajjāl," *Dābiq*, No. 12, January 2016, p. 3.

[155] Lorenzo Vidino, Francesco Marone, and Eva Entenmann, *Fear Thy Neighbor: Radicalization and Jihadist Attacks in the West*, the Hague: International Centre for Counter-Terrorism, June 14, 2017.

Of course, this recent trend should not suggest that groups have abandoned complex plots that can achieve greater consequences. Al Qaeda propaganda published in 2017 stated that transportation, including maritime, was still a key priority for the group.[156] And Australian authorities foiled an attempted ISIS attack in July 2017 that sought to target an Abu Dhabi–bound aircraft with a novel explosive device shipped to Australian operatives by group members in Turkey.[157] But simpler attacks likely occur more frequently than complex attacks because they require less technical skill to develop and shorter planning cycles to execute and often provide fewer trip wires that would allow authorities to identify would-be operatives.

The Frequency of Terrorist Attacks Inside the United States

The contention of top counterterrorism experts that the terrorism threat is lower in the United States today than after 9/11 is consistent with the data on actual terrorist attacks on domestic targets. The definition of *terrorism* varies greatly, so one study that attempts to evaluate the trend of terrorism over time might consider an event or actor to be representative of terrorism while another study does not. However, most measures suggest that the threat to the United States is low, and some reflect a decrease in the threat since the 9/11 attacks.

A previous RAND analysis of terrorist trends using the GTD found that, since 9/11, terrorist attacks have been less frequent in the United States (and, in fact, worldwide).[158] The GTD identifies 414 attacks inside the United States since 9/11, resulting in 304 fatalities (33 perpetrators and 271 nonperpetrators). Just six of these attacks killed more than ten people (Table 4.1). As we mentioned earlier, the GTD errs on the side of inclusivity in its data. GTD's data also separate attacks that others might lump together—for example, the four 9/11 hijackings are listed as four separate terrorist attacks. For these reasons, the GTD's number of total events could be higher than those from other sources.[159]

---

[156] Adam Kredo, "Al Qaeda Publishes Blueprint for Attacks on Key U.S. Transportation Systems," *Washington Free Beacon*, August 15, 2017.

[157] "Australian Terror Plan to Hide Plane Bomb in Barbie Revealed," BBC, August 21, 2017; Jacqueline Williams, "Australia Details 'Sophisticated' Plot by ISIS to Take Down Plane," *New York Times*, August 4, 2017.

[158] Meagan Smith and Sean M. Zeigler, "Terrorism Before and After 9/11: A More Dangerous World?" *Research and Politics*, October–December 2017, pp. 1–8.

[159] This bias does not affect our ability to judge trends related to GTD data over time: The GTD's definitions remain consistent. The GTD's data are also useful in that they include attacks by both domestic and foreign-associated actors.

Table 4.1. Attacks Since 9/11 with Ten or More Fatalities, per the GTD

Date	Event	Fatalities
October 1, 2017	A gunman opened fire using multiple firearms on concertgoers from a hotel room in Las Vegas, Nevada.	59
June 12, 2016	A gunman opened fire using multiple firearms on customers at a night club in Orlando, Florida.	50
December 2, 2015	Two assailants used multiple firearms and a failed explosive device to attack a workplace holiday party in San Bernardino, California.	16
April 17, 2013	Unidentified people set fire to a fertilizer plant, causing an explosion.	15
November 5, 2009	An Army major opened fire using multiple firearms on civilians and fellow soldiers in Fort Hood, Texas.	13
October 1, 2015	A gunman used multiple firearms to hold a college classroom hostage in Roseburg, Oregon.	10

Other studies have looked at the frequency of terrorist attacks since 9/11 and the number of fatalities caused. Research by New America identified 56 attacks that caused fatalities, regardless of whether they were conducted by jihadist, far-right wing, or other ideological actors.[160] Together, these attacks killed 206 people (see Figure 4.2).

Figure 4.2. Deadly U.S. Terrorist Attacks, by Year and Actor

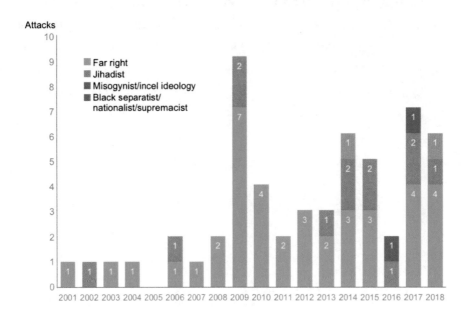

SOURCE: New America, "Terrorism in America After 9/11," undated.

---

[160] New America, "What Is the Threat to the United States?" *Terrorism in America After 9/11*, Washington, D.C., c. 2017, Part IV.

A previous RAND report on the frequency of foreign terrorism–related attacks in the United States using a more stringent definition of terrorism incidents and only attacks tied to foreign terrorist groups found that, between September 12, 2001, and December 31, 2017, only 25 such plots successfully advanced to the operational phase. The attacks killed 102 people; in 60 percent of cases, no casualties occurred.[161] These research studies all considered plots that resulted in attempted terrorist attacks and, in the case of the New America information, only attacks that led to fatalities. This does not reflect how many terrorist plots might have existed but been foiled by law-enforcement action.

A Possible Rise in the Threat of Domestic Terrorism

Several terrorist attacks in recent years perpetrated by white nationalist and white supremacist entities have propelled the subject of domestic terrorism into the public discourse. Some scholars and experts have argued that domestic terrorism is a greater threat to the U.S. homeland and national security than jihadist groups are. According to Peter Bergen and David Sterman, "Jihadist organizations are no longer the main terrorist threat facing the country. Since 9/11, no foreign terrorist group has successfully conducted a deadly attack in the United States."[162] Bergen and Sterman noted a web of drivers, including "[u]biquitous firearms, political polarization, images of the extensive apocalyptic violence tearing apart societies in the Middle East and North Africa, racism, and the rise of populism," along with the advances made in online communication.[163] The authors contended that the U.S. counterterrorism apparatus has been largely successful in preventing lethal attacks by foreign jihadist groups since 9/11—although ISIS has successfully recruited U.S. citizens on American soil—and that terrorism today is less common than in the 1970s. Besides white nationalists and white supremacist groups, other threats from domestic terrorism include far-right, far-left, and black nationalist ideologies. As mentioned earlier, however, it is difficult to determine whether government vetting mechanisms are as effective against domestic terrorism threats as they are against foreign-associated terrorist threats.

Threats of Crime in the Port Environment

MTSA also raised concerns about the threat of federal crime, particularly trafficking of people and illicit material and theft, in the port environment. This was raised as a particular concern given that "United States ports are international boundaries;" although, not all MTSA-

---

[161] These fatalities do not include the deaths of 13 perpetrators (Heather J. Williams, Nathan Chandler, and Eric Robinson, *Trends in the Draw of Americans to Foreign Terrorist Organizations from 9/11 to Today*, Santa Monica, Calif.: RAND Corporation, RR-2545-OSD, 2018, p. 13).

[162] Peter Bergen and David Sterman, "The Real Terrorist Threat in America: It's No Longer Jihadist Groups," *Foreign Affairs*, October 30, 2018.

[163] Bergen and Sterman, 2018.

regulated facilities engage in international business. *The National Security Strategy for Maritime Security* raises concerns that terrorists could use criminal smuggling networks to circumvent border security measures and smuggle agents, materials, or revenue.[164] It reports that ports were particularly vulnerable to security threats, given their location and accessibility. TSA has also expressed that the TWIC STA is concerned with more than just terrorism and criminal acts within ports; it also addresses the potential for a TWIC holder to use their access in a maritime facility to facilitate a terrorist act in another location through smuggling of firearms or explosives or by providing material support to terrorists.[165]

MTSA references the autumn 2000 findings of the Interagency Commission on Crime and Security in U.S. Seaports, which remains one of the most comprehensive studies of crime in the maritime environment. In this study, researchers focused on 12 major ports and benefited from data provided directly by dozens of federal and local law-enforcement agencies. This data-collection effort was necessary because "federal agency databases do not adequately collect and report crime data by seaports, and state and local law enforcement agencies do not specifically collect and report crime data by seaports."[166] We were unable to find any improved system of seaport crime data statistics,[167] which limits our ability to ascertain the extent to which crime has changed since the 2000 report and to which the commission's findings extend to MTSA-regulated facilities that might not be part of major ports.

Although we recognize the limitations in our ability to expand on the interagency commission's report, its findings are still very informative of the criminal threats in the maritime environment. The commission found that "U.S. seaports are major conduits for serious crime."[168] The most prevalent and reported crime problem was drug smuggling, but the commission also found consistent problems with "smuggling of contraband and prohibited or restricted merchandise, stowaways and alien smuggling, trade fraud and commercial smuggling, environmental crimes, and the unlawful exportation of controlled commodities and munitions, stolen property, and drug proceeds."[169] Illegal activity, particularly drug smuggling, was aided by the use of internal conspirators among transportation workers: "Internal conspiracies were reported at 9 of the 12 seaports surveyed—Charleston, Gulfport, Los Angeles, Miami, New

---

[164] DHS, *The National Security Strategy for Maritime Security*, Washington, D.C., September 2005, p. 4.

[165] Multiple conversations between the authors and representatives from the TSA Office of Chief Counsel, June–July 2019.

[166] Interagency Commission on Crime and Security in U.S. Seaports, *Report of the Interagency Commission on Crime and Security in U.S. Seaports*, Fall 2000, p. 57.

[167] For example, the Uniform Crime Reporting (UCR) program, along with its successor, the National Incident-Based Reporting System, breaks down data by state but not locality or by port. Moreover, law-enforcement authorities responsible for maritime facilities might not always report their statistics to the UCR program.

[168] Interagency Commission on Crime and Security in U.S. Seaports, 2000, p. 57.

[169] Interagency Commission on Crime and Security in U.S. Seaports, 2000, p. 57.

Orleans, New York/New Jersey, Port Everglades, Philadelphia, and San Juan."[170] Drug trafficking organizations used "dockworkers, employees of ocean carriers, security firms, freight forwarders, brokers, and other companies involved in the importation or transportation of goods." The full extent of such conspiracies was unknown, and other people were also identified as involved in trafficking, such as ship crew members and cruise passengers. The commission assessed that criminal background checks for people in secure or restricted port areas and the display of distinctive ID badges would be highly beneficial to physical security.

Summary

The threat environment for the maritime environment is diverse, with threats coming from nation-state actors, terrorists, and transnational criminal organizations. Fortunately, the United States has not seen a repeat of large-scale, coordinated attacks akin to the 9/11 attacks. Foreign terrorist groups have pushed adherents and sympathizers toward opportunity-driven attacks with higher chances of success but potentially lower consequence. These actors often lack sophisticated capabilities and direct aid from terrorist groups. This trend suggests that security measures, such as access control programs, could deter radicalized actors who would not be capable of carrying out a sophisticated attack. In our research, we found that threats that could cause TSIs are assessed to be less likely to occur today than they would have been at the inception of the TWIC program, and the terrorism threat is low. Although we were unable to determine how criminal threats in the maritime environment have changed over time, past evidence suggests that smuggling and theft have been previously identified as major concerns in the maritime environment. The 2000 Interagency Commission on Crime and Security in U.S. Seaports report called for more-consistent tracking of crime in the maritime environment; however, because there is still no clear system of seaport crime data statistics, we are unable to determine whether or how the prevalence of crime has changed since that study.

Findings from congressional legislation, the Interagency Commission on Crime and Security in U.S. Seaports, and *The National Security Strategy for Maritime Security* assert that identity verification methods and background checks contribute to improving the maritime security environment. In later chapters, we consider the costs and benefits of how identity verification and background checks are currently conducted. Our findings regarding the diverse and dynamic nature of threats within the maritime environment are also relevant to our discussion in Chapter 7 of the threats for which TWIC can play a mitigating role and those that exceed its risk-mitigation potential.

---

[170] Interagency Commission on Crime and Security in U.S. Seaports, 2000, p. 36.

5. The Risk-Mitigation Value of the TWIC STA

TSA's STA provides a common standard for background checks on people seeking unescorted access to facility secure areas. Public Law 114-278 instructs that a program evaluation determine whether the TWIC program's current vetting standards, which are set forth in 46 U.S.C. § 70105, are "appropriate." To determine the appropriateness of vetting standards, one must understand the function they are intended to serve. In this chapter, we discuss STA standards set in regulations, including references to the objective of the TWIC program, as well as discussion about the program's purpose according to the congressional record. Because Section 70105 specifically addresses the fact that the vetting process is one intended to determine "*Terrorism* Security Risk" (emphasis added), and the legislative history has often emphasized the counterterrorism value of the TWIC program, we considered the standards set forth in Section 70105 specifically in terms of their relevance to determining terrorism risk. In particular, we surveyed existing research on whether criminal history and immigration status are useful risk factors in identifying whether someone poses a terrorist threat and the role of incarceration in terrorist radicalization. Given that other parts of the statute speak to a general concern about crime and TWIC's ability to enhance security, we also considered the appropriateness of vetting standards for the broader purpose of reducing security risks. In this chapter, we also provide information from interviewees on the perceived value of the STA process and opportunities that could exist to enhance the program's security value. Last, we discuss the efficiency of the current federal process in terms of the costs of vetting and time taken to do so. We conclude with a summary of our findings. The material in this chapter directly addresses Public Law 114-278's questions regarding the appropriateness of vetting standards (Section 1[b][3][A][i]), the cost of vetting (Section 1[b][3][A][ii]), and the length of time needed to review an application (Section 1[b]).

The Purpose of the STA

Public Law 114-278 states that the evaluation must determine whether TWIC's vetting standards are "appropriate," but it does not define the term. In this analysis, we assumed that *appropriate* means *suitable or fitting for the intended purpose*. Thus, to determine whether the standards are appropriate, we needed to identify the nature and intent of the STA standards.

Standards of the STA

The language in MTSA, as initially enacted in 2002, provided broad guidance for how DHS should determine whether someone should be granted a transportation security card, and it emphasized terrorism security risk or risk of causing a severe TSI. The initial language in the law read as follows:

> I DETERMINATION OF TERRORISM SECURITY RISK.—(1) An individual may not be denied a transportation security card under subsection (b) unless the Secretary determines that individual—(A) has been convicted within the preceding 7-year period of a felony or found not guilty by reason of insanity of a felony—(i) that the Secretary believes could cause the individual to be a terrorism security risk to the United States; or (ii) for causing a severe transportation security incident; (B) has been released from incarceration within the preceding 5-year period for committing a felony described in subparagraph (A); (C) may be denied admission to the United States or removed from the United States under the Immigration and Nationality Act (8 U.S.C. 1101 et seq.); or (D) otherwise poses a terrorism security risk to the United States.[171]

The final rule that initially required the TWIC card to be used at maritime facilities also established TWIC's specific qualification standards.[172] In the rule, TSA determined that the criminal disqualifications used for HME, which were derived from 49 U.S.C. § 44936 (employment investigations and restrictions for aviation personnel), would also apply to TWIC applicants.[173] The Uniting and Strengthening America by Providing Appropriate Tools Required to Intercept and Obstruct Terrorism (USA PATRIOT) Act similarly called on TSA to conduct an STA to determine whether someone holding an HME presented a "security risk." According to the final rule, TSA "interpreted the language 'security risk' to mean a risk of terrorism or terrorist activity."[174] The final rule further reads,

> MTSA, enacted a year later, requires a security threat assessment to determine whether an applicant poses a 'terrorism security threat.' We believe the security threat assessment required under MTSA is the same threat assessment required under the USA Patriot Act, even though the actual language differs slightly.[175]

The initial HME standards were determined by TSA

> in consultation with the Department of Justice (DOJ) and DOT [the U.S. Department of Transportation], to include those offenses that are reasonably indicative of an individual's predisposition to engage in violent or deceptive behavior that may be predictive of a security threat.[176]

---

[171] 46 U.S.C. § 70105.

[172] USCG, 2007.

[173] Public Law 107-56, Uniting and Strengthening America by Providing Appropriate Tools Required to Intercept and Obstruct Terrorism Act of 2001, October 26, 2001, more commonly called the Patriot Act.

[174] USCG, 2007, p. 3501.

[175] USCG, 2007, p. 3501.

[176] TSA, "Security Threat Assessment for Individuals Applying for a Hazardous Materials Endorsement for a Commercial Driver's License," interim final rule and request for comments, *Federal Register*, Vol. 69, No. 226, November 24, 2004, pp. 68719–68749.

Under the SAFE Port Act of 2006, anyone convicted of any of four specified felonies—treason, espionage, sedition, or crime of terrorism—is permanently disqualified from being issued a transportation security card. Anyone convicted of any of these offenses is not eligible for a waiver. On August 3, 2007, President Bush signed Public Law 110-53, adopting the STA standards established in the *Federal Register*, which were then codified at 46 U.S.C. § 70105. (The complete list of disqualifying offenses can be found in Appendix B.) The new law amended MTSA to add those disqualifying offenses and the additional crimes TSA promulgated in the TWIC final rule: Crimes related to explosives, murder, and organized crime were added as permanently disqualifying but eligible for waiver.[177] It also added 16 other broad categories of felony offenses (e.g., smuggling, arson, rape) as interim disqualifying offenses.[178] An interim offense is disqualifying if, within seven years of the date of the TWIC application, the applicant has been convicted, has pleaded guilty, or was found not guilty by reason of insanity. It is also disqualifying if the applicant has been incarcerated for the crime and released within five years of applying for the TWIC. The same disqualifying factors appear in 49 C.F.R. Part 1572, which provides rules on credentialing and STAs for maritime and land transportation security.[179]

STA Standards That Are Relevant to TWIC's Purpose

MTSA, as noted earlier, tied security risk to two criteria: (1) the risk of terrorism and (2) the risk of causing a severe TSI. *Terrorism* is not further defined, but *TSI* is. As we introduced in Chapter 1, *TSI* is defined as "a security incident resulting in a significant loss of life, environmental damage, transportation system disruption, or economic disruption in a particular area."[180] However, the term *significant* is subject to interpretation. The TWIC/MTSA Policy Advisory Council's Policy Letter 01-08 indicates that a TSI would have on the order of 150 deaths or a critical disruption to area economic activity or the area's transportation system.[181] The USCG uses this standard to review security procedures (i.e., to assist in identifying facilities and areas where a TSI could occur). This is not to imply that the USCG would find the deaths of 149 people to be insignificant, simply to point out that the USCG has established, by this definition, a sense of scale for what the magnitude of an incident would need to be to be considered a TSI. It is also a definition that suggests that a TSI would very likely be an act of terrorism or an act of war, in that it is hard to envision an alternative actor motivated to cause such harm. In addition, some federal laws and executive orders require agencies to perform cost–benefit analyses, find alternative solutions, and minimize the effect that regulatory costs

---

[177] GAO, 2011a, p. 23.

[178] Misdemeanor convictions are not disqualifying factors.

[179] 49 C.F.R. Part 1572.

[180] Pub. L. 107-295, 2002, § 102.

[181] TWIC/MTSA Policy Advisory Council, U.S. Coast Guard, "Redefining Secure Areas and Acceptable Access Control," Policy 01-08, January 7, 2008.

have on small entities. The USCG performed an analysis and applied other requirements when determining the applicability of security standards and regulations. Because each facility and vessel is unique in its location and operation, the USCG has developed regulations, standards, and policies that satisfy important federal requirements to limit the impact of economic and security standards to areas where significant events might occur. TSA, in contrast, has not further refined the term *significant loss of life* in the context of a TSI. They have chosen instead (as permissible under the principles of administrative law) to evaluate the term in context of whether a particular conviction, arrest, or indictment is disqualifying under the statute and regulation. They do not have an established definition used internally to the organization or a list of incidents that are defined as TSIs. This difference in interpretation by the two agencies implementing the TWIC program suggests that there might not be a common understanding or clear standard of the degree of risk that TWIC is intended to mitigate.

The legislative record regarding the TWIC program and TWIC standards generally emphasizes the counterterrorism purpose of the program. During the original discussion of MTSA, Senator Fritz Hollings stated,

> The bill also will require criminal background checks of employees with access to ocean manifests or access-controlled areas of a port or terminal. These background checks are designed to ensure that individuals with access to our terminals and cargo facilities are not a terrorism security threat.[182]

In 2007, in a prepared statement, Representative Sheila Jackson Lee—then chair of the U.S. House of Representatives Committee on Homeland Security's Subcommittee on Transportation Security and Infrastructure Protection—stated,

> the TWIC program was created to ensure the security of [key transportation] facilities by issuing identification cards only to workers who are not known to pose a terrorist threat, and allow these workers unescorted access to secure areas of the transportation system.[183]

In a Subcommittee on Border and Maritime Security hearing on June 18, 2013, committee chair Representative Candice Miller stated that MTSA was passed "to prevent acts of terrorism that might impact our Nation."[184] The TWIC card was described as "designed to prevent terrorists from gaining access to sensitive parts of the Nation's ports." In discussion of the SAFE Port Act on May 4, 2006, Representative Peter King, in reference to the initially proposed disqualifying crimes for the TWIC program, stated that these standards should "accurately identify individuals

---

[182] In U.S. Senate, "Maritime Transportation Security Act of 2002: Conference Report," *Congressional Record*, Vol. 148, No. 147, November 14, 2002, p. S10975.

[183] Sheila Jackson Lee, representative, U.S. House of Representatives, "Homeland Security Failures: TWIC Examined," remarks before the U.S. House of Representatives Committee on Homeland Security, October 31, 2007.

[184] Subcommittee on Border and Maritime Security, Committee on Homeland Security, U.S. House of Representatives, *Threat, Risk, and Vulnerability: The Future of the TWIC Program*, hearing, Serial No. 113-23, June 18, 2013.

that pose a terrorism security risk."[185] The Congressional Record suggests that some policymakers saw criminal history as inextricably linked to terrorism risk. Senator Jim DeMint, speaking in 2007 about a bill to codify the criminal standards that TSA proposed in its TWIC rulemaking, stated that such prohibitions were connected to "the threat our ports face when traditional criminals, particularly organized criminals, work with terrorists."[186] He further stated,

> The threat not only comes from criminals working directly with terrorists, it also
> comes from criminals who may look the other way when a suspect container
> comes from a port . . . The nightmare scenario here is where a criminal at one of
> our ports who may think he is just helping a friend smuggle in drugs
> inadvertently helps smuggle in a weapon of mass destruction.[187]

Because TWIC is clearly intended to address terrorism risk, we focused on considering the STA's standards (set by statute for vetting someone for terrorism risk, criminal history, and immigration status) in terms of that risk—that is, we considered each standard as to whether it reduced terrorism risk, regardless of whether it might have value in reducing other risks, such as crime. We also considered the appropriateness of these standards broadly in relation to reducing crime, given the broad definition of *security risk* in the statute and legislative record and the reference specifically to federal crimes in MTSA's findings.

MTSA's introductory language also suggests that reducing crime could have been on policymakers' minds, given that Congress's findings include reference to crimes in such statements as, "Ports often are a major locus of Federal crime, including drug trafficking, cargo theft, and smuggling of contraband and aliens" and "[b]iometric identification procedures for individuals having access to secure areas in port facilities are important tools to deter and prevent port cargo crimes, smuggling, and terrorist actions."[188]

According to 49 C.F.R. § 1572.5, which stipulates the standards for the STA, an applicant is vetted to determine whether they present a security threat, a term defined in 49 C.F.R. § 1570.3 as "an individual whom TSA determines or suspects of posing a threat to national security; to transportation security; or of terrorism." This definition speaks to risks beyond terrorism, to include grave threats—those that might threaten national security or transportation networks. The fact that the list of disqualifying crimes does not include crimes of larceny or theft also suggests that TWIC's purpose is narrower than reducing crime generally.

---

[185] Peter King, representative, U.S. House of Representatives, comments made during a debate about the Security and Accountability for Every Port Act, *Congressional Record*, Vol. 152, No. 52, May 4, 2006, p. H2121.

[186] U.S. Senate, "Improving America's Security Act of 2007," *Congressional Record*, Vol. 153, Part 4, February 28, 2007, p. 4899.

[187] U.S. Senate, 2007, p. 4899.

[188] Pub. L. 107-295, 2002.

The STA's Use of the Terrorism Watch List

The primary tool that the U.S. government uses to identify someone who presents a terrorism risk is the terrorist watch list—also known as the TSDB—a consolidated database of people "known to be or reasonably suspected of being involved in terrorist activities."[189] Much of the information in the TSDB is derived from the Terrorist Identities Datamart Environment (TIDE) the U.S. government's central classified database, maintained by NCTC, of known and suspected international terrorists. This information is married with the identities of known and suspected domestic terrorists in a data set maintained by the FBI and populated directly into the TSDB.[190] As of November 2014, the TSDB listed approximately 800,000 U.S. and foreign identities.[191]

This is not to suggest that every person currently on the watch list presents a threat to the maritime environment. Some people who are on the watch list because of suspected terrorist connections are ultimately determined not to be terrorists and are removed from the list. NCTC's fact sheet on watch-listing states that more than 228,000 records in TIDE had been deleted in the past six years of people no longer meeting the criteria for inclusion.[192] Further, some people on the terrorist watch list are assessed to present less risk than others. For example, an FBI official testified in 2014 that only about 8 percent of the people in the TSDB were on the "No Fly List"—people who presumably present a threat specifically to aviation.[193] The remaining people are still allowed to use commercial airlines, although they are usually subject to enhanced screening when flying.[194] Although not everyone on the terrorist watch list is actively a threat to the maritime sector, there are reasonable grounds to conclude that the watch list as a whole is a relevant resource for identifying terrorism risk. The TSDB is therefore a relevant tool for TSA to use in determining whether someone could present a risk of terrorism, in investigating their possible risk to the maritime sector, and in making a risk-based decision on whether to issue a credential.

---

[189] Terrorist Screening Center, "Frequently Asked Questions," January 2017.

[190] Jerome P. Bjelopera, Bart Elias, and Alison Siskin, *The Terrorist Screening Database and Preventing Terrorist Travel*, Washington, D.C.: Congressional Research Service, R44678, November 7, 2016, p. 3.

[191] Not all of the records in TIDE are included in the TSDB because some records do not include sufficient identifying information. Each record in the TSDB must include at least a surname and another piece of identifying information. As of February 2017, NCTC indicated that TIDE contained 1.6 million identities. U.S. persons (citizens and lawful permanent residents) accounted for appropriately 16,000 of that total. The FBI also maintains separate records on domestic terrorists who have no international connections. We do not know the number of these records. Therefore, we cannot determine what proportion of people in the TSDB would meet the citizenship eligibility requirements for a TWIC card (NCTC, "Terrorist Identities Datamart Environment [TIDE]," 2017).

[192] NCTC, 2017.

[193] Bjelopera, Elias, and Siskin, 2016.

[194] Steve Sadler, assistant administrator, Transportation Security Administration, U.S. Department of Homeland Security, "TSA's Role in the Transportation Worker Identification Credential (TWIC) Program," statement before the U.S. House of Representatives, Committee on Homeland Security, Subcommittee on Border and Maritime Security, June 18, 2013.

To perform its screening, TSA maintains an in-house screening system, the Transportation Vetting System (TVS), that receives biographic information for identities in the TSDB and other federal databases and can perform near-real-time screening. This system continuously evaluates whether there are any potential matches with TSA's credentialed populations, including TWIC cardholders.[195] TSA identifies additions to the terrorist watch list related to current TWIC cardholders in less than 24 hours, typically in a few hours, and as rapidly as within minutes. If the government determines that the holder now presents a terrorism security risk and should not hold a TWIC, the TWIC card number would be added to the CCL. TSA has stated that it attempts to recover the credential card if it suspects terrorism risk.[196]

Although we were not privy to the specifics of cases in which individuals have been identified to have possible terrorist connections, which is sensitive security information, our understanding based on conversations with TSA is that the numbers are very low. A March 2019 report from the DOJ Office of the Inspector General was critical of the FBI's process for determining whether to issue a TWIC card to someone with a known or suspected connection to terrorism, in that FBI agents making such determinations might not be fully aware of the access granted to TWIC holders and the related risk.[197] The FBI has stated that it will strengthen policies and procedures regarding its coordination with TSA to enhance the vetting and scrutiny of TWIC applicants and cardholders. The STA's use of the TSDB is directly relevant to identifying a terrorism-related threat to the maritime environment and, as we discuss further in the next section, is a process that requires a federal role in screening programs.

Federal Terrorism Checks Versus Private-Sector Terrorism Checks

The federal government has a unique ability to check the terrorist watch list. Only authorized agencies and officials can check the TSDB; TSA is one of five major federal agencies that are authorized.[198] Although some consumer reporting agencies that provide background checks claim in their marketing material that they can identify terrorist connections, they are not checking *the* terrorist watch list. Private companies' terrorism checks—sometimes referred to as Patriot Act checks—are generally checking identities against the Office of Foreign Assets Control's (OFAC) list of Specially Designated Nationals. OFAC's list is intended primarily to combat terrorism financing and enforce economic sanctions. The list involves mostly companies

---

[195] The same system is used for other TSA credentialing populations, such as TSA Pre✓®, HME, and SIDA.

[196] HSOAC interviews with personnel from the TSA Law Enforcement Investigative Unit, July 2017; conversations with TSA Office of Chief Counsel, June 2019.

[197] Office of the Inspector General, U.S. Department of Justice, *Audit of the Federal Bureau of Investigation's Management of Maritime Terrorism Threats*, Audit Division 19-18, March 2019, redacted for public release.

[198] The other organizations are Department of State, the FBI, Customs and Border Protection, and the Department of Defense (Terrorist Screening Center, 2017).

and organizations but includes 10,634 individuals, none of whom is a U.S. person.[199] Compare that with TIDE, which contains 1.6 million individuals, 16,000 of whom are U.S. persons. Examples of individuals on OFAC's list are Hasan Nasrallah, secretary-general of Hizballah, and Ayman al-Zawahiri, the operational and military leader of al Qaeda. It seems relatively safe to assume that no one on this list would be granted a U.S. work visa, much less seek employment at a port.

Commercial background check vendors could also seek information on whether someone has been charged specifically with a crime of terrorism. This approach also does not provide information on people suspected to be terrorists—only on those who have been successfully charged with acts of terrorism. Someone the federal government (principally the FBI) considers a terrorist might not ultimately be charged under terrorism statutes, a problem that is particularly true for domestic terrorists.[200] *The Washington Post* recently reported that its review of internal FBI figures suggests that, of the thousands of people suspected of being domestic terrorists and investigated each year, only hundreds were charged with crimes, and only dozens were actually recognized as terrorist threats.[201]

Prior Criminal History as a Terrorism Risk Factor

Most people who are denied TWICs are denied on the basis of past criminal history. Given that one possible interpretation of MTSA's language is that TWIC's criminal standards could have some value in determining terrorism risk, we examined literature for any evidence that a criminal history suggests a greater risk of terrorism. Our review found a series of scholarly studies that identify risk factors by comparing individuals who engaged or attempted to engage in terrorism with those who did not. We discuss these studies in detail below.

These analyses provide compelling evidence showing that prior criminal history—among other risk factors analyzed—is more prevalent among the terrorists studied than among the general U.S. population or among a comparison group of nonviolent extremists. This research might suggest that using prior criminal history for vetting purposes could be one risk factor to identify people more likely to commit acts of terrorism.

However, when evaluating this research to determine whether the 46 U.S.C. § 70105 criminal history standards are appropriate in identifying risk of terrorism, we found both practical and methodological limitations that raise questions about the degree to which the standard can reliably predict whether someone will engage in terrorism. We should also recognize, as we discuss in greater depth, that using criminal history as a terrorism risk factor

---

[199] U.S. Department of the Treasury, "Specially Designated Nationals and Blocked Persons List (SDN) Human Readable Lists," last updated June 28, 2019.

[200] Bjelopera, 2017.

[201] See Devlin Barrett, "Arrests in Domestic Terror Probes Outpace Those Inspired by Islamic Extremists," *Washington Post*, March 9, 2019. We did not independently verify these figures.

still has an incredibly high false-positive rate—by which we mean that someone could be assessed to be a security risk because of a disqualifying criminal history but present no actual threat of terrorism. Someone who conducts a terrorist act might be more likely to have a criminal history than the average U.S. person, but the overwhelming majority of people with criminal histories do not conduct or facilitate acts of terrorism.

Research Studies on the Correlation of Criminality and Terrorism

Our literature survey identified some research projects that have attempted, with varying degrees of success, to empirically identify risk factors associated with committing extremist violence. This work has typically been done outside the United States, in order to validate other countries' specialized risk-assessment tools for dealing with terrorism-related crime and ideological violence.[202] More recently, a series of studies sponsored by the National Institute of Justice (NIJ) produced findings about potential risk factors associated with U.S.-based terrorists.[203] In these studies, researchers explored whether certain characteristics, experiences, or behaviors—such as criminal history, mental health issues, unemployment, or single relationship status—are more prevalent among people who have engaged or attempted to engage in terrorism than among those who have not.

It is important to note that these analyses varied in their approach in terms of the terrorists examined and with whom these individuals were compared (see Table 5.1). Altogether, the samples of terrorists included a wide range of group-based and lone-actor terrorists of varied ideologies, including Islamist, antigovernment, anticapitalist, nativist, and other political and social terrorist movements (often referred to in the literature as *religious*, *left-wing*, *right-wing*, or *single-issue* terrorism).[204] The NIJ-sponsored research focused on extremists who were based in the United States and embraced a range of extremist ideologies, but the studies differed in terms of other criteria used to develop the samples. An additional study that we reviewed (not part of the NIJ-sponsored research) that resulted in similar findings included a sample of U.S.- and Europe-based extremists. Researchers in three of those studies compared those individuals with the general population, and one study compared the samples with other extremists who did not conduct violent acts.

---

[202] For a more detailed discussion of these risk-assessment tools and their performance, see Allison G. Smith, *Risk Factors and Indicators Associated with Radicalization to Terrorism in the United States: What Research Sponsored by the National Institute of Justice Tells Us*, Washington, D.C.: U.S. Department of Justice, National Institute of Justice, NCJ 251789, June 2018, and Brian A. Jackson, Ashley L. Rhoades, Jordan R. Reimer, Natasha Lander, Katherine Costello, and Sina Beaghley, *Practical Terrorism Prevention: Reexamining U.S. National Approaches to Addressing the Threat of Ideologically Motivated Violence*, Santa Monica, Calif.: RAND Corporation, RR-2647-DHS, 2019.

[203] A. Smith, 2018.

[204] For greater detail about how the samples differed and overlapped, see a summary of them in A. Smith, 2018.

Table 5.1. Summary of Findings on Prior Criminal History as a Risk Factor

Research Study	Actor Type	Sample	Findings on Criminality
START[a]	Lone, group	Random sample of 1,475 from a larger population meeting its inclusion criteria between 1965 and 2013[b]	Found consistent evidence that criminal activity prior to radicalization was associated more with those engaging in violent political activity than those who did not
University of Massachusetts Lowell[c]	Lone	Includes all 71 people who, between 1990 and 2013, engaged in violence in the United States in support of a broader ideological group but acted alone	Found higher rates of previous criminal convictions (**58%**), and a wider range of illegal activities, among lone-actor terrorists than in the general U.S. population (the researchers compared solo mass murderers and lone-actor terrorists, but we can use those data to compare the latter with the general population)
Indiana State University[d]	Lone	Includes all 98 people who, between 1940 and 2013, engaged in terrorism in the United States but acted alone, did not belong to a group, and were not directed by others	Found high rates of previous criminal records among the sample of lone-actor terrorists (**55%**)
Gill, Horgan, and Deckert, 2014[e]	Lone	Analyzed 119 people who, between 1990 and 2014, engaged or planned to engage in lone-actor terrorism in the United States or Europe.	Found high rates of previous criminal convictions (**41.2%**) among the terrorists and attempted terrorists sampled

NOTE: START = National Consortium for the Study of Terrorism and Responses to Terrorism.

[a] Gary LaFree, Michael E. Jensen, Patrick A. James, and Aaron Safer-Lichtenstein, "Correlates of Violent Political Extremism in the United States," *Criminology*, Vol. 56, No. 2, May 2018, pp. 233–268.

[b] The project included people who radicalized in the United States; who espoused ideological motives and acted on these motives; and who had been (1) arrested, (2) indicted, (3) killed in action, (4) members of or associated with designated terrorist organizations, or (5) members of or associated with organizations whose leaders or founders had been indicted for ideologically motivated terrorism.

[c] John G. Horgan, Paul Gill, Noemie Bouhana, James Silver, and Emily Corner, *Across the Universe? A Comparative Analysis of Violent Radicalization Across Three Offender Types with Implications for Criminal Justice Training and Education*, Washington, D.C.: National Institute of Justice, June 2016.

[d] A. Smith, 2018.

[e] Paul Gill, John Horgan, and Paige Deckert, "Bombing Alone: Tracing the Motivations and Antecedent Behaviors of Lone-Actor Terrorists," *Journal of Forensic Sciences*, Vol. 59, No. 2, March 2014, pp. 425–435.

Specific Findings of Previous Studies

Research conducted at START, based at the University of Maryland, examined the radicalization processes and trajectories of violent and nonviolent (both criminal and noncriminal) extremists and included both group-based and lone actors. The research randomly sampled 1,475 people from the larger population who met its inclusion criteria (as described in Table 5.1) between 1965 and 2013.[205] START's analysis found consistent evidence that criminal activity prior to radicalization was associated with engaging in violent political activity. It is important to note that this association was true regardless of whether the prior criminal activity itself was violent: The measure of past criminality included nonviolent crimes, such as drug

---

[205] LaFree et al., 2018.

offenses and larceny. Further, the researchers identified more than a dozen other risk factors associated with a higher likelihood of engaging in terrorism, including having less education, being unemployed, and being a loner.

Research conducted at the University of Massachusetts Lowell examined whether differences exist between lone-actor terrorists and mass murderers by comparing demographic, psychological, and behavioral variables among 115 solo mass murderers and 71 lone-actor terrorists who engaged in ideologically inspired violence in the United States between 1990 and 2013.[206] The researchers found higher rates of previous criminal convictions, and a wider range of illegal activities, among lone-actor terrorists than in the general population. Of the sample of lone-actor terrorists, 58 percent had previous criminal convictions and 59 percent served time in prison. Much like in START's findings, the nature of the crimes committed by the sampled terrorists varied from severe to petty and included both nonviolent and violent offenses, such as counterfeiting, disorderly conduct, robbery, concealed weapon, counterfeiting, possession of child pornography, and firearms. The researchers concluded that, given the wide range of illegal activities, they could not identify such criminality as an escalatory "trigger" for subsequent lone-actor terrorism or for nonterrorist mass murder.[207]

A study conducted by researchers at Indiana State University, which sought to distinguish lone wolves from those who are radicalized in group settings, analyzed a sample of 98 people who engaged in terrorism alone in the United States between 1940 and 2013. Although the researchers concluded that there was no standard profile of the American lone-actor terrorist, the analysis provides evidence that most are unemployed, single white males with criminal records. And, like those at University of Massachusetts Lowell, the researchers found higher rates of previous criminal records among the sample of lone-actor terrorists (55 percent) than in the general U.S. population.[208]

Similarly, a study conducted by Paul Gill, John Horgan, and Paige Deckert in 2014 analyzed 119 people who engaged or planned to engage in lone-actor terrorism between 1990 and 2014 in the United States and Europe and found higher rates of previous criminal convictions (41.2 percent) among the terrorist sample than in the general U.S. population.[209] Like in other studies, the criminal offenses varied widely, including first-degree robbery, criminal damage, custodial and second-degree assault, firearm offenses, obstructing law-enforcement officers' activities, drunk driving, drug possession, criminal use of explosives, vandalism, income tax

---

[206] Horgan et al., 2016.

[207] Horgan et al., 2016.

[208] Mark Hamm and Ramon Spaaj, *Lone Wolf Terrorism in America: Using Knowledge of Radicalization Pathways to Forge Prevention Strategies*, Washington, D.C.: National Institute of Justice, February 2015.

[209] Gill, Horgan, and Deckert, 2014.

issues, possession of child pornography, graffiti, and (somewhat strangely) "possession of a carcass of a protected barn owl."[210]

The findings suggest some evidence that prior criminal history is more prevalent among the violent terrorists studied than in the general U.S. population or a comparison group of nonviolent extremists. This suggests that using criminal history as a risk factor for screening and vetting is relevant for evaluating terrorism risk. It does not, however, make this factor on its own a strong predictor of terrorism risk. According to a report from the Brennan Center for Justice, as of 2015, between 70 million (22 percent) and 100 million (31 percent) Americans had criminal records.[211] If we average percentages from the three studies that identified the percentages of people with criminal convictions (see Table 5.1), we could assume that roughly 50 percent of people who engage in terrorist attacks have criminal histories. Suppose further that 27 percent of U.S. residents have criminal histories (the median of the Brennan Center study's range). Then, for a given number of terrorists in the United States, the odds that an arbitrarily selected person with a criminal history is a terrorist are roughly 2.7 times those for an arbitrarily selected person with no criminal history. However, given that the baseline odds of being a terrorist (in the full U.S. population) are so low, this increase in odds likely has a negligible difference in successfully identifying someone who presents terrorism risk.

To illustrate how the low baseline rate of terrorism and the wide prevalence of criminal history make criminality a poor predictor when used as a singular risk factor, let us consider a hypothetical number of terrorists in the United States. Recognizing that we do not know how many terrorists are in the United States, we can make assumptions that allow us to consider orders of magnitude. On the low end, let us assume that 100 people present terrorism risk in the United States; on the high end, let us assume that 10,000 people do.[212] If we compare this to the U.S. population of 327 million, that means the odds of being a terrorist are between 1 in 3.27 million and 1 in 32,700—that is, between 99.99997 percent and 99.997 percent of the U.S. population are *not* terrorists.[213] Using the statistics cited above, among those with criminal backgrounds, the odds are between 1 in 1.77 million and 1 in 17,700 (or, between 99.99994 percent and 99.994 percent are not terrorists). And, even if we exclude people with criminal histories, there is a still a chance of between 1 in 4.77 million and 1 in 47,700 that any arbitrarily selected person is a terrorist. The point is that terrorists are so rare in the general population that, even if we were to exclude a subgroup that accounts for 50 percent of terrorists,

---

[210] Gill, Horgan, and Deckert, 2014, p. 428.

[211] Matthew Friedman, "Just Facts: As Many Americans Have Criminal Records as College Diplomas," New York: Brennan Center for Justice, November 17, 2015.

[212] The FBI arrested around 200 people per year in 2017 and 2018 for domestic and foreign terrorism. Conversely, TIDE has the identities of 16,000 U.S. persons as known or suspected terrorists or as having some connection to a known or suspected terrorist (Barrett, 2019; NCTC, 2017). Ultimately, however, the numbers used in our analysis are notional.

[213] U.S. Census Bureau, 2010 Census of Population, P94-171 redistricting data file, undated.

the remaining pool of people has decreased its propensity for terrorism by, at best, 0.001 percentage points. This small reduction comes at the cost of potentially excluding tens of millions of people from eligibility. (Because we cannot break down the prevalence of criminal history by specific crime, we cannot determine how many people have disqualifying criminal histories.)

Further, there are some methodological and practical limitations with using this research to inform the STA standards used for TWIC, which we outline in the next section.

Limitations to Applying the Literature Findings to the TWIC Vetting Standards

Evaluating this research in the context of TWIC's vetting standard, we found both practical and methodological limitations that raise questions about the degree to which the standard can reliably *predict* whether someone will engage in terrorism. First, given the relatively small numbers of people who engage in terrorism compared with the large numbers of Americans with criminal backgrounds, we found that the screening standard would invariably lead to significant numbers of false positives (i.e., disqualification of applicants who would not subsequently engage in terrorism). Second, the research we discuss here studied a much broader set of crimes than the TWIC program uses, so we cannot confirm that those findings remain valid in the context of the STA's narrower set of criminal offenses. We discuss these issues in more detail next.

Few people with risk factors engage in terrorism, meaning that the great majority of people with disqualifying criminal histories present no terrorism risk. Although research that analyzes samples of terrorists can help identify characteristics and experiences that are generally associated with a particular outcome, evaluating whether the use of such risk factors is appropriate for screening and vetting purposes requires examining their probability of success in identifying at-risk people. Literature evaluating the performance of risk-assessment tools—that generally include a basket of risk factors, including prior criminal history—suggest that they are better than chance but not by much.[214] Many of the tools rely on the structured professional judgment of clinicians or analysts about the importance of different risk factors on a case-by-case basis.[215] These risk-assessment tools are not intended to provide reliable results for large-population screening. *Therefore, reliance on criminal history as an isolated risk factor of terrorism to indiscriminately disqualify all applicants with criminal backgrounds will invariably lead to overwhelming numbers of false positives—that is, someone assessed to be a security risk who presents no actual terrorism threat.* Radicalization is a complex process, and numerous studies have shown that such pathways vary based on the ideologies that people embrace, the

---

[214] Jackson, Rhoades, et al., 2019.

[215] J. Monahan, "The Individual Risk Assessment of Terrorism," *Psychology, Public Policy, and Law*, Vol. 18, No. 2, 2012, pp. 167–205.

time periods in which they radicalize, and the peoples' own characteristics and experiences.[216] Scholars have therefore cast doubt on whether the profiles of those at risk for engaging in relatively rare types of violence will ever be "sufficiently specific" and argue that, even if profiles are identified, "an over-reliance on the use of such a profile would be unwarranted because many more people who do not engage in lone-actor terrorism would share these characteristics."[217] The studies discussed in the previous section underscore that very few people engage or attempt to engage in terrorism in the United States.

Past studies considered criminality broadly, and we cannot determine their consistency with TWIC's specific disqualifying offenses. Many of the research findings summarized above suggest that the samples of terrorists studied committed both petty crimes and felonies and both violent and nonviolent offenses. The TWIC criminal standard (see Appendix B), however, involves a narrower set of criminal offenses that generally involves felonies and violent crimes. This criminal standard also includes interim disqualifying offenses that apply only to applicants who were convicted, pleaded guilty, or were found not guilty by reason of insanity within seven years of application.

Because the studies discussed above considered a much broader set of crimes, we cannot confirm whether their findings that criminal history might be more prevalent among terrorists than in the general population remain valid when using TWIC's narrower set of disqualifying criminal offenses. It is also unclear whether a narrow set of crimes can reliably predict whether someone is at greater risk of engaging in terrorism. For example, the University of Massachusetts Lowell researchers concluded that, given the wide range of illegal activities committed by the terrorists studied, they could not identify an escalatory "trigger" for any specific type of crime for subsequent behavior into lone-actor terrorism. These studies have also compared criminal history with numbers in the general population, which is not equal to the TWIC population. TSA has indicated in its conversations with us that criminality is much higher among the credentialed TWIC population than the general U.S. population, as high as 40 percent. Therefore, although the research discussed above suggests that people with prior criminal histories are associated with a higher likelihood of engaging or attempting to engage in terrorism than the general population, it does not support a finding that people who have committed the criminal offenses that the TWIC program uses for vetting are more likely to engage in such activity.

Incarceration as a Risk Factor for Terrorism Radicalization

We also reviewed literature regarding the extent to which incarceration in the United States leads to an increased risk of radicalization and mobilization to ideological violence. Although we did not find specific reference to this concern in the regulatory history of TWIC specifically, a possible link between incarceration and radicalization has been raised in other contexts. The

---

[216] Hamm and Spaaj, 2015; Horgan et al., 2016.

[217] Gill, Horgan, and Deckert, 2014, p. 433.

literature we reviewed revealed a diversity of perspectives regarding the prevalence and seriousness of the risk of radicalization in U.S. prisons. Although there was general agreement that radicalization occurs to some extent in U.S. prisons, there is considerable uncertainty about the pervasiveness of the issue and the extent to which incarceration contributes to someone's commitment to pursue ideological violence. Studies also highlight the challenges in drawing definitive conclusions about these issues given the lack of open sources, the individual and private nature of the radicalization process, and reluctance of correctional facilities to allow the access necessary for in-depth studies of these issues.

One strand of literature we reviewed raised concerns that U.S. prisons serve as ideal incubators for terrorism and suggest that vulnerable inmates form captive audiences for recruitment by terrorist offenders.[218] These sources also suggest that religious converts—particularly inmates adopting Islam—might be more likely to embrace extremist views. Scholarly sources also raised concern that the imprisonment of known terrorists could produce a greater threat by bringing them together with hardened criminals, creating "a potential toxic mix of extremist ideology."[219] And governmental sources have also underscored the significant danger that radicalization in U.S. prisons poses to national security. For example, in 2006, then–U.S. Attorney General Alberto Gonzales suggested that homegrown terrorists who radicalized online or in prisons "may be as dangerous as groups like al-Qaeda, if not more so."[220] One example is John Georgelas, an American ISIS propagandist who joined the group in Syria following his incarceration. Georgelas had already been initially radicalized prior to his incarceration, and he was sentenced for infiltrating websites on behalf of the global jihadist movement.[221] Such examples are often cited in literature as evidence suggesting a more systemic problem of radicalization in U.S. prisons.

This literature, however, mostly identifies a potential link between incarceration and radicalization, sometimes by pointing to specific cases in which someone might have converted to Islam in prison, radicalized, and conducted or aspired to commit a violent act.[222] However, these statements often generalize the threat, frequently without data about prevalence or a causal link between incarceration and terrorism. For example, shoe bomber Richard Reid, who had been incarcerated in England, and attempted dirty bomber Jose Padilla, who had been imprisoned in

---

[218] Frank J. Cilluffo, Sharon L. Cardash, and Andrew J. Whitehead, "Radicalization: Behind Bars and Beyond Borders," *Brown Journal of World Affairs*, Vol. 13, No. 2, Spring–Summer 2007, pp. 113–122; Ian M. Cuthbertson, "Prisons and the Education of Terrorists," *World Policy Journal*, Vol. 21, No. 3, Fall 2004, pp. 15–22.

[219] Basia Spalek and Salah el-Hassan, "Muslim Converts in Prison," *Howard Journal of Criminal Justice*, Vol. 46, No. 2, May 2007, p. 100.

[220] Alberto R. Gonzales, U.S. Attorney General, "Stopping Terrorists Before They Strike: The Justice Department's Power of Prevention," prepared remarks, World Affairs Council of Pittsburgh, Pittsburgh, Pennsylvania, August 16, 2006.

[221] Graeme Wood, "The American Climbing the Ranks of ISIS," *The Atlantic*, March 2017.

[222] Amna Akbar, "Policing 'Radicalization,'" *UC Irvine Law Review*, Vol. 3, No. 4, December 2013, pp. 809–884.

the United States, have been presented as examples of prison radicalization. Researcher Gaetano Joe Ilardi with the Victoria, Australia, police has challenged the causality of imprisonment in these individuals' radicalization, pointing to other driving factors, particularly related to their postrelease activity.[223] Other research has highlighted the success of prison gangs in recruiting in U.S. prisons, suggesting that terrorist organizations can use the same techniques to find new supporters.[224]

Research studies have found that, although inmates can be recruited to terrorist causes, such recruitment occurs infrequently. In 2009, the Federal Bureau of Prisons found no evidence of widespread radicalization nor any indication of organized recruitment efforts by terrorist organizations in U.S. federal prisons.[225] NIJ studies found that moving from radicalization to actual recruitment for terrorism and ideological violence is a rare event and that only a small percentage of converts to white supremacist groups and to Islam turn radical beliefs into terrorist action.[226] Research built on these studies, albeit only about Islamic radicalism, identified only 14 people who, between 2001 and 2010, committed acts of terrorism-related violence or were prosecuted for terrorism-related offenses and appear to have been possibly influenced by Islamic radicalism while in U.S. prisons.[227] In another study of U.S. prisons, researchers found high levels of patriotism among American prisoners and that, although they might be Muslim or converted to Islam in prison, they did not want to commit violence against the United States.[228] They quoted one inmate as saying, "Even though we're criminals, we see ourselves as Americans." He "couldn't turn against this country."[229]

Other researchers have pointed out that prison experiences can have different effects on inmates. Indeed, no two imprisoned people's experiences in state or federal correctional systems are likely to be the same, given the intrinsic diversity of inmates and of prison facilities. In some cases, exposure to religious information while incarcerated can have *deradicalizing* effects on

---

[223] Gaetano Joe Ilardi, Victoria Police, adjunct research associate, Global Terrorism Research Centre, "Prison Radicalisation: The Devil Is in the Detail," paper presented at the Australian Research Council Linkage Project on Radicalisation Conference, Understanding Terrorism from an Australian Perspective: Radicalisation, De-Radicalisation and Counter Radicalisation, Monash University, Australia, November 8, 2010.

[224] Cuthbertson, 2004; Scott Decker and David C. Pyrooz, "'I'm Down for a Jihad': How 100 Years of Gang Research Can Inform the Study of Terrorism, Radicalization and Extremism," *Perspectives on Terrorism*, Vol. 9, February 2014, pp. 104–112.

[225] Bert Useem and Obie Clayton, "Radicalization of U.S. Prisoners," *Criminology and Public Policy*, Vol. 8, No. 3, August 2009, pp. 561–592.

[226] Mark S. Hamm, *Terrorist Recruitment in American Correctional Institutions: An Exploratory Study of Non-Traditional Faith Groups—Final Report*, Rockville, Md.: National Institute of Justice, December 2007; Mark S. Hamm, "Prisoner Radicalization: Assessing the Threat in U.S. Correctional Institutions," *NIJ Journal*, No. 261, October 2008.

[227] Bert Useem, "U.S. Prisons and the Myth of Islamic Terrorism," *Contexts*, Vol. 11, No. 2, 2012, pp. 34–39.

[228] Useem, 2012.

[229] Useem and Clayton, 2009, p. 566.

inmates, especially when it is to mainstream interpretations of religions. A 2019 RAND study exploring terrorism prevention, which interviewed officials familiar with radicalization trends, described cases in which inmates' commitment to violence weakened during their prison sentences.[230] Likewise, criminological evidence indicates that there is no relationship between terrorism and prisoner conversions to Islam.[231] Criminologists generally agree that religion offers prisoners a way to adjust to institutional life by providing natural means to cope with unnatural surroundings.[232]

This diversity of views likely stems in part from the challenges evaluating the prevalence of radicalization in U.S. prisons. In a study on radicalization in European prisons, for example, RAND researchers found that it was not possible to draw any definite conclusion because of the lack of open sources and reluctance on the part of authorities to discusses these issues.[233] A report released in 2006 by the George Washington University Homeland Security Policy Institute and the University of Virginia's Critical Incident Analysis Group echoes the RAND researchers' findings: "At present there is insufficient information about prisoner radicalization to qualify the threat. There is a significant lack of social science research on this issue."[234] The report, authored by a panel of law-enforcement experts, also highlights the lack of information about prisoners prior to their incarceration and the limited ability to track activities following their release to present a full assessment of the impact of prison.[235]

The Value of the STA Process to Counterterrorism Efforts

The STA could also serve a possible role in counterterrorism efforts by intelligence and law-enforcement officers. Understanding how frequently people on the terrorist watch list seek authorized access to ports is a possible indicator of threat to the maritime sector. For example, a rapid increase in the number of people seeking TWIC cards, particularly ones with connections or shared ideology, could suggest an ongoing plot to penetrate maritime facilities. Security officials investigating someone for possible terrorist connections might want to put higher priority on the case in which the person had access to critical infrastructure, which they might not determine as rapidly without a federal database of credential holders.

---

[230] Jackson, Rhoades, et al., 2019.

[231] Hamm, 2007.

[232] Todd R. Clear, Bruce D. Stout, Harry R. Dammer, Linda Kelly, Patricia L. Hardyman, and Carol Shapiro, "Does Involvement in Religion Help Prisoners Adjust to Prison?" *NCCD Focus*, San Francisco, Calif.: National Council on Crime and Delinquency, November 1992.

[233] Greg Hannah, Lindsay Clutterbuck, and Jennifer Rubin, *Radicalization or Rehabilitation: Understanding the Challenge of Extremist and Radicalized Prisoners*, Santa Monica, Calif.: RAND Corporation, TR-571-RC, 2008.

[234] F. Cilluffo and G. Saathoff, *Out of the Shadows: Getting Ahead of Prisoner Radicalization—A Special Report*, Washington, D.C.: George Washington University Homeland Security Policy Institute and University of Virginia Critical Incident Analysis Group, 2006, p. iv.

[235] Cilluffo and Saathoff, 2006.

Furthermore, as we discussed earlier in this chapter, the terrorist watch list is not a static database. People are added to the terrorist watch list as new investigations are opened with the FBI or otherwise nominated by intelligence authorities. The recurrent vetting process allows the federal government to quickly identify that someone who is suspected of terrorism connections might have access to a maritime facility. This could affect FBI decisions about how to prioritize investigations and otherwise take actions to appropriately protect critical infrastructure.

Immigration Status as a Risk Factor for Crime or Terrorism

Under 49 C.F.R. § 1572.105, anyone applying for a credential that requires an STA must be a national of the United States or be admitted to the country under one of several immigration categories, such as lawful permanent resident (LPR), refugee, or alien granted asylum. This requirement is derived from 46 U.S.C. § 70105(d)(2)(B). Aliens are often eligible for TWICs based on work authorization status or possession of skills that might be particularly important for obtaining a transportation security card (i.e., crewman or commercial driver licensed in Canada or Mexico). At least two immigration categories that are deemed ineligible for a TWIC appear to be specifically related to security risk: an alien granted lawful immigration status because they were an informant on a criminal (an S-5 visa holder) or terrorist organization (an S-6 visa holder).

Additionally, the TWIC criminal standard (49 C.F.R. § 1572.103) indicates that a conviction for felony violation of immigration law is an interim disqualifying offense, and 46 U.S.C. § 70105 states that an applicant can be denied a transportation security card if "denied admission to the United States or removed from the United States under the Immigration and Nationality Act." These disqualifying offenses, as well as the requirement that an applicant possess legal status in the United States, raise questions about whether disqualifying an applicant based on immigration status is relevant in assessing security risk. Therefore, in the next section, we review scholarly literature that evaluates whether any relationship exists between someone's immigration status and the propensity to commit violent and nonviolent criminal acts, including terrorism.

Research on the Relationship Between Immigration and Terrorism

Researchers in several studies have also analyzed the national origins and immigration statuses of people involved in terrorism in the United States. Overall, these researchers have found that terrorist plots and attacks are more frequently committed by U.S. citizens than by foreigners holding immigration status in the country. For example, in a 2018 RAND study examining the demographics of people recruited or inspired by ISIL or al Qaeda in the United States, researchers found that, "[o]verwhelmingly, most individuals connected to U.S. jihadist terrorism since 9/11 have been U.S. citizens."[236] Of the 476 people the study identified, 209 were U.S.-born, 129 were naturalized U.S. citizens, 18 others were U.S. citizens who might or might not have been naturalized.[237] So 75 percent of the people connected to U.S. jihadist terrorism since 9/11 were U.S. citizens. Additionally, the researchers found that 26 people were responsible for 23 domestic attacks in the United States between September 2001 and September 2017, only two of whom were nonresidents (both had entered the country legally), while 13 were U.S.-born citizens, seven were naturalized U.S. citizens, and four were LPRs.[238]

In another RAND study with results published in 2017 examined jihadist terrorist attacks and plots in the United States since 9/11, concluding that "American jihadists are made in the United States, not imported."[239] Specifically, the author identified 86 plots and 22 attempted attacks by a total of 178 people in the post-9/11 period. These 178 people included 86 U.S.-born citizens, 46 naturalized U.S. citizens, another U.S. citizen who might or might not have been naturalized, 23 LPRs, eight temporary-visa holders, three asylum seekers, four who had been brought into the country illegally as minors, and two who were refugees. Three others were foreigners who were part of a plot but did not enter the country, while the statuses of the remaining two are unknown.

Additionally, in a New America project that examined jihadist terrorist activity in the United States since 9/11, researchers found that the large majority of such terrorists have been U.S. citizens or legal residents.[240] Specifically, the researchers tracked the citizenship statuses of people who were charged with terrorism or related crimes or who died but were reportedly involved with jihadist criminal activity, finding that—at the time of charge or death—84 percent were citizens or LPRs, while 16 percent were nonresidents or unknown.[241] The report notes that, "while a range of citizenship statuses are represented, every jihadist who conducted a lethal attack inside the United States since 9/11 was a citizen or legal resident."[242]

Moreover, in a 2010 analysis[243]—using a Heritage Foundation list of 30 terrorist plots foiled between October 2001 and 2010[244]—authors conducted independent research into 63 people directly associated with those plots who were arrested in the United States. They found that those associated with the plots consisted of 31 U.S.-born citizens, 14 naturalized citizens, one dual

---

[236] H. Williams, Chandler, and Robinson, 2018, p. x.

[237] H. Williams, Chandler, and Robinson, 2018, p. x.

[238] H. Williams, Chandler, and Robinson, 2018, p. x.

[239] Brian Michael Jenkins, *The Origins of America's Jihadists*, Santa Monica, Calif.: RAND Corporation, PE-251-RC, 2017, p. 1.

[240] New America, 2017, Part II.

[241] New America, 2017, Part II.

[242] New America, 2017, Part II.

[243] Edward Alden, "National Security and U.S. Immigration Policy," *Journal of International and Comparative Law*, Vol. 1, No. 1, Fall 2010, Art. 3.

[244] Jena Baker McNeill, James Jay Carafano, and Jessica Zuckerman, "30 Terrorist Plots Foiled: How the System Worked," Washington, D.C.: Heritage Foundation, Backgrounder 2405, April 29, 2010.

citizen, nine legally present immigrants or visa holders, seven illegally present immigrants, and one whose situation was not determinable.[245]

In our literature review, we also identified studies that evaluated terrorism plots and attacks in the United States by perpetrator visa category. Two reports published by the Cato Institute in 2016 and 2019, for example, present a terrorism risk analysis based on the visa the plotter or attacker was *first issued* to enter the United States—not necessarily the status that the person possessed at the time of the attack.[246] This is an important distinction as we think about applying these findings to the TWIC regulatory immigration standards because many of the perpetrators adjusted their statuses and gained citizenship or permanent residency once in the country. Nevertheless, the Cato researcher found that, from 1975 through the end of 2017, 192 foreign-born terrorists planned, attempted, or carried out attacks on U.S. soil.[247] Nine were illegally present immigrants, 57 were LPRs, 21 were students, one entered on a K-1 fiancé(e) visa, 25 were refugees, 11 were asylum seekers, 41 were tourists on various visas, and 11 were from Visa Waiver Program countries.[248] The visas for the remaining 16 terrorists could not be determined. In the same time frame, 788 native-born terrorists planned, attempted, or carried out attacks on U.S. soil.[249] In drawing implications of this research for the TWIC regulatory immigration standard, we found that it suggests that native-born Americans are much more likely than others to participate in terrorist activity on U.S. soil. And, in examining the immigration status of the foreign-born terrorists, nearly half would be eligible to obtain TWICs given that LPRs, asylees, and refugees are not disqualified based on the standard.

Of course, this research also highlights that several people who conducted terrorist attacks in the United States held immigration statuses that would have disqualified them from applying for TWICs. But, when evaluating these numbers in the context of the total number of foreigners who entered the country during the same time period, we see clearly that ideologically motivated violence is a statistically rare event. According to Cato's 2016 study, the U.S. government had

---

[245] Alden, 2010, p. 26.

[246] For the 2016 study, see Alex Nowrasteh, *Terrorism and Immigration: A Risk Analysis*, Washington, D.C.: Cato Institute, Policy Analysis 798, September 13, 2016, p. 2.

> This report counts terrorists who were discovered trying to enter the United States on a forged passport or visa as illegal immigrants. Asylum seekers usually arrive with a different visa with the intent of applying for asylum once they arrive, so they are counted under the asylum category. For instance, the Tsarnaev brothers, who carried out the Boston Marathon bombing on April 15, 2013, traveled here with a tourist visa but their family immediately applied for asylum, so they are included in that category. (Nowrasteh, 2016, p. 3)

See pp. 3 and 7 of Nowrasteh, 2016, for further inclusion criteria, information on how various items were counted, data sources, and data limitations. For the 2019 study (which updated and expanded on the prior analysis), see Alex Nowrasteh, *Terrorists by Immigration Status and Nationality: A Risk Analysis, 1975–2017*, Washington, D.C.: Cato Institute, Policy Analysis 866, May 7, 2019.

[247] Nowrasteh, 2019, p. 1.

[248] Nowrasteh, 2019, p. 2.

[249] Nowrasteh, 2019, p. 1.

issued 1.14 billion visas under the categories that 154 foreign-born terrorists used to enter the country between 1975 and the end of 2015. Of those, only 0.0000136 percent (or approximately 1 in 7.4 million) actually participated in terrorism.[250] Therefore, given that the overwhelming majority of foreigners are unlikely to conduct or facilitate acts of terrorism, the use of immigration standards as proxy for terrorism risk leads to an incredibly high rate of people being incorrectly identified as possible security risks. In our conversations with TSA, TSA officials have raised that an immigrant could present an increased risk from having an unidentified disqualifying criminal factor, given that TSA has less insight into an immigrant's full past criminal history. However, as we mentioned in the preceding section, criminal history is not a strong predictor of terrorism risk.

As for the connection between immigration status and terrorism, we can calculate some hypothetical effects of policies that restrict TWIC eligibility to different groups of immigrants. For measures of the total population of immigrants with different types of visas, we use recently compiled statistics from the Migration Policy Institute (MPI), which analyzed data from the American Community Survey (ACS) (the same survey used by most of the studies cited above), along with visa information from DHS and asylum information from the Department of State.[251] The population-level data show that 44.5 million immigrants reside in the United States, which is 13.7 percent of the population. Of those, 22 million are naturalized citizens (49 percent of all immigrants and 7 percent of the total population). The MPI researchers also estimated 11.3 million unauthorized immigrants in the United States.[252] In addition, a DHS researcher estimated 13.2 million LPRs (as of 2015, the most recent year available).[253]

The studies cited above imply that roughly 50 percent of all terrorists are U.S.-born, an additional 25 percent are naturalized citizens, an additional 10 percent have LPR status (including refugees and asylees), and roughly 2 percent are undocumented immigrants. If the

---

[250] Nowrasteh, 2016, pp. 7–8.

[251] Jie Zong, Jeanne Batalova, and Micayla Burrows, "Frequently Requested Statistics on Immigrants and Immigration in the United States," Washington, D.C.: Migration Policy Institute, March 14, 2019. See also the associated data report, Jeanne Batalova, Andriy Shymonyak, and Michelle Mittelstadt, *Immigration Data Matters*, Washington, D.C.: Migration Policy Institute, March 2018.

[252] There is no single universally accepted way to estimate the number of illegally resident immigrants based on representative population data. The MPI team's methods are documented in Jeanne Batalova, Sarah Hooker, and Randy Capps, *DACA at the Two-Year Mark: A National and State Profile of Youth Eligible and Applying for Deferred Action*, Washington, D.C.: Migration Policy Institute, August 2014. Other commonly referenced numbers come from the Pew Center, which counted 10.7 million undocumented immigrants as of 2016 (Jeffrey S. Passel and D'Vera Cohn, "U.S. Unauthorized Immigrant Total Dips to Lowest Level in a Decade," Pew Research Center, November 27, 2018), and DHS, which estimated 12 million as of 2015 (Bryan Baker, "Estimates of the Illegal Alien Population Residing in the United States: January 2015," Washington, D.C.: U.S. Department of Homeland Security, Office of Immigration Statistics, Office of Strategy, Policy and Plans, December 2018). It is reasonable to focus on MPI's estimate given that it is close to the average of the other two.

[253] Bryan Baker, "Estimates of the Lawful Permanent Resident Population in the United States: January 2015," Washington, D.C.: U.S. Department of Homeland Security, Office of Immigration Statistics, Office of Strategy, Policy and Plans, May 2019.

baseline number of terrorists in the population is between 100 and 10,000, between 99.99998 percent and 99.998 percent of U.S.-born citizens are *not* terrorists; for all citizens, including naturalized immigrants, the rate is between 99.999975 percent and 99.9975 percent. For citizens and LPRs combined, between 99.99997 percent and 99.997 percent are not terrorists, and the same range holds for all legal residents combined. Recall from the discussion of criminality that these assumptions imply a baseline range of 99.99997 percent to 99.997 percent in the general population, so, *at best*, a policy of excluding immigrants from eligibility for a credential could achieve an improvement of 0.001 percentage points over the baseline propensity for terrorism. As with criminal background, because of very low rates of terrorism in the population at large, it is virtually impossible for an eligibility policy based on immigration status to appreciably change the risk profile of the TWIC card–holding population.

The analyses of both criminality and immigration status have the same overall takeaway: Even a "good" predictor of terrorism will be too coarse a measure to yield a large change in the risk profile of the eligible population based on a reasonable exclusion measure. The rate of terrorism in the population is too low, and the occurrence of predictive traits, such as criminal background or visa category, is too high, to effectively eliminate even one terrorist from the eligible applicant pool without also eliminating tens of thousands or even millions of other people.

Research on the Relationship Between Immigration and Crime

In our literature review, we sought to identify relevant scholarly studies that explored whether people deemed *ineligible* for TWICs based on immigration criteria present a higher security risk than those who are *eligible*. As noted above, the TWIC regulatory immigration standard disqualifies some foreigners who hold legal status in the country while allowing some foreigners with different legal immigration statuses to apply. It would also disqualify people with no legal status, and an immigration violation is an interim disqualifying offense. We were unable to identify literature evaluating the security risk specific to each of these narrow immigration categories that qualify or disqualify an applicant for a TWIC. We did, however, identify literature that broadly addressed the risk of crime that people legally and illegally in the United States pose to the country.

In our review, we found little credible evidence that immigrants—whether of legal or unauthorized status—are more likely to commit crimes than U.S. citizens or natives. Rather, researchers in several empirical studies found no significant relationship between immigration and crime. Results from others suggest that immigrants in the United States legally or without authorization are less likely to engage in violent and nonviolent criminal activity than their native-born peers and are less likely to be incarcerated than native-born Americans. In addition, results of multiple studies that relied on longitudinal analyses suggest that U.S. cities with more immigrants—including those of unauthorized status—tend to have lower crime rates than areas with fewer immigrants. These findings suggest that disqualifying foreign applicants based on their immigration statuses alone presents few security benefits.

In 2018, given the number of studies that have explored the immigration–crime relationship, relying on a diversity of research designs and samples, researchers Graham Ousey and Charis Kubrin synthesized findings from 51 such studies conducted between 1994 and 2014 to examine immigration's average effect on crime rates in the United States.[254] In their research, they employed a two-pronged approach to reviewing and assessing the body of literature, combining the qualitative method of narrative review with the quantitative strategy of systematic meta-analysis. *Their findings indicate that, overall, the immigration–crime association is negative but very weak.* However, the researchers highlighted significant variation in findings across studies and concluded that study design features, including measurement of the dependent variable, units of analysis, temporal design, and locational context, affect the immigration–crime association in varied ways.

In addition, several studies have examined immigration's effect on violent and nonviolent crime in cities over time. For example, researchers in a peer-reviewed empirical study reported in *Criminology* in 2018 found no link between violent crime and illegal immigration.[255] This research combined estimates of the unauthorized population in all 50 states and Washington, D.C., from 1990 to 2014, with multiple data sources, including police reports and victimization data, to provide a longitudinal analysis of the macro-level relationship between undocumented immigration and violence. The results from fixed-effect regression models revealed that undocumented immigration does not increase violence. Rather, the researchers concluded that the relationship between undocumented immigration and violent crime is generally negative, although significantly so in only some specifications. Importantly, the researchers found little evidence that these results are due to decreased reporting or selective migration undocumented immigrants to low-crime areas.

Similarly, in a 2016 study, researcher David Green found that undocumented immigration is generally not associated with violent crime but that there appears to be a small but significant association between undocumented-immigrant populations and drug-related arrests.[256] In the study, Green examined rates of violent crime and drug arrests, by state, for 2012 through 2014. He compared these data with pooled statistics on foreign-born and Mexican nationals living in the United States, as well as estimates of undocumented foreign and undocumented Mexican populations, by state. He first tested the research question by running correlations with immigrant populations and crime rates, regressing immigrant population data against violent-

---

[254] Graham C. Ousey and Charis E. Kubrin, "Immigration and Crime: Assessing a Contentious Issue," *Annual Review of Criminology*, Vol. 1, 2018, pp. 63–84.

[255] Michael T. Light and Ty Miller, "Does Undocumented Immigration Increase Violent Crime?" *Criminology*, Vol. 56, No. 2, 2018, pp. 370–401.

[256] David Green, "The Trump Hypothesis: Testing Immigrant Populations as a Determinant of Violent and Drug-Related Crime in the United States," *Social Science Quarterly*, Vol. 97, No. 3, September 2016, pp. 506–524.

crime rates and drug-related arrests, and finally running expanded regressions controlling for a variety of economic and demographic factors at the state level. *According to Green, the data uniformly show no association between immigrant population size and increased violent crime. The data, however, do suggest that undocumented-immigrant associations with drug-related crime are minimal, although significant.*

In another study, Robert Adelman, a sociologist at the State University of New York at Buffalo, and his colleagues compared immigration rates with crime rates for 200 metropolitan areas over a 40-year period from 1970 to 2010.[257] The researchers stratified the sample based on region and population size, so that it was broadly representative of the regional distribution of U.S. metropolitan areas. In 136 metro areas, almost 70 percent of those studied, the immigrant population increased between 1980 and 2016 while the crime rate stayed stable or fell. The number of areas where crime and immigration both increased was much lower—54 areas, slightly more than a quarter of the total. The ten places with the largest increases in immigrants all had lower levels of crime in 2016 than in 1980. *Given these findings, the researchers concluded that, for property crime, immigration has a consistently negative effect. For violent crime, immigration has no effect on assault and a negative effect on robbery and murder. In addition, the authors concluded that there is strong and stable evidence that, at the macro level, immigration does not cause crime to increase in U.S. metropolitan areas and might even help reduce it.*

In our literature review, we also identified studies in which researchers compared the incarceration rates of immigrants with those of native-born Americans during different time periods. In a Cato Institute study reported in 2019, researchers found that all immigrants—legally and illegally present—are less likely to be incarcerated than native-born Americans relative to their shares of the population.[258] The study relied on ACS data from the U.S. census to analyze incarcerated immigrants according to their citizenship and legal statuses in 2017.[259] According to the data, an estimated 1,926,390 native-born Americans, 106,431 illegally present immigrants, and 52,424 legally present immigrants were incarcerated that year. The incarceration rate in 2017 for native-born Americans was 1,471 per 100,000; 756 per 100,000 for illegally present immigrants; and 364 per 100,000 for legally present immigrants. Thus, according to

---

[257] Robert Adelman, Lesley Williams Reid, Gail Markle, Saskia Weiss, and Charles Jaret, "Urban Crime Rates and the Changing Face of Immigration: Evidence Across Four Decades," *Journal of Ethnicity in Criminal Justice*, Vol. 15, No. 1, 2017, pp. 52–77.

[258] Michelangelo Landgrave and Alex Nowrasteh, "Criminal Immigrants in 2017: Their Numbers, Demographics, and Countries of Origin," Washington, D.C.: Cato Institute, Immigration Research and Policy Brief 11, March 4, 2019.

[259] The ACS data include illegally present immigrants incarcerated for immigration offenses and in U.S. Immigration and Customs Enforcement detention facilities. Removing the immigration offenders by subtracting the 13,000 convicted for immigration offenses and the 38,000 in Immigration and Customs Enforcement detention facilities on any given day lowers the incarceration rate for illegally present immigrants to 397 per 100,000—only 9 percent above the incarceration rate for legally present immigrants.

these data, the researchers found that illegally present immigrants were 49 percent less likely than native-born Americans to be incarcerated. Legally present immigrants were 75 percent less likely than native-born Americans to be incarcerated.

These findings are consistent with those from a different Cato study analyzing ACS incarceration data for 2014.[260] In that year, an estimated 2,007,502 natives, 122,939 illegally present immigrants, and 63,994 legally present immigrants were incarcerated. The incarceration rate was 1.53 percent for natives, 0.85 percent for illegally present immigrants, and 0.47 percent for legally present immigrants. Illegally present immigrants were 44 percent less likely than natives to be incarcerated. Thus, informed by these data, the researchers found that legally present immigrants were 69 percent less likely than natives to be incarcerated. Legally and illegally present immigrants were underrepresented in the incarcerated population, while natives were overrepresented.

A 2007 study by researchers Kristin Butcher and Anne Morrison Piehl found that, in addition to having lower rates of institutionalization than the native-born, immigrants' relative rates of institutionalization fell between 1980 and 2000. The authors also examined whether the improvement in immigrants' relative incarceration rates during this period is linked to increased deportation, immigrant self-selection, or deterrence. Their evidence suggests that deportation does not drive the results. Rather, the researchers found that the process of migration selects people who either have lower criminal propensities or are more responsive to deterrent effects than the average native.[261]

Criminal History as a Risk Factor for Security Threats in General

In the previous section, we discussed the appropriateness of vetting standards considering that the purpose of the STA is to reduce terrorism risk. However, as we discussed previously, one interpretation of MTSA's language is that it implies that TWIC is also intended to reduce the risk of other federal crime, such as smuggling and trafficking.

Ports, particularly those engaged in significant international commerce, naturally elicit concern among policymakers as a source of potential crime, as we discussed in Chapter 4. For reasons also discussed in Chapter 4, it is difficult to determine whether crime has decreased since the introduction of the TWIC program. We can, however, look at general literature about the value of criminal-history vetting in reducing crime in the context of TWIC's vetting standards. Someone who has been arrested in the past is more likely than the average person to be arrested

---

[260] Michelangelo Landgrave and Alex Nowrasteh, "Criminal Immigrants: Their Numbers, Demographics, and Countries of Origin," Washington, D.C.: Cato Institute, Immigration Research and Policy Brief 1, March 15, 2017.

[261] Kristin F. Butcher and Anne Morrison Piehl, *Why Are Immigrants' Incarceration Rates So Low? Evidence on Selective Immigration, Deterrence, and Deportation*, Cambridge, Mass.: National Bureau of Economic Research, Working Paper 13229, July 2007.

in the future,[262] and a small number of chronic offenders make up the majority of arrests.[263] But the criminology literature also finds that one-time offenders often age out of criminal activity.

Recency has been identified as an important factor in criminal recidivism. In a 2007 study reported in *Crime and Delinquency*, researchers found that, "if a person with a criminal record remains crime-free for a period of about 7 years, his/her risk of a new offense is similar to that of a person without any criminal record."[264] Researchers in a 2009 study found that a crime-free period of ten years resulted in ex-offenders presenting risk equal to that of nonoffenders, caveating that be some offenses could be considered "so obnoxious or potentially harmful that we should never countenance their obliteration."[265] Other factors, such as age of first offense, current age, and number and type of prior incidents, are statistically relevant for determining someone's risk level.[266] Recidivism risk, for example, is statistically higher for younger offenders. At some level, even factors that are empirically relevant in ascertaining risk might be practically irrelevant in estimating risk. For example, it could be understandably impractical for a program, such as TWIC, to have different standards depending on the age of the applicant. TWIC's current standards—certain permanently disqualifying offenses and interim disqualifying offenses that disqualify someone for seven years after the time of conviction and five years after the time of release—are generally consistent with research in this area. However, TSA does not appear to use any more-refined risk-prediction tools, of which there are multiple in practice with similar predictive results, in making decisions of security risk, either in initial evaluation of security risk or in evaluating waiver applicants.

Research in this area is less informative in reaching conclusions on the specific crimes included in TWIC's vetting standards, both because existing research does not always consider the variance between crimes and because the STA's disqualifying offenses do not meet any specific criterion that a researcher might have used in a study (e.g., they do not encompass violent offenses). Further, there is significant emerging research on the predictive value of criminal history and recidivism, given the increasing accessibility of criminal-history information and trend toward employee background checks. Therefore, there might be value in revising the specifics of vetting standards on a routine basis, such as each decade, to benefit from new research findings.

---

[262] Megan C. Kurley, Robert Brame, and Shawn D. Bushway, "Scarlet Letters and Recidivism: Does an Old Criminal Record Predict Future Offending?" *Criminology and Public Policy*, Vol. 5, No. 3, August 2006, pp. 483–504.

[263] Megan C. Kurley, Robert Brame, and Shawn D. Bushway, "Enduring Risk? Old Criminal Records and Predictions of Future Criminal Involvement," *Crime and Delinquency*, Vol. 53, No. 1, January 2007, pp. 64–83.

[264] Kurley, Brame, and Bushway, 2007.

[265] Keith Soothill and Brian Francis, "When Do Ex-Offenders Become Like Non-Offenders?" *Howard Journal of Criminal Justice*, Vol. 48, No. 4, September 2009, pp. 373–387.

[266] Samuel E. DeWitt, Shawn D. Bushway, Garima Siwach, and Megan C. Kurlychek, "Redeemed Compared to Whom? Comparing the Distributional Properties of Arrest Risk Across Populations of Provisional Employees with and Without a Criminal Record," *Criminology and Public Policy*, Vol. 16, No. 3, August 2017, pp. 963–997.

Anecdotal Insights on TWIC's Impact on Crime

We heard anecdotally in several interviews with security officers that they perceived a decline in crime since the introduction of TWIC. For example, one interviewee explained, as a result of TWIC, "I believe we have significantly increased our stance against common criminals, employee thefts, things like that. We went from chasing bad guys with loaders [people trying to steal aluminum] to now where we haven't had that in 15 years."[267] One reason given was the direct vetting of people with criminal histories. We learned in our interviews that, before TWIC implementation, some companies operating in the maritime industry were not conducting any kind of criminal background checks.

Another reason cited is the general enhancement of security at facilities and the introduction of access control. Some facilities had no access control program prior to MTSA and TWIC, meaning that someone seeking to commit a crime could more easily access some facilities than they might today. Multiple interviewees, particularly from non–risk group A facilities, highlighted this benefit. One stated,

> Before MTSA regulations, this was the Wild West out here. When I used to drive by this place, there were no fences, limited gates, we had people all over the terminals everywhere. MTSA came in and boom that shut everything down, and we've got the standards, so it's a much more safe and secure environment.[268]

Another stated,

> All these guys that work at refineries know the rules. And we don't get many people that have failed their background [check]. We get maybe one or two a year. Most people know obviously a DUI [driving under the influence] [violation] is a mistake.[269]

This interviewee said that the TWIC background check had made a difference: "Before . . . you had some outlaw motorcycle gang types, there was always fights going on in the parking lot . . . .[TWIC] brought in a higher level of worker."[270] Finally, some interviewees said that the TWIC program—and the federal administration of it—led employees to be more compliant with the law, lest they lose their eligibility for a credential and the employment opportunities that require it. One interviewee noted, "It makes people vested in wanting the job. We use it as a weeding-out [tool]. We also have a company background check, but TWIC is another layer."[271]

---

[267] Interview with the FSO of a container facility.

[268] Interview with the chief of security for a mix of facilities at a hybrid port.

[269] Interview with the security supervisor of an oil refinery.

[270] Interview with the security supervisor of an oil refinery.

[271] Interview with an FSO of a ferry terminal.

Facility Perceptions of the STA Process

In the course of our interviews, we asked those in the port environment about their perceptions of the security value of the STA. Stakeholders' perceptions do not tell us the true value of the STA process in mitigating risk. However, these perceptions are relevant in that facilities have latitude in integrating the TWIC program into their access control programs, as we introduced in Chapter 2. In Chapter 6, we discuss the specifics of TWIC's integration at the port facilities from which we interviewed personnel. Perceptions of the STA's security value could affect choices that facilities make when determining whether to integrate TWIC into a PACS, invest in using the CCL, or expand the use of biometric technologies. We often heard critical comments in our interviews about the lack of value of the STA process in mitigating the perceived risks to maritime facilities, but, given that there were also often misperceptions of the content of the STA or the waiver process, it was difficult for us to determine whether stakeholders would find greater value in the STA if they understood its full security benefits.

Facilities generally endorsed the need for someone with unescorted access to have a background check conducted. In the words of one interviewee,

> I agree we should have a system to vet people. It may not be what it could be, but I like having a federally vetted ID that is tied to a biometric tag and is bounced off of a database that is hopefully kept current.[272]

Many accepted the standards of the government's STA and appreciated the standard identity assurance credential that TWIC provides. FSOs interviewed generally reported seeing TWIC standards as low. One interviewee stated, "It seems like you have to commit treason to not get [a TWIC]."[273] In the words of another, despite the validity of the concept of TWIC, it was "watered down to the No Truck Driver Left Behind Act. Industry would have stopped, so, unless you're a terrorist or a serial killer, you can have TWIC."[274] A similar sentiment was expressed as, "If [the background investigation] was tighter, we wouldn't have any labor. So, there's probably a trade-off in what TSA decided was appropriate to check."[275]

Officials from some facilities, particularly those who saw their facilities' security risk as higher, felt that the criminal background standards of the STA were too low to meet their needs and, therefore, conducted or required additional background checks on people seeking access. Interviewees frequently raised, in relation to the specific vetting standards, concerns about the fact that TWIC did not vet all violent offenses.[276] Facility operators were frequently unaware that TSA's ability to check for potential links to terrorism differs from that of private vendors.

---

[272] Interview with the FSO of a hybrid port facility.

[273] Interview with the port authority of a cruise facility.

[274] Interview with the FSO of a cruise facility.

[275] Interview with the FSO of a hybrid port facility.

[276] Interviews with the terminal manager and FSO for a cruise facility.

Facilities rarely mentioned without prompting that TWIC included a terrorist watch-list check, but, when asked whether they saw this as a value of the credential, the answer was a nearly universal yes.

We found that many FSOs were operating under inaccurate information about the content of the STA. Two misperceptions we heard about the STA process related to the databases checked and whether TWIC holders were subject to recurrent vetting for new disqualifying information. Some facility operators reported doing additional background checks because they perceived that the STA process did not go far enough in identifying people who present security risk.

A Lack of Understanding About TWIC Recurrent Vetting

As we stated earlier in this chapter, the STA process has included recurrent vetting for all credential holders against the terrorist watch list since the inception of the program. Automated recurrent vetting for terrorism occurs whenever the terrorist watch list or applicant records change.[277] These results are reviewed within a 24-hour period for appropriate action. TSA also uses IDENT for continuous terrorism, criminal, and immigration checks. IDENT can identify potentially disqualifying information on TWIC holders using both biometric and biographic records. This would include active wants and warrants; federal, state, and local alerts; and pending immigration removal orders. If TSA identifies new derogatory criminal information, it reevaluates a cardholder's rap sheet. If information is disqualifying, TSA is a preliminary letter of ineligibility to the cardholder and—barring a successful appeal or waiver petition by the cardholder—cancel the card.

TSA also intends to use the FBI's Rap Back service in the future for criminal-history monitoring. The Rap Back subscription service provides "notification of subsequent activity or updates to an individual's criminal history record after the initial request for Criminal History Record Check (CHRC)."[278] The service alerts the subscriber "of any future reported events selected as Rap Back Triggering Events, which could be criminal or civil.[279] TSA has provided information regarding these processes through a variety of channels, including area maritime security committee meetings, quarterly stakeholder calls, and industry conferences, but, during our interviews, we still found misperceptions of recurrent vetting. For example, one interviewee stated, "The NCIC [National Crime Information Center] isn't connected to TWIC;"[280] however, this system is checked in the STA process.

---

[277] TSA, business year 2018 Transportation Worker Identification Credential business case provided to the authors, August 15, 2016a.

[278] Richard Conrad, program manager, Aviation Program Management Division, Office of Intelligence and Analysis, Transportation Security Administration, "TSA Rap Back Overview Brief," presented at Transportation Security Administration/Federal Bureau of Investigation Rap Back Workshop, March 28, 2017.

[279] Conrad, 2017.

[280] Interview with the FSO of a CDC facility.

Others stated that recurrent vetting was not occurring, including for terrorism checks.[281] We heard such statements as "the TWIC cards—certainly they're not real time,"[282] and, "If you're running a background check only five years, it's only a glorified ID check. It's possible for someone to get their TWIC, go to prison for two years for a disqualifying crime and come back here."[283] When we asked one facility official whether they were aware of recurring background checks under TWIC, they responded, "We haven't heard anything and always asked what happened if I radicalized in the next two years."[284] Another example was when a different interviewee stated, "I don't know if TSA has a routine vetting process for somebody. You could be clean slate five years ago but could become a terrorist two years ago."[285] We also heard in interviews that TWIC would not identify existing wants and warrants, but TVS does identify potential new criminal information from federal wants and warrants.

Concerns About the TWIC Waiver Process

Multiple interviewees raised the topic of TSA's waiver process. MTSA requires TSA to implement a waiver process for people who are initially deemed ineligible for TWIC and to consider a variety of factors when making waiver decisions. Respondents often expressed concern about the high percentage of people who had been granted waivers. Embedded in these concerns appeared to be an assumption that someone who had been granted a waiver presented a greater risk than someone who had not. For example, one FSO suggested that the CCL should include whether someone had been granted a waiver—implying that the risk of a waivered person on the CCL was greater than for someone who did not receive a waiver. These concerns were generally about the waiver process in theory. When asked as a follow-on question whether the interviewee knew of a specific person who had been granted a waiver and, if so, whether they agreed with that waiver decision, respondents agreed with TSA's decision to issue waivers in the specific cases with which they were familiar.

In our conversations with TSA personnel regarding their waiver processes, we were told that security risk is considered per the definition of security threat in 49 C.F.R. § 1570.3: "an individual whom TSA determines or suspects of posing a threat to national security; to transportation security; or of terrorism." TSA would not issue a waiver to anyone it determined presented such a security threat. TSA does evaluate whether someone could present a criminal risk beyond this threshold. A TWIC holder, for example, could present an increased risk of theft to a facility, and this would not alone be sufficient reason for the cardholder to be denied a

---

[281] Interviews with FSOs of three CDC facilities, security managers of a container facility, security professional of a container facility, officials at the port authority of a medium-sized port involved in container and bulk operations, and officials at a landlord port authority.

[282] Interviews with security personnel of CDC facilities.

[283] Interview with the FSO for a port with a mix of facilities.

[284] Interview with the safety specialist of a CDC facility.

[285] Interviews with FSOs and security personnel of container facilities.

TWIC card or a waiver. TSA did not share any policy documents or precedent that would further expand how these distinctions have been implemented in practice.

TSA has, understandably, voiced the need to protect the privacy of anyone who requests a TWIC. MTSA also stipulates that TSA may not share information related to the results of an STA, including whether a waiver was granted or denied, with the public or the employer. However, facility operators' confidence in the waiver process—and therefore the STA process as a whole—could be improved by greater transparency about the process. First, TSA could provide greater insight into the criteria under which it gives a waiver, which could help facility operators understand how TSA determines that someone does not present a security risk. Second, emphasizing the overall numbers of people who have been granted waivers and the percentage they compose of the overall TWIC workforce might provide reassurances, given that the waivered population is very small. Third, efforts could be taken to test the assumption that someone who been granted a waiver presents greater risk than someone who had not. For example, further research could be done into breaches of security at facilities or TWIC revocations to determine whether someone who received a waiver was more or less likely to conduct a crime or incur a violation in the future. Ultimately, however, given that people who are granted waivers can still present risk to facilities—although not a security risk per the definition in 49 C.F.R. § 1570.3—some facility operators might still perceive the waiver process as a weakness in the STA process, given that their goals for the TWIC program might differ from those of the federal government.

Efficiency of the STA Process

The Adequacy of TWIC Enrollment Fees

Public Law 114-278 states that an evaluation should assess whether the costs of the credential are commensurate with the costs of the vetting process. People we interviewed also sometimes commented on the cost of the TWIC card. To determine whether costs were adequate given the costs of vetting, an HSOAC team reviewed the costs of the TWIC program in relation to the fee charged to applicants. We performed this analysis using enrollment, fee revenue, and cost data covering fiscal years (FYs) 2016, 2017, and 2018. We found that TWIC user fees have aligned reasonably well with per-enrollment costs. In FYs 2016 and 2017, TWIC revenue exceeded costs, and the surplus was used as a carryover to maintain liquidity from year to year. In FY 2018, revenue fell short of costs, but the deficit was covered by carryover funds. In each year, user fees remained within 25 percent of the underlying per-enrollment costs.

Table 5.2 compares fees and costs for each enrollment type. In FYs 2016 and 2017, user fees exceeded average cost per enrollment by 13 to 23 percent. In FY 2018, user fees aligned more closely with the underlying costs. Fees for standard enrollments, renewals, and comparable enrollments fell short of per-enrollment costs, but the margin was less than 2 percent. The fee for replacement cards continued to exceed per-enrollment cost, but the margin shrank to 9 percent. For a complete review of our analysis of TWIC user fees, please see Appendix E.

Table 5.2. TWIC User Fees and Costs per Enrollment, in Dollars

FY	Fee or Cost	Standard Enrollment	Renewal	Comparable Enrollment	Replacement Card
2016	User fee	128.00	128.00	105.25	60.00
	Cost per enrollment	111.83	111.83	92.42	49.54
2017	User fee	125.25	125.25	105.25	60.00
	Cost per enrollment	110.58	110.58	91.59	48.99
2018	User fee	125.25	125.25	105.25	60.00
	Cost per enrollment	126.35	126.35	106.64	54.96

SOURCE: Administrative data provided by TSA.
NOTE: A comparable enrollment is offered to an applicant with an active HME on a commercial driver's license.

Although the $125.25 enrollment fee is higher than the typical cost of a commercial background check, we highlight that these fees cover additional costs, which include check of the terrorist watch list, check of immigration status, and the cost of printing and mailing a physical credential. TWIC fees also include continuous monitoring of (terrorist and) criminal history; in contrast, most commercial background checks are one-time services.

The Length of Time for TWIC Issuance

GAO and OIG reports have raised concerns about the length of time required for the STA process, and Public Law 114-278 Section 1(b)(3)(B) requests that this study review the length of time taken to process a TWIC application, including requests for redress.[286] TSA submitted a report to Congress in 2019 reflecting an analysis of the STA process.[287] The authors of the TSA analysis found that the system adjudicates applications for 50 to 55 percent of applicants favorably within two days, with applicants receiving their TWIC cards three to four days later. It adjudicates most of the remaining cases within 30 days of application. Less than 1 percent of all adjudication cases require more than 30 days to reach preliminary determination of qualification. From January through October 2018, 2,284 appeals were processed in an average of 26 days. During the same time frame, 1,700 waivers were processed in an average of 75 days. The average for appeals had decreased significantly from an average of 106 days in 2016; waivers took an average of 112 days in 2016. From our previous study on the STA process, we found

---

[286] Public Law 114-278's specific language reads, "(B) review the process for renewing applications for Transportation Worker Identification Credentials, including the number of days it takes to review application, appeal, and waiver requests for additional information." However, there is no process for renewal of a TWIC application. Instead, all applicants are treated equally regardless of whether they have previously held TWICs. Therefore, we considered the length of time for the TWIC application process for all applicants.

[287] TSA, 2019.

these numbers consistent with our understanding of the typical timeline. During interviews in our previous study, TSA personnel indicated that delays in the STA process can often come from incomplete case data in NCIC. Researchers in a GAO study in 2015 identified this as a chronic issue in NCIC.[288] TSA indicated that delays in a final decision in the redress process can often result from awaiting applicants' efforts to gather material relevant to their case. For this reason, requiring that TSA complete every case within a limited period of time could limit applicants' efforts to successfully seek redress. In our interviews, the length of time taken to process TWIC applicants was rarely, if ever, brought up as a current concern about the TWIC program. Interviewees did sometimes comment that TSA had significantly improved this process.

Summary

Statute establishes the vetting criteria used by the STA process, which fall roughly into three bins: known or suspected ties to terrorism, past felony criminal history, and legal immigration status. TSA evaluates whether an applicant meets these explicit criteria and whether each applicant might be eligible for an appeal or waiver if requested, according to the requirements of the law. Our task, per Public Law 114-278, was to consider how effectively the law was achieving its intent of identifying people who pose a risk to the maritime environment. To do so, we reviewed legislative records to describe the risks that TWIC is intended to mitigate, and we evaluated past studies on the relevance of those risk factors to achieving TWIC's stated objectives.

Reducing the risk of terrorism is an explicit objective of the TWIC program. Past studies suggest that prior criminal history could be one risk factor relevant to determining whether someone poses a greater-than-average risk of engaging or attempting to engage in terrorism. However, we found both practical and methodological limitations when attempting to use that research to evaluate whether TWIC's vetting standards were appropriate in identifying whether someone presents a terrorism risk. Our analysis of this research raised several questions that cast doubt on the predictive value of criminal history broadly, and STA standards specifically, as a single risk factor in determining, absent other risk factors, someone's threat as a potential terrorist. Previous research has focused on a broader set of crimes than the TWIC program uses; these inconsistences raise questions about whether those findings remain valid when using the narrower set of criminal offenses specified in TWIC standards. The TWIC population also has a greater rate of criminality than the general population. Therefore, we cannot assume that even the increased chance of a terrorist having a criminal history among the general population means that a TWIC applicant would have the same increased probability. If the sole purpose of the program is to reduce terrorism risk, then, informed by the literature, we find it difficult to justify the use

---

[288] GAO, *Criminal History Records: Additional Actions Could Enhance the Completeness of Records Used for Employment-Related Background Checks*, Washington, D.C., GAO-15-162, February 12, 2015.

of criminal history (except terrorism-specific crimes) as a vetting criterion, given its low predictive value.

TWIC's criminal-history standards would have merit in considering a broader STA goal to reduce federal crime at maritime facilities for its own sake, separate from the value it might have in reducing other security risks, although, for the reasons discussed in Chapter 4, we are unable to determine whether a reduction in crime has occurred and, if so, quantify the extent to which that is true.

We found the process itself—in terms of both time and cost—to be generally efficient. Ninety-nine percent of TWIC applications are initially adjudicated within 30 days, and around half within a couple of days. TWIC enrollment fees are generally consistent with TSA's costs in conducting the STA and issuing the card.

6. TWIC Use at Maritime Facilities

As we introduced in Chapter 2, the TWIC program can reduce risk at maritime facilities. In Chapter 4, we provided an overview of threats in the maritime environment, and, in Chapter 5, we discussed the vetting standards intended to identify people who might present a threat. In this chapter and Chapters 6 and 7, we examine the TWIC program's relevance in reducing facilities' security risk. We focus first on examining facility access control vulnerabilities. Two sources of information are relevant to facility access control vulnerabilities. The first comes from FSOs, who are the experts in the specific vulnerabilities at their facilities. Per 33 C.F.R. § 105.205, the FSO is responsible for ensuring that a facility security assessment is conducted for their facility, which is used to develop and implement an FSP; maintaining security awareness at the facility; recording and reporting any security-related events; and implementing the TWIC program.[289] USCG facility inspectors review facility security assessments and FSPs for completeness, but, ultimately, the FSOs are the most-knowledgeable sources on any facility's specific vulnerabilities. Given their extensive knowledge, we focused our interview recruitment efforts on FSOs; as a result, FSOs were the majority of those we interviewed. A second source is the information USCG PSSs gather on facilities, which is used to populate MSRAM, and includes information on facility vulnerabilities (see Appendix C for more information on MSRAM). We interviewed multiple PSSs, and we reviewed some aggregated data on facility vulnerability scores, as we discuss in Chapter 7. Our use of MSRAM was limited by the fact that certain information becomes classified when compiled.

This chapter summarizes findings from our port and facility interviews about how facilities covered in our sample have implemented TWIC, insights about the TWIC program from the perspective of security professionals and facility operators, and how TWIC has reduced facility security risk. As we introduced in Chapter 1, we conducted 200 interviews with facility operators, security professionals, industry representatives, and labor representatives, covering 164 facilities in 45 port areas. Figure 6.1 depicts the locations of these port areas, and Appendix A provides background on our sampling and coding methods. We found that, for many reasons, the way maritime facilities have implemented TWIC varies widely. One of the fundamental drivers for this variability seems to be the differences in maritime facilities themselves (e.g., physical configuration, type of commodity, volume of business), which have implications for security vulnerabilities and consequences of attack, which, in turn, inform decisions on investments in mitigation measures. For some facilities, TWIC is integral to their operations as the primary ID credential. Others view it as not adding much value to the facility,

---

[289] 33 C.F.R. § 105.205.

given that it is an additional security mechanism apart from and on top of otherwise-robust security measures.

Figure 6.1. Port Areas Covered in Interviews

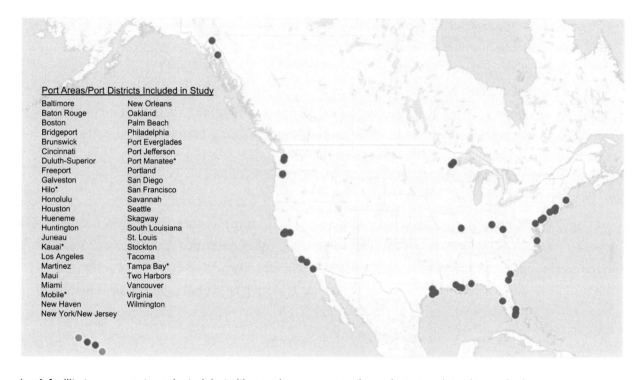

Port Areas/Port Districts Included in Study

Baltimore	New Orleans
Baton Rouge	Oakland
Boston	Palm Beach
Bridgeport	Philadelphia
Brunswick	Port Everglades
Cincinnati	Port Jefferson
Duluth-Superior	Port Manatee*
Freeport	Portland
Galveston	San Diego
Hilo*	San Francisco
Honolulu	Savannah
Houston	Seattle
Hueneme	Skagway
Huntington	South Louisiana
Juneau	St. Louis
Kauai*	Stockton
Los Angeles	Tacoma
Martinez	Tampa Bay*
Maui	Two Harbors
Miami	Vancouver
Mobile*	Virginia
New Haven	Wilmington
New York/New Jersey	

* = A facility tour was not conducted, but either a phone conversation or in-person interview took place.

These differences in how ports and facilities have implemented TWIC directly affect TWIC's potential risk-mitigation value. For example, the robust security features of TWIC that make it difficult to counterfeit is relevant only if a TWIC card is used as the access control credential (or otherwise checked closely at time of entry). Another example is the use of the CCL, which identifies cards that have been reported lost or stolen or have been revoked because the holder is no longer qualified. Some facilities have chosen to integrate the CCL into their PACSs and, as a result and given that the process is automated, have a better chance of detecting whether someone attempted to use a stolen or revoked card.[290] The specifics of TWIC use at facilities address questions in Public Law 114-278 about how the program addresses known and likely maritime security risks (Section 1[b][3][C][i]), TWIC's operational impacts (Section 1[b][3][C][iii]), and the costs and benefits of the TWIC program (Section 1[b][3][C][iv]).

---

[290] TSA has recently made a list of canceled-card CINs available on its website, which would allow someone to manually reference the CCL by searching for the unique eight-digit code physically printed on the card.

Facility Personnel's and Users' Experiences with the TWIC

TWIC's report card from cardholders and facility operators is decidedly mixed. Around one-third of risk group A facility operators we interviewed saw some security value in the program (equally split between CDC and large–passenger vessel facilities), while a similar proportion perceived little to no security value (slightly more operators at large–passenger vessel facilities held this view than those at CDC facilities). Perceptions were more favorable at non–risk group A facilities, with nearly half seeing security value and 20 percent finding little to none. As we later discuss at greater length, the majority of risk group A operators we interviewed had unfavorable opinions of the reader rule, so those opinions might have been factors in their less favorable response to TWIC overall. The views of the remaining facility operators were ambivalent or neutral. Despite the criticisms we often heard, few interviewees—particularly among FSOs—actively advocated eliminating TWIC.

The federal background check was most frequently cited as a benefit, with one interviewee stating, "We can be reassured that anyone with [a TWIC card] has been through a background check."[291] According to interviewees, the background check provides some reassurance that personnel working at the port have gone through a level of security vetting. Although some interviewees advocated for more-stringent standards—such as including all violent offenses—even those who assess the standards as low expressed some version of the statement, "something is better than nothing." As one interviewee stated,

> . . . it is nice that everyone who shows up at my gate has a standard ID and they aren't on the No-Fly List. Instead of a truck driver showing up from Oklahoma having nothing—at least they walk in the door with something. That is a benefit. We have something to start from and code up from our readers. There is some value.[292]

Interviewees perceived some other security benefits, including the standardization of ID, provision of a security deterrent, and supplying an additional layer of security.

Interviewees who spoke negatively about TWIC perceived it as a regulatory requirement rather than a security benefit. That is, they saw TWIC as just another check that is required by law—providing no added benefit to the security procedures already in place and incurring additional costs to the facility, employer, or individual. They also brought up that non–TWIC holders are able to use escorts, which effectively bypasses the intention of TWIC, and suggested that TWIC is redundant to the background check conducted for the HME program. FSOs with small numbers of staff felt that TWIC was not really useful for them because the staff all know each other. In the words of one manager of a risk group A facility with five staff, it felt

---

[291] Interview with the safety specialist for a CDC facility.

[292] Interview with a group of FSOs and security managers for chemical and petroleum facilities.

"counterproductive" to have to check a photo ID every day.[293] Interviewees also noted a perceived lack of risk or threat of terrorism to their facilities.

Facility Use of the TWIC

As we presented in Chapter 2, facilities have many options for integrating TWIC into their access control programs. In determining whom to authorize for access to their facilities, facility operators can use the STA as their standard for personnel vetting, or they can conduct additional vetting. This is because a TWIC does not entitle its holder to access a facility; that decision lies with the facility operators. In determining how to verify the identities of people presenting themselves as authorized personnel, an operator can use visual or electronic inspection of a TWIC or integrate the TWIC card into a PACS. Also, facility operators have a variety of methods available to verify business purpose. Not only did these standards and methods vary between facilities; they often varied *within* facilities, with different standards and methods used for different categories of people. Direct employees, for example, were often held to a higher standard and given greater access than contracted staff or people making deliveries.

We found that the use of TWIC and the management of access control points at facilities varied widely in our sample. Around 75 percent of facilities in our sample used other credentials in addition to TWIC for at least some portion of the population seeking access to the facility[294]— direct facility employees might use a different credential from those for contract employees, who use a different credential from those for longshoremen or truck drivers. Often, these other credentials are used as a primary form of ID, but someone might be required to present more than one credential at the access control point. Facilities that use other credentials as primary forms of ID indicated that these credentials are used to verify business purpose in addition to identity. Whether one needs to present a valid TWIC to be issued one of these other credentials varied by type of credential. For example, the Pacific Maritime Association and the ILA issue cards to all their members, irrespective of whether those members have TWIC cards. To obtain a Merchant Mariner Credential, one must apply first for a TWIC card because the TWIC STA serves as the background check. Some facilities also issued credentials to people without TWIC cards because significant portions of those facilities were not secure areas or not regulated by MTSA. Facilities issuing company badges or IDs (including ship and ferry IDs, port authority IDs, and facility cards) almost always conducted separate background checks as part of the hiring process for their direct employees; for contractors, most often, the contract stipulates the level of background check that must be conducted prior to employment. We discuss these facility-specific credentials more in the next section.

---

[293] Interview with the regional manager of a CDC facility.

[294] Nearly 100 percent of risk group A facilities in our sample used other credentials in addition to the TWIC card, and the breakdown for non–risk group A facilities was roughly 80/20 (other credential/TWIC card only).

Facility-Specific ID Cards Are Common

As mentioned above, more often than not, facilities used some kind of facility-specific credential. Sometimes these credentials are issued to everyone accessing the facility; other times, they are issued only to direct facility employees or contractors. In some cases, if a facility is in a public port, the credential is issued by the port and can be used at multiple facilities within the port. In other cases, a company might operate multiple facilities in different geographic areas, so they have a company credential that can be used at these facilities.

Interview subjects provided multiple reasons that a facility would continue to use an ID card in addition to TWIC. Facility-specific credentials usually served to demonstrate business purpose. For example, one facility that relied on the TWIC's STA rather than conducting a separate background check still issued a port credential, accepting that this meant that it would need to check both credentials, because the port credential "proves you have a reason to be at the port."[295] Facility-specific credentials could also serve a purpose unrelated to access control in secure areas: Some were used for timekeeping or to certify the user's credentials to operate sensitive equipment. (TSA's proposed next data model would have undedicated storage that would allow facilities to store information related to their business purposes directly on the TWIC card.) Facility-specific cards could also be cheaper to replace than a TWIC card, given that they had fewer security features. Because cards are particularly susceptible to wear and tear in the maritime environment and given the physical nature of many maritime jobs, replacing a $5 company card was seen as preferable to requiring a $60 TWIC replacement card.[296]

TWIC cards are valid for up to five years.[297] In some cases, facilities that use facility-specific credentials to demonstrate business purpose shorten the time the credential is valid so that people have to reestablish business purpose more frequently. For example, facility-specific credentials might be valid for a year, six months, or, in at least one case, a matter of days. Some FSOs also appreciated the ability to revoke facility-specific ID cards, which they could not do with TWICs. As we discuss later in this chapter, many facilities do not use the CCL, making it difficult for them to otherwise determine whether a TWIC card is still valid.

In terms of physical security features, no facility-specific ID cards that we observed were as resistant as TWIC is to counterfeiting. Many that we observed had no security features, and

---

[295] Interview with the FSO of several cruise facilities.

[296] Per regulation, TWIC cards would still need to be on one's person or easily accessible but could be kept in a wallet, protective sleeve, or locker during daily use at the facility.

We would caveat that the cost of printing a company card was often given to us as a ballpark figure and did not necessarily provide a true accounting of the associated costs of printing a local card. For example, in addition to card stock, there are also costs for printers, ink, personnel, and physical space.

[297] A TWIC card would be issued for a five-year period, with the exception of HME credentials, for which holders apply for reciprocal credentials. In this circumstance, the TWIC card would be issued for whatever period of time is remaining under the initial STA.

others had only chips or holograms.[298] TWIC, in contrast, has a chip, holograms, color-shifting ink, microtext, and reflective text, among other security features.

Many Facilities Already Use Electronic Verification for the TWIC

Although facilities currently are not required to do more than visually inspect the card, many facilities we visited have implemented more-robust controls for identity verification and access control.[299] The most common investment was in a PACS (just under 50 percent of our sample), which we observed most frequently at bulk liquid facilities (62 percent of the facilities that have invested in PACSs). In 8 percent of the sample, these PACS also verified identity using biometric systems—either fingerprints, facial recognition, or matching the vascular pattern of a hand.[300] Some facility operators believe that using a PACS is beneficial because it allows them to further limit access control permissions, such as limiting access to specific areas or to certain times of day. Respondents also cited benefits of PACSs unrelated to security. For example, a PACS allows an operator to easily generate a list of people currently on the facility, which is useful in the case of emergencies and evacuations.

Around 14 percent of facilities we interviewed have invested in portable readers, but only 2 percent were using portable readers on a regular basis to verify TWIC cards.[301] Some of these portable readers had the capability to check the biometric information saved on the card, but we are unsure how frequently they were being used for this purpose. (Facilities typically were not checking biometrics as routine practice.) The remaining 50 percent of our sample still relied on visual inspection of the TWIC card on a daily basis.[302] Figure 6.2 shows these findings.

---

[298] Not all of our interviews were conducted in person, so this finding does not apply to all facilities covered in our sample.

[299] Any numbers presented in this section represent the mode of access control implemented during the scope of this study and do not reflect past modes of access control (which might have been more or less stringent) or planned future investments.

[300] The 8 percent breaks down across facility types as follows: four container, three bulk liquid, three mixed use, two cruise terminals, and one break-bulk and solids.

[301] The 14 percent breaks down across facility types as follows: 5 percent mixed use, 4 percent bulk liquid, 3 percent break-bulk and solids, 2 percent cruise or ferry, and no container facilities.

[302] This 50 percent breaks down across facility types as follows: 15 percent bulk liquid, 12 percent cruise, 10 percent mixed use, 8 percent break-bulk and solids, 4 percent container, and 2 percent ferry.

Figure 6.2. TWIC Verification Methods Used by Facilities Whose Officials We Interviewed

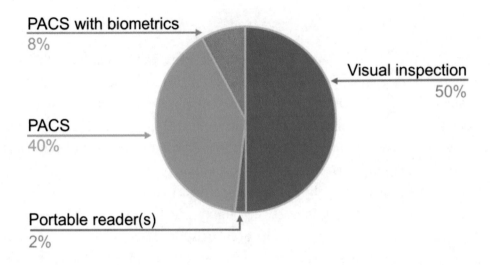

It is important to note that the results shown in Figure 6.2 might not be generalizable to the entire MTSA-regulated facility population because our sample does not precisely mirror the distribution of facility types within the full MTSA-regulated population (see Table 6.1), and our sample contains a higher proportion of high-risk facilities than the full MTSA-regulated population (34 percent and roughly 16 percent, respectively). Our sample covers 164 facilities (5 percent of MTSA-regulated facilities) consisting of a range of facility sizes (a few employees to thousands of employees) and facility types, including barging, launch services and provisions, general cargo and break-bulk, bulk solid (including hazardous material, or hazmat), bulk liquid (including hazmat), RORO, petrochemical refineries, chemical manufacturers, OCS facilities, passenger terminals (cruise and ferry), containers, and mixed-use facilities (often a combination of container, general cargo or break-bulk, and RORO). For ease of comparison, we consolidated facility types into the same categories used in the USCG 2015 regulatory analysis (and consistent with our approach for the break-even analysis described in Chapter 8): break-bulk and solids, bulk liquids, container, mixed use, passenger (cruise), and passenger (ferry).[303] Table 6.1 shows how our sample compares with the breakdown of facility types for all MTSA-regulated facilities. Given that that our sample consists of a higher proportion of high-risk facilities and included some facilities because they are using unique technologies to verify TWIC cards, it is likely that we observed a higher rate of facilities using more than just visual inspection for verification than the general MTSA population, which would likely has a higher proportion of facilities using only visual inspection.

---

[303] Office of Standards Evaluation and Development, 2015.

Table 6.1. Facilities Whose Officials We Interviewed Compared with Facilities in the Maritime Transportation Security Act–Regulated Population

Facility Type	Percentage in Our Sample	Percentage of MTSA-Regulated Facilities
Break-bulk and solids	11	17
Bulk liquids	45	38
Container	10	4
Mixed use	15	25
Passenger		
Cruise	15	6
Ferry	4	10

The Need for a Physical Card Affects Facility Operations

Respondents, depending on how long they had worked at the facility, were sometimes able to speak to how the introduction of TWIC has changed the access control programs in place at their facilities. For some facilities, there was little semblance of an access control program prior to the introduction of the TWIC program, and the introduction of TWIC brought notable changes to facility operations. One respondent who reported that TWIC appropriately improved access control told us that, prior to TWIC, their facility "was wide open . . . . It was pretty seedy . . . . There was no control."[304] For others, the facility already had a system of verifying identity and conducting background checks, and TWIC changed very little in terms of who was authorized personnel at the facility and how the process of allowing access worked. In the words of one interviewee, "All we've done is go from driver's licenses to TWIC. Both tell me nothing—just who they are." GAO reports discussed in Chapter 3 note issues with TWIC's early implementation; interviewees also raised many of these issues, but they were positive about the improvements that had been made in card durability, availability of enrollment centers, time for enrollment, and ease in receiving the card. Recognizing that these problems might have had greater operational effects in the past, we focus here on issues relevant today and under the current implementation of the TWIC program. In the next section and in Chapter 8, we address the impacts of using TWIC readers.

The major operational effects that respondents mentioned were related to the physical TWIC, which we have grouped into three concerns: (1) the need to escort someone who might have forgotten or lost their TWIC card, (2) the inability to fully transition to a facility-specific card, and (3) the wear and tear on the TWIC card, particularly the card antennae. A TWIC holder is required to have their card on their person or accessible within ten minutes; otherwise, both the holder and the facility could suffer fines. No policy or practice allows the holder of a valid TWIC to be issued a temporary card or otherwise be virtually checked by the facility and granted

---

[304] Interview with the FSO of a mixed-use port.

authorized access. A TWIC holder who is not in possession of their card would need to retrieve their card (e.g., drive home to get it) or enlist an escort who should remain with them at all times that they are in the secure area of the facility.[305] This issue also comes into play when considering a facility's use of a facility-specific card. If a facility has registered that card in its PACS, linked its credential to TWIC expiration dates, and actively uses the CCL, it has a way to virtually maintain knowledge of an authorized person's TWIC. However, because the USCG could still hold a facility accountable if someone did not have their card on their person, facilities end up checking both the TWIC card and the facility-specific card upon a person's entry.

TWIC requirements do allow for TWIC cards to be retrieved within a reasonable time, rather than carried by the holder, as articulated in TWIC/MTSA Policy Advisory Council Policy Letter 08-09.[306] Under this guidance, a facility operator can store TWIC cards somewhere on the facility, which could minimize the wear and tear on cards and the potential for loss or theft. NVIC 03-07 specifically articulates this regulation in its enclosure, where it states,

> Individuals granted unescorted access should carry the TWIC on their person when they are in a secure area and the TWIC must be available for inspection if requested by owners/operators, security personnel, or Coast Guard inspectors. However, if owners/operators determine that having their personnel physically maintain the TWIC on their person is impractical, the credentials may be secured in a convenient location where they can be retrieved and presented within a reasonable amount of time for inspection or examination. Ten minutes or less is considered a reasonable amount of time.[307]

We did observe one facility at which the operator had opted to implement such a policy. During some interviews, we asked facility personnel whether they had considered such an operational configuration. Reasons presented for considering such an operational configuration not ideal included that some TWIC holders need to retain their cards because they used them to access multiple facilities; that TWIC holders might wish to use their TWIC cards as general ID documents in settings other than at the facility; or generally that the TWIC cards were seen as the property of the cardholders and they should be able to retain possession of them. Some facilities were large enough that the 10-minute rule would not be feasible, and it is not clear that all facilities recognized that such an operational configuration was permissible.

In the next section, we discuss durability of the TWIC cards.

---

[305] If a card has been reported lost and a replacement card has been applied and paid for, the holder can use a paper receipt from the transaction for entry.

[306] TWIC/MTSA Policy Advisory Council, "Incorporating TWIC into Existing Physical Access Control Systems," Policy Letter 08-09, July 15, 2009.

[307] Commandant, USCG, 2007, Enc. 3.

Interviewees Expressed Concern About the Durability of TWIC Cards

The physical TWIC card was mentioned in about one-fifth of interviews as a concern because of previous issues with durability of the card; bad card batches related to production quality and manufacturing issues; and problems with the antenna, chip, or fingerprint. Some concerns were that the card was generally fragile given that it is used in a harsh maritime environment and often by those doing physical labor. Some users stated that extensive exposure to water and heat can affect the card's features.[308] Interview respondents also told us that TWIC holders might not always take care in handling their TWIC cards, such as by leaving them on dashboards, which causes pictures to fade.[309] As one interviewee said, "We made fairly delicate cards for a robust workforce."

The most frequent concern we heard was about the card antenna, which is damaged easily and prevents the card from working with a proximity reader. Facility personnel voiced a preference for proximity readers over contact readers because proximity readers are completely contained (versus having a slot to insert the card) and therefore more durable given the exposure to moisture and dirt common at maritime facilities in harsh environments. At least one facility had gone so far as to purchase multiple electronic card readers to ascertain whether problems were because of readers or cards. Interviewees from multiple facilities along the southern coast suggested that these problems might be exacerbated by high summer temperatures affecting connectivity of the card antenna. One interviewee pointed out that, when users carry their TWIC cards, the cards "get bent, the chips get cracked or break, and they can't get verified." Some interviewees also expressed concern about the cost burden that faulty cards place on TWIC cardholders or their employers (many employers cover the costs of the credential) if the card needs to be replaced.

One facility's interviewees told us that initial problems in reading cards were actually determined to be problems with the electrical and wireless connections of the reader technology. It did appear that facilities might be quick to fault the card for problems that might, in fact, be problems with power, connectivity, reader integration, or the reader equipment itself—which can also be susceptible to harsh environmental conditions. The Secure Technology Alliance, a nonprofit association, has issued a troubleshooting guide for using TWIC cards with readers; the guide identifies several possible issues related to the field deployment of readers.[310] As noted, at least one facility we visited was testing cards using multiple readers to ascertain whether issues in reading cards were the fault of the card or the reader. Because most facilities were not

---

[308] Interviews with a senior leader at a port operating company at a major port and with multiple supervisors at a chemical facility.

[309] Interview with the harbor master of a medium-sized port; supervisors of multiple state ports; and multiple FSOs at a medium-sized port, which together are involved in container, cruise, and bulk operations.

[310] Secure Technology Alliance, *TWIC® Card/Reader Use with Physical Access Control Systems: A Field Troubleshooting Guide*, version 1.0, May 2018.

collecting systematic data on card read errors, this is an area vulnerable to cognitive bias: These events might have seemed notable because they were unusual and might not have been as frequent as remembered. For example, one interviewee believed that the new TWIC Next Generation Card Design had a more robust antenna and was experiencing errors less frequently; however, the antenna is the same as in the previous version. TSA has told us that it has done extensive testing on the card and has confidence in its durability. As we discussed in the previous section, a facility has the option to store TWIC cards somewhere on the facility if using a PACS and separate credential for entry. Such an operational configuration could minimize the wear and tear on cards, recognizing our earlier stated points as to other possible drawbacks of this operating model.

Facility Personnel's and Users' Observations About TWIC Readers

In the course of our interviews, we asked respondents about the security benefit and operational costs of biometric readers used with the TWIC program. We prioritized asking this question of interviewees from risk group A facilities and asked those from non–risk group A facilities if time allowed. We would note that interviewees often equated "TWIC reader" with "biometric, electronic reader," and we sought to be specific in the course of our interviews. However, it could be that, at times, respondents were referring to electronic biometric readers in terms of their ability to electronically verify cards as valid but not necessarily the biometric component of their identity verification.

Perceptions Were Mixed on the Degree to Which Readers Enhanced Security

Approximately one-third of respondents from risk group A facilities agreed with the notion that readers provide a security benefit to their facilities (split equally between CDC and large–passenger vessel facilities). The overall perception they shared with us was that, *if readers are working properly*, they are an effective tool and provide an additional level of comfort and security. This general sentiment was also true with non–risk group A facilities whose personnel expressed support for the use of readers. Respondents identified a range of benefits from the use of electronic readers, such as the ability to verify that a card is valid, expediting the validation of TWIC holders, and helping track who is inside a facility. Biometrics were seen as adding benefit in identity verification. In the words of one respondent specifically about the value of biometrics, "If you have the ability to read a TWIC and confirm that it's valid and belongs to the person actually holding it, it's exponentially greater in its effectiveness to prevent unauthorized access."[311] More than half of the respondents from non–risk group A facilities who identified readers as a beneficial tool specifically noted the effectiveness of biometrics.

---

[311] Interview with a port authority officer who managed security for multiple facilities, including a cruise facility.

Approximately 40 percent of respondents from risk group A facilities disagreed that readers provide a security benefit at their facilities (slightly more from large–passenger vessel facilities than from CDC facilities). These respondents felt that readers do not provide any additional benefit or sufficient return on investment in improving facility security. With regard to biometrics, the majority of personnel indicated that they did not see how the use of biometrics would reduce the threat or improve security at their facilities. Others, however, said that biometrics would be useful, but only if used at higher MARSEC levels. One respondent pointed out that the requirement for vessels to also use TWIC readers means that staff would be required to validate their TWICs at both the facility entrance and at the vessel, a process seen as unnecessarily redundant.[312] (We note that the TWIC-reader rule states that a TWIC holder entering the vessel from a secure area where their TWIC has been electronically inspected does not need to be inspected again—provided that they have not entered an insecure area in the interim.)

For facilities with relatively small staff where the security personnel know all the staff, facilities in largely public areas, or facilities with limited activity, respondents noted, TWIC readers either do not provide additional security benefits or are not needed.

The Coast Guard personnel with whom we spoke also expressed mixed feelings about the use of TWIC readers at facilities. Some personnel stated that readers play an important role in helping verify personnel, while others did not see a security value and experienced challenges when previously using readers. In the USCG's and TSA's use of readers, there have been difficulties historically in maintaining current CCLs for readers, given that some of the previous equipment in use could not be updated using USCG or TSA systems.[313] TSA has stated that it resolved these issues for its readers in December 2017 by adding security to the communication protocol used by the Universal Enrollment Services (UES) website. (The USCG is in the process of fielding new reader equipment and did not have readers in active use at the time of this writing.)

Facilities Have Experienced Several Technological Challenges with Electronic Readers

Risk group A facilities have experienced issues with the implementation of readers, ranging from technology failures (including those related to the use of biometrics) to increased screening time at the gate and issues associated with vendors. Some issues were related to readers failing to properly read TWICs. One respondent, who praised the security value of readers, estimated that the readers their facility purchased had a 25-percent failure rate.[314] Others had issues with readers freezing or restarting or other general software issues causing the readers to malfunction. Respondents expressed concern about the inability to maintain normal business operations with

---

[312] Interviews with supervisors of a large passenger vessel.

[313] Interviews with Coast Guard units in relatively large cities.

[314] Interview with a port authority speaking about a cruise facility.

readers in place. They raised particular concerns about how they should operate if readers were to fail. Because the current version of the reader rule does not allow for a facility to revert to visual inspection, even temporarily, if reader technology fails, respondents felt that there were excessive costs in maintain backup readers for such contingencies.

Respondents noted that these technology challenges have caused delays in verifying TWICs, and some noted that, even when the technology is working as expected, they have experienced increased screening time at the gate when compared to visual inspections. Interviewees from risk group A facilities expressed concern about the lack of available vendor options from which to choose, which, some argue, is partially due to the postponement of the reader rule. Respondents from risk group A facilities also described challenges that they have encountered with scanning biometrics at their facilities, primarily in scanning fingerprints. In Chapter 9, we provide additional information about known limitations of biometrics.

Personnel from non–risk group A facilities that elected to use TWIC readers reported similar challenges, such as technology failures, increased screening time (particularly during adaptation), and resistance from the labor population. The reported degree of these problems varied dramatically, so we cannot determine an average or typical experience. In addition to challenges in scanning cards, several facilities encountered software issues in connecting to the CCL or maintaining network connectivity, causing the readers to malfunction. For example, one facility found, after using readers for a period, that it could no longer update the software or coordinate with the CCL, prompting it to return to only visual inspections.[315] Interviewees from several non–risk group A facilities highlighted, in addition to these challenges, issues with using fingerprint biometrics, such as not being able to consistently read the prints. For at least two facilities, the use of other biometric measures, such as vascular scans, have been more reliable.

The Qualified Technology List (QTL) provides information about TWIC readers that have passed independent lab testing and found to be compliant with TSA's TWIC Reader Hardware and Card Application Specification. Facilities are not required to use QTL readers, even under the pending TWIC-reader rule, but the QTL ensures that readers meet certain standards, such as conforming with environmental specifications for temperature range, humidity, shock, and vibration, and are intrinsically safe.[316] In our interviews, vendors said that, in the past few years, many readers on the QTL are now outdated or no longer available. Vendors also said they had not submitted newer models for QTL approval because testing is expensive and regulations are uncertain. Specifically, they noted that the delay in the TWIC-reader rule has affected demand for readers. In some cases, vendors continue to sell now-outdated readers to facilities and vessels that want to ensure that they are using QTL-approved models.

---

[315] Interview with the FSO from a liquid storage facility.

[316] Because industrial and chemical facilities deal with flammable materials, they require intrinsically safe technology, which is technology that has been found incapable of releasing sufficient electrical or thermal energy under normal or abnormal conditions to cause ignition of a specific hazmat.

Some Facilities Have Had Largely Positive Experiences with Readers

Despite the challenges with using readers, facilities that had effectively integrated readers into their operations found they had little negative operational impact or have improved the flow of traffic. According to one facility that recently integrated readers, "We were very worried initially that [using] TWIC [readers] would slow things down, but it hasn't. It just takes the first time or two learning it."[317] Interviewees from all facilities relayed that there was a learning curve and initial time investment in getting readers online and staff comfortable with using readers. A variety of factors affected the difficulty of fully integrating readers. Not only are there different vendors of readers; multiple system integrators facilitate their installation. Effective readers also required a variety of supporting infrastructure, such as sustained internet connectivity, electrical networks, and database integration.

Confidence in the CCL

Respondents who had chosen not to integrate the CCL into their PACS provided a range of reasons. The most common concern we heard about the CCL was that facilities do not know why a user's card is listed on the CCL.[318] Because facilities were unaware of the specific reasons for a card being on the CCL, the reason was assumed to usually relate to the card itself rather than the qualification of the cardholder. In most cases, cards are on the CCL because they are reported lost or stolen. TSA informed us that 900 cards had been canceled for cause based on recurrent vetting from IDENT. Recognizing that IDENT is not the only source of information that could drive someone's credential to be canceled and on the list for cause, even if we assume that double that number—1,800 cards—have been canceled for cause, this represents only 1.4 percent of the entities on the CCL.[319]

We heard anecdotally that it is not uncommon for TWIC holders to recover their cards and continue using them for access. Although TSA's website states that one cannot use a card after reporting it missing, the website does not specify that the card will be added to the CCL after it is reported missing.[320] The USCG's Homeport website's section on replacing lost or stolen TWIC cards does not say that cards reported lost or stolen cannot continue to be used if they are later found. The UES website, which is used to request replacements for lost and stolen cards, does not inform a user prior to reporting a lost card that it cannot be used if later found. Because a new card will be issued with the same picture and expiration date as the previous card, a user

---

[317] Interview with the director of security operations at a state port.

[318] Interviews with supervisors of a large passenger vessel.

[319] In conducting this calculation, we considered only entries listed on the CCL going back five years—from June 9, 2015, to June 9, 2019—for a total of 130,826 entries. The CCL does include some cards with earlier issuance dates, which would now be expired as well as canceled.

[320] This statement was true as of the time of this writing; however, we have brought this to TSA's attention, and it has stated an intent to adjust the website to add such a disclosure.

who has maintained their card in like-new condition might not even be able to tell which card is the currently valid one. There was also one previous occurrence when a large number of cards were canceled because of faulty production. Although that occurred some years ago, at least one facility still saw this as a reason the CCL would return many false positives. As previously discussed, some facilities are unaware that credential holders are continuously monitored and that new derogatory information could result in their cards being canceled.

These issues together seem to contribute to some facilities believing that someone carrying a canceled card is of low risk and that the CCL is not a worthwhile security investment. In the words of one respondent implying that the number of false positives would present an operational burden, "Ninety-nine percent of the time I lost my card, I found it, and now I'm using it again."[321] Creating a list of cards that are lost and stolen, separate from a list of revoked cards, could lead facilities to make greater efforts to treat someone with a revoked card as high risk.

Counterfeit Cards Were Seen Infrequently

Interviewees seemed unconcerned about counterfeit TWIC cards primarily because their use does not appear to be very common. Facility operators indicated that their security staff regularly catch expired TWIC cards, but they did not say the same about counterfeit cards. Interviewees seemed very confident in the ability of security staff to visually recognize a counterfeit TWIC card, so they did not think counterfeit cards were going unnoticed. We did hear, anecdotally, about counterfeit TWIC card rings in the past, but these interviewees characterized such rings as rare or nonexistent, with only one interviewee perceiving them as common. In the rare case in which a counterfeit TWIC card is identified, facility operators rely on law enforcement, the USCG, or TSA (or some combination of these) to investigate and determine whether to assess any fines.[322]

In analyzing past breaches of security at maritime facilities, we found few instances in the five-year period we analyzed in which a reported breach of security was attempted with a counterfeit TWIC card.[323] This, of course, is vulnerable to reporting biases; someone with a credible fake could have entered a facility undetected.

---

[321] Interview with a group of FSOs and security managers for chemical and petroleum facilities.

[322] TSA assesses fines against individuals; USCG assesses fines against facilities.

[323] Chapter 7 describes our analysis of the total 11,961 attempted and potential breaches of security in the past five years; however, not every incident report includes enough detail about the nature of the breach for us to completely rule out the possibility that a counterfeit TWIC card was been involved.

Summary

We found that perceptions of TWIC varied widely among the users and facility operators with whom we spoke during our port and security visits. Interviewees' positive comments about the benefits of TWIC included that TWIC provides a background check, standardization of ID, security deterrence, and an additional layer of security. Negative comments centered on perceptions that TWIC was a regulatory requirement rather than a security benefit and incurred additional costs.

We observed that the use of TWIC and the management of access control points varied among the facilities we interviewed. Many facilities used other credentials in addition to TWIC. Although visual inspection is currently all that is required, around half the facilities we interviewed used electronic verification for TWIC, often in the form of a PACS. Interviewees cited both security benefits (e.g., greater identity assurance) and nonsecurity benefits (e.g., timekeeping and accountability in an emergency) of using a PACS. We found some facilities voluntarily using their PACSs to verify users' identities using biometric systems—fingerprints, facial recognition, or vascular scans of the hand. We found that variations in the TWIC verification methods that we observed seemed to result from differences in the characteristics of the facilities themselves, which affect facility vulnerability, potential attack consequences, and thus decisions on where to invest in security measures. Some facilities had found that using the TWIC card in coordination with a PACS and biometric identity verification could both enhance security and bring operational efficacies. This suggests that enhanced biometric assurance measures are not necessarily at odds with operational efficiency, although these facilities were high-traffic container facilities, and some elements of their operating model do not necessarily apply to all facilities. The number of accessing individuals, the frequency with which the same people passed through access points, the dispersion over time of accessing individuals, and the technology investments already being made by the facility all appeared to be important factors in these differences between facilities and the impact on access control programs.

We did not find many facilities electing to integrate the CCL into their PACSs. Interviewees sometimes perceived that someone with a canceled card might be of low risk because a card can be on the CCL because it is reported lost or stolen, not necessarily because new derogatory information has resulted in the card being canceled. Additionally, some interviewees were unaware of key benefits of the CCL: that credential holders are continuously monitored and that new derogatory information could result in their cards being canceled. Interviewees did not appear to be particularly concerned about the prospect of counterfeit TWIC cards, which had been identified infrequently.

7. TWIC's Limits in Addressing Risks to Maritime Security

In the preceding chapters, we discussed how the TWIC STA can help identify people who present a threat and how TWIC is integrated into facility access control programs. We also discussed the practical ways in which facilities use TWIC as part of their access control programs.

In this chapter, we discuss the limitations of the TWIC program in mitigating risk in the maritime sector. We also explain why TWIC's risk-mitigation value is related to and conditional upon the broader security architecture. In doing so, we first discuss how adaptive adversaries complicate the ability to measure the value of security measures. Then we turn specifically to the case of TWIC and its limitations in preventing attacks in the maritime sector. Last, we look at practical evidence from past breaches of security at maritime facilities and what it suggests about the vulnerabilities of such facilities. We include interviewees' perspectives on other risks they saw as beyond those that can be managed with TWIC.

Security Measures Affect Adversary Attack Choices

The TWIC program seeks to protect the maritime environment from actors who might seek to threaten U.S. national security or transportation security or conduct an act of terrorism. A TSI does not necessarily need to be an act of terrorism—a cyberattack, for example, on the U.S. maritime sector could come from a state actor. In either circumstance, however, we should assume that an adversary who wishes to disrupt the maritime sector is adaptive when encountering security measures.[324]

Even terrorist actors, for example, are generally not irrational when choosing where and how to attack. Past research has found that terrorists are sensitive to risk but "highly motivated to achieve operational objectives," meaning that they "must at least implicitly undertake a kind of cost–benefit analysis of the available alternative operations."[325] Even if engaged in suicide operations, terrorists "do not wish to waste their own lives or other resources on missions that are doomed to fail or unlikely to achieve their intended results."[326] In anticipating adversary preferences, we can assume that an actor seeks to conduct an attack they believe has a chance of success. Security measures can deter a terrorist actor from attempting an attack when they reduce

---

[324] Brian A. Jackson, Peter Chalk, Kim Cragin, Bruce Newsome, John V. Parachini, William Rosenau, Erin M. Simpson, Melanie W. Sisson, and Donald Temple, *Breaching the Fortress Wall: Understanding Terrorist Efforts to Overcome Defensive Technologies*, Santa Monica, Calif.: RAND Corporation, MG-481-DHS, 2007.

[325] Andrew R. Morral and Brian A. Jackson, *Understanding the Role of Deterrence in Counterterrorism Security*, Santa Monica, Calif.: RAND Corporation, OP-281-RC, 2009, p. 3.

[326] Morral and Jackson, 2009, p. 2.

the terrorist's estimation of success in conducting that specific attack.[327] (Although research cited here focused specifically on terrorist actors, it is logical to assume a state actor would be similarly affected.) We purposely draw a distinction here between an adversary perspective and reality—a would-be attacker might miscalculate their own prospective of success. Therefore, a security measure could deter an adversary, even if the adversary actually had the capability to overcome the security measure but did not realize it. Conversely, an adversary might underestimate a security measure's ability to prevent their success and attempt their attack but be defeated by the security measure.

Ultimately, adversaries make choices about why, whether, where, and how to attack a target based on their perceptions of potential gains relative to potential costs and risks.[328] Security measures can deter attacks by decreasing an individual's or organization's belief that an attack will succeed or by increasing the risk of apprehension and thus exposure of an organization or network. Security measures can also increase the detectable "signature" of attackers and plots, in that harder targets demand larger, more-complex operations to overcome them.[329] Deterrence occurs when security measures that cause shifts in the perceived utility, cost, or uncertainties associated with specific types of attack operations (or classes of operations) result in an adversary being persuaded that a particular attack attempt should be abandoned, reevaluated, or aborted.[330] Perception matters significantly here. As stated above, adversaries could misperceive their own capability (e.g., believing themselves incapable of overcoming security barriers that they might have breached if tested).[331]

Adversaries do not typically abandon their aspirations entirely when faced with security measures. They often respond by choosing an alternative attack mode with a greater chance of success or by focusing their efforts on attacking a less-secure target, processes to which we refer as attack mode substitution and risk displacement, respectively. Attack mode substitution and risk displacement can reduce the deterrent value of security measures, such as access control programs.

Because of this, "security systems cannot be characterized as having an *inherent* level of overall deterrent effect."[332] To determine the extent to which substitution and risk displacement come into play, we must understand the characteristics of the broader security architecture. If a security system "denies one type of attack but permits another equally destructive attack that is

---

[327] Morral and Jackson, 2009.

[328] Morral and Jackson, 2009.

[329] Morral and Jackson, 2009, p. 11.

[330] Morral and Jackson, 2009.

[331] Conversely, terrorists could overstate their own capabilities, believing that they can overcome security barriers that, in reality, they cannot. In this case, the security measures have mitigated the probability of an attack not because they have reduced the threat but because they have reduced the target's vulnerability.

[332] Morral and Jackson, 2009, p. 19.

no more difficult to mount," that substitution or risk displacement has not led to a net security benefit.[333] Instead, a truly effective security measure would need to push an adversary to choose an attack method that is less likely to succeed or would be of lesser consequence.

TWIC's Contribution to Vulnerability Reduction Is Inherently Limited

Access control measures, such as TWIC, could play a role in reducing the risk of attack to port facilities and vessels by deterring or denying some attacks. The TWIC STA, for example, could deter an adversary from seeking a TWIC to gain authorized access to a facility, or it could identify that someone presents a terrorism risk and deny them a credential. For a potential adversary without a TWIC card, TWIC's integration into access control programs could similarly deter them from gaining entry to a facility or deny them the ability to pose as an authorized person.

However, it is useful to understand that access control measures' role is limited and that even a perfect access control system will not eliminate all risk. To illustrate why this is the case, we return to the definition of *risk*, as it appears in the DHS risk lexicon. Risk is "the potential for an adverse outcome assessed as a function of threats, vulnerabilities, and consequences associated with an incident, event, or occurrence."[334]

The three components of risk are

- threat: the likelihood that an adversary will attempt to carry out an attack
- vulnerability: the likelihood that an attack succeeds, given an attempt by the adversary
- consequence: the severity or magnitude of the effects—be they injuries or deaths, damage or destruction of property, or costs of business interruption—given a successful attack.

These three components of risk are not independent of one another; they are interrelated. A facility could be under greater threat because adversaries see its damage as producing greater consequence—for example, a facility in New York City might be a more appealing target to adversaries because of the association with 9/11. A facility could be more appealing to attackers because they see it as more vulnerable and, therefore, the attack more likely to succeed. Enhanced security measures are most likely to affect both threat and vulnerability, in that they could deter adversaries and reduce threat and reduce the likelihood that an attack succeeds by denying an adversary access or increasing the chance of detection. In this assessment, we assumed that an adversary has decided to attempt an attack, thus turning from *adversary* to *attacker* in our terminology.

The component of risk most affected by access control measures is vulnerability. Access controls do not completely determine facility vulnerability; they relate only to *an attacker's ability to access the target*, not to whether the attacker is able to carry out the attack once on the

---

[333] Morral and Jackson, 2009, p. 19.

[334] DHS, 2017, p. 562.

facility. This is consistent with how MSRAM models the role of security measures. (See Appendix C for more information about MSRAM.) To the extent that an attacker needs physical access to the secure area to carry out an attack, access control measures can play a role in reducing the likelihood that the attack succeeds (i.e., vulnerability). However, as we describe in this section, not every attack on a facility or vessel requires the attacker to have physical access to the secure area (i.e., some areas are vulnerable to remote attacks). Moreover, an attacker could gain entry to a secure area by defeating access controls other than TWIC (e.g., climbing a fence).

Not Every Attack Method Requires Access to a Secure Area

It is a requirement of 33 C.F.R. Part 105 that a facility have a method of restricting access to only authorized personnel, including verifying and authorizing those seeking access and having physical barriers to otherwise impede access to secure areas. For a maritime facility, physical barriers typically come in the form of fencing around the shoreside—in either the facility's entirety or around secure areas—and access points or gates to control entry. These security measures are meant to impede an adversary who needs to gain physical access to a facility's secure area from the shoreside. The TWIC program, in theory, provides a way to distinguish between people who are deemed to be of lower risk—and thus may be granted authorized access to secure areas—from people who are known to present a higher level of risk or who present an unknown level of risk and should therefore be denied access or granted limited access.

However, not all attack methods require an attacker to gain physical access to a secure area. Other attack methods include standoff attacks, which could be carried out by an attacker just outside or, for that matter, well outside the secure area, such as sniper attacks, attacks on ships by small watercraft, aerial attacks via drone, or a cyberattack. Regardless of how effective TWIC is at preventing attacks from within secure areas, these standoff attack modes are beyond TWIC's ability to play a risk-mitigation role.

TWIC Affects One of Multiple Means of Entry to a Secure Area

For attack methods that would necessitate someone gaining physical access to a secure area, TWIC can play a risk-mitigation role. However, even here, TWIC's role is limited because use of the TWIC is not the only way for an attacker to gain physical access to a secure area. It might be one of the best methods for an attacker to gain access to a secure area undetected with operational freedom. However, conceptually, there are other means of doing so:

- An attacker could enter the area using an invalid TWIC card. This could be a fake, stolen, borrowed, expired, or canceled TWIC card.
- An attacker could also quietly circumvent an entry point (e.g., gate) by climbing a fence or entering from the water side, for example.
- An attacker could be escorted in by a valid TWIC cardholder with escort privileges and elude or overcome their escort.

Although these pathways might not provide the attacker the equal assurance that they can operate undetected, these pathways might be easier and more appealing than others, depending on other security measures in place, and sufficient to achieve the attacker's objective. An attacker might also be able to successfully conduct an attack in the secure area despite being detected as a threat. For example, an attacker could physically overcome security measures by brute force, such as overpowering a guard, crashing a gate, or crashing some other portion of a fence.

Figure 7.1 depicts the fact that there can be multiple options available to adversaries and that not all require physical access, but also that not all pathways bring equal assurances about detection.

Figure 7.1. Notional Pathways for Attacking a Maritime Facility

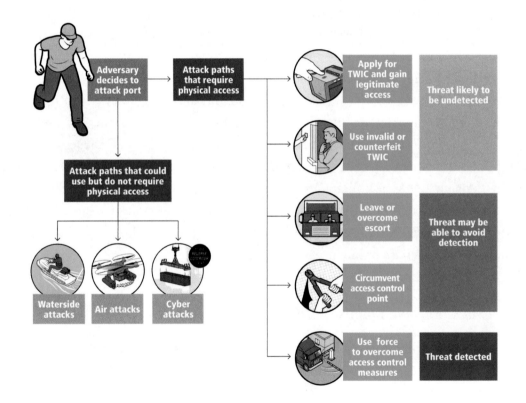

Let us assume that an adversary has chosen to conduct an attack using physical access. Their decision on what attack method to use and their probability of success depend not just on the TWIC program but on the suite of security measures at a facility that together limit an adversary's ability to successfully execute an attack that leads to adverse consequences. Several factors will determine the success of the adversary's attempt, and the extent to which elements of the TWIC program could influence this probability depends on the mode of attack. Let us consider a notional example in which an adversary wishes to use a truck bomb at a maritime

106

facility with the intent to destroy or seriously damage that facility. An adversary who wants to achieve this outcome could do so in several ways:

- **option A:** Apply for and obtain a valid TWIC card, use it to gain authorized access, drive the truck filled with explosives through the front gate and to the target site, and blow up the facility.
- **option B:** Acquire a fraudulent TWIC card, show it at the gate to illicitly gain authorized access, drive the truck filled with explosives through the front gate and to the target site, and blow up the facility.
- **option C:** Hire or coerce an escort to get through the gate, drive a truck filled with explosives through the front gate and to the target site, and blow up the facility.
- **option D:** Drive a truck filled with explosives through the front gate, overpowering any access control measures along the way, and blow up the facility.

These correspond to the first three and the last pathways of Figure 7.1—applying for a TWIC and gaining legitimate access, using an invalid or counterfeit TWIC, leaving or overcoming an escort, and using force to overcome access control measures. Now suppose that the TWIC program were perfect, meaning that no good actors would be denied the credential and no bad actor would be issued the credential. Additionally, nobody with a fraudulent or otherwise invalid TWIC card would be able to get through the facility gate undetected, and everyone with a proper credential would. In a perfect TWIC world, options A and B would not be available to the adversary. The vetting process would have ensured that a TWIC card was not issued to anyone with nefarious intent, eliminating option A. Identity verification systems at the facility gate would have recognized a bad actor's credential as fraudulent and denied access to the facility, eliminating option B. However, the TWIC program cannot do anything to stop the adversary from pursuing options C and D, leaving these options open to the adversary and allowing for the possibility that the incident could occur. The security value of TWIC in this instance would be the differential probability of success and likely consequence distribution between options C and D versus those that allowed the adversary alone to clandestinely enter the site and position their explosive-laden vehicle. Depending on the port and its security measures (e.g., efforts of gate guards to determine whether someone else is hiding in the vehicle or physical barriers that could stop a truck crashing through the gate), that difference could be substantial or negligible. Ultimately, however, this example illustrates that not only is TWIC's risk-mitigation value limited by the fact that it cannot address all threats; its value is conditional on other security measures in place at facilities. In Table 7.1, we provide a further exploration of these pathways, distinguishing between the type of access level that would be required and whether the pathways would be available to an attacker. This list is not exhaustive but provides a wide range of examples.

Table 7.1. Pathways That Various Actors Might Choose

Type of Access Desired	Examples of Actor Objectives	Apply for a Valid TWIC (Pass an STA)	Use a Counterfeit TWIC	Use Someone Else's TWIC	Use an Expired TWIC	Use a Revoked TWIC	Circumvent the Gate and Guard (Sneak In)	Get Then Elude an Unwitting Escort	Apply Brute Force to Guard, Gate, or Fence	Attack Outside the Secure (TWIC) Area
Continued access to a secure area	Perform reconnaissance and gather intelligence	x	x	x	x	x				
	Sabotage using inside knowledge	x	x	x	x	x				
	Steal	x	x	x	x	x				
	Smuggle material	x	x	x	x	x				
	Obtain a job, having no nefarious intent	x	x	x	x	x				
One-time access to a secure area	Be an individual shooter	x	x	x	x	x	x	x	x	
	Detonate a person-borne IED	x	x	x	x	x	x	x	x	
	Attack with an assault team	x	x	x	x	x	x	x	x	
	Detonate a vehicle-borne IED	x	x	x	x	x	x	x	x	
Access to a crew area	Hijack a ship	x	x	x	x	x	x	x	x	x
	Smuggle a weapon	x	x	x	x	x	x	x	x	x
Access to a passenger area	Be an individual shooter	x	x	x	x	x	x	x	x	x
	Detonate a person-borne IED	x	x	x	x	x	x	x	x	x

108

An Attempt to Estimate the Limit of TWIC's Role Using MSRAM

In December 2018, the USCG conducted a simulation to estimate the maximum possible impact that incremental security improvements, such as introducing TWIC readers, can have on MSRAM risk scores for a limited number of facilities. We further expanded on this analysis to explore the sensitivity of MSRAM's scoring of risk (measured in risk index numbers, or RINs) to hypothetical reductions in the vulnerability of MTSA-regulated facilities. The RIN in MSRAM is the product of threat, vulnerability, and consequence for a given scenario.

MSRAM's unit of analysis is a scenario, defined as an attack mode coupled to a target; thus, each maritime facility can have multiple relevant scenarios. MSRAM represents the threat as "the likelihood of an attempted attack."[335] Threat has four components: intent, capability, geographic threat, and confidence. Vulnerability in MSRAM is represented by factors related to achievability of an attack, target hardness, and system security. Consequence factors "represent the impacts of a successful attack across an array of impact types" related to death and injury, primary economic damage and business interruption, environmental impacts, national security, symbolic value, and response capability.[336]

In the USCG's simulation and our sensitivity analysis, the threat and consequence terms in the RIN were held constant. We did this for two reasons. First, our focus was on exploring the *relative* impact that an incremental improvement in security would have on risk reduction. Second, we wished to conform to the calculation of the RIN in MSRAM. MSRAM has no built-in parameter or relationship that could be used as a surrogate for representing TWIC's effect on threat through deterrence or denial of access to a facility or on consequence. Indeed, MSRAM's timeline, as shown in Appendix C, begins after an attacker makes a decision to attack, so MSRAM has no capacity to account for the deterrence value of security measures of any kind, not just TWIC. Similarly, TWIC and any other security feature have no bearing on the calculation of the consequence term in MSRAM. MSRAM uses the value of the consequence term from only the worst-case scenario to calculate the RIN for a facility, regardless of whether it is TWIC relevant or not.

Because TWIC is not included as a specific parameter in MSRAM, the USCG's simulation exercise and our sensitivity analysis assumed that changes in the TWIC program could be represented through changes in MSRAM's vulnerability score, particularly in the system security parameter, which accounts for a variety of security measures the facility might have in place. The system security parameter is one of several categorical parameters that contribute to a facility's overall vulnerability score in MSRAM. A PSS selects it using one of three options:

- Option 1 assumes that three "stakeholders" (as MSRAM describes owners and operators, the USCG, and local law enforcement) act independently to provide system security to

---

[335] USCG, *MSRAM 2018 User Manual*, c. 2018a, p. 15, Not available to the general public.

[336] USCG, 2018a, pp. 21–23.

the target. The system security parameter is a single value for option 1 and one of seven categories representing a probability range. The categorical value represents the probability that the target's owner or operator, the USCG, and local law enforcement each independently fails "to interdict the attack on the target given that the attack is achievable."[337] Category 1 represents a 95- to 100-percent probability that a stakeholder responsible for security interdicts the attack; category 2, 85 to 95 percent; category 3, 65 to 85 percent; category 4, 35 to 65 percent; category 5, 15 to 35 percent; category 6, 5 to 15 percent; and category 7, 0 to 5 percent. Note the difference in the widths of the probability range across the categories.

- Option 2 also assumes that the target's owner or operator, the USCG, and local law enforcement act independently and each fails to interdict the attack on the target.[338] In contrast to option 1, option 2 requires the analyst to make an independent judgment about each stakeholder's capabilities to "detect, decide, engage and defeat, and models the capabilities independently."[339] MSRAM uses nine roughly equal probability ranges to characterize a stakeholder's capabilities to detect, decide on, engage in, and defeat an attack. (This probability distribution is different from that for option 1.)

- Option 3 assumes that the three stakeholders are working in concert, not independently. It is used to score facilities with extensive security cooperation between system security providers, such as extensive memoranda of understanding and joint drills. As a result, option 3 facilities are assumed to have more-extensive security than option 1 and 2 facilities. In this option, the system security parameter represents the "probability of a combined USCG, LEA [law-enforcement agency], [and] owner operator [security posture] failing to interdict the attack on the target given that the attack is achievable." In contrast to how it handles options 1 and 2, for option 3, MSRAM then uses a multistep "fault tree" analysis to calculate the joint probability of the stakeholders failing to interdict or detect an attack.[340]

By assuming that changes in the category of the system security parameter represent varying levels of "hardening" in the TWIC program, the USCG was able to show, in its limited simulation exercise, that such changes would have a relatively small effect on the vulnerability score for individual facilities and, by extension, on the relative risk rankings of facilities. Making use of the details provided in the USCG's analysis of how the system security parameter is calculated in MSRAM,[341] we sought to gain a more general understanding of the sensitivity of a facility's vulnerability (and, by extension, the scenario risk score) across the full set of MTSA-regulated facilities, not just the ones used in the limited USCG simulation. In our sensitivity analysis, we considered the three attack modes that were assumed to be TWIC-relevant in the USCG's 2015 regulatory analysis: passenger or passerby IED, truck bomb, and terrorist assault team. We also included results for sabotage because we considered that this would also be a

---

[337] USCG, 2018a, p. 18.

[338] USCG, 2018a, p. 18.

[339] USCG, 2018a, p. 19.

[340] USCG, 2018a, p. 19.

[341] Written communication from CG-PSA-2 to HSOAC, January 4, 2019.

relevant scenario for TWIC. However, even if we used an expanded set of attack modes for each MTSA-regulated facility in MSRAM, the threat and consequence terms would remain the same in our relative comparison of the RIN before and after changes in TWIC and thus have no bearing on the calculation of a change in the RIN. MSRAM itself encompasses a wider range of risks beyond those that TWIC could possibly affect through a limited number of scenarios.

The sensitivity analysis, which we conducted outside of the MSRAM tool itself, replicates the calculation carried out in MSRAM: a translation of several categorical judgments about the level of system security into a single value of vulnerability, expressed as a probability of a successful attack given an attempt. As a first step in MSRAM, the user chooses one of the three system security options described above related to the level of cooperation and coordination among the three stakeholders: owner or operator, local law enforcement, and the USCG. The calculation of the system security parameter in MSRAM's vulnerability module differs by option. As previously noted, option 1 assumes stakeholder independence and uses a single input to categorize system security attributed to each stakeholder. Option 2 also assumes stakeholder independence but requires users to enter four inputs that categorize the level of system security provided by each stakeholder. Option 3 assumes stakeholder coordination and prompts users for four inputs to categorize system security attributed to each stakeholder. By knowing the distribution of scenarios among the three system security options and the range of probability of interdicting an attack, we were able to infer or bound how much vulnerability would be reduced by increased hardening of system security in MSRAM across all scenarios, keeping constant other terms in the vulnerability equation (e.g., target hardness and achievability of the attack). Appendix C provides further details of our approach and assumptions.

For the 1,788 TWIC-relevant scenarios that used option 1 in MSRAM, nearly all (99.6 percent) had been placed in either category 7 (1,256 in the range of probability of interdiction between 0 and 5 percent) or category 6 (525 in the range of probability of interdiction between 5 and 15 percent) for system security. Assuming that a strengthening of the TWIC program could be represented by, at most, a downward shift in category,[342] we found that using a weighted average across these option 1 scenarios, vulnerability and hence the scenario risk score would be reduced by a maximum of 10 percent. The assumption of a shift of only one category conforms with the USCG's assumption in its sensitivity analysis. We used the same assumption in the absence of empirical evidence that TWIC *on its own* could have a larger impact on system security. To place this reduction in perspective, for example, a RIN for a given

---

[342] For the purposes of this exercise, we assumed that introducing TWIC readers could shift the category rating by one interval, which might be an overly generous adjustment. In conversations with USCG personnel, we determined that the introduction of TWIC readers—depending on the details of the scenario—might not lead to any adjustment in the system security parameter. At most, however, it was not anticipated under any scenario to lead to an adjustment of more than one interval.

facility would need to change by about 90 percent to change a facility's overall risk level from very low to low.[343]

The calculations for options 2 and 3 are different and more complicated. For example, rather than a direct shift in the category for the system security parameter, the adjustment is through a shift in the probability category for detecting an attack, where the probability categories for deciding on, engaging in, and defeating an attack are assumed unaffected. For the 798 scenarios scored under option 2, we estimated that shifting the category for probability of detecting an attack down one level would result in a reduction of vulnerability and hence the scenario risk score of only around 0.5 percent. For the 391 scenarios scored under option 3, we found that the corresponding reduction of vulnerability and hence the scenario risk score is around 1.9 percent. The vulnerability reduction is much smaller for options 2 and 3 (around 0.5 and 1.9 percent, respectively) than for option 1 (around 10 percent) as a result of MSRAM's mathematical formulation. Options 2 and 3 require more attributes to describe vulnerability, but we assumed that only one of those attributes (detection capability) was relevant to TWIC, as explained in Appendix C.[344]

This analysis was in relative, not absolute, terms. The conclusion we draw from these results is that, in the MSRAM construct, hardening of TWIC can have only a marginal impact on reduction in vulnerability and hence the RIN for MTSA-regulated facilities. Even considering a broader range of scenarios would not change the outcome. It should also be noted that these results reflect the particular mathematical structure of MSRAM's RIN calculations and, as a result, cannot be used to draw inferences about the relative value of the three system security options.

Although MSRAM is the definitive tool that the U.S. government uses to estimate risk in the maritime sector, these results should be interpreted with caution. MSRAM's analysis is limited to the worst-reasonable-case versions of scenarios with a short timeline. As such, this analysis does not indicate TWIC's full potential for risk reduction through deterrence or interdiction. Rather, the results indicate the maximum expected change in risk profiles as measured by MSRAM. The system security parameter itself bundles multiple dimensions of system security, including access control, of which TWIC is just one part. That said, the potential impact of further improvements in TWIC would be unlikely to significantly change the risk profile in MSRAM for maritime facilities at which TWIC is required.

---

[343] MSRAM risk levels are categorized as follows: very high is more than 10,000 RINs; high is 500 to 10,000 RINs; medium is 100 to 500 RINs; low is ten to 100 RINs; and very low is fewer than RINs.

[344] For example, for option 2, because of multiplicative effects in the system security element of MSRAM's vulnerability module, a change in only one of the four attributes leads to a much smaller reduction in vulnerability than for option 1, in which TWIC affects the only attribute of the system security element.

Empirical Evidence of Breaches of Access Control Measures

To better understand the vulnerabilities of access controls, we analyzed five years of data on breaches of security at maritime facilities. The USCG defines *security breach* as "an incident that has not resulted in a TSI but in which security measures have been circumvented, eluded, or violated."[345] By law, owners and operators are required to report suspicious behavior and breaches of security to the USCG National Response Center.[346] The USCG also records security breaches the MISLE system, which is "a steady-state system designed to capture information required to support the Coast Guard's marine safety, security, environmental protection and law enforcement programs."[347] We do not suggest that a breach of security necessarily constitutes an attack. Indeed, the MISLE data suggest that, in most cases, the person's intent is not malicious. Analysis of MISLE data does, however, suggest in broad terms where there might be common vulnerabilities to breaches among facilities' access control programs. In the next section, we discuss our approach to analysis of these data and the results of our analysis.

Our Approach to the Analysis

We analyzed MISLE data for October 2013 to September 2018 for all events in the database coded as a security breach or potential security breach at a U.S. facility. The data set contained a total of 1,961 security breaches at 571 unique facilities across the United States.[348] Data for each breach came from a report typically filed by a USCG officer but filed in a few instances by local law-enforcement officers.

We began by reviewing the event narratives and characterizing each breach in the spreadsheet using five attributes: intent, method, type of breach, consequence, and whether TWIC was explicitly mentioned. Intent of the breach is a judgment made by the reporting officer and does not necessarily represent a verified fact. A significant portion—390, or nearly 20 percent—of these events were lacking significant details, including the breach method and consequence. (In 193 of those cases, MISLE data lacked information that would allow us to code any of four variables: the breach's intent, method, consequence, or whether a breach even actually occurred.) We used double-blind coding and tested intercoder reliability on a random subset of 200 incidents. In the case of multiple attempts to breach the facility, we coded the actual cause of the breach. We determined that nine events were duplicates, so we removed them

---

[345] Assistant Commandant for Prevention Policy, USCG, "Reporting Suspicious Activity and Breaches of Security," Policy Letter 08-16, December 14, 2016.

[346] Code of Federal Regulations, Title 33, Navigation and Navigable Waters; Chapter I, Coast Guard, Department of Homeland Security; Subchapter H, Maritime Security; Part 101, Maritime Security: General; Subpart C, Communication (Port–Facility–Vessel); Section 101.305, Reporting.

[347] USCG, 2009, p. 2.

[348] Note that, if entries in the database were eliminated in which either the breach method or success of the breach was recorded as "unknown," the total would be 1,571 security breaches at 426 unique facilities.

from the analysis (for a total of 1,952 incidents). Of the 1,952 incidents, 1,933 occurred at waterfront facilities, followed by other areas: barge fleeting areas (14), nonmarine facility or location (three), and marina or boat ramp (two). We conducted a basic exploratory data analysis to understand the frequency of occurrence of each of the five attributes and their relationship to one another.

Results

Table 7.2 provides a detailed list of access methods in reported attempted breaches. The most–commonly attempted methods involved circumventing the access point entirely: going over or through the fence line, gaining waterside access, or taking photos or using a drone. For a significant portion of the reported breaches, no access method was given. Specific numbers of each breach by access method, including known success rates for each, is provided in an Unclassified/Sensitive Security Information version of this report.

Table 7.2. Access Methods of Attempted and Successful Breaches

Access Method Used
Entered with an escort
Used water access
Tailgated
Hid in a vehicle
Overcame security at a gate
Went over or through a fence in some way
Entered at an unattended gate
Used an expired TWIC to pass through security
Made other illicit entry
Used a bad or fake ID other than a TWIC
Use a borrowed or stolen TWIC to pass through security
Use a fake TWIC to pass through security

SOURCE: MISLE data resulting from a coding exercise.

Of the 1,952 incidents, 428 incidents (22 percent) mentioned TWIC. Some of these cases mention TWIC only to state that this was "not a TWIC related incident." A much smaller portion involve incidents related to someone attempting to gain authorized access using a fraudulent ID card (but not a TWIC card), an expired TWIC card, or a stolen or fake TWIC card. These incidents included both cases in which security was breached and cases in which no breach occurred, typically because the person was identified and security officers turned them away. None of the events reported any death, injury, damage to the environment, or reputational loss; very few events resulted in either theft or harm of goods or other items.

114

A small number of events involved people who were first denied entry because they lacked valid TWIC cards but then attempted a second or third time to circumvent security and breach the facility another way. Each of these events involved using a method other than TWIC on the second attempt (and, in most cases, security was then successfully breached). Some cases involved trucks being turned away but then proceeding onto the facility because of a misunderstanding of directions. In other cases, people were stopped at gates for not having valid TWICs, subsequently escorted onto the facility, then separated from their escort—thus causing a security breach. Other attempts included climbing a fence, gaining waterside access, sneaking by or charging past guards, or circumventing security at the gate in some other way. Although TWIC-related measures played a role in each of these breaches, the introduction of more-robust requirements to validate TWIC cards, such as electronic biometric readers, would likely not have led to different results. Instead, the results suggest that other paths were accessible to intruders despite TWIC-related requirements at access control points.

We cannot say with certainty how representative or accurate the MISLE data are, nor have we performed tests to determine the statistical significance of our findings. The data are very susceptible to a reporting bias because unauthorized people might have gained access undetected. It also seems plausible that, although a truck through the gates would not have escaped notice, someone might have been able to frequently use a faulty ID to gain access and might even have done so on a routine basis. For these reasons, these findings should be interpreted cautiously. At the most basic level, the data seem to lend support to the idea that people determined to breach security make use of multiple pathways to gain access to maritime facilities. In this particular data set, a small percentage of all of the attempted breaches were directly tied to the form of ID presented at the gate and only a portion of those events were successful.[349]

Recognizing our earlier stated caveats about the potential bias in the data, we suggest a few hypotheses about facilities' vulnerabilities in relation to TWIC. The first is that the access control measures used to identify authorized personnel, including TWIC, often successfully deter or deny people seeking to gain illicit entry to maritime facilities. People who have been identified breaching or attempting to breach a facility's security perimeter have been more likely to have used other methods. These data are also suggestive when considering the value of further enhancing the security measures surrounding TWIC—specifically, requiring electronic or biometric readers. Electronic readers would likely be more successful than human guards at identifying expired or fake credentials. Electronic biometric readers would likely be more successful than human guards at identifying stolen or borrowed credentials. But our analysis suggests that other methods of gaining access to the facility—such as entering with an escort or circumventing security—could be a greater source of vulnerability in access control programs. A

---

[349] Specific numbers on the success rates of breach attempts related to TWIC and IDs are provided in an Unclassified/Sensitive Security Information version of this report.

biometric reader at gates could be successful at preventing access from the least capable adversaries, but more-capable adversaries would likely seek to exploit other methods of breaching security with a high likelihood of success. Investing further in hardening security measures at the gate might be more successful at catching less capable adversaries, but such an adversary would also have been less able to achieve a maximum consequence effect.

The low number of facility breaches attempted in relation to the TWIC program and the lower success rates of people using invalid TWICs in accessing facilities could be a success attributable to the TWIC program as currently implemented. One possible meaning of these data is that people seeking to breach facilities have sought to use other access methods because they lacked valid TWIC cards.

Limitations of TWIC Inspection Data

Our review of breach-of-security data suggests in broad terms where there might be common vulnerabilities among facilities' access control programs. However, as stated previously, there is a potential reporting bias in these data. We do not know how many people might have gained unauthorized access to facilities but went undetected or unreported. It is possible to answer this question through carefully designed statistical sampling approaches when inspecting for TWIC compliance. Both the USCG and TSA conduct intermittent inspections at facilities to check for TWIC cards, either individually or in tandem, and we reviewed these inspection data going back several years. However, neither the USCG nor TSA uses a structured sampling approach in gathering these data. Facility inspections are sometimes announced—implying that compliance would be higher than expected otherwise—or targeted toward facilities where compliance is suspected to be low.

The USCG conducts at least two inspections per year at each facility, one announced and one unannounced. TWIC inspections could also be performed in the course of normal operations—for instance, safety audits, security plan reviews, or MTSA compliance examinations. TWIC violations that are found incidentally during these activities should not be used as evidence of the typical rate of such violations because such violations might be observed in a nonrandom way. Even for cases in which large numbers of TWIC checks were performed—during MTSA compliance examinations, for example—we could not determine whether the checks were performed on a random sample of facility workers or were based on a convenience sample of whoever was nearby at the time. Therefore, we cannot be certain that any evidence from the inspection data provides a valid estimate of the rate of TWIC violations at a given facility.

Unlike the USCG case, the sole purpose of TSA inspections is to conduct TWIC checks. Although TSA inspections are conducted either in tandem with USCG inspections or by themselves, they suffer the same shortcoming as inspections that are conducted in a nonrandom way, so the results cannot be readily extrapolated. Our study team directly observed some of these activities. TSA officers often checked TWIC cards at the entrance to a facility, announced

116

their presence with signs, and checked TWICs for a limited window of hours. If someone knew that their TWIC was not in compliance, they could wait to enter or exit the facility until inspection activities had ceased (or potentially use another entry point). None of this is to criticize the methods by which TSA and the USCG are conducting inspections—which are important activities to encourage regulatory compliance and provide a measure of deterrence. However, such collection methods impede our ability to extrapolate real numbers of TWIC compliance from inspection data.

TWIC's Strengths and Weaknesses in Mitigating Risk

The TWIC program is strongest in reducing the risk presented by someone who is a known or suspected terrorist and who seeks to conduct an attack on a maritime facility that would require persistent insider access. These people would be detected by the STA process and presumably denied a TWIC; it would be difficult for such people to maintain continual access to a facility without a valid TWIC card. The TWIC card is similarly effective in reducing the risk from someone with a disqualifying criminal history who would have been willing to engage in illicit activity at the facility, such as smuggling, that might aid a terrorist group. TWIC's effectiveness in achieving this goal is largely similar with or without an electronic card reader. Although readers would reduce human error in detecting a counterfeit TWIC or a TWIC that had been issued to another person, competent security guards should, at some point, detect these people seeking to gain entry. The major exception to this case would be someone who had initially passed the STA, had been issued a valid TWIC, and was found to have possible terrorist ties prior to the card's expiration. In circumstances in which such a person's TWIC card was revoked but could not be recovered by law-enforcement officials, use of an electronic card reader in conjunction with the CCL would dramatically increase the chances of detection.

The TWIC program is less effective at stopping threats where an attacker (or attackers) seeks one-time access to a facility to conduct an attack and is not easily deterred from attempting to gain entry. Even if such an attacker were unable to legally obtain a TWIC, they could attempt to present an invalid card and test the access control system. The would-be attacker could also engage the services of an escort, if permitted by the facility, to gain access and then depart from or overcome the escort. Alternatively, the attacker could use brute force to overcome any access control measures presented at the gate, including any mechanism to verify TWIC cards. The TWIC program might provide some additional ability to detect these threats, but the ability to prevent such a threat is dependent on other mechanisms of the access control program, such as the guard, PACS, or deployable physical barriers. A TWIC card reader could increase the likelihood that an invalid TWIC card will be detected, but it alone does not increase the access control program's ability to prevent entry. Figures 7.2 and 7.3 are conceptual diagrams that provide a relative ordering of the likelihood of detecting a threat when using visual inspection and when using an electronic TWIC reader. On the left side, we acknowledge that access control programs—using visual inspection or TWIC readers—are simply unable to detect threats outside a secure area. They are also equally poor at detecting someone circumventing the access control program, eluding an escort once inside the secure area, or using brute force to overcome the access control program. Visual inspection is also poor at detecting a revoked TWIC because the TWIC would seem visually authentic. Visual inspection could identify someone using a counterfeit TWIC or someone else's TWIC, if the guard or inspecting authority were looking closely at the card for security features or matching the picture to the user. An expired TWIC would seemingly be easier to identify via visual inspection, particularly on the newest TWIC cards, on which this information is in large text with a color-coding system by year. A properly functioning electronic reader would likely be better at checking for counterfeit or expired cards, given that it would not be subject to human error or negligence. A reader also using biometric means to verify identities would also likely be more capable than visual inspection of identifying someone using a card issued to another person.

Figure 7.2. Access Control Programs' Ability to Detect Threats Using Visual Inspection

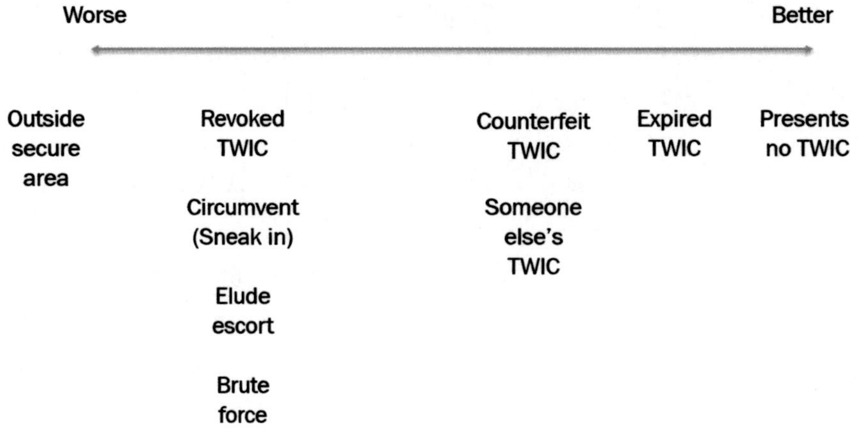

Figure 7.3. Improvement in Access Control Programs Detecting Threats Using TWIC Readers

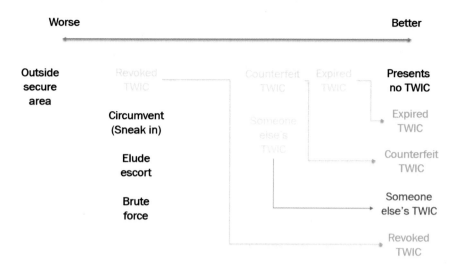

NOTE: Text in green reflects performance improvements that could, in theory, be achieved by use of an electronic reader. Text in purple reflects performance improvements brought by using an electronic biometric reader.

A TWIC program with robust access control technology would still fail to detect the threat posed by someone with a "clean" history (i.e., someone who was not known to authorities). As we discussed in Chapter 4, the most likely terrorist attack within the United States today is seen as coming from HVEs. Because HVEs are often self-radicalized using terrorist propaganda available online, they might. elude the attention of intelligence and law-enforcement authorities. The TWIC's program's broad net of criminal-history factors could disqualify someone who did not pose a threat to the facility; however, TWIC's waiver process provides recourse for these people to demonstrate that they do not pose such a threat. The requirement for everyone to have their physical card credential on hand also affects a population of people who do not pose a threat to facilities: credential holders who have forgotten or misplaced their cards. Because there is no ability to virtually verify credentials, these people must recover their TWICs, apply for replacement TWICs, or use escorts.

Facility Security Personnel Reiterated the Limitations of TWIC

Our interviews with facility security personnel are relevant to understanding access control vulnerabilities at facilities. We frequently asked facility operators about their primary security concerns and how they would prioritize security investments if they had additional security resources. Facility operators might have a limited understanding of threat—for example, they might have limited access to classified information regarding active threats, or they might not understand the statistical likelihood of attack types. However, they are subject-matter experts (SMEs) on their facilities' vulnerabilities, and their security concerns might reflect which vulnerabilities they see as most pressing. The most-frequent security concerns raised were those related to the cyber realm and to an active shooter (that is, someone—possibly a disgruntled employee with insider access—committing an act of mass violence). Although the term *active shooter* is generally used imprecisely, the context in most interviews suggested that respondents believed that an active-shooter threat was something independent and separate from terrorist-based threats and that TWIC would have limited utility in mitigating this threat. The perspectives of facility security personnel are broadly consistent with our summary of TWIC above.

Facility Personnel's Security Concerns Transcend Terrorism

Few interviewees completely dismissed the threat of domestic or international terrorism to their ports or facilities, although it was not often the top security concern.[350] Interviewees across risk groups prioritized such concerns as an active shooter, insider threat, explosives, domestic violence, safety, and theft and other criminal activity over terrorism. Some interviewees mentioned other targets that might be more attractive than a facility, including bridges outside of the port environment. Respondents expressed skepticism that the TWIC program or biometric readers would play much of a role in reducing the risk of terrorism, deterring an attack, or stopping an active terrorist incident.

Many interviewees expressed concerns about an insider threat or an active shooter, and several of them described an insider threat, regardless of motivation, as their biggest concern and the hardest to mitigate. For example, many interviewees at chemical and petroleum facilities indicated that insider knowledge of a facility's layout, coupled with an understanding of dangerous chemical mixtures and the ability to release them, would allow a perpetrator to create an event affecting a large number of people.[351] One interviewee noted,

> The one threat vector that has high potential for damage and is difficult to mitigate is insider threat . . . . [It] doesn't have to be [someone with a] religious ideology—just someone who is willing to damage and kill other people and create a TSI.[352]

Similarly, another facility representative said that his greatest concern was someone with a high-powered weapon and insider knowledge.[353] None stated they felt that TWICs or electronic readers would be of much use to combat either threat.

Those working in cruise and ferry facilities felt that active shooters were their biggest threats and stated that TWIC would play little role in mitigating that threat. This is due in part to typical cruise and ferry facility configuration: At many terminals, an active shooter would not even need to breach security to cause harm. In the words of a port security manager, "It's the easiest thing

---

[350] In many cases, we had to ask specifically whether interviewees were concerned at all about terrorism because they did not bring it up when being asked a general question about security concerns for the facility or port.

[351] Interview with a group of FSOs and security managers for chemical and petroleum facilities.

[352] Interview with a group of FSOs and security managers for chemical and bulk liquid facilities.

[353] Interview with the terminal manager of a CDC facility.

to do and has the greatest potential for loss of life."[354] Passenger vessel facility operators were also very concerned about explosives. As one ferry operator said,

> A fear that I have . . . is an actor that goes onto the terminal with a bomb or gun or goes onto a vessel and does harm, like an active shooter . . . TWIC doesn't stop a lone wolf.[355]

Some Interviewees Saw an Escort Option as a Possible Source of Vulnerability

Most facilities we visited typically allow escorts as a routine course of business,[356] although escort policies varied considerably. Escorting allows a non–TWIC holder to enter a secure or restricted area with a TWIC holder who has been approved as an escort for the facility. Escorting is typically done for people who need access to perform nonroutine work and who would not otherwise need a TWIC for work purposes (e.g., gardener, maintenance technician) or for truck drivers who do not normally drop off or pick up containers at ports. Although regulations require "regular workers" to have TWICs to have unescorted access, some respondents indicated ambiguity about what constitutes a "regular worker." Because the USCG has not issued policy guidance on this matter, the definitions vary across facilities: Some facilities defined regular access as more than five times a year; others as once a month. Sometimes, someone with an expired or canceled TWIC card is able to engage an escort and access the secure area, although interviewees stated that, to the best of their knowledge, security guards knowingly allow this only when the person can present evidence (e.g., UES receipt) that he or she had initiated the TWIC reenrollment process or had applied for a replacement card.[357]

Although some facilities explicitly required guards to serve as escorts, others allowed anyone who had completed the required escort training to do so. At some ports, an approved escort is given a special escort card, or their company badge identifies them with an icon, the word "escort," or a different color; at others, a security office maintains a list. Escort training is typically provided through a third party (although some facilities provide this in-house) and consists of a short class. We also learned that, at some facilities, one can hire an escort for a fee of $75 to $80 per occurrence. Some facilities allow only known people onto the facility, even with an escort; at others, anyone who can demonstrate a business purpose would be able to engage the services of an escort.

Some FSOs, particularly at container facilities, raised concerns that an escort could allow someone to circumvent the TWIC STA. One interviewee pointed out that someone denied a TWIC could just "turn around and get a TWIC escort and can come on [the facility]." Another

---

[354] Interview with a port security manager who operates a cruise terminal.

[355] Interview with the director of a ferry facility.

[356] This is permissible under current TWIC regulations.

[357] Interviewees from facilities that allow this specified that they would not do so if the TWIC had been expired for some time and that, in those circumstances, they would deny the person access entirely.

interviewee explained that most of the trucks entering the facility do so with escorts, which defeats the purpose of requiring TWIC.[358]

Other concerns were about how TWIC escort requirements could affect safety and security at facilities. One interviewee said escorts present a safety concern because they could get in the way of heavy equipment. One unintended consequence mentioned by a facility interviewee was that people without TWICs would not bother to get TWICs in the first place because the escort policy allowed all those without TWICs to be escorted.

Forced Entry Is Also a Concern at Facilities

We asked interviewees about opportunity costs associated with spending money on TWIC requirements and adhering to the reader rule as opposed to other security features. About half of the interviewees who answered this set of questions mentioned a preference for spending money on increased visibility on their own property by, for example, adding cameras along with smart analytics, motion sensors, or facial recognition abilities, as well as improving lighting capabilities (e.g., "high-intensity LED lights"). About one-fifth of those who said they would spend money on increasing visibility noted that they would focus on their perimeter security (e.g., fencing, gates, entry barriers) and increase training and the use of canine teams. These measures appeared to be driven by a concern about a person's ability to gain access through the perimeter. One respondent said that he would hypothetically target the "chain link fence that common sense tells me, with a bolt cutter and a few minutes, I'm in the facility."[359]

Summary

In this chapter, we have explored the extent of TWIC's risk-reduction value through interdiction and deterrence. TWIC's value in interdiction is difficult to quantify for several reasons. First, access control is one of several complementary components of system security. Second, TWIC is one of several elements of access control. Third, adversaries have several choices of pathways to gaining access to a facility, some of which to not entail defeating TWIC. For attacks in a secure area, TWIC's denial value is limited because a would-be attacker has a variety of pathways to entering a secure area, and TWIC can deny only a few of them. Further, TWIC can do nothing to deny attacks that originate outside a secure area.

The problem of deterrence is similar. To the extent that adversaries perceive that they are denied certain pathways, they will be deterred from attempting entry in that manner. However, they might choose another pathway for entering a secure area or choose to attack from outside the secure area. Further, it is also possible that deterrence simply shifts the adversary's attack from a maritime target to another target entirely. This might be beneficial for the owner or

---

[358] Interview with FSOs from a port complex.

[359] Interview with the regional manager of a CDC facility.

operator of the maritime facility but might be unsatisfactory for a policymaker concerned about terrorism risk reduction generally.

Our analysis of the system security component of MSRAM's vulnerability module showed *in relative terms* the limited reductions in vulnerability and risk that are theoretically possible by simulating the hardening of TWIC in the MSRAM model. The mathematics of the MSRAM tool constrains the effects that TWIC could have to improvements in the likelihood of interdiction; TWIC's deterrence value cannot be simulated in MSRAM. In reality, TWIC is one of several components of access control that is itself one of several components of system security. It is therefore difficult to isolate TWIC's benefits in deterring or interdicting attacks, particularly when multiple pathways exist to gaining access to a facility, only a subset of which TWIC could possibly affect.

Available data on the effectiveness of current access control systems are fragmentary, subject to bias, or anecdotal, so definitive conclusions cannot be drawn from the information summarized in this chapter. However, circumstantial evidence supports some observations. For example, facility-specific security experts identified many sources of potential vulnerability for their own facilities other than those related to the presentation of TWIC at access points, including from adversaries who seek landside physical access to secure areas and from adversaries who could attack virtually or via other means (such as a drone or from the water).

Security is only as good as its weakest link. Regardless of how robust security measures might be, they would not produce a net security benefit at a facility if other attack paths that offer the same or better prospects of success at lower cost are available to an adversary. Hence, the value of the TWIC program must be assessed in the context of the larger system of security measures in place at a facility and at the larger class of maritime facilities.

8. A Cost-Effectiveness Analysis of the TWIC-Reader Rule Requirements

As we described in Chapter 2, DHS implemented the TWIC program in two phases. The first phase, the TWIC rule, focused on the initial issuance of TWIC cards, and facility and vessel operators were not required to purchase or install electronic TWIC readers.[360] In 2013, DHS issued a second NPRM for the TWIC-reader rule to require owners and operators of certain types of vessels and facilities to conduct electronic inspections of TWIC cards as an access control measure.[361] The USCG conducted a preliminary economic regulatory analysis in February 2013, in support of the second-phase NPRM, to assess the costs, benefits, and other potential impacts of the proposed rule requiring stronger access control technology.[362] The analysis was informed by a pilot program that used biometric TWIC readers and the USCG's MSRAM database and tool. The pilot program was used to inform the USCG's calculations of the costs of biometric readers, including business processes, technology, and operational impacts. The USCG used MSRAM—a tool that evaluates maritime facilities' threat and vulnerability to a variety of attack modes and scenarios (which include an attack mode and a target), as well as the estimated consequences of an attack—to provide risk scores for facilities and estimate losses that could result from terrorist attacks. The USCG used these numbers to estimate the potential benefits of the TWIC-reader rule. In this chapter, we refer to *terrorist attack*, given that this is the terminology that the USCG used in the initial reader rule analysis; however, the fact that a high-consequence attack might or might not have been motivated by terrorism is largely immaterial to the costs and benefits.[363]

Following interagency review and a public comment period, the USCG published a final regulatory analysis in November 2015 in support of the rulemaking.[364] According to the regulatory analysis, the final TWIC-reader rule, promulgated on August 23, 2016, limited the application of electronic TWIC inspection requirements to all facilities and one vessel deemed at

---

[360] USCG and TSA, 2008.

[361] USCG, 2013.

[362] Office of Standards Evaluation and Development, Standards Evaluation and Analysis Division, U.S. Coast Guard, *Transportation Worker Identification Credential (TWIC)–Reader Requirements: Notice of Proposed Rulemaking—Preliminary Regulatory Analysis and Initial Regulatory Flexibility Analysis*, Washington, D.C., USCG-2007-28915, February 2013.

[363] The 2015 regulatory analysis referred to the rule as seeking "to prevent terrorist attacks by enhancing access control" (Office of Standards Evaluation and Development, 2015, p. 74). MSRAM, furthermore, is "an analysis tool designed to assess risk for potential terrorist targets in the U.S. maritime domain" (Office of Standards Evaluation and Development, 2015, p. 75).

[364] Office of Standards Evaluation and Development, 2015.

"high risk" for a potential TSI.[365] The USCG subsequently published an NPRM in the *Federal Register* on June 22, 2018, to delay the effective date by three years for certain facilities until August 23, 2021.[366]

This chapter provides a cost-effectiveness analysis of the TWIC-reader requirements, building on the framework of the 2015 regulatory analysis, and offers an alternative assessment of the costs and benefits of the TWIC-reader rule based on additional data inputs and potential alternatives to the final rule. In the first section, we discuss the methodological approach, including the framework for conducting a break-even analysis.[367] We then provide an overview and assessment of key assumptions and data inputs.[368] Ultimately, we provide alternative and improved estimates of the overall costs of the TWIC-reader rule, as well as a revised break-even analysis, to assess how large the benefits would need to be to justify the costs of the rule. This analysis responds to Sections 1(b)(3)(C)(iii) and 1(b)(3)(C)(iv) of Public Law 114-278.

Methodology for Determining Costs and Benefits of the TWIC-Reader Rule

Ideally, in the case of the TWIC-reader rule, the benefits of the regulation could be quantified by estimating how much the regulation reduces the probability of a terrorist attack. By combining this incremental reduction in the probability of a terrorist attack with monetary estimates about the consequences of an attack, one could produce an estimate of the economic value of the benefits of the regulation and compare it directly to the costs of the regulation. However, data do not exist to estimate the current (or baseline) probability of a terrorist attack and the potential reduction in that probability due to the regulation. Terrorist attacks in general are very infrequent events; as we discussed in Chapter 3, this is particularly true in the maritime sector. Moreover, historical data on past terrorist attacks do not provide information about whether deficiencies in access control enabled attacks or whether stronger access controls could have prevented them. Therefore, not only can we not determine the likelihood that a terrorist attack will occur under the current state of TWIC implementation; we cannot determine how enhanced access control requirements would affect the likelihood of a terrorist attack.

The Rationale for the Break-Even Analysis

Because of the inability to perform a cost–benefit analysis, the 2015 regulatory analysis used a break-even approach to answer the question of whether TWIC should require stronger access controls. We assessed that the USCG's use of break-even analysis to evaluate the costs and benefits of the TWIC-reader rule was appropriate because it is well established in the cost–

---

[365] USCG, 2016.

[366] USCG, 2018b.

[367] Appendix F provides additional background information on the rationale for the break-even analysis.

[368] Appendix G provides a detailed analysis of the quantified costs and benefits.

benefit literature and has been widely used to support past DHS rulemakings. The Office of Management and Budget (OMB) recommends a break-even or threshold analysis when quantifying or monetizing a regulation's benefits is not possible.[369] This can help to frame the question in a different way by asking, how large would the benefits have to be to equal or exceed the costs of the regulation? When it is not possible to quantify benefits, the annualized costs represent the threshold at which the annualized benefits would break even with the costs of the regulation. The break-even threshold can be expressed in terms of the number of undesirable events that would have to be avoided each year for a regulation's benefits to equal the costs. In Appendix F, we present further rationale for the break-even analysis, provide past examples, and discuss the relevance of break-even analysis for decisionmakers. Given that a break-even analysis provides only some of the information necessary to determine whether a regulation will be cost-effective, the results of this analysis do not lead to a clear decision about desirable options to improve access controls for maritime facilities and vessels. Rather, they provide useful information about the relationship of costs and benefits that, when supplemented with credible threat and hazard information and overlaid on a decisionmaker's risk propensity, can contribute to risk-informed decisions.

Alternatives to a Break-Even Analysis

Break-even analysis is not the only method available for informing a risk-based decision. In circumstances in which a risk is perceived but cannot be quantified, the precautionary principle is an alternative to which regulators often turn as a justification for regulatory action.[370] For example, the European Union and the United States have decided that regulating the commercial use of thousands of chemicals that are presumed, but not proven, to be toxic is a prudent course of action from a public health perspective.[371] A precautionary approach might be justified where plausible threats of harm are known but there is insufficient evidence of the nature or scale of likely undesirable events. Similarly, policymakers might justify the TWIC-reader rule as a precautionary action, even though the frequency and likelihood of success of terrorist attacks in the maritime environment is unknown.

---

[369] OMB, "Regulatory Analysis," Washington, D.C., Circular A-4, September 17, 2003.

[370] Science for Environment Policy, *The Precautionary Principle: Decision-Making Under Uncertainty*, prepared for the Directorate-General of the European Union for Environment and the Science Communication Unit at the University of the West of England, Future Brief 18, 2017.

[371] Jonathan B. Wiener and Michael D. Rogers, "Comparing Precaution in the United States and Europe," *Journal of Risk Research*, Vol. 5, No. 4, 2002, pp. 317–349; Nicholas A. Ashford, "The Legacy of the Precautionary Principle in US Law: The Rise of Cost–Benefit Analysis and Risk Assessment as Undermining Factors in Health, Safety and Environmental Protection," in Nicolas de Sadeleer, ed., *Implementing the Precautionary Principle: Approaches from the Nordic Countries, EU and USA*, Sterling, Va.: Earthscan, 2007, pp. 352–378.

Similarly, less formalized and technical alternatives include qualitative approaches that discuss underlying risk and assess whether an uncertain event is reasonably likely to occur.[372] Such a discussion might be more readily understandable and less likely to be misconstrued by readers unfamiliar with break-even analysis. Break-even analysis should also include such a qualitative discussion of risk and likely outcomes but further formalizes a threshold over which benefits will exceed the costs of a regulation.

Another alternative is a scenario-based approach that also seeks to quantify costs and benefits. In this case, costs and benefits can be described under plausible scenarios characterizing the evidence and assumptions underlying each alternative scenario.[373] This approach avoids projecting a single probable future when different outcomes are possible but does not address the limitation that the likelihood or distribution of individual outcomes is unknown.

Finally, more-formal and -technical approaches would involve assigning probabilities to each outcome. The USCG's MSRAM database and tool could be used to provide distributions of attack mode, vulnerability, and consequence—and, combined with probability estimates, could inform a probability distribution of maritime terrorist attacks. Alternatively, expert elicitation with a wide pool of security experts could be used to inform a probability distribution of undesirable events. If additional information of the probability of each attack mode were known, a probabilistic approach could be used.[374] This alternative approach would consider the regulation's effect on the overall terrorism risk posed by several different types of attacks that could occur on many different targets. In this approach, the overall risk would be derived from the outcomes of numerous individual attack scenarios, each weighted by the probability that a successful attack will occur.

Foundations of the TWIC-Reader Rule Regulatory Analysis

The initial TWIC-reader rule regulatory analysis drew on information from a TWIC-reader pilot program, conducted from 2008 to 2011. Facilities voluntarily participated in this pilot program, which TSA conducted in collaboration with the USCG and under the direction of the DHS Science and Technology Directorate (S&T). We discuss the pilot program in greater detail in Appendix G. The structure and administration of the TWIC-reader pilot program, however, led to unreliable results, as extensively documented in GAO, 2013a, *Transportation Worker Identification Credential: Card Reader Pilot Results Are Unreliable; Security Benefits Need to Be Reassessed.* We focus here specifically on how those results directly relate to the subsequent

---

[372] Daniel A. Farber, "Breaking Bad? The Uneasy Case for Regulatory Breakeven Analysis," *California Law Review*, Vol. 102, No. 6, December 2014, pp. 1469–1493.

[373] Farber, 2014.

[374] Tom LaTourrette and Henry H. Willis, *Using Probabilistic Terrorism Risk Modeling for Regulatory Benefit–Cost Analysis: Application to the Western Hemisphere Travel Initiative Implemented in the Land Environment,* Santa Monica, Calif.: RAND Corporation, WR-487-IEC, 2007.

regulatory analysis for the TWIC-reader rule. We identified four main areas in which either the pilot program or the assumptions in the regulatory analysis might have led to inaccurate estimates of the TWIC-reader rule's effects:

- **unrepresentative sample of facilities:** As GAO concluded, the facilities that volunteered to participate and ultimately completed the pilot were not representative of the maritime industry or the facilities subject to the TWIC-reader rule. GAO noted, "No specific unit of analysis, site selection criteria, or sampling methodology was developed or documented prior to selecting the facilities and vessels to participate in the TWIC reader pilot."[375] This implies that results about the costs of the reader requirements would not necessarily be generalizable to the facilities subject to the final rule.
- **miscalculation of capital costs:** When replicating the cost calculations from the 2015 regulatory analysis, we found that the analysis incorrectly calculated the average capital costs associated with acquiring and installing readers. The net impact is an underestimate of the amount of capital expenditures required to comply with the TWIC-reader requirements by nearly 50 percent. Similar calculation errors result in slightly underestimating the number of readers that we assess will be required, which further biases the capital cost estimate downward.
- **faulty assumptions about the number of readers required at facilities:** We assess, based on our review of pilot program data and FEMA port security grant data and our observations of access point configurations at high-risk facilities, that the 2015 regulatory analysis underestimated the average number of readers required per facility for compliance.[376]
- **combination of maximum consequence scores possibly overstating benefits:** The 2015 regulatory analysis attributed the highest maximum consequence score across multiple attack modes to the potential benefits of the regulation. This does not accurately reflect potential outcomes for the universe of facilities subject to the TWIC rule and the attack modes for which improvements in access controls could plausibly avert a terrorist attack. This approach obscured differences in the magnitude of benefits that would be needed to offset the costs of the regulation for the lower average consequence of a particular set of terrorist attack scenarios.

Building on the Framework in the Regulatory Analysis for the TWIC-Reader Rule Using Additional Cost Data

As a general matter, regulatory analysis relies on assumptions for certain inputs to calculate the costs and benefits where the actual values are unknown or measuring them precisely is impractical. These assumptions should be validated with evidence. In the case of the TWIC-reader rule, we do not have precise information for every facility and vessel subject to the final rule. However, we can make informed assumptions about these inputs, building on the

---

[375] GAO, 2013a, pp. 13–14.

[376] Underestimation could be due, in part, to the broad review of FSPs that USCG used to inform assumptions about the configuration of access points and the number of readers that would be required for compliance with the final reader rule. The review included facilities not in the pilot program and not subject to the TWIC-reader rule.

framework in the 2015 regulatory analysis. We sought to validate previous assumptions by reexamining the data used in that analysis, primarily the pilot program results. We then collected data from other independent sources to inform our assumptions about cost inputs.

Data Sources

The HSOAC team conducted interviews and collected data from various SMEs, including FSOs and vendors of readers capable of reading TWIC cards. We also looked at past federal security grants and industry reports and gathered additional information on the costs of access control systems. Here we summarize the data sources used to validate assumptions about the costs and benefits of the TWIC-reader rule:

- **site visits and interviews with facility operators:** As discussed in Chapter 1 and Appendix A, we conducted interviews with personnel from 164 MTSA-regulated facilities, considering several port attributes as selection criteria to develop a sample of ports, including geographic location and size, volume of traffic, commodity type, organization management, risk classification, and TWIC enrollments. During these interviews, we asked operators about actual costs they had incurred to install electronic readers or PACSs and any estimated costs that resulted from evaluating the feasibility of acquiring and installing readers or other final reader rule compliance measures. We received qualitative information, and some participants provided invoices or other supporting information for TWIC-related purchases.[377]
- **interviews with vendors:** We spoke with vendors of readers capable of reading TWIC cards, including hardware, software, and PACS integration systems. Vendors provided insights into reader pricing, installation, and integration costs, as well as other considerations, such as equipment availability.
- **FEMA port security grants:** We analyzed data provided by FEMA's Port Security Grant Program on awards for TWIC-related security improvements for FY 2007 through FY 2018, which includes funding under the American Recovery and Reinvestment Act of 2009 and other supplemental appropriations. For FYs 2007 to 2016, awarded dollar amounts was the only information available. For FYs 2017 and 2018, more-detailed information was available, including partially itemized project descriptions for TWIC-related investments.
- **the International Biometrics and Identity Association (IBIA) reader rule analysis:**[378] IBIA, a trade group representing the ID technology industry, performed its own cost analysis of TWIC reader requirements in 2011. The analysis, which predated the NPRM, assessed a small sample of facilities and extrapolated the numbers of readers required and certain TWIC-related costs to a larger number of MTSA-regulated facilities.

---

[377] We note that, although our sample might be better than the sample used in the 2015 regulatory analysis, it is not necessarily representative.

[378] In Appendix G, we discuss the differences in key assumptions between the IBIA analysis and the 2015 regulatory analysis, such as assumptions about the average cost of hardware and software.

A Comparison of the 2015 Regulatory Analysis and Our Break-Even Analysis

In this section, we compare the results of our revised break-even analysis using the additional cost information collected in our research with those from the 2015 regulatory analysis. We believe that this update gives policymakers a more accurate representation of the final rule's potential economic impacts. Our comparison "moves the needle" significantly regarding the break-even threshold at which the regulation's benefits would equal or offset the costs. We performed a separate break-even analysis for each attack mode for which improved access controls could plausibly avert a terrorist attack. This approach makes the simplifying assumption in each case that the regulation would affect only one type of attack. In reality, the regulation might simultaneously reduce the risk of more than one type of attack, so it is possible for the regulation's benefits to equal or offset the costs by averting a relatively small number of terrorist attacks combining different attack modes (i.e., the number of events could be smaller than implied by any of the individual break-even thresholds, but the overall impact would be larger).

A Definition of Performance Metrics

To clarify the interpretation of the results of the break-even analysis, we first define the relevant performance benchmarks.

- *required avoidance rate:* This is the number of events per year that must be avoided for the net costs of the regulation to equal 0. This is calculated by dividing the annualized cost by the monetized estimate of the consequences of a TSI. The "required" part of the avoidance rate refers only to how often an undesirable event would need to be averted to equal or offset the costs of the rule. It does not imply any actual reduction in the probability of a successful terrorist attack but rather provides a hypothetical threshold at which the benefits of the regulation would equal its costs.
- *required frequency of attacks averted:* The avoidance rate can alternatively be expressed in terms of the number of years between events, whereby one TSI would have to be averted to offset the costs of the rule. This is calculated as the inverse of the avoidance rate described above. A longer time horizon (i.e., a lower required avoidance rate) is generally favorable for justifying a regulation. That is to say, additional years between events provides a less stringent criterion for the benefits of a regulation to outweigh its costs. A shorter time horizon provides a more stringent threshold to justify a regulation because it means that, to equal or offset the costs, TSIs would have to be averted more frequently as a direct result of the regulation.

An Estimation of Costs

Building on the framework used in the 2015 regulatory analysis, we estimated the total industry costs for 525 facilities and one vessel initially estimated to be subject to the TWIC-reader rule.[379] The 2015 regulatory analysis identified ten primary cost components for the final rule, as shown in Table 8.1. Unless otherwise noted in this chapter, all costs and benefits are reported in 2012 dollars (using a 7-percent discount rate), for direct comparison with the 2015 regulatory analysis.

Table 8.1. Components of Regulatory Costs of the TWIC-Reader Rule

Cost Category	Cost Component
Capital	TWIC readers, including hardware and software
	Installation of TWIC readers
	Infrastructure updates required for the TWIC readers to operate or be installed in appropriate locations, including costs to integrate TWIC readers with existing PACSs
Maintenance	Maintenance
Operational	Amending FSPs
	Recordkeeping systems
	Updating the CCL
	Training personnel to perform electronic TWIC inspections
Additional	Delay costs due to reader failures
	Additional delay, travel, and TWIC replacement costs due to TWIC failures

SOURCE: Office of Standards Evaluation and Development, 2015.

We estimated that the total (ten-year) industry costs of the final reader rule, as written, are $321 million (in undiscounted 2012 dollars)—or approximately $610,000 per facility and $450,000 per vessel.[380] In comparison, the 2015 regulatory analysis estimated that the total industry costs of the rule are $192.5 million on an undiscounted basis—or approximately $370,000 per facility and $70,000 per vessel.[381] Our estimate is between 1.6 and 1.7 times higher than that in the 2015 regulatory analysis.

To validate cost estimates, we examined the key assumptions and inputs for each cost category that contributed to the overall estimate. Our review of the methods employed in the 2015 regulatory analysis and the data that we collected demonstrate that the prior cost estimates,

---

[379] Office of Standards Evaluation and Development, 2015. We noted in Chapter 2 that there is uncertainty about the classification of CDC facilities and, therefore, how many facilities would meet the criteria for risk group A and be subject to the rule. Complicating this confusion is our observation during facility visits that operations were sometimes different from those described in the facility description in the list of facilities (derived from MISLE) that the USCG provided and therefore poses challenges for generating a precise list of facilities that will be subject to the final reader rule. To compensate for data limitations, we conducted a sensitivity analysis of the total number of facilities potentially subject to the rule, which we discuss later in this chapter.

[380] Our total (ten-year) industry costs are $264.8 million using a 7-percent discount rate and $294.1 million using a 3-percent discount rate.

[381] The 2015 regulatory analysis total (ten-year) industry costs are $153.7 million using a 7-percent discount rate and $173.8 million using a 3-percent discount rate.

particularly the predicted capital costs, underestimate the total costs of the final reader rule. (See Appendix G for a detailed analysis of the costs of the final reader rule.)

Table 8.2 summarizes our estimation of the total industry costs of the final reader rule, by year, based on the additional cost information we collected. We do not include governmental costs because the incremental governmental costs associated with the reader requirements are minimal compared with the overall costs of implementing and operating the TWIC program. The USCG estimated that the total additional government costs are approximately $100,000 on an undiscounted basis and will be incurred during the first two years of the rule's implementation.[382] It is important to note that some of the costs to industry tabulated in Table 8.2 might be subsidized by government funds, including through the Port Security Grant Program.[383]

Table 8.2. Industry Costs of the TWIC-Reader Rule, by Year, in Millions of 2012 Dollars

Year	Capital Costs	Maintenance Costs	Operational Costs	Additional Costs	Total
1	105.4	0.0	1.5	2.5	109.5
2	105.0	2.8	1.7	2.5	112.0
3	0.0	5.6	0.4	2.5	8.5
4	0.0	5.6	0.4	2.5	8.5
5	0.0	5.6	0.4	2.5	8.5
6	15.9	5.6	0.4	2.5	24.4
7	15.9	5.6	0.4	2.5	24.3
8	0.0	5.6	0.4	2.5	8.5
9	0.0	5.6	0.4	2.5	8.5
10	0.0	5.6	0.4	2.5	8.5
Total cost	242.2	47.3	6.1	25.5	321.0
Annualized cost	30.0	4.5	0.7	2.5	37.7

NOTE: We do not show discounted costs by year. Annualized costs are calculated using a 7-percent discount rate. Totals have been rounded, so some do not sum precisely.

Table 8.3 summarizes our estimation of the total industry costs, by facility or vessel type.

---

[382] Office of Standards Evaluation and Development, 2015, Chapter 4.

[383] As discussed in Appendix G, FEMA port security grants have funded more than $200 million (in 2018 dollars) in TWIC-related improvements at U.S. maritime facilities. Many of the expenditures were not only for TWIC readers but also for structural, technological, and personnel investments to improve the overall TWIC program. Federal funding also contributed to TWIC-related improvements at nonregulated facilities and those voluntarily installing TWIC readers. Therefore, it is not feasible to separate expenditures directly associated with the final reader rule because funding also contributed to improving the baseline TWIC program (e.g., streamlining operations for visual inspection of TWIC cards) and voluntary adoption of TWIC readers at nonregulated facilities.

Table 8.3. Industry Costs of the TWIC-Reader Rule, by Facility or Vessel Type

Facility or Vessel Type	Number of Facilities or Vessels	Cost, in Millions of 2012 Dollars	
		Total, Undiscounted	Annualized, with 7-Percent Discount Rate
Bulk liquid facility	290	229.1	27.5
Break-bulk or solids facility	16	8.9	1.1
Container facility	3	9.8	1.1
Large–passenger vessel facility	92	46.4	5.0
Small–passenger vessel facility	63	9.2	1.0
Mixed-use facility	61	17.2	2.0
Vessel	1	0.4	0.1
Total	526	321.0	37.7

NOTE: Totals have been rounded, so one does not sum precisely.

Estimation of Benefits

To estimate the magnitude of the benefits required to equal or offset the costs of the final reader rule, we analyzed the break-even threshold for three attack modes in MSRAM for which the USCG has assessed that improvements in access controls could plausibly avert a terrorist attack: terrorist assault team, truck bomb, and passenger or passerby explosive or IED.[384] Benefits are estimated using the consequence scores assigned to attack modes in MSRAM, which is assessed as equivalent economic consequence to provide a single measure of potential losses.

The break-even analysis in the 2015 regulatory analysis is based on the worst-case scenario across these attack modes and estimated that the maximum consequence of a successful terrorist attack for risk group A facilities was $5 billion. We assessed that the 2015 regulatory analysis overestimated the potential benefits by using only the maximum consequence of any attack scenario for each facility regardless of the attack mode. This approach obscured differences in the magnitude of benefits that would be needed to offset the costs of the rule for lower-consequence TSIs.[385] For example, even if access controls do nothing to mitigate the threat of a terrorist assault team attack or a truck bomb, they could still mitigate the threat of a passenger or passerby explosive or IED to such a degree that it is cost-effective *solely on the basis of mitigating that one type of incident.* However, in this example, improved access controls would

---

[384] We analyzed these attack modes in order to be consistent with the framework used in the 2015 regulatory analysis. See Appendix C for more information on the MSRAM framework and its application to the TWIC-reader rule.

[385] The average consequence for risk group A facilities across all attack modes for which improvements in access controls could plausibly avert a terrorist attack is considerably lower than the average maximum consequence.

need to avert several IED attacks (which have a lower average maximum consequence) to realize the same benefits as averting a single terrorist assault team attack. Thus, the rule would be considered more cost-effective if it averted a single higher-consequence terrorist attack than if it averted a single lower-consequence event. This distinction is lost when considering only the worst-case scenario and makes the break-even analysis appear overly favorable for the regulation.

To illustrate a range of ways in which improved access controls could achieve the break-even threshold, we estimated the required avoidance rate separately for each of the attack modes evaluated. If decisionmakers believe that the final reader rule could plausibly achieve just one of these required avoidance-rate thresholds in the break-even analysis, they might judge that the benefits are likely to exceed the costs of the regulation. In reality, the final reader rule might reduce more than one type of risk simultaneously, so it is possible for the regulation to break even by achieving an appropriate combination of events avoided across multiple types of attacks.[386]

As shown in Tables 8.2 and 8.3, we estimated that the annualized costs of the TWIC-reader rule are $37.7 million. This implies that the required avoidance rate of a successful terrorist attack to justify the costs of the rule is between 0.005 and 0.019 events per year. Expressed in terms of years between avoided events, the regulation would have to avert one event every 54 years (for a lower-consequence event) or one event every 195 years (for a higher-consequence event) to equal or offset the costs of the rule. This does not mean that a terrorist attack would need to occur during this time frame to justify the costs of the regulation. It means that at least one terrorist attack that would otherwise have been successful must now be averted because of the security enhancements brought by the TWIC-reader rule.

In comparison, the 2015 regulatory analysis estimated annualized costs of $21.9 million, which implies that the required avoidance rate is 0.0043 events per year; that is, the regulation would have to avert one event every 229 years to equal or offset the costs of the rule. Relative to the 2015 regulatory analysis, our analysis represents a more conservative approach and a more stringent threshold for the final reader rule to be considered a cost-effective regulation.

Summary of the Revised Break-Even Analysis

In Table 8.4, we summarize the results of our revised break-even analysis compared with those from the 2015 regulatory analysis. Because our cost estimates were higher than those in the 2015 regulatory analysis, the benefits would also need to be higher to justify the costs of the regulation. This implies that, to equal or offset the costs, TSIs would have to be averted more

---

[386] For example, consider a regulation that would break even by averting losses of $10 million per year. The regulation could break even either by avoiding event type A ($1 billion in losses) at a rate of 0.01 events per year (or one event every 100 years) or event type B ($200 million in losses) at a rate of 0.05 events per year (or one event every 20 years). It could also break even by avoiding both A *and* B at certain rates below 0.01 and 0.05 events per year, respectively, so long as the combined impact exceeded the break-even threshold of $10 million per year.

frequently as a direct result of the regulation. We estimated the annualized cost of acquiring and installing TWIC readers to be $37.7 million (using a 7-percent discount rate). For the higher-consequence event—one by a terrorist assault team, with an average maximum consequence of $7.3 billion—this implies that, to equal or offset the costs, the regulation would have to avoid 0.005 events each year, or one event every 195 years. For the lower-consequence event—one using a passenger or passerby explosive or IED, with an average maximum consequence of $2.0 billion—this implies that, to justify the costs, the regulation would have to avoid 0.019 events each year, or one event every 54 years. We used the average maximum consequence scores for the three attack modes from the 2015 regulatory analysis because we could not access the underlying data to use more-appropriate information regarding the distribution of consequences across facilities to estimate the average consequence, rather than the average *maximum* consequence.[387]

Table 8.4. A Comparison of the 2015 Regulatory Analysis and Our Break-Even Analysis

Factor	2015 Regulatory Analysis	Our Break-Even Analysis		
		Terrorist Assault Team	Truck Bomb	Passenger or Passerby Explosive or IED
Maximum consequence, in millions of dollars	5,014.1	7,341.4	3,287.2	2,027.2
Annualized cost, in millions of dollars[a]	21.9	37.7	37.7	37.7
Required avoidance rate (events avoided per year)	0.004	0.005	0.011	0.019
Required frequency of attacks averted (years between attacks)	229	195	87	54

[a] We calculated annualized cost using a 7-percent discount rate.

Decisionmakers should use their informed judgment to assess whether it is plausible that the regulation's benefits will exceed the break-even threshold—whereby, given their assessment of threat and vulnerability, the regulation is likely to achieve the required avoidance rate (i.e., a certain number of events avoided each year or a single event avoided over a particular time frame) to justify the costs of the rule. As previously discussed, decisionmakers might have a sense of an upper bound (or ceiling) for the regulation's benefits—for example, an estimated number of planned or attempted attacks in the maritime environment each year. If this upper bound (i.e., successfully averting every plausible attack because of the regulation) is

---

[387] Although these values were originally reported in Table 5.4 of USCG's 2015 regulatory analysis (based on an outdated VSL estimate of $6.3 million), USCG subsequently provided revised figures (based on a VSL estimate of $9.1 million) on May 24, 2019. Monetary consequence values based on the $9.1 million VSL estimate were properly reported in Table 5.6 and other sections of that report.

insufficiently high to justify the costs of the rule, the regulation would not meet the break-even threshold.

Limitations of the Use of MSRAM Data in the 2015 Regulatory Analysis

In this section, we discuss issues concerning the use of the consequence scores in MSRAM and the factors that can lead to under- and overestimation of benefits in a break-even analysis.

Consequence Scores in MSRAM

USCG PSSs provide facility-specific information and inputs for various attack scenarios to MSRAM, including estimated numbers of casualties and economic impacts. This information is used to inform the consequence score assigned to an attack mode in MSRAM. An attack scenario is the combination of a target and an attack mode. The 2015 regulatory analysis indicated that an attack by a terrorist assault team had the highest average maximum consequence score, but, in MSRAM, this scenario was assessed for only approximately one-third of the targets evaluated. The two other scenarios, truck bomb and passenger or passerby explosive or IED, had lower average maximum consequence scores and were evaluated for more than 90 percent of targets. As part of normal practice, the USCG does not evaluate the consequences associated with every attack mode at every facility, so estimates do not necessarily exist in MSRAM for all attack modes at each facility. Additionally, other attack modes (besides those identified in the 2015 regulatory analysis) in MSRAM—such as active-shooter and hostage-taking scenarios—are arguably also relevant for access control, but, because inputs for these scenarios are not required, these are assessed for only a limited number of targets and are not validated by the USCG at the headquarters level. This made it infeasible for the USCG to include them in the regulatory analysis.

Factors That Could Lead to an Underestimation of the Benefits of the Reader Rule

The 2015 regulatory analysis report describes each of the consequence factors included in MSRAM.[388] These include death or serious injury, primary economic, environmental, national security, symbolic, and secondary economic. (See Appendix G for more information on the value of a statistical life, which is relevant for monetizing the first category: death or serious injury.) However, the 2015 regulatory analysis omitted all of the other categories of impact. This exclusion of other potential benefits likely results in an understatement of the total benefits of the TWIC-reader rule. In the interest of completeness, we note that it would be desirable if the quantified benefits also included the prevention of any (not just serious) injury, property damage, and other direct economic impacts—but it does not need to include business losses from transactions that could be diverted to another port or facility because these can be considered

---

[388] Office of Standards Evaluation and Development, 2015, Chapter 5, Table 5.2.

transfers and not direct impacts. In the rest of this section, we discuss the implications of excluding each of these categories.

Omission of Economic Impacts. The MSRAM tool prompts the PSS to provide estimates of direct economic impacts, such as property damage; hence, these data exist in MSRAM. However, the 2015 regulatory analysis indicated that the primary economic impact category "represents the expected property damage and immediate business interruption from a successful attack. This includes the actual costs of replacing or repairing maritime infrastructure, as well as business losses resulting from the attack."[389] Because this category combines property damage with business losses (i.e., passengers or cargo) that, in the event of a closure, could likely go to another port or facility, it was excluded in the USCG's and our analyses to avoid counting transfers. Therefore, direct (and indirect) economic effects are likely underestimated.

Without data from MSRAM to validate the value of other direct and indirect economic impacts, we did not include these impacts in our calculation. Using the literature review discussed in Appendix G, we can only approximate that these costs are roughly equivalent to 20 to 30 percent of the equivalent-fatalities estimate.

Underestimation of the Value of Avoided Injuries. As described in the 2015 regulatory analysis report, in its consequence estimates, MSRAM considers only serious, severe, and critical injuries.[390] It would be appropriate to include less severe injuries in addition to the more-severe injuries, which would increase the overall consequence score. However, because the monetary value of less severe injuries is substantially lower, this would be unlikely to significantly affect the overall estimate. In assessing the economic value of more-severe injuries, MSRAM assigns an equivalency of ten injuries to one fatality (i.e., one injury is equal to 10 percent of the value of a statistical life, or VSL) for all injury types. In comparison, the Abbreviated Injury Scale counts serious injuries as 10.5 percent of a VSL, severe injuries as 26.6 percent, and critical injuries as 59.3 percent of a VSL.[391] This suggests that MSRAM might be underestimating the consequence of terrorist attacks, both by excluding less severe injuries and by underestimating the monetary value of more-severe injuries. The magnitude of the underestimation depends on the distribution of fatal and nonfatal injuries in the equivalent-fatalities estimate.

Inability to Estimate the Benefits of Reduced Crime. As discussed in Chapter 4, it is difficult to determine what TWIC's benefits are in reducing crime broadly and whether electronic readers would create enhanced benefits. The initial regulation also included the

---

[389] Office of Standards Evaluation and Development, 2015, Chapter 5.

[390] Office of Standards Evaluation and Development, 2015, Chapter 5.

[391] Molly J. Moran, acting General Counsel, U.S. Department of Transportation, and Carlos Monje, Assistant Secretary for Transportation Policy, U.S. Department of Transportation, "Guidance on Treatment of the Economic Value of a Statistical Life (VSL) in U.S. Department of Transportation Analyses: 2016 Adjustment," memorandum to secretarial officers and modal administrators, Washington, D.C., August 8, 2016.

potential for the rule to reduce crime but did not include it as a benefit given the inability to quantify it.

Factors That Could Lead to an Overestimation of the Benefits of the Reader Rule

Information on the distribution of consequence scores across facility types could be used to more accurately reflect risk for the population of facilities subject to the TWIC-reader rule—rather than combining maximum consequence scores across all attack modes. By using a maximum, the current approach artificially inflates the consequence score, thereby biasing the break-even estimate and making the rule appear more favorable on a cost–benefit basis. That is, the benefits of the final reader rule appear much larger than a more conservative approach would suggest and thus also appear more likely to equal or offset the costs.

If the USCG intends to revise its analysis, it has the opportunity to use more-recent MSRAM data to calculate the average consequence for each relevant attack mode in the break-even analysis. Changes in the consequence estimates would alter the results of the break-even analysis, as demonstrated above. We also note that, in 2016, DOT revised its VSL estimate for the value of avoided fatalities to $9.6 million (for a 2015 base year). Using a different base year will therefore increase the maximum consequence values in MSRAM.[392] However, this adjustment on the benefit side could be offset by corresponding inflation-driven adjustments on the cost side.

In the next section, we present an additional alternative considering different access control requirements and a sensitivity analysis contemplating a larger number of facilities falling under the broader definition of *CDC facility*.

Consideration of Regulatory Alternatives

In its 2015 regulatory analysis, the USCG considered several regulatory alternatives. These included differences in the number and types of facilities and vessels subject to the TWIC-reader rule.[393] Table 8.5 summarizes the regulatory alternatives considered in the 2015 regulatory analysis and their estimated costs.

---

[392] According to conversations with USCG personnel in November 2018, the revised VSL estimate has already been applied in MSRAM and is reflected in more-recent consequence data.

[393] Office of Standards Evaluation and Development, 2015, p. 90.

Table 8.5. Regulatory Alternatives in the USCG's 2015 Regulatory Analysis

| Regulatory Alternative | Description | Population | | Cost, in Millions of Dollars, with 7% Discount Rate | | Maximum Consequence, in Millions of Dollars |
		Facilities	Vessels	Total	Annualized	
Final rule preferred	All risk group A facilities and risk group A vessels with more than 20 crewmembers [each]	525	1	153.8	21.9	5,014.1
NPRM	All risk group A facilities and risk group A vessels with more than 14 crewmembers [each]	532	38	153.5	21.9	5,014.1
2	All risk group A facilities and risk group A vessels (except barges)	532	138	158.2	22.5	5,014.1
3	Risk group A and all container facilities and risk group A vessels with more than 14 crewmembers [each]	651	38	182.6	26.0	4,158.7
4	All risk group A facilities, plus additional high consequence facilities including petroleum refineries, non-CDC bulk hazardous materials facilities, and petroleum storage facilities, and risk group A vessels with more than 14 crewmembers [each]	1,174	38	309.5	44.1	2,211.3
5	Risk group A and B facilities and risk group A vessels with more than 14 crewmembers [each]	2,173	38	548.9	78.1	1,647.1

SOURCE: Office of Standards Evaluation and Development, 2015, pp. 90, 93. The descriptions are verbatim except as indicated.

The 2015 regulatory analysis compares each alternative with a baseline, whereby—in the absence of the TWIC-reader rule—facilities would use TWIC only as minimally required: visually inspecting TWIC cards to allow access to the site. In practice, however, during our facility interviews, we found that many facilities opt to do more than verify TWIC through visual inspection only and use a variety of methods to do so. Table 8.6 reports the distribution of TWIC verification methods among the 164 facilities whose personnel we interviewed, weighted by facility type, to extrapolate to the MTSA-regulated population.[394] If a facility used multiple verification methods, the table indicates the highest level of TWIC verification used at that facility. The table suggests that there is no single standard to which facilities adhere. In particular, even among facilities that would be subject to the final reader rule, at least some still perform visual inspection, while others who would not be subject to the rule have opted to use biometric verification.

---

[394] Several facilities use different verification methods for different populations entering. For example, a facility might use a PACS for employees but do visual verification for contractors. We categorized facilities by the highest form of verification used.

Table 8.6. Highest Level of TWIC Verification Among Facilities from Which We Interviewed Personnel, by TWIC-Reader Rule Applicability

	Percentage of Facilities	
Verification Method	Subject to TWIC-Reader Rule	Not Subject to TWIC-Reader Rule
Biometric reader	15	13
Electronic reader or PACS	44	42
Portable reader only (not using biometric validation)	18	10
Visual inspection only	23	35

SOURCES: Facility interviews; data on MTSA-regulated facilities.
NOTE: Tabulations are weighted by facility type. The table differs from Table A.5 based on the facility characteristic being tabulated. This table shows the highest level of TWIC verification that a facility could use, based on technology available. Table A.5 shows the TWIC verification method actually in use on a daily basis.

Because facilities already use a variety of TWIC verification methods, we considered the relative operational effectiveness of the TWIC-reader rule and potential alternatives. A variety of access control measures could plausibly be used to achieve the same policy objectives as in the TWIC-reader rule. To illustrate different access control requirements, we define three representative tiers:

- **visual inspection only (baseline):** As required by the 2008 TWIC rule, facilities and vessels must conduct visual inspection of TWIC cards.
- **electronic authentication:** As an additional access control measure, TWIC cards must be authenticated using an electronic reader, but the reader is not required to verify the TWIC holder's identity using biometric data.
- **biometric verification:** The preferred alternative of the 2015 regulatory analysis requires facilities and vessels to verify cardholder identities using biometric readers capable of reading TWIC cards.

Using the additional information on costs and benefits we examined, we evaluated the impact of requiring electronic authentication in lieu of biometric verification to potentially reduce the risk of terrorist attacks in a more cost-effective way. In the rest of this section, we compare the costs of electronic authentication requirements with the costs of the preferred alternative in the 2015 regulatory analysis. This represents just one potential alternative; we anticipate that a variety of options could be utilized to improve access controls above and beyond the baseline of visual inspection only. For example, an additional access control measure taking a step beyond electronic authentication might be to require dual-factor authentication, such as a PIN. Alternatively, a less stringent option might require electronic authentication but not maintenance of an up-to-date CCL and checking credentials against it before granting each TWIC cardholder access to a facility.

Representation of an Electronic Authentication Alternative

To illustrate an intermediate level of access control requirements, we estimated the costs of electronic authentication, which would require the use of electronic readers with a PACS or portable readers as an alternative to more-expensive readers with biometric verification capabilities. Currently, as shown in Table 8.6, approximately half of MTSA-regulated facilities can use comparable methods for TWIC verification as a primary access control measure or in addition to visually inspecting TWIC cards.[395] In addition, nearly 20 percent of facilities in our sample were using more–technologically sophisticated biometric readers. Although we could not compare the benefits of biometric validation with other access control measures, such as electronic authentication, we were able to conduct a break-even analysis to provide a benchmark for the effectiveness of each, assuming that the benefits are equal.

Using the cost information presented in this chapter, we estimated that the cost of electronic readers was about $600 per reader, or approximately 10 percent of the cost of biometric readers currently on the market. We estimated that facilities would still incur installation and related infrastructure costs; however, we assumed that these costs would be less. As a proxy for the cost premium, we looked at the difference between the FEMA port security grants that did and did not include investments in specific infrastructure or equipment associated with expanding access points. Using a limited sample of FY 2017 and FY 2018 awards, we estimated that up-front capital costs, excluding readers, would be approximately 20 percent less than the installation and infrastructure costs associated with biometric readers.

We also estimated that maintenance costs would decline proportionally. Personnel at facilities stated that electronic proximity readers without moving parts were less prone than those with moving parts to breaking or malfunctioning. We estimated that delay costs were unlikely to change, with the exception that an invalid inspection due to a biometric failure would no longer cause a delay. The 2015 regulatory analysis identified seven "failure modes" that resulted in an invalid electronic TWIC inspection.[396] According to data from the TWIC pilot program, 17.1 percent of electronic TWIC inspections were invalid—however, the data did not provide information on the distribution of invalid inspections. The 2015 regulatory analysis therefore assumed a uniform distribution of invalid inspections across the seven failure modes, or 2.4 percent for each. Thus, we estimated that the rate of invalid inspections would decline by 2.4 percent if biometric failure were eliminated as a reason for a delay.

---

[395] We note that not all these facilities would be compliant with the access control requirements in the TWIC-reader rule, even excluding the biometric verification requirement. For example, some facilities use a combination of visual inspection of TWIC cards and electronic authentication of other credentials, such as a private company's employee ID card.

[396] The failure modes included the card being on the CCL, the card being invalid, biometric failure, card failure, otherwise-unreadable card, user error, and the reader failing. Note that the term *failure mode* is misleading because the first two modes indicate the success of access control measures in rejecting invalid TWIC cards. See additional information on failure modes in Office of Standards Evaluation and Development, 2015, p. 65.

Different levels of access control could result in costs that are higher or lower than those described here. We endeavored to select an alternative for which the costs differed sufficiently from the preferred alternative in the 2015 regulatory analysis as to materially affect the break-even analysis. We considered additional alternatives to illustrate the range of access control measures but believed that minor differences in costs did not justify an analysis of multiple alternatives. Furthermore, the cost information we collected was not sufficiently detailed to calculate cost differences due solely to the technical configurations of TWIC readers.

Representation of a Broader Universe of CDC Facilities

As described earlier in this report, we anticipated that the lack of clarity regarding the definition of *CDC facility* could increase the number of facilities potentially subject to the final reader rule. We estimated that up to three times as many facilities could fall under the broader definition of *CDC facility*. To derive this estimate, we included the following facility types: risk group A facilities; non–risk group A (nonexempt) bulk liquid or bulk oil facilities; non–risk group A (nonexempt) facilities receiving or transferring hazardous, explosive, or radioactive materials;[397] and all non–risk group A (nonexempt) container facilities.[398] Using these criteria, we estimated that about 1,500 facilities could fall under the broader definition of *CDC facility* and therefore be subject to the TWIC-reader rule. Most of the additional facilities that would fall under the broader definition of *CDC facility* are bulk liquid facilities. Some container facilities and mixed-use facilities might also fall under the broader definition of *CDC facility* because of the presence or transfers of specific hazmat. Table 8.7 provides a representation of a larger number of facilities potentially subject to the TWIC-reader rule, including risk group A facilities and other nonexempt facilities that might fall under the broader definition of *CDC facility*.[399]

---

[397] This includes any facility designated a "facility of particular hazard."

[398] Approximately 20 percent of container facilities meet at least one of the other criteria. However, descriptive information was not available to evaluate each of the nonexempt container facilities. Therefore, we might have overestimated the number of container facilities that would fall under the definition of *CDC facility*.

[399] USCG provided facility-level data with limited descriptive information.

Table 8.7. Number and Types of Facilities Potentially Subject to the TWIC-Reader Rule

Facility Type	Risk Group A	Other Potential CDC Facilities	All
Bulk liquids	290	780	1,070
Break-bulk and solids	16	62	78
Container	3	119	122
Passenger			
Cruise	92	0	92
Ferry	63	0	63
Mixed Use	61	20	81
Total	**525**	**981**	**1,506**

For a sensitivity analysis, we estimated the impact of the TWIC-reader rule for all facilities that might fall under the broader CDC definition. Many of the estimated costs would increase proportionally to the number of regulated facilities, by facility type. For example, to estimate the up-front capital costs, we used the average capital cost per facility for each facility type from Table G.3.[400] However, we estimated that delay costs would increase because the number of affected TWIC cardholders would significantly increase. For example, in the 2015 regulatory analysis, estimates were approximately 39,000 TWIC cardholders at risk group A container facilities and nearly 1.6 million TWIC cardholders at all container facilities. To account for this, we relied on the estimated annual cost of delay for container facilities as calculated in the 2015 regulatory analysis, approximately $7.5 million per year.[401] We also estimated the increased delay costs for all facility types due to invalid inspections based on the proportion of TWIC cardholders at risk group A and other, nonexempt facilities that would fall under the broader definition of *CDC facility*. In addition, given the USCG's assumption that 5 percent of TWIC cards would become damaged or defective each year, we calculated an increase in the potential cost of replacing TWIC cards. In both cases, delay costs and TWIC card replacement costs would increase by an order of magnitude to millions of dollars per year.

Expanded Break-Even Analysis Results

Table 8.8 reports the costs of the preferred regulatory alternative as reported in the 2015 analysis, biometric verification (as calculated for this report), electronic authentication, and sensitivity analyses regarding the number of facilities that fall under the definition of *CDC*

---

[400] This could overestimate costs for bulk liquid facilities if the non–risk group A facilities require fewer readers or less infrastructure and PACS improvement than risk group A facilities. We estimated that the average capital costs for container facilities were likely the same as those for the risk group A container facilities—which are higher than for all other facility types—as shown in Table G.3.

[401] See the discussion of the annual delay costs for container facilities in Office of Standards Evaluation and Development, 2015, p. 89.

facility. With the broader definition of a CDC facility, we estimated that the total cost of biometric verification requirements would increase by almost a factor of 4. For the electronic authentication alternative, we estimated that the total cost of the reader requirements would be approximately 60 percent of the costs of the biometric verification requirements.

Table 8.8. The Costs of Regulatory Alternatives

| | | Cost, in Millions of Dollars | | | |
| | | Undiscounted | | 7% Discount Rate | |
Alternative	CDC Facility	Total	Annualized	Total	Annualized
2015 regulatory analysis		192.6	19.3	153.8	21.9
Biometric verification	Limited CDC definition	321.1	32.1	264.9	37.7
	Including all CDC facilities	1,241.8	124.2	985.0	140.2
Electronic authentication	Limited CDC definition	182.6	18.3	157.8	22.5
	Including all CDC facilities	736.2	73.6	601.8	85.7

NOTE: Costs are reported in 2012 dollars and rounded to the nearest hundred thousand for direct comparison with the 2015 regulatory analysis.

When comparing these alternatives, we also used the results of the break-even analysis to assess the potential effectiveness of different access control requirements. Figure 8.1 shows the break-even curves implied by the two regulatory alternatives (biometric verification and electronic authentication) using the limited CDC-facility definition. The blue line illustrates the break-even threshold for biometric verification, as required in the TWIC-reader rule, and the orange line illustrates the threshold for a lower-cost electronic authentication requirement. The vertical dotted lines illustrate the monetary consequence of the three attack modes used in the analysis, and the points on the curves show the avoidance rates that would be required in order for the regulation to break even.

Figure 8.1. Break-Even Points for Three Attack Modes Under Alternative Regulations, Assuming Regulation Applies to Facilities Based on Limited CDC Definition

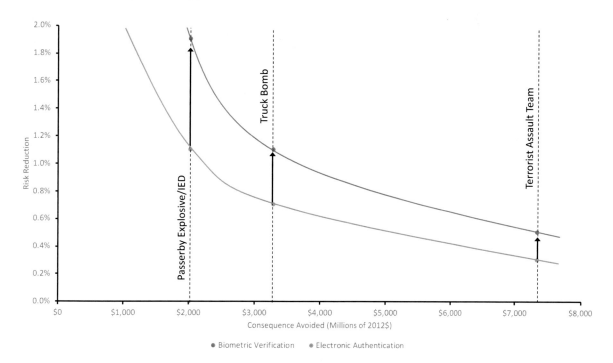

NOTE: The blue line illustrates the break-even threshold for biometric verification, as required in the TWIC-reader rule, and the orange line illustrates the threshold for a lower-cost electronic authentication requirement. The vertical dotted lines illustrate the monetary consequence of the three attack modes used in the analysis, and the points on the curves show the avoidance rates that would be required in order for the regulation to break even.

The figure shows that, for each attack mode, the required avoidance rate is higher under the biometric verification requirement (blue) than under the electronic authentication requirement (orange). This is because the biometric requirement would result in a higher-cost regulation and therefore must avoid more events per year (for a given-size event) than the lower-cost electronic requirement to achieve the same net benefit. According to our estimates, avoiding 0.019 passerby explosives per year would justify the biometric rule, but so would avoiding 0.005 terrorist assault team attacks; the regulation need only achieve one of these thresholds—not both.

Figure 8.1 also shows that less consequential events would require a larger change in the avoidance rate to justify the higher-cost biometric requirement over an electronic authentication requirement. This is shown by the length of the solid black arrows, which indicate the amount by which the aversion rate would need to increase to justify the higher-cost rule: The arrow is longest for the lower-consequence event (passenger or passerby explosive or IED) and shortest for the higher-consequence event (terrorist assault team). Thus, costlier regulations must meet a higher bar to be justified based on the aversion of a low-consequence event.

Table 8.9 compares the costs, required avoidance rates, and required frequency of attacks averted for each regulatory alternative and the two definitions of *CDC facility*. Because we could not recalculate updated or alternative consequence estimates using MSRAM,[402] we used information from the 2015 regulatory analysis to use the most reasonable approximation. Alternative 4 in the 2015 regulatory analysis (described in Table 8.5) provides the closest approximation for the average maximum consequence score for a grouping of facilities similar to that in our proposed alternative scenario with the expanded definition of *CDC facility*. Because this alternative includes many non–risk group A facilities, the average maximum consequence score is lower than for risk group A. Even with the reduced maximum consequence scores for lower-risk facilities, there is still an upward bias in the calculation of break-even points because we are relying only on maximum consequence scores. Using updated estimates of average consequence scores (which would be lower than the maximum consequence score) would result in an even higher required avoidance rate to equal or offset the costs of the TWIC-reader rule.

Table 8.9. Break-Even Analysis, by Regulatory Alternative

		Biometric Verification				Electronic Authentication			
		Limited Definition of *CDC Facility*			All CDC Facilities	Limited Definition of *CDC Facility*			All CDC Facilities
Characteristic	2015 Regulatory Analysis, All Attack Modes	Terrorist Assault Team	Truck Bomb	Passenger or Passerby Explosive or IED	All Attack Modes	Terrorist Assault Team	Truck Bomb	Passenger or Passerby Explosive or IED	All Attack Modes
Annualized cost, in millions of dollars, 7% discount rate	21.9	37.7			140.2	22.5			85.7
Average maximum consequence, in millions of dollars	5,014.1	2,027.2	3,287.2	7,341.4	2,211.3	2,027.2	3,287.2	7,341.4	2,211.3
Required avoidance rate (events per year)	0.004	0.019	0.011	0.005	0.063	0.011	0.007	0.003	0.039
Required frequency of attacks averted (one event every . . . years)	229	54	87	195	16	90	146	327	26

NOTE: Costs are reported in 2012 dollars and rounded to the nearest hundred thousand for direct comparison with the 2015 regulatory analysis. Because of data limitations, we were not able to recreate break-even analyses for individual attack modes and the expanded definition of *CDC facility*.

---

[402] Because of classification requirements on aggregate MSRAM data, the USCG was unable to provide more-detailed consequence data or information for more-recent years. This limited our ability to recalculate and update alternative consequence scores.

Under the broader definition of a CDC facility, we estimated that the magnitude of the benefits needed to offset the costs of the rule would substantially increase and that the break-even threshold would require that at least one TSI be averted every 16 years, as opposed to one passerby-explosive incident every 54 years, one truck bomb every 87 years, or one attack by a terrorists assault team every 195 years under the limited CDC definition. This change is due, in part, to the maximum consequence score (i.e., the corresponding magnitude of benefits) being much lower across a larger number of facilities. For the electronic authentication requirements, the break-even threshold for the broader definition of a CDC facility would require averting at least one TSI every 26 years. This means that, for the rule to be cost-effective, the baseline frequency of attempted terrorist attacks would have to be relatively high, rather than terrorist attacks being "once-in-a-century" events.

Other Factors That Might Influence the Cost-Effectiveness of the TWIC-Reader Rule

A variety of factors could shift the break-even threshold to make the cost-effectiveness regulation more favorable. First, the USCG could further limit the number of facilities subject to the regulation by using a more stringent definition to determine what is part of risk group A. Rather than generalizing facilities by type, the regulation could categorize facilities by additional drivers of risk. These could relate to consequence, such as proximity to population sector or volume of dangerous material. These could also relate to vulnerability—for example, the TWIC-reader rule could be more beneficial at facilities with large numbers of personnel. (Currently, there is no relationship between number of staff and TWIC-reader rule requirements. During our site survey, we visited one facility that would be subject to the regulation that had fewer than ten staff members, who would be required to use electronic biometric readers to verify their identities to each other under the rule as currently written.) We learned from the USCG that the quality of data in MSRAM has increased over time; therefore, a more refined analysis would be possible today than when the initial data were derived from MSRAM.

The TWIC-reader rule would also be more favorable from a cost–benefit perspective if the costs were lower. For example, requiring facilities to have portable readers on-site and use them intermittently and at random to verify identity, rather than at every entry point to the secure area at all times, would reduce capital and operational costs and could still bring some deterrent value. Costs could also decrease over time as biometric technology becomes more prevalent. We heard in our interviews that uncertainty regarding the TWIC-reader rule has led to market instability for vendors of readers capable of reading TWIC cards, which affects prices in addition to availability and investment in new technology development. One facility interviewee stated, "Since the implementation [of the reader rule] has been delayed again, vendors aren't showing up to conferences as actively for marketing and selling products."[403] Some facility personnel

---

[403] Interview with a port authority official speaking about a cruise facility.

have noted that they are now holding off or delaying the purchase of readers to see what happens with the next iteration of the TWIC-reader rule.

Summary

To address Sections 1(b)(3)(C)(iii) and 1(b)(3)(C)(iv) of Public Law 114-278, this chapter provided an assessment of the costs and benefits of TWIC access control requirements, building on the framework in the USCG's 2015 regulatory analysis using additional cost information collected from site visits, interviews, industry reports, and federal grants for port security improvements. We assessed that the ten-year industry costs of the TWIC-reader rule are likely to be 1.6 to 1.7 times higher than the USCG previously estimated: $321.0 million (measured in 2012 dollars), or approximately $610,000 per facility and $450,000 per vessel. We then conducted a break-even analysis to help policymakers assess whether stronger access control requirements are likely to be cost-effective given the potential benefits of the TWIC-reader rule. Specifically, we calculated the frequency (i.e., the number of events per year) with which access control measures would have to avert or mitigate a terrorist attack for the benefits to justify the costs. We used MSRAM data on the maximum consequence (i.e., potential economic losses) for three types of terrorist attacks that could plausibly be mitigated by stronger access controls.

We found that the TWIC-reader rule would be cost-effective if it resulted in one of the following scenarios: averting a passenger or passerby explosive or IED attack at least once every 54 years, averting a truck bomb attack at least once every 87 years, or averting a terrorist assault team attack at least once every 195 years. We also calculated the break-even thresholds for alternative regulatory scenarios, including a lower-cost regulation mandating electronic access controls (without a biometric authentication requirement) and a higher-cost regulation mandating stronger access controls for a universe of facilities expanded by a broader definition of *CDC facility*.

Given the relative infrequency of terrorist attacks in the maritime environment historically, it is not possible to determine whether the TWIC-reader rule would equal or exceed the break-even thresholds calculated in this study to justify the regulation on a cost–benefit basis. Although break-even analysis does not affirm whether a policy is appropriate or not, the more stringent break-even threshold we calculated does present a substantive challenge to the estimated or perceived benefit of the regulation. This is particularly true if the universe of facilities subject to the TWIC-reader rule were to increase to around 1,500, which yields a break-even threshold of averting one attack every 16 years. Alternative access control requirements that would lower the costs of the rule while achieving a similar level of benefits would increase the likelihood that the rule's benefits will exceed its costs. Furthermore, using additional metrics in MSRAM to identify facilities and vessels at high risk of a terrorist attack because of specific threats or vulnerabilities associated with a deficiency in access controls could result in a more narrowly focused rule that achieves an improved cost–benefit ratio. At the same time, limiting the number of high-risk facilities using stronger access controls would make it less likely that such benefits would be achieved. To improve future cost–benefit analysis, the USCG might be able to utilize more-granular MSRAM data to further assess risk and potential outcomes.

9. Alternative Models and Redundancies

Public Law 114-278 directs that an evaluation ask about alternative credentialing models and potential redundancies of the TWIC program (Sections 1[b][3][A][iii], 1[b][3][A][iv], and 1[b][3][C][ii]), questions that we address directly in this chapter. MTSA requires that anyone "entering an area of a vessel or facility that is designated as a secure area" hold "a transportation security card."[404] The transportation security card must also have biometric information about the user. Public Law 114-278 instructs that this study review TWIC's security value by "evaluating the potential for a non-biometric credential alternative."[405] The study was also to consider "whether there is unnecessary redundancy or duplication with other Federal- or State-issued transportation security credentials"[406] and "the appropriateness of having varied Federal and State threat assessments and access controls."[407] Previous GAO reports have also suggested that an alternative model that should be considered would be one in which the federal government conducts the STA but does not directly issue a card credential. This chapter discusses such alternatives.

Using Biometrics in the TWIC Program

Biometrics are relevant for the TWIC program in two ways. The first is the capture of biometric (fingerprint) data at the time of enrollment in order to check the Next Generation Identification database, a federal repository of criminal-history information based on arrest records, and IDENT, a DHS database that can help verify identities and find potential derogatory information. The second is the storage of biometric information—two primary fingerprints captured at time of enrollment—on the card itself, allowing the holder to verify their identity. This biometric information can be used by portable TWIC readers or integrated into a facility PACS.[408] Storing such information on the card is also consistent with NIST standards for personal identity verification of federal employees and contractors at federal facilities.[409] We

---

[404] 46 U.S.C. § 70105(a).

[405] Section 1(b)(3)(C)(ii).

[406] Section 1(b)(3)(A)(iii).

[407] Section 1(b)(3)(A)(iv).

[408] A facility does not need to use the stored biometric data on the card as its form of identity assurance for daily use. It can use stored fingerprint information to verify identity when enrolling a cardholder into its PACS and capture alternative biometric information at that time (for example, an infrared scan of the vascular hand pattern or a facial photograph) to be used at points of entry.

[409] NIST, *Personal Identity Verification (PIV) of Federal Employees and Contractors*, Federal Information Processing Standards Publication 201-2, August 2013.

presumed that, in Public Law 114-278, Congress is interested primarily in a nonbiometric alternative credential that does not store this biometric information on the card itself but still involves the capture and use of fingerprint data to run the underlying criminal-history check. We made such an assumption given that fingerprints are a well-established and efficient method of checking criminal records and because the primary concern we heard in an interview with labor organizations about biometrics was not the use of biometrics at time of enrollment but the fact that biometric data were seen as highly personal information that could be compromised if stored on the TWIC's integrated circuit chip.

Biometrics as an Authentication Measure

Biometric sensors are often considered a state-of-the-art component of security systems. NIST, for example, has cited biometrics as one component of identity proofing methods of superior strength and has noted that biometrics can be a method of detecting fraudulent enrollments and establishing credential ownership.[410] Biometric collection is mandatory for NIST's highest level of identity assurance. Biometrics are not, however, the only method of authenticating someone's identity. There are three canonical types of authentication factors: knowledge, possession, and inherence factors. A knowledge factor—something the person knows—could be a PIN or passcode. A possession factor—something the user has—could be a card credential or an authentication token. An inherence factor—something the user is—is a biometric measure. Although fingerprint readers are perhaps the most pervasive today— particularly with the widening adoption of fingerprint readers as a replacement for passcodes in mobile devices—they are not the only biometric measure. Others include facial, iris, heartbeat, vascular, vocal, and gait scans.

Biometrics are often considered the best method of verifying identity. Other common authentication measures that are not biometric (e.g., key cards, PINs, passcodes) have well-known flaws. For example, they are inherently transferable, meaning they can be shared with adversaries attempting to gain false entry either intentionally or unintentionally. Furthermore, they can be lost. Biometric credentials, on the other hand, are not transferable or easily lost; they are on each person's individual body carried with them at all times. Fingerprints, in particular,

---

[410] Paul A. Grassi, James L. Fenton, Naomi B. Lefkovitz, Jamie M. Danker, Yee-Yin Choong, Kristen K. Greene, and Mary F. Theofanos, *Digital Identity Guidelines: Enrollment and Identity Proofing Requirements*, Gaithersburg, Md.: National Institute of Standards and Technology, U.S. Department of Commerce, Special Publication 800-63A, June 2017. According to Grassi and his colleagues, identity proofing is a process in which

> an applicant provides evidence to a credential service provider (CSP) reliably identifying themselves, thereby allowing the CSP to assert that identification at a useful identity assurance level. (p. ii)

are a commonly recognized method of identity assurance. It is an appealing system given that there is nothing for the user to remember or lose.[411]

However, biometric verification methods, like other security measures, also carry flaws. Past research has shown that use of fingerprints is not as efficient or as unassailable as popularly thought. On efficiency, fingerprint readers have been shown to carry higher error rates than conventional passwords and PINs; are prone to common issues, such as failing to register prints; often carry a high cost; and, when used alone, provide no backup measure when a user is unable to provide the required fingerprint.[412] On security, it is possible to create false images that replicate the biometric ID of the intended user. A research team was able to defeat mobile fingerprint readers using a set of artificial fingerprints that was able to match real fingerprints 65 percent of the time (although the success rate would be lower in real life than in experimental conditions).[413] Other researchers were able to use readily available photos to replicate fingerprints.[414] Similar weaknesses have been found with other biometric measures. Mahmood Sharif and his colleagues were able to defeat facial security measures at a rate of 90 to 100 percent using a technique in which an imposter wears a specific set of eyeglass frames.[415] In another case, a week after the launch of Apple's Face ID system on mobile devices, researchers began cracking the system by using a 3-D–printed artificial mask.[416] Although these various spoofing techniques—fingerprint replication, special glasses, and masks—would be quite obvious and observable at a manned checkpoint, they could pose vulnerabilities at unmanned or un–photo-monitored checkpoints. Although biometrics might require such additional sophistication to defeat, ultimately, the most robust security system is one that uses multifactor authentication rather than any one single measure.

Alternative Authentication Measures

The TWIC, if visually inspected properly, already provides for multifactor authentication. This is because the TWIC card itself provides a possession factor, and the card contains a photograph of the credential holder, an inherence factor. Yet, matching unknown faces to

---

[411] Joseph Bonneau, Cormac Herley, Paul C. van Oorschot, and Frank Stajano, "The Quest to Replace Passwords: A Framework for Comparative Evaluation of Web Authentication Schemes," *2012 IEEE Symposium on Security and Privacy*, Institute of Electrical and Electronics Engineers, 2012, pp. 553–567.

[412] Bonneau et al., 2012.

[413] Vindu Goel, "That Fingerprint Sensor on Your Phone Is Not as Safe as You Think," *New York Times*, April 10, 2017.

[414] "Japan Researchers Warn of Fingerprint Theft from 'Peace' Sign," *Phys.org*, January 11, 2017.

[415] Mahmood Sharif, Sruti Bhagavatula, Lujo Bauer, and Michael K. Reiter, "Accessorize to a Crime: Real and Stealthy Attacks on State-of-the-Art Face Recognition," *CCS '16: Proceedings of the 2016 ACM SIGSAC Conference on Computer and Communications Security*, 2016, pp. 1528–1540.

[416] Andy Greenberg, "Hackers Say They've Broken Face ID a Week After iPhone X Release," *Wired*, November 12, 2017.

photographs is a difficult and error-prone task, even under the best viewing conditions.[417] People vary greatly in their ability to recognize faces.[418] This variation appears to be explained by inherent ability, and face ID appears to be a difficult skill to improve.[419] A past study of passport officers also suggested that security professionals, even with training and experience, are not better than the general public at this task.[420] These studies, however, do not necessarily dictate how effective or ineffective security guards are at conducting visual inspection of TWIC cards. This is in part because not all security officers are matching TWIC photographs to *unknown* faces. Although they are doing just that at facilities with very large throughput or large staffs, at many facilities, security guards are verifying the identifies of *known* faces. By that, we mean that many facilities have limited staff or a moderate number of repeat individuals accessing their facilities. Security guards might also have the benefit of additional inherence factors on which to verify identities (e.g., voices or gaits) or other possession factors (e.g., a known vehicle).[421]

Knowledge factors could be an alternative method of providing for a multifactor authentication system using TWIC. The TWIC card also stores a unique PIN, either generated randomly or chosen by the holder. Under current regulations, however, a facility is not allowed to use the PIN in lieu of a visual inspection of the photograph or biometric identity authentication. We found no instances of facilities otherwise using the PIN for access control purposes during our site survey. Given its widespread disuse, many TWIC holders are unaware of their PINs (or maintain cards with their PINs with the TWIC cards themselves).[422] As discussed in the earlier section, knowledge factors have an inherent weakness in their transferability, purposefully or not, and their ability to be forgotten. So, although knowledge factors would be an alternative method of dual-factor authentication, they would require less sophisticated means to defeat and could be difficult to adopt, given their sparse use at this time.

Facilities also have the latitude to adopt other biometric features, including ones that users might feel are less intrusive than fingerprints. To do so, facilities use the stored fingerprints on

---

[417] David White, Richard I. Kemp, Rob Jenkins, Michael Matheson, and A. Mike Burton, "Passport Officers' Errors in Face Matching," *PLoS ONE*, Vol. 9, No. 8, 2014, e103510; Markus Bindemann, Meri Avetisyan, and Tim Rakow, "Who Can Recognize Unfamiliar Faces? Individual Differences and Observer Consistency in Person Identification," *Journal of Experimental Psychology: Applied*, Vol. 18, No. 3, September 2012, pp. 277, 286.

[418] Brad Duchaine, Brad, "Individual Differences in Face Recognition Ability: Impacts on Law Enforcement, Criminal Justice and National Security," *Psychological Science Agenda*, June 2015; Bindemann, Avetisyan, and Rakow, 2012, pp. 286–287.

[419] Alice J. O'Toole, "Psychological and Neural Perspectives on Human Face Recognition," in Stan Z. Li and Anil Jain, eds., *Handbook of Face Recognition*, New York: Springer, 2005, pp. 349–369; Bindemann, Avetisyan, and Rakow, 2012, p. 288.

[420] White et al., 2014.

[421] However, guards benefiting from other information to recognize personal identities could introduce a new vulnerability, in that they might be less likely to examine the TWIC card itself and fail to notice such facts as the card's expiration date.

[422] We would highlight that a user can reset their PIN at any time at a TSA enrollment center.

the card to verify an identity at the time of enrollment, then capture separate biometric information for routine use at access points. Some facilities are doing this using facial recognition technology, and TSA officials have told us that the Next Generation TWIC data model will better support facial matching by facilities. A few ports—notably, the Port of Savannah, the single largest container facility in the United States—use infrared pictures of the vascular hand pattern. Savannah has used this system for nine years and was highly complimentary of its utility. In Savannah's experience, the vascular hand scan provides rapid, reliable results; is durable in a maritime environment; and feels less intrusive for users than fingerprints. We did not test the difference between biometric reader technologies to evaluate efficiencies between them, but we bring up these comparative options to highlight that fingerprints are not the only available biometric in use at ports for identity assurance.

Biometrics in the Maritime Environment

In our site visits, we observed a range of biometrics in use in the maritime environment, including fingerprints, facial recognition, and vascular scans. A common concern raised about TWIC readers is the need for technology to operate in a harsh maritime environment—where equipment will likely be exposed to the elements, salt water, large mechanical equipment, and a workforce disinclined to handle readers gently. Regional climate is also an important concern. Examples we were given about factors that facilities found affected reader reliability of readers include vascular scanners working less effectively in cold weather[423] and facial recognition having trouble with beards.[424] We cannot independently confirm these facts, or how prevalent they might be between readers, because we did not directly test reader technologies.

A Consequence of Removing Biometric Data from the TWIC Card

Removing the stored fingerprint data from the TWIC card would eliminate some options and flexibility currently available to facilities in using the card. A facility might use biometric verification when enrolling someone into a PACS; removing the stored biometric data on the card would eliminate this method of identity verification. Per current regulation, a facility using a PACS at an unmanned access point must use biometric ID of some kind to provide identity assurance (unless regulation were to also change to allow PINs to provide identity assurance). The biometric information can be referenced in the PACS servers or compared with the biometric information stored locally on the TWIC's chip.

If no biometric information were stored on the card itself, a facility could still collect biometric information at the time of enrollment into a PACS and store that information in a local system. However, the facility would have less assurance that the person it is enrolling in its system is the properly issued holder of the card, in that it would be able to verify the person's

---

[423] Interview with the director of security operations at a state port.

[424] Interview with the director of operations at a state port.

identity only through a visual verification of the card's photograph and verifying the card's PIN. We still find these controls robust, provided that the enrolling officer carefully checks the photograph. Fraudulent use of a TWIC in this scenario would require a conspiracy between two people: one who was able to pass an STA and acquire a TWIC, who then transferred the card and PIN to someone with a similar physical likeness who could use it as their own to enroll in a PACS.

The biometric information currently stored on the TWIC card's chip, however, gives the facility an alternative IT option in configuring a PACS. Rather than storing biometric information for all users in a single place, the access control system could compare the data stored locally. This configuration eliminates the need for the facility to maintain biometric information on its authorized personnel. Locally stored information also provides the USCG and TSA the ability to do spot checks and inspections that provide greater identity assurance than can be provided with a visual match of the card's photo. A facility that has not invested in a PACS but still wants to be able to intermittently use enhanced identity assurance measures, including authenticating identities with biometrics, could do so with only the investment in a portable biometric reader. Removing the fingerprint at this point—after it has been an attribute of the TWIC program for the past ten years—would incur costs both for the government and for those facilities that use the biometric, in that they would have to alter programs to accommodate for its absence.

Other Transportation Credentials

Public Law 114-278 Section 1(b)(3)(A)(iii) directs that this evaluation assess potential unnecessary redundancy and duplication with other transportation credentials. We therefore considered other transportation security credentials that might be required of TWIC holders in terms of their purpose, function, and standard. We did not find any credentials to be duplicative of TWIC; by *duplicative*, we mean having the same purpose, function, and standard. We defined *redundancy* as whether other credentials are significantly similar to TWIC in purpose, function, and standard. We defined *unnecessary redundancy* as providing a risk-reduction effect similar to TWIC's and not providing additional benefits.

In terms of federal credentials, some TWIC holders also possess HMEs, which are a necessary credential for commercial drivers carrying hazmat over U.S. roads. TSA estimates that around 280,000 people have both TWICs and HMEs—around 21 percent of the HME total population and 12 percent of the total TWIC population. GAO raised concerns that TWIC and HME are credentials with "redundant background check investigations," which is an accurate description: The information used in and standards applied for the STA for these credentials is the same.[425] These programs are not completely redundant, given functional differences between

---

[425] GAO, 2007.

them. The HME, which is actually state issued, also requires the holder to have passed a knowledge-based test on handling hazmat. The TWIC fee also includes a card credential, but this is not the case for an HME, which appears on the holder's state-issued commercial driver's license.

There is also some reciprocity between TWIC and HME, and the TSA Modernization Act of 2018 would further promote this reciprocity.[426] Under current rules, someone with an HME can apply for a TWIC at a reduced rate and vice versa. The implementation of the TSA Modernization Act of 2018 would allow a TWIC holder to satisfy the HME requirements for an STA without having to pay a separate fee for an HME. We do not know when TSA will adjust its enrollment process to allow for these reciprocal benefits to be conferred or whether any changes will be made to the reciprocal process for someone who has an HME and applies for a TWIC. One opportunity to further integrate the TWIC and HME credentials would be to allow someone to apply for both credentials simultaneously at a reduced cost. Currently, an applicant would have to apply for the credentials subsequently at full cost because there is no method to enroll once and be conferred multiple credentials. Alternatively, an applicant can apply for one credential and await its award before requesting reciprocal recognition for the other. The fees are reduced for doing so but only marginally—around 15 percent in applying for a TWIC and 25 percent in applying for an HME—because the fee portion for enrollment process is paid in full each time. Allowing an applicant to apply the STA to multiple TSA-managed credentialing programs could reduce costs and hassle for users. This could also include the TSA Pre√® program, which has very similar standards,[427] although its redress process is limited to record correction.

We identified no state that currently has a statewide maritime credential, but some state and local port authorities use a separate credential in addition to TWIC in their operations. Port-specific credentials often serve a purpose different from that of the TWIC card. For example, the Georgia Ports Authority (GPA) operates two ports (Savannah and Brunswick) with a total of five terminals and uses a port authority badge in addition to TWIC at all five. Even though GPA is a state authority, this is not a statewide credential, given that is not required for anyone working at a privately owned maritime facility in Georgia. For GPA facilities that used electronic access points, the TWIC card was used as the access control credential, and business purpose was established by enrollment in a facility PACS. The GPA badge was used for entry points without electronic systems and for other purposes, such as timekeeping and to operate certain secure equipment. In Florida, 15 public ports operate under the administration of county-level port authorities. We found that at least some of these ports similarly issue a port-specific credential.

---

[426] U.S. Senate, TSA Modernization Act, Bill 1872, 115th Congress, placed on legislative calendar under general orders, June 6, 2018.

[427] Whereas immigrants with certain work visas can apply for TWIC cards, only U.S. citizens and LPRs are eligible for the TSA Pre√® program.

These cards were often used to establish business purpose at a facility. In the case of the Port of Tampa Bay, some port users do not require TWIC cards because they are not accessing secure areas; therefore, a port credential provides a cheaper alternative ID badge for those users. Those at the Port of Tampa Bay who do have TWIC cards are issued port credentials at no cost.

One difference between a port authority's credential and a credential issued by a private company is that some port authorities have the ability to have background checks conducted by law-enforcement authorities. This means that, for some port authorities, law enforcement could check data sources similar to those that TSA uses in the STA, rather than those port authorities depending fully on commercial vendors for their background checks. Otherwise, port authority credentials are akin to facility- or company-specific credentials. Table 9.1 lays out these differences.

Table 9.1. Overlapping Transportation Credentials and Threat Assessments

Issuer	Credential	Purpose	Function of Credential	Data Source	Standard
Federal entity	TWIC	Identify threats to national security, to transportation security, or of terrorism.	Verify the STA and identity.	Federal criminal-history databases; the terrorist watch list	As established by 49 C.F.R. § 1572.5
	HME	Identify threats to national security, to transportation security, or of terrorism.	Verify the STA; ensure that safety standards are met.	Federal criminal-history databases; the terrorist watch list	As established by 49 C.F.R. § 1572.5
State or local entity	Port authority	Identify threats specific to port security, safety, or business interests.	Verify identity and business purpose	Varies; federal criminal-history databases or commercial vendors or a combination	Varies between port; often also varies with employee type
Private entity	Facility- or company-specific	Identify threats specific to the facility or company security, safety, or business interests.	Verify identity and business purpose.	Commercial vendors	Varies between facility and company and often by employee type

Alternative Operating Models for the Transportation Security Card

The current model of the federally issued TWIC card is not necessarily the only model under which the transportation security card program could operate. At least two other credentialing models are in use at critical infrastructure in the United States. One is a hybrid credentialing model that airports use—the SIDA badge, for which TSA provides information about possible terrorist ties—which provides an input into a risk-based access decision that the airport makes. Another is a privatized model, similar to the one used at Chemical Facility Anti-Terrorism Standards–regulated chemical facilities called the Personnel Surety Program, which sets requirements for facilities in doing their own background checks for facility personnel and visitors and requires facilities to inform the federal government of all employees and contractors accessing secure areas so as to check for terrorist history. (Notably, TWIC provides one acceptable means for facilities to satisfy that background check requirement.) In the rest of this chapter, we discuss the regulatory requirements related to alternative models, as well as the possible differences in risk reduction between these frameworks. It is also relevant to consider the differences in cost and logistics of these alternative models.

Regulatory Barriers to a Hybrid or Privatized Model

Before turning to the characteristics of these alternative models and the differences between them, it is necessary to consider regulatory barriers to their adoption. Under both the hybrid credentialing model and the privatized model, facilities themselves would need to have access to STA results and make a determination about each applicant's eligibility for access credentials. MTSA explicitly requires DHS to determine whether an applicant is eligible to receive a TWIC card. Adoption of either of these alternative models would require that MTSA be amended to permit facilities to make their own credentialing decisions. This amendment might mirror the language of 49 C.F.R. Part 1542, which authorizes airport operators to "establish and carry out a personnel identification system."[428] Airport operators "must ensure that no individual is granted unescorted access authority unless the individual has undergone a fingerprint-based criminal history records check (CHRC) that does not disclose that he or she has a disqualifying criminal offense."[429] Similarly, MTSA could be amended to authorize each maritime facility, rather than DHS, to establish and carry out a credentialing process, including the issuance of a biometric transportation security card.

The privacy provisions contained in MTSA represent an additional regulatory barrier to the adoption of either the hybrid credentialing model or the privatized model. Under MTSA, information obtained in the course of the credentialing process "may not be made available to the public, including the individual's employer."[430] An additional regulatory issue is posed by the requirement that "any information constituting grounds for denial of a transportation security card . . . shall be maintained confidentially by the Secretary . . . An individual's employer may only be informed of whether or not the individual has been issued the card."[431] We can presume that this limitation in information sharing extends to the maritime facility—regardless of whether

---

[428] Code of Federal Regulations, Title 49, Transportation; Subtitle B, Other Regulations Relating to Transportation (Continued); Chapter XII, Transportation Security Administration, Department of Homeland Security; Subchapter C, Civil Aviation Security; Part 1542, Airport Security; Subpart C, Operations; Section 1542.205, Security of the Security Identification Display Area; Paragraph (b)(1).

[429] Code of Federal Regulations, Title 49, Transportation; Subtitle B, Other Regulations Relating to Transportation (Continued); Chapter XII, Transportation Security Administration, Department of Homeland Security; Subchapter C, Civil Aviation Security; Part 1542, Airport Security; Subpart C, Operations; Section 1542.209, Fingerprint-Based Criminal History Records Checks (CHRC); Paragraph (b), Individuals Seeking Unescorted Access Authority.

[430] 46 U.S.C. § 70105(e)(1).

[431] 46 U.S.C. § 70105(e)(2).

the maritime facility is the direct employer of the person in question. A hybrid credentialing model, however, would require that the results of an STA be provided to the maritime facility. Such a model would require the employer to access and analyze information, necessarily including derogatory information, pertaining to someone's eligibility for access credentials. To overcome this regulatory hurdle, MTSA could be amended to mirror the language of 49 C.F.R. Part 1542, which requires airport operators to maintain records "in a manner that is acceptable to TSA and in a manner that protects the confidentiality of the individual."[432] Such a provision would permit maritime facilities to collect and assess the information necessary for the credentialing process while also mandating the protection of an individual's information.

Considerations in a Privatized Model

In a privatized model, a facility or employer could use a background check provided by a commercial vendor, known as a consumer reporting agency (CRA), and evaluate individuals based on a set of government standards. Such a system would still require a role for government in ensuring facility compliance. This model would have greater differences than the aforementioned hybrid model because different sources of information are checked in a CRA background check and in an STA. We lay out a summary of these differences in Table 9.2. One of the most significant differences is the inability of CRAs to check the terrorist watch list, which we discussed in Chapter 4. Recognizing that only a small number of people who are in the TSDB have sought TWICs, some people have been denied credentials for this reason, which is an important benefit that could not be replicated without federal involvement in a credentialing process.

Table 9.2. Differences Between TSA's and CRAs' Criminal-History Record Checks

Criterion	STA	CRA
Source of identity check	Biometric (fingerprints) and biographic data (name, DOB)	Biographic data (name, DOB, social security number)
Primary source of record	Rap sheets	Court records
Consolidation of data set	Consolidated data set	Federal, state, or county-specific
Consistency of record check	Limited case resolution data, which can create false positives that must be resolved through appeals	Sources vary by firm
Ability to check the terrorist watch list	Yes	No
Recurrent vetting	Yes	Generally no
Cost	$125 for a five-year period	$50–100 per check

NOTE: DOB = date of birth.

---

[432] 49 C.F.R. § 1542.209(k)(4).

TSA currently, under its authorities in 46 U.S.C. §70105(d), can conduct a wider-reaching criminal record check than a CRA can, given its ability to access FBI data. This assumes that the facility is not capable of doing an NCIC check—which a facility operator might be able to do, depending on their relationship with law enforcement. Further, the difference between results from a criminal record check and a CRA's check of court records might narrow as court records become increasingly digitized and centralized.

An NCIC check performed by TSA and a background check conducted by a CRA draw on different sources of data to identify an applicant's criminal history. The NCIC is an automated, nationally accessible criminal justice information system maintained by the FBI.[433] NCIC's data content draws information from the Interstate Identification Index, which includes criminal records from all 50 states and the District of Columbia. This data set should include everyone arrested for felonies and serious misdemeanors. Although NCIC has a large repository of information, with more than 12 million active federal records and 85.9 million state criminal-history records, it is not necessarily comprehensive. Federal, state, local, and tribal authorities are responsible for data entry, modification, and removal.[434] The update frequency, thoroughness, and reliability of the records depend on their sources; many of these sources classify crimes differently; and criminal records often lack final case results. A report by SEARCH and the National Center for State Courts documented that state and local warrant systems fail to report a significant number of their records to NCIC, and SEARCH has also found that the NCIC system exhibits technical issues that result from its age and initial design.[435]

CRAs typically use the applicant's name, DOB, and social security number to gather criminal-history information from court data. Although it has always been possible for the public to access and examine court records, the lack of a national database of these records had made it impractical to use them as source for more-comprehensive criminal record checks historically.[436] Therefore, although "publicly accessible, [court records] enjoyed a 'practical obscurity' before statewide court-record centralization and, more importantly, the advent of digitized records."[437] Now, they are increasingly centralized and electronically accessible.[438] Although some CRAs would inspect local court records manually, increasingly popular methods include searching

---

[433] SEARCH, *Improving the National Instant Background Screening System for Firearms Purchases: Recommendations by SEARCH*, version 2, February 2013, p. 6.

[434] FBI, "National Crime Information Center (NCIC)," undated b.

[435] Dennis DeBacco and Richard Schauffler, "State Progress in Record Reporting for Firearm-Related Background Checks: Fugitives from Justice," Washington, D.C.: Bureau of Justice Statistics, National Center for State Courts, and National Consortium for Justice Information and Statistics, February 2017, p. 9; SEARCH, 2013, p. 12.

[436] James B. Jacobs, James B., *The Eternal Criminal Records*, Harvard University Press, 2015.

[437] Jacobs, 2015.

[438] Jacobs, 2015.

online public records and purchasing and examining data from courts and state repositories.[439] According to the National Center for State Courts, 44 states have at least some electronic access to court records, but they vary in terms of rules for bulk use and the extent of information provided. Not only do states vary in whether criminal record information is accessible for private companies to search;[440] in some states, state searches would not include all county-level information, requiring a county-level search as well. "Companies that sell criminal background checks range from large national firms that download bulk court data to their own proprietary criminal record databases to small companies that [search] publicly available data [online]."[441] The accuracy of their information varies greatly by vendor. The costs for private commercial checks vary significantly by vendor and jurisdiction[442] but typically ranged between $50 and $100 per check.[443] Unfortunately, little research has been done on how the results differ between NCIC and CRA background checks.

Another major difference between a privatized model and the current federal model is that the CHRC provided by the FBI now provides a recurrent vetting capability through the availability of Rap Back and TSA receives new derogatory criminal history information through IDENT. We found that not only were many facility operators unaware that TSA does continuous monitoring for TWIC holders; they believed specifically that TSA did not do so and that there was no continuous monitoring of criminal history.

A privatized model could introduce significant challenges in regulation and enforcement. A privatized model could theoretically make employers responsible for background checks. However, the employment structure in the maritime environment is highly complex, with a variety of subcontractors, individual contractors, and unionized labor and a mix of dedicated, part-time, and occasional laborers. This would make it extremely difficult for the USCG to ensure compliance with background check requirements. Alternatively, the burden could be put on facilities to ensure that a background check had been conducted. As we discuss in greater detail in the next section, a nonfederalized model would introduce redundancies for credential users who access multiple facilities.

---

[439] Marina Duane, Nancy G. La Vigne, Emily Reimal, and Mathew Lynch, *Criminal Background Checks: Impact on Employment and Recidivism*, Washington, D.C.: Urban Institute, March 1, 2017, pp. 7–8.

[440] GAO, 2015.

[441] Jacobs, 2015.

[442] Duane et al., 2017, p. 8.

[443] This range is per "Background Check Company Comparisons," *The Best Background Check Companies of 2019*, last modified January 30, 2018. This source notes, "Some providers charge set-up fees, while others make you commit to conducting a certain number of checks each year." For further information on how these prices can range depending on such factors as desired level of detail and location, see Ryan Howard, "Cost of a Background Check: How Much Should You Pay?" *VeriFirst*, June 2, 2017.

Considerations in a Hybrid Model

A hybrid credentialing model would represent a system in which TSA conducts an STA and provides the results to a maritime authority to provide a local maritime credential, rather than providing the credential directly. This is similar to the system used in the aviation industry to issue airport credentials (the SIDA badge). Each airport issues its own SIDA badges that are specific to that airport. Airports must ensure that standards similar to those of TWIC are in place for anyone with access to the SIDA. Airport authorities can also use the results of the STA to hold a more stringent standard for authorized personnel because the SIDA vetting process allows local airport authorities to see the criminal background check information pulled in the STA.[444] Unlike the example of a privatized model—in which a commercial company would not be able to check the same information used by TSA—in a hybrid model, the same derogatory information would be identified. The difference with a hybrid credentialing model is primarily one of process and cost. There is also a difference in the extent to which the credential would demonstrate business purpose. The government could also lose some of the situational awareness and quality assurance provided by a centralized issuance model. For example, TSA would have a record of people with active STAs but not necessarily of who has been issued a credential. Conversely, even though TSA currently has a list of everyone who holds a valid credential, it does not know where or even whether those credentials are in use.

In many ways, TWIC, as used by facilities, essentially operates as a semihybrid model. Because a facility is not necessarily required to permit access to anyone with a TWIC card or use the TWIC card as its primary ID card, facilities already can appreciate some of the benefits from a hybrid model. This includes setting a lower risk-tolerance standard (i.e., accepting less risk than the federal government) by conducting more-stringent background checks or considering other criteria (such as drug tests) before granting people authorized access to the facility secure area.

A truly hybrid model, in which TSA would provide STA results to a facility to evaluate applicants, could allow facilities that wish to set a lower risk-tolerance standard to do so more easily. If potentially derogatory criminal information is shared with an employer, that information can allow that employer to make a facility-specific risk-based determination about personnel access without requiring it to pay for a criminal background check to directly acquire that information. (A facility might still seek to conduct a commercial background check to identify possible criminal offenses that were not reported to the federal government, such as local misdemeanors.)

However, a completely hybrid model would likely then introduce redundancies for an unknown portion of credential holders who access multiple facilities. (The portion is unknown because self-reported positions of TWIC holders at time of enrollment are not reliable or clear

---

[444] Subcommittee on Border and Maritime Security, 2013.

162

sources of data; however, we believe that it is a sizable portion of the TWIC-holding population.) This is one area in which the maritime industry has important differences from the aviation sector. SIDA rules apply at the 440 U.S. federalized airports, which are generally distributed geographically across the United States. MTSA regulations affect 3,300 facilities that are more likely to be clustered around U.S. coastlines and major waterways. Whereas a SIDA credential holder is likely to need access to only one airport, a TWIC holder—such as a longshoreman, trucker, or support contractor—may work at multiple facilities and would need to maintain multiple credentials. In multiple interviews, respondents expressed appreciation for the consolidation provided by a single credential. Because there is no means to track where TWIC cards are being used in practice and by whom, we have no method of determining whether the efficiencies gained for facilities would outweigh the inefficiencies introduced to the population of TWIC holders. A written statement from the American Trucking Associations, the largest national trade association for the trucking industry, to Congress emphasizes the value that a universal credential, rather than multiple background checks, has for truck drivers.[445]

The government could make changes to allow greater flexibility to industry under the current semihybrid construct. Although a facility may integrate TWIC into its PACS, both the facility and the credential holder are held accountable if an unescorted person in the secure area fails to have their TWIC card with them. Therefore, many facilities that enroll TWIC holders into their PACSs and use facility credentials as the primary access badge still often ask TWIC holders to see their cards, to protect the facility from liability. The government could consider a change in regulation to require a facility to take measures to ensure that an authorized person has an active TWIC card (i.e., enrolling the TWIC card into a PACS using biometric identity verification, tracking the card's expiration date, and using the CCL to ensure that the credential is still active) but puts the responsibility of ensuring that a TWIC is physically on the person only on the shoulders of the cardholder. This could also allow greater flexibility if a card is forgotten or is inaccessible on a given day: A facility that has stored TWIC card numbers in its PACS, has biometrically identifying information, and uses the CCL could be allowed to issue temporary access cards to users on an occasional and temporary basis given that it can virtually authenticate each person's credential. Currently, the person would need to retrieve their card or be escorted in the secure area. Similar to how the USCG maintains a standard that a person accessing a facility on a regular basis should not be escorted, the USCG could require that facilities log the frequencies of these occurrences to ensure that such an accommodation is not abused.

---

[445] Subcommittee on Border and Maritime Security, 2013.

Summary

This chapter responds to questions in Public Law 114-278 about the potential for a nonbiometric credential alternative and potential redundancies between the TWIC and other transportation credentials.

The most robust security system is one that uses multifactor authentication rather than any one single measure. Given that the TWIC card is itself a possession factor and it contains a knowledge factor (the stored PIN), it would be possible to use dual-factor authentication without using a biometric factor (the stored fingerprint). Unlike knowledge and possession factors, however, inherence factors are not transferable, forgotten, or easily lost. Thus, biometric verification methods are generally considered to require more sophistication to defeat than nonbiometric ones and make for a more robust security system. This is not to say that biometrics cannot be defeated by a skilled adversary. But storing a user's biometrics on the card provides greater assurance that the holder is the same person to whom the card was issued, and it gives facilities greater flexibility in configuring their security systems.

To examine potential redundancy, we also considered other transportation security credentials that might be required of TWIC holders. We did not identify any states that currently have statewide maritime credentials, but some port authorities do issue credentials. These port credentials are not duplicative of TWIC because they are often used to establish business purpose at a facility, which TWIC does not do. With respect to other federal credentials, such as the HME, we note that allowing applicants to apply the STA to multiple TSA-managed credentialing programs could reduce costs and hassle for users. TSA is already taking steps to provide greater reciprocity for TWIC holders in acquiring HMEs.

With respect to alternative models for transportation security cards, other possible credentialing models are a hybrid model, whereby the government performs the STA but facilities apply qualifying standards, or a private model by which facilities do their own background checks. Adoption of either of these types of models would require amendments to MTSA to permit facilities to make their own credentialing decisions and to alter privacy provisions. We found that a truly hybrid model, in which TSA would provide STA results to facilities to evaluate applicants, could allow facilities that wish to set a lower risk-tolerance standard to do so more easily, but it could introduce redundancies for some credential holders who need to access multiple facilities and thus maintain multiple credentials. Given that a significant portion of the TWIC population likely moves between facilities, this is an important consideration in determining the optimal models. A privatized model would mean loss of important benefits of federal involvement in the STA process—namely, the abilities to (1) check the terrorist watch list, (2) conduct a national criminal record check using arrest records, and (3) conduct recurrent vetting for new terrorism or criminal information.

Ultimately, the TWIC program already operates somewhat in a semihybrid construct. We say that because facilities still make the ultimate decisions on whom to allow entry—a TWIC card does not entitle a person to access to a maritime facility. Furthermore, facilities can conduct additional background checks or other security inquiries, allowing them to set risk-tolerance standards most appropriate for their operations. They can also use their own physical credentials for entry to their facilities. Some options available to the government could provide greater flexibility to industry under this semihybrid construct. Currently, both TWIC holders and facilities are liable for ensuring that every unescorted person in a secure area have not only an active TWIC but also a physical TWIC card on or near their person. This means that facilities are generally still checking for TWIC cards, even if they use facility credentials, and have no ability to issue temporary unauthorized access to a credentialed cardholder who might have forgotten or be unable to access their card for the day. The government could establish a mechanism by which facilities using PACS could virtually authenticate that a person holds an active TWIC to accommodate for these circumstances.

10. Conclusion

Our efforts to provide a straightforward answer to the question of TWIC's risk-mitigation value is complicated by the fact that TWIC cannot be empirically separated from the access control programs in which it is integrated. Moreover, those access control programs and the facilities where they are used vary dramatically, so risk differs by where TWIC is employed. However, we can establish a few parameters for TWIC's potential risk-mitigation value. First, TWIC cannot mitigate all risks in the maritime environment. Instead, it can significantly influence risk only where someone must gain physical access to a facility through an entry point. TWIC might have a deterrent effect on people who do not require such access, but such a value is determined by these individuals' perceptions and is not easily estimated. Furthermore, facilities face many threats for which gaining physical access through entry points is not necessary. For example, attacks in the cyber realm, launched from the water, or using a drone would not require someone to gain physical access through an entry point. TWIC—no matter how stringent the STA standards or how robust the verification methods used at entry points— cannot reduce the risk presented by these threats.

Second, as TWIC is only a component of access control programs, TWIC's ability to mitigate threats where gaining physical access is necessary is directly related to the quality of that access control program. Let us consider the example of a truck bomb. Someone seeking to gain access to a facility with a truck bomb could attempt to enter the facility through an entry point using a valid TWIC card. But that person could also try to overcome the access control program—by using an invalid TWIC card[446] or by simply driving through the fence or access control point. The STA relates to the risk presented by the first attack pathway in that it determines who has a *valid* TWIC card. The TWIC card and the reader rule relate to the risk presented by the second attack pathway in that they could prevent someone from using an *invalid* TWIC card.[447] But the level of risk presented from this attack scenario also depends on other pieces of the access control program: the strength of the fence, the presence of bollards or a gate arm that can forcibly stop a truck from entering the facility. In these cases, TWIC cannot mitigate risk from these types of threats alone, and the extent to which it can do so is directly related to these other security measures. Yet, in these cases, TWIC can provide the benefit of

---

[446] A TWIC card could be invalid for any of a variety of reasons. It could be counterfeit, expired, canceled, or issued to a different person.

[447] The TWIC-reader rule would require that facilities use electronic biometric readers to provide greater assurance that cards were valid and belonged to the users presenting them. However, the TWIC card itself does allow for these functions using visual inspection: The card has a photograph, many security factors to verify its authenticity, a printed expiration date, and a unique ID number that can be matched to the visual CCL, a public list of canceled cards.

alerting facility personnel of an unauthorized entry, which could have an immediate benefit (e.g., if security forces could interdict the entrant) or a future benefit (e.g., by denying the entrant future access).

TWIC's risk-mitigation value could be directly related to attack scenarios in which an attack could be conducted only by an authorized person, an "insider." But even here, TWIC does not determine who facility insiders are; this decision rests with the facility operator.[448] Ideally, it would determine who they are *not* (i.e., by denying a known high-risk person a TWIC card and, thereby, facility access). However, we should caveat that a facility operator can grant anyone access—including someone denied a TWIC card—provided that a TWIC holder is escorting the person. Because a facility operator has no clear way of knowing whether someone has been denied a TWIC card, they would be unaware that such a person presented higher risk.

A determined adversary is not likely to be entirely deterred by one closed or challenging attack pathway; instead, they would seek alternative methods for conducting their attack. However, TWIC does impose costs on the adversary. A sophisticated attack of maximum consequence can require persistent insider access and multiple actors. An actor who sought to conduct this type of attack would likely need to develop a complex plan of attack and overcome the obstacles that the TWIC program presents. This conspiracy could increase the chances of detection by intelligence and law-enforcement officers and reduce the actor's likelihood of success. This is particularly true for known or suspected terrorists, who might be detected in applying for TWICs or in communicating with TWIC holders. TWIC, therefore, likely contributes to pushing threatening actors toward simpler and potentially less harmful attacks.

When considering TWIC's use at facilities and the pending requirements for high-risk facilities to further harden TWIC controls at access points, facility operators point to other potentially more-pressing vulnerabilities. Examples we heard included cybersecurity, vulnerabilities from the waterside, threats from drones, weak fencing, and threats posed by trusted insiders. Our analysis of breaches of security at facilities in the past five years suggests that detected breaches have more frequently come from means other than TWIC. This could be a testament to the success of TWIC in deterring or denying adversaries. But the frequency of use of alternative access modes is particularly important to consider given the pending rule to require more-robust security measures for TWIC.

We found that benefits brought by the TWIC-reader rule are unlikely to outweigh its costs. We assessed that the initial regulatory analysis underestimated the costs to facilities and might affect a significantly larger universe of facilities, making the rule overall more expensive to industry than initially assessed. A more favorable break-even point could be achieved by reducing the costs of compliance—for example, by requiring a facility to use an electronic reader but not require biometric identity assurance—or by reducing the number of facilities subject to

---

[448] A facility need not grant someone access simply because they have a TWIC—and in fact it should not: That person still needs a valid business purpose.

the rule. Break-even analysis, however, will never be able to tell us whether the TWIC-reader rule is "worth it," because it cannot establish how frequently a terrorist attack might occur. Terrorist attacks have occurred infrequently in the maritime realm. The TWIC-reader rule, as currently promulgated, would affect facilities that handle dangerous cargo—where dangerous materials could be released or stolen—and large–passenger vessel facilities—where an adversary would have access to a large number of people. In neither case, however, is the threat specific to the maritime arena. The same dangerous cargoes might be accessible in more-vulnerable environments (for example, when being driven out of the facility, or at a facility without a dock). If an adversary wished to cause a massive loss of life by attacking a large–passenger vessel facility, they could do it as passengers are embarking or disembarking. If an adversary wished simply to find a cluster of people, there are many more-vulnerable targets, including malls, parks, sporting events, and tourist attractions. That is to say, these locations could be targets of deadly attacks but for reasons separate and distinct from their maritime character.

The TWIC program affects a very large population—nearly 2.3 million people, 3,300 facilities, and 14,000 vessels. In establishing the TWIC program, Congress highlighted ports' vulnerability to risks of terrorism and federal crime, such as trafficking. Congress also highlighted how ports are international boundaries, where hazards from abroad could enter the United States. In considering examples, such as San Pedro Bay Port Complex—the adjacent ports of Los Angeles and Long Beach, which combined create the sixth-busiest container complex in the world and affect an estimated 32 percent of U.S. market share[449]—or the Houston Port Complex—moving 247 million tons of cargo through a sometimes-narrow 52-mile-long ship channel—it is easy to see how ports can be vital to the U.S. economy and be critical infrastructure to protect. Conversely, it can be difficult to see why a dock receiving barges located on an inland waterway 1,000 miles from the ocean and accessed by a half-dozen company employees would be the target of an adversary or facilitate drug trafficking, and especially why it would require an electronic biometric reader.

In establishing TWIC requirements, Congress spoke to concerns about TSIs. What constitutes a TSI—particularly a "significant loss of life"—is defined very differently by even the organizations implementing the TWIC program. The extent to which TWIC is intended to mitigate risk in the maritime environment is unclear. This leaves us without a standard by which to judge TWIC's success.

It also leaves us unable to determine whether TWIC is exceeding its mandate. We suggest that, even if TWIC were significantly reducing the risks of violent or property crime at maritime facilities—and, with the lack of systematic data on this issue, we cannot judge its contributions to this end—that reduction would not be sufficient to justify the TWIC program, given that this is not a stated objective of the TWIC program. The federal government's regulations regarding

---

[449] Caltrans, "Freight Planning Fact Sheet: Port of Los Angeles," January 2014; Port of Los Angeles, "2018 Facts and Figures," c. 2019.

access control programs at maritime facilities inherently put limitations on private industry, so any security gains inherently come with trade-offs that Congress should consider.

We would further suggest that TWIC is strongest when it provides flexibility and options to the maritime industry. Examples of such accommodations are USCG regulations that allow facilities to integrate TWIC into their PACSs, TSA's development of a mobile application that allows cards to be checked against the CCL, the provision of waivers for people who have disqualifying criteria but are found not to pose a security risk, and the planned provision for facility-specific data to be stored on the TWIC card. To further provide flexibility to industry, DHS and its components could explore the feasibility of other initiatives. This could include furthering reciprocity between federally issued credentials and benefit programs (such as HME and TSA Pre✓). Another possibility is providing an option other than escorting for facilities to allow access to credential holders who might be temporarily without their TWIC cards.

Summary of Conclusions About Public Law 114-278

The purpose of this study was to satisfy the requirements for a comprehensive security assessment of the TWIC program called for in Section 1(b) of Public Law 114-278. In the preceding chapters, we have covered a variety of elements of the TWIC program relevant to Congress's questions. In conclusion, we present the law's questions in sequence and recap our previous findings related to each. Section 1(b)(3) lays out the necessary contents of this report:

> (3) CONTENTS.—The assessment commissioned under paragraph (1) shall—
> (A) review the credentialing process by determining—(i) the appropriateness of vetting standards; (ii) whether the fee structure adequately reflects the current costs of vetting; (iii) whether there is unnecessary redundancy or duplication with other Federal- or State-issued transportation security credentials; and (iv) the appropriateness of having varied Federal and State threat assessments and access controls; (B) review the process for renewing applications for Transportation Worker Identification Credentials, including the number of days it takes to review application, appeal, and waiver requests for additional information; and (C) review the security value of the Program by—(i) evaluating the extent to which the Program, as implemented, addresses known or likely security risks in the maritime and port environments; (ii) evaluating the potential for a non-biometric credential alternative; (iii) identifying the technology, business process, and operational impacts of the use of the transportation security card and transportation security card readers in the maritime and port environments; (iv) assessing the costs and benefits of the Program, as implemented; and (v) evaluating the extent to which the Secretary of Homeland Security has addressed the deficiencies in the Program identified by the Government Accountability Office and the Inspector General of the Department of Homeland Security before the date of enactment of this Act.

Section 1(b)(3)(A)(i): Review the Appropriateness of the Vetting Standards

To determine whether vetting standards are appropriate, we considered their suitability for the program's intended purpose. An inappropriate standard could be one that does too much or too little to achieve program goals. The law and congressional record related to the TWIC program lay out a few purposes for the TWIC program:

- Help prevent a high-consequence attack in the transportation environment (i.e., a TSI).
- Identify people who pose a national security, transportation security, or terrorism threat.
- Help deny those people access to the maritime sector.

Such a threat could likely come from a nation-state actor, a terrorist actor, or criminal organization. Our interviews suggest that many facility operators sought another benefit from their access control programs: to enhance security generally at their facilities. In our study, we considered the consistency, and sometimes mismatch, among the vetting standards, congressional goals, and industry goals.

In Chapter 2, we laid out the vetting process of the TWIC program. TWIC applicants are screened for ties to the population of known or suspected terrorists, for certain criminal offenses, and for legal immigration status, as required by 46 U.S.C. § 70105 and according to the standards in 49 C.F.R. § 1572.5. The initial determination of eligibility assumes that anyone with a disqualifying criminal history or immigration status could present a security risk. An applicant can seek redress via appeal if they feel that they have been improperly disqualified for a TWIC card or via a waiver if they feel that, despite meeting certain disqualification criteria, they do not present a security risk. It is only in the case of someone seeking a waiver or initially being identified as having possible ties to terrorism that TSA would investigate or evaluate the security risk presented by a specific person, given the specific details of their character or personal history, as opposed to basing a risk decision on the existence of a risk factor. TWIC holders are continuously monitored for connections to terrorism, and most—and, in the future, all—of the TWIC population is monitored for new criminal convictions via the DHS IDENT database. Credentials are valid for a period of five years. Credential holders who lose eligibility per recurrent vetting are added to the CCL, as is the holder of any credential reported lost or stolen.

Around 98 percent of people who apply for TWICs are granted one.[450] We cannot determine the number of people who decided not to seek TWIC cards—for either employment or nefarious purposes—because they believed that they might not be granted and therefore did not see the benefit in providing a nonrefundable $125.25 application fee or PII to the federal government.

Some people we interviewed argued that standards were insufficient to identify applicants who present a *general security risk*. Industry respondents were often speaking about their

---

[450] This number is based on TWIC enrollments for January 1, 2015, through October 1, 2018, for people who were initially approved, approved on appeal, or approved with waivers. For a breakdown of these numbers, see Figure 2.2 in Chapter 2.

expectations of the TWIC program—namely, their security standards, which included reducing the risk that an employee would harm other people at, damage material at, or steal from the facility. In the words of one respondent, even if

> it's quite unlikely that a guy that beats his wife will have any links to terrorism ... you [don't] want to work with that guy though, because he's violent. You don't want to work with that guy if he may beat you with a hammer. At the end of the day, I just don't think [TWIC vetting standards are] sufficient.[451]

Similarly, some respondents stated that they believed that the vetting standards would not protect them from an active-shooter threat, such as a disgruntled employee, which they saw as more likely than terrorism. Facilities who felt the standards were insufficient would therefore contract for a separate criminal record check (performed by a commercial vendor) to identify criminal offenses that were not disqualifying for a TWIC or perform other types of checks—such as drug tests—to determine whether someone presented a security (or safety) risk.

The sentiment that TWIC's standards do too little was not universal, and some facilities found TWIC's standard sufficient, particularly for those with limited levels of access at a facility. For example, some facilities rely solely on the TWIC vetting for truck drivers making deliveries but conduct separate background checks for company employees with sustained access to the facility. At approximately two-thirds of facilities whose representatives we interviewed, the facility conducted a separate background check for at least some part of the population. Given that we weighted our interview sample toward high-risk facilities, we would anticipate there being a higher proportion of low-risk facilities that accept TWIC as the vetting standard.

Alternatively, an argument is sometimes made that TWIC standards do more than meet their intended purpose. The criminal vetting standards likely disqualify a significant number of people who do not present a threat to national security or transportation security or of terrorism, given that the number of people who present such a threat is very small. Our review of the literature suggests that past criminality and incarceration are not strong predictors of future terrorism. As described above, some in industry value criminal standards to reduce the risk that an employee would cause harm to another, damage material at the facility, or steal from the facility. However, other facility operators are willing to accept significant risk from such people—given that the facility might have goods of low value and few employee interactions—and, in these cases, criminal-history standards sometimes disqualify prospective job candidates. In the words of one respondent, "the disqualifying offenses? I'm not saying they're not serious—they are—but is there a nexus to terrorism?"[452]

Determining whether standards are as appropriate as possible requires a clear understanding of what TWIC is—and is not—intended to achieve. Most people we interviewed felt that the TWIC program made some contribution to the security of the maritime environment and,

---

[451] Interview with the terminal manager and FSO for a cruise facility.

[452] Interview with a member of a labor association.

therefore, that the vetting standards were not wholly inappropriate. Recognizing that the federal government and industry might sometimes have different objectives also means that there might be inherent trade-offs between (1) how stringent the criminal-history standards are and (2) how satisfied stakeholders are with the TWIC program. Overall, TWIC standards and the redress process attempt to strike a balance between the two. This balance trends toward a higher risk tolerance given that a single vetting standard must apply to the entire population working in the maritime sector—a population of around 2 million people—and that facilities can choose to adopt additional criteria beyond TWIC vetting standards to satisfy their specific security needs.

Section 1(b)(3)(A)(ii): Review the Fee Structure and the Cost of Vetting

Informed by our review of program's revenue, cost, and carryover data for FYs 2016, 2017, and 2018, we assessed that the TWIC fee structure is currently adequate. TWIC user fees have aligned reasonably well with per-enrollment costs. In FYs 2016 and 2017, user fees exceeded average cost per enrollment by 13 to 23 percent. In FY 2018, costs exceeded revenue by about $600,000, but the deficit was covered by the $60 million the program was holding as carryover.

Section 1(b)(3)(A)(iii): Find Any Unnecessary Redundancy or Duplication with Other Transportation Credentials

In considering whether there are unnecessarily redundant or duplicative transportation credentials, we defined *duplicative* as the same in purpose, function, and standard; *redundant* as similar in purpose, function, and standard; and *unnecessarily redundant* as providing a similar risk-reducing effect without providing additional benefits.

We found no duplicative credentials. An overlapping federal credential to TWIC is HME, with around 21 percent of the total HME population and 12 percent of the total TWIC population carrying both credentials. HME also requires a knowledge-based test on hazmat, and the TWIC fee adds a card credential. There is redundancy between these programs in that they use the same vetting standards. The current process provides a marginal reduction in fees for anyone seeking a reciprocal credential and has no process for an applicant to seek both credentials at the same time for a single fee. The 2018 TSA Modernization Act, if implemented, would improve reciprocity by allowing someone with a TWIC to get an HME without an additional TSA fee; it is unclear whether there will be changes in reciprocity for HME holders seeking TWICs. Given that these credentials confer different benefits on users and that there is also a need to determine whether an HME holder has knowledge of how to handle the HME, we would not describe these credentials as unnecessarily redundant.

We found no state that issued a statewide maritime credential. Some port authorities, operated at the state, county, or municipal level, issue port-specific credentials. Private facilities also often issue facility- or company-specific credentials. Whereas the TWIC card serves primarily as an ID badge and proof of an STA, these port- and facility-specific credentials serve primarily to establish business purpose at facilities or relate to company-related business (such as managing timekeeping). We would not consider these credentials redundant of TWIC because they have different purposes, functions, and standards.

Section 1(b)(3)(A)(iv): Determine the Appropriateness of Having Varying Threat Assessments and Access Control

As discussed in our review of the appropriateness of vetting standards, industry and the federal government can have different objectives for the threat assessments conducted as part of the TWIC program (beyond national security risks, transportation security risks, and terrorism risks). Further, the USCG has determined that security risk varies among maritime facilities based on the facility's specific threats, vulnerabilities, and consequences. For example, the national security risk presented by a facility handling a toxic, airborne substance is higher if that facility is adjacent to a large population area than it would be in an isolated location. Therefore, it is appropriate that there would be different standards applied at the federal and facility levels so that facilities may choose standards that best match their risk profile. Similarly, it is appropriate for states to apply different threat assessment standards from federal standards when objectives go beyond the scope of the TWIC program. As discussed in Chapter 9, there are several options for conducting background checks outside of TSA's STA. However, we are not privy to the extent to which the outputs of these background checks differ from the output of TSA's STA, and little research has been done in this area to compare the results between federal and commercial background checks. Therefore, we did not evaluate the substitutability of these different background checks.

Facilities also vary in their levels of risk tolerance, which would affect their levels of investment in security measures. Let us take the example of a RORO facility that exports and imports luxury vehicles. Although the government might assess this facility to be low risk in terms of a TSI, the facility might put significant investment in security measures that prevent one of its expensive vehicles from being stolen. Given these facility-by-facility differences in nature of the risk, level of risk, and risk tolerance, it is wholly appropriate that their access control systems would vary, and be customized, to best meet the needs of each facility.

TWIC establishes the standard for acceptable risk to national security, transportation security, and of terrorism, in terms of authorized personnel in secure areas. A facility may hold authorized personnel to additional standards—by having additional disqualifying criteria for access—but it cannot grant unescorted access to the secure area to someone whom the government has deemed a security risk. Insofar as TWIC provides facilities options in how it can be integrated into existing access control systems, TWIC allows facility operators flexibility in customizing an access control system that is appropriately suited to risk type, risk level, and risk tolerance of a particular facility.

Section 1(b)(3)(B): Assess the Length of Time to Review TWIC Applications

Public Law 114-278 instructs that the assessment ask about the length of the process for renewing applications for TWICs, but, given that there is no renewal specific process for the TWIC program—the application process is the same for new and former TWIC holders—we considered this question in the context of the application process for all applicants. As we discussed in Chapter 5, TSA provided a report to Congress in February 2019 addressing the concerns raised in the law on the length of time to review applications.[453] This report illustrates that almost every TWIC application receives an initial adjudication result within 30 days. TSA determined that the average processing time for redress applications for the first nine months of 2018 was 26 days for appeal requests and 47 days for waiver requests. These averages have improved considerably since passage of Public Law 114-278 in 2016.

Section 1(b)(3)(C)(i): Assess TWIC's Addressal of Known and Likely Maritime Security Risks

There is a large number of combinations of potential: threat actors, desired outcomes of attacks, and methods of attack. TWIC is designed for and is capable of protecting against some of these combinations more than others. The TWIC program is strongest in reducing the risk presented by someone who is a known or suspected terrorist who seeks to conduct an attack on a maritime facility that would require persistent insider access via possession of a TWIC. The STA process would detect such an individual, which would presumably result in the TWIC being denied, and it would be difficult for such an individual to maintain continual access to a facility without a valid TWIC card. The TWIC card is similarly effective in reducing the risk from a criminal with a disqualifying criminal history who would have been willing to engage in illicit activity at the facility, such as smuggling, that might aid a terrorist group. TWIC's effectiveness in achieving this goal is largely similar with or without an electronic card reader. Although readers would reduce the human error in detecting a counterfeit TWIC or a TWIC being used by someone other than the person to whom it was issued, competent security guards should, at some point, detect these people seeking to gain entry over an extended duration of time. The major exception to this case would be someone who had initially passed the STA, been issued a valid TWIC, and been found to have possible terrorist ties prior to the card's expiration. In circumstances in which this person's TWIC card was revoked but could not be recovered by law-enforcement officials, use of an electronic card reader in conjunction with the CCL would dramatically increase the chances of detection.

---

[453] TSA, 2019.

The TWIC program is less effective at stopping threats for which an attacker (or attackers) seeks one-time access to the facility to conduct an attack and is not easily deterred in gaining entry. Even if such an attacker were unable to legally obtain a TWIC, they could attempt to present an invalid card and test the access control system. The attacker could also engage the services of an escort, if permitted by the facility, to gain access and then depart from or overcome the escort. Alternatively, the attacker could use brute force to overcome any access control measures presented at the gate, including any mechanism to verify TWIC cards. The TWIC program might provide some additional ability to detect these threats, but the ability to *prevent* such a threat is dependent on other mechanisms of the access control program, such as the guard, PACS, or deployable physical barriers. An TWIC card reader could increase the likelihood that an invalid TWIC card is detected, but it alone does not increase the access control program's ability to prevent entry. The attacker could also attempt to gain access to the secure facility via a route that did not require a TWIC card (e.g., a remote section of fence or a waterside entry point).

A TWIC program with robust access control technology would still fail to detect the threat posed by someone with a "clean" history (i.e., someone who was not known to authorities). As we discussed in Chapter 4, the most likely terrorist attack within the United States today is seen as coming from HVEs. Because HVEs are often self-radicalized using terrorist propaganda available online, they might elude the attention of intelligence and law-enforcement authorities.

Section 1(b)(3)(C)(ii): Assess the Potential for a Nonbiometric Alternative

Regarding a nonbiometric credential alternative, we considered the benefits brought by the current storage of biometric information (two fingerprints) on the integrated circuit chip of the TWIC card. Biometrics have been found a superior method of identity verification. This is not to say biometrics are not invulnerable to spoofing or defeating, but they do provide a sophisticated mechanism for dual-factor authentication. Without the biometric information, TWIC cards would still have the means of assisting in dual-factor authentication options using the saved PIN; however, these PINs are generally not used at this time and are more transferable to other users, such as a bad actor improperly using someone else's TWIC card. Our analysis of past breaches of security suggests that there are instances in which people have attempted to use other people's cards. We cannot determine the extent to which the stored biometric information might provide an added deterrence to this type of activity.

The stored biometric information also gives facilities flexibility in how to integrate TWIC into their access control procedures. Facility management seeking to use biometric verification methods could still collect biometric information at time of enrollment, but it would not have the same level of assurance that the person presenting the credential was the person who initially applied for a TWIC card and was processed through the STA. Removing the biometrics would also eliminate the ability for portable, stand-alone readers to be used to conduct spot checks using biometrics, which TSA, the USCG, and facilities can currently do.

Section 1(b)(3)(C)(iii): Determine the Impact of TWIC Cards and TWIC Readers

The flow of commerce and security in the maritime and port environment differ from those in other environments in quite a few significant ways. However, what is not unique is the tension between security on the one hand and, on the other, ease of movement and doing a job. This tension is common in physical security, as well as cybersecurity and classified security. We take as an inherent assumption of any transportation security card program that it would have some negative impact on the flow of commerce, but such a program could be tailored so that the negative impacts are outweighed by the benefits brought by reducing the risk that commerce would suffer catastrophic shocks or chronic strain from illegal actions. At issue, then, is whether the TWIC program has found that balance.

The transportation security card program was introduced more than ten years ago, and there have been significant improvements in the enrollment process and card quality since then. Given this extended evolution, it was difficult for us to ascertain what the operational impact has been of the introduction of the transportation card program. This impact is further varied depending on facility practice prior to the introduction of the TWIC program. For some facilities, there was little semblance of an access control program prior to the introduction of the TWIC program, and facility operators often found the establishment of clear access control procedures a security benefit. For respondents from facilities that already had robust access control measures, differences brought by the program appear to be less apparent. Indeed, if we suppose that the facility might have had similar, or higher, criminal-history standards in place prior to TWIC and that the facility has continued to use a facility-specific access control credential, the major impact of introducing TWIC is the exclusion of people with known or suspected ties to terrorism. Because people with such ties are rare, the TWIC program might present no realized difference in who is accessing these facilities.

Given improvements made in the enrollment process, the operational impact of applying for TWICs did not appear to be a major concern across facilities. Operational impacts of the current implementation of the TWIC program primarily related to (1) the durability of the TWIC card and (2) the necessity of a TWIC holder physically having their credential, which could introduce redundancies for a facility using a PACS and facility-specific credential and extra costs when a credential holder forgets or loses their card.

In Chapter 8, we reviewed the cost and benefit of requiring TWIC readers at maritime facilities. We replicated the method that the USCG used to examine the costs to facilities in using readers. The previous regulatory analysis had only limited data from a TWIC pilot; our incorporation of additional data sources shows that the costs of TWIC readers are higher than originally estimated. This, in combination with the fact that the TWIC-reader rule could affect many more facilities than originally estimated, suggests that the rule could put a high cost burden on industry that is unlikely to be recovered in benefit. Industry has also had mixed experiences in the reliability of reader technology. The pending status of the TWIC-reader rule has contributed to volatility in the demand for TWIC readers. Some of the readers previously identified as on the QTL are outdated or no longer available.

Section 1(b)(3)(C)(iv): Review the Costs and Benefits of the TWIC Program

As we identified in Chapter 7, the TWIC program cannot alone have a security benefit. The TWIC program exists as one security measure in a complex system facing an adaptive adversary. TWIC plays a role in mitigating only some threats. According to our site survey and as presented in Chapters 4 and 5, most facility interviewees did see some practical benefit from access control programs and background checks, including TWIC. For some, the specific standards of the STA were sufficient. For others, the STA set too low of a bar in reducing security risk broadly. For management at those facilities, who might not recognize or put a high value in the federal government's unique capabilities in terrorism vetting, TWIC is redundant with the private background checks conducted internally and a regulatory cost rather than a security benefit.

Section 1(b)(3)(C)(v): Address Previous GAO and OIG Concerns

Public Law 114-278 also requires that the assessment consider the extent to which the deficiencies in the TWIC program that GAO and OIG identified prior to 2017 have been remedied. As we discussed in Chapter 3, themes in those reports related to the need to demonstrate TWIC's risk-reduction value, better calculate TWIC costs, improve internal controls and management practices of the TWIC program, and consider alternative models to the program. According to our previous study on the TWIC program and the feedback we received in our interviews regarding TWIC holders' experiences with the program, many of the issues related to the program's management have been improved. In conducting this study, we sought to address many of GAO's other questions: Appraise the risk-reduction value of the program, examine the appropriateness of TWIC vetting standards, and assess the trade-offs in using alternative models.

GAO's open recommendations relate primarily to the need to conduct a comprehensive assessment on the TWIC program—recommendations we aimed to satisfy through this study. Those questions focus on the extent to which TWIC, as currently implemented and as envisioned under the TWIC-reader rule, enhance the security posture of maritime facilities. As discussed at great length in this report, such a question is not simple to answer. The TWIC program as currently implemented can enhance facilities' security posture by improving identity assurance and vetting people who are higher risk. The extent to which TWIC enhances a specific facility's security posture depends on what access control procedures it was using prior to TWIC's introduction or would use in TWIC's absence. It also depends on the extent to which the facility takes advantages of options provided by the TWIC program beyond simply visual inspection of the TWIC card. We are skeptical that, under the regulation's current parameters, the TWIC-reader rule would bring greater benefits than its costs. Our assessment suggests that there is not a one-size-fits-all solution for improving security at maritime facilities, given their broad differences in risk and operations. The current process of facility-specific security assessments and security plans is designed to enable flexible solutions specific to each facility's needs. Greater identity assurance methods might be appropriate for some facilities, given their risk profiles. Transparent management of the TWIC program with a focus on how to effectively support TWIC's stakeholders could incentivize industry to maximize TWIC's potential security benefit.

Appendix A. Port and Facility Interviews

This appendix describes our site selection and facility interview sampling approach. To develop the initial list of ports, we used a combination of publicly available data sets, internal federal agency data, and subject-matter expertise from the USCG, TSA, and DHS overall. The goal of this effort was to identify a sample of ports and facilities that might best represent typical and relevant atypical TWIC operations (such as an innovative use of the TWIC card or an early technology adopter). However, because the maritime space is so complex, we were not able to develop a representative sample that covered the entire space of relevant attributes within the timeline and scope of this assessment. We instead focused on a few attributes to develop our sample (with input from DHS, USCG, and TSA SMEs) with the intent of speaking to facility operators and security managers who might represent the diversity of opinions about the TWIC program and of facility operations but not necessarily the preponderance of either of these.

We begin by describing the data sources and the candidate selection criteria that informed our site selection. Next, we outline our sampling methods and the final list of ports that were visited.[454] We then briefly discuss our interview approach and formal interview coding methods.

Data Sources

We used a combination of publicly available data sources and data sets internal to TSA and the USCG to inform our port selection process. No publicly available data sets addressed the universe of MTSA-regulated facilities, some of which do not fall under the authority of a port. Instead, data sets typically covered the largest ports, as defined by various measures. Table A.1 summarizes the data sources and briefly describes the data elements.

---

[454] To protect participants' identities, we do not include the final list of specific facilities that we visited within those ports.

Table A.1. Summary of Data Sources

Source	Description	Number of Ports Covered
Port Performance Freight Statistics Program, Bureau of Transportation Statistics[a]	Annual report provided to Congress on port capacity and throughput on 25 U.S. ports with the highest total tonnage, most TEUs, and most dry bulk	49[b]
	Port profiles for 49 ports, including data on cargo (total tonnage and TEUs) and throughput capacity (commodities and vessel calls)	
NDC, Waterborne Commerce Statistics Center[c]	Several data sets managed by the U.S. Army Corps of Engineers that focus on total tonnage and TEU, by port	Total tonnage: 150 TEUs: 71
U.S. Census Bureau trade data[d]	Customs value of imports and exports, in U.S. dollars, by commodity type and by port	374
American Association of Port Authorities[e]	Cruise industry statistics from 2016, including numbers of ship calls and annual passengers	44
Port websites	Individual port websites providing general descriptions of ports, including geography, industry and commodities supported, organizational management, and additional statistics on cargo and throughput capacity	
TWIC card enrollment data[f]	Enrollment data, by enrollment center	N/A
USCG facility risk category[g]	List of facilities, by risk group (A, B, and C) according to the TWIC-reader rule	All applicable ports with MTSA-regulated facilities

NOTE: TEU = 20-foot-equivalent unit. NDC = Navigation and Civil Works Decision Support Center. N/A = not applicable.
[a] Bureau of Transportation Statistics, U.S. Department of Transportation, "Port Profiles," undated.
[b] At a minimum, the report needs to include data on the nation's 25 top producing ports but can include more. We used the 2018 annual report (Chambers et al., 2019). The reference for the 49 port profiles is Bureau of Transportation Statistics, undated.
[c] Institute for Water Resources, "NDC: Navigation and Civil Works Decision Support," undated.
[d] USA Trade, "USA Trade Online," undated.
[e] American Association of Port Authorities, "Port Industry Statistics," undated.
[f] TSA I&A, Maritime Branch.
[g] USCG Headquarters, Cargo and Facilities Division, Office of Port and Facility Compliance.

Site Selection Criteria

We considered several port and facility attributes as candidate selection criteria. We generated the list of attributes through a combination of efforts, including exploratory analysis of the data sets described in the prior section; expert judgment from the Maritime Branch of TSA I&A and the USCG for attributes that might best capture the maritime and port security environment and TWIC program operations; and discussions with internal experts on risk-assessment approaches and important maritime threats.

The port environment is a complex space with many dimensions, so developing a representative sample from ports to answer the set of research questions relevant to this assessment quickly became very difficult. To support analytic rigor and to be able to complete port visits within the project timeline and budget, we decided to limit the number of dimensions used to choose ports. As stated above, we developed our sample with the intent of speaking with facility operators and security managers who might represent the diversity of opinions about the TWIC program and of facility operations. Table A.2 provides a list of the attributes we considered, a description of each attribute, and a brief summary of why we used or did not use the attribute to inform our initial site selection sample. (We discuss our sampling method in more detail in the following section.) Using the study team's subject-matter expertise, we narrowed our primary dimensions to volume of traffic, commodity type, and geographic region, using the USCG district organizational structure as a guide. Where feasible, we considered additional dimensions, such as TWIC enrollments and facility risk group, to round out the list to ensure that our sample captured the diversity of ports.

Table A.2. Summary of Candidate Port and Facility Attributes for Site Selection

Attribute	Description	Included	Reason for Decision
Location	Geographic location, with latitude and longitude coordinates	x	Accounting for regional differences in the sample was important
Physical size	The acreage of the port or facility and whether that acreage was contiguous		No comprehensive data on the physical sizes of ports or facilities were readily available
Volume of traffic	The average annual throughput, in tonnage or TEUs, at the port or facility[a]	x	This was important for capturing variable rates of operations across the United States.
Facility or commodity type	The primary type of commodity transported through the facility		This can vary dramatically by port, so we deemed it not well suited as a dimension at the port level. We did use this before each visit to inform which specific facilities we visited at each port.
Foreign versus domestic commerce breakdown	The share of foreign versus domestic commerce reported for a port		We deemed this not particularly relevant for characterizing the variability in port operations or understanding how TWIC has been implemented.
Organizational management	The ownership structure (i.e., operating port, landlord port, or hybrid)		No comprehensive data on organizational management structures at ports were available.
Incidents and reported terrorism threats	The number of credible (as determined by a federal agency) reported terrorism threats or incidents		No terrorism incidents have occurred in the U.S. maritime environment.
Attack value	A target's significance to a would-be terrorist; could be symbolic value or the value of maximizing loss of life or economic disruption		No comprehensive data exist on ports and facilities to assign an attack value, a priori.

Attribute	Description	Included	Reason for Decision
Accessibility	The ease of access to the port, based on such factors as the geographic location of the port, the physical security measures in place, and the use of access control technologies		There was no readily available way to assess this prior to visiting the port or facility.
USCG facility risk classification	The risk category that the USCG assigned to a facility in its analysis that informed the TWIC-reader rule	x	Although risk category is not assigned at the port level, we still used this to inform port selection to ensure that the sample sufficiently characterized the perspective on the program and the implications of the pending TWIC-reader rule.
TWIC enrollments	TWIC enrollment numbers, by enrollment center and by job identification	x	This was important for determining the distribution of TWIC holders.
Innovative use of TWIC or access control measures	This could include early adopters of reader technologies and biometrics or other access control measures beyond what MTSA or TWIC requires or the pending TWIC-reader rule would require.	x	This was important for understanding the full range of how TWIC has been implemented and what drives decisions about to innovative uses of TWIC.

[a] We did consider including vessel calls as a measure of volume of traffic, but, informed by SME opinion, we limited this measure to tonnage or TEUs.

Sampling Methods

To develop our initial sample of ports, we used a combination of stratified, judgment and expert, and extreme and deviant case sampling. The stratified sampling method helped us ensure that our sample of ports reasonably covered the range of port sizes and geographic characteristics. Because the port environment is a complex space, we also elicited expert judgment from the USCG and TSA to ensure that our stratified sample appropriately covered the diversity of TWIC operations and the relevant maritime threat environment. Finally, we used extreme and deviant case sampling to include certain locations where we learned of innovative implementations of the TWIC program or other access control measures to provide an opportunity to observe outliers.

Using the NDC data set for total tonnage and TEUs, we first analyzed the summary statistics for volume of traffic and commodity, then assigned a size (small, medium, or large) to each port on the list.[455] We then used the USCG district as a geographic dimension, selecting as least one large and one medium port from each district.[456] We also included some small ports in the

---

[455] We also reviewed U.S. Census Bureau trade data on imports and exports for U.S. ports but chose to use the NDC data as the primary source for the size of the port because the customs value might not necessarily be an accurate representation of the volume of traffic at any given port or facility. We note, however, that customs value could have implications for the level of crime or a target's attractiveness to a terrorist wanting to inflict economic harm.

[456] We treated USCG District 8 differently because of its geographic spread, which spans 26 states, including the Gulf of Mexico coastline from Florida to Mexico; the adjacent offshore waters and OCS; and the inland waterways

182

sample but did not include one from each district because our data set did not have a small port in each district and because we were limited by the number of visits we could realistically complete within the project timeline and budget.

We sampled more heavily from large ports because they have high volumes of both commodities and people, which might make them higher-value targets for a terrorist attack or other TSI. Additionally, large ports handle different types of cargo, which allowed the study team to observe, at a single port differences, in TWIC operations for different cargo types and how potential vulnerability might vary across cargo types.

Cruise terminals were also important to consider in our sample, given the unique nature of the cruise industry and the fact that cruise ships are typically, although not exclusively, the vessels and facilities affected by the final TWIC-reader rule stipulation on vessels certified to carry more than 1,000 passengers. Because cruise terminals are not represented in the NDC data set, we separately selected cruise terminals of different sizes of operations (high, medium, and low) using passenger and ship call data from the American Association of Port Authorities and our team's subject-matter expertise. We then compared this stratified list of cruise operations with the list of ports we selected using the tonnage data from NDC. There was significant overlap between the lists; where there appeared to be a gap in the strata, we added a port from the cruise list to our sample list.

We also included some ports with unique characteristics. For example, we included Savannah, Georgia, because we learned of an innovative use of a biometric-enabled PACS. We also sought to include at least some ports and facilities that participated in the initial reader pilot program.

Finally, to round out our sample, we used TWIC enrollment data, by geographic location of enrollment center, as a proxy marker for location of TWIC users and USCG facility risk group categories for insight into risk variance across ports. To ensure that, in this initial site selection process, we did not miss any unique aspects of the industry, we vetted our initial list of ports for field visits with USCG representatives at the regional level, as well as with TSA and DHS overall.

Port and Facility Interviews

The HSOAC research team conducted 200 semistructured interviews that covered 164 facilities across 45 ports and port districts (characterized below). Each interview was conducted by one interview lead with one or more notetakers. Interviews were conducted over the phone or in person during site visits and could include one or more interviewees. Participation in our study was voluntary, and we provided each interviewee an assurance of confidentiality. We made an effort to ask questions in a structured, consistent manner from the

---

of the Mississippi, Ohio, Missouri, Illinois, and Tennessee River systems. Given that, we selected more facilities in this district than in the others.

interview discussion guide (discussed briefly at the end of this appendix), which we organized around themes that we believed were important in answering the questions in Public Law 114-278. However, for several reasons, including time constraints, the respondent's knowledge of the topic, or the applicability of the question to the facility or port, we were not always able to ask the same set of questions to every respondent in the same way. As such, we cannot provide quantitative analysis for every theme addressed in the interviews. Almost every member of our research team participated in a site visit, and at least one member of a core travel team was on every site visit, ensuring that we had a core team who had observed consistencies and differences across the maritime environment.

Participants

Our interviews were predominantly with FSOs and security managers. By law, an FSO is required to have knowledge of the security organization of the facility, security systems and their operational limitations, security assessment methodology, current security threats, and TWIC requirements.[457] Many FSOs have prior experience in the military, the USCG, or law enforcement. The FSO is an important data source for understanding how the TWIC card is validated and authenticated at a facility, the PACS that a facility has in place, what additional background checks that facility might perform, and the specifics of a facility's security plan and security assessment. The FSO can also speak to facility-specific security concerns and give their thoughts on how the TWIC program plays a role in mitigating risks at the facility, but not necessarily TWIC's risk-mitigation value overall. We also conducted interviews with local facility operators; corporate security personnel; union representatives of labor groups and trade associations; and representatives from law enforcement, the USCG, and TSA. In the following sections, we list the final sample of ports that we visited, briefly describe our team's development of the interview discussion guide, and discuss our approach to qualitative coding of the interview notes and theme extraction.

Facility Sample Description

The set of ports we actually visited varied slightly from our initial selection. In some cases, we added ports near those we had originally selected (for example, Houston was on our list, and contacts there connected us with FSOs at Freeport, which had not been on our original list). To maintain the integrity of our stratified sample, when we could not visit a selected port, we substituted another port with similar characteristics. Figure A.1 shows a map of the port areas covered in our interviews. In each case, we visited one or more facilities in the port area; we might or might not have interviewed the port authority, if any, in that location.

---

[457] 33 C.F.R. § 105.205.

Figure A.1. Final List of Port Areas Covered in Interviews

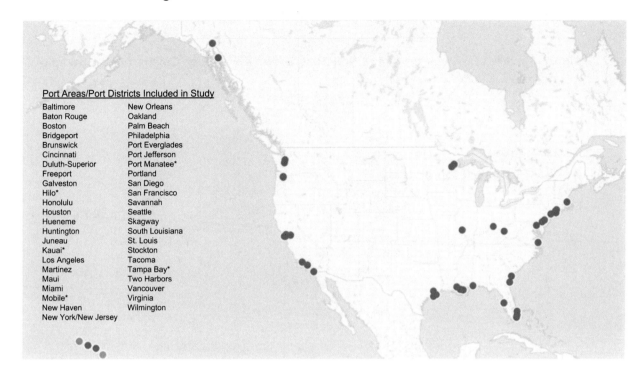

Port Areas/Port Districts Included in Study

Baltimore	New Orleans
Baton Rouge	Oakland
Boston	Palm Beach
Bridgeport	Philadelphia
Brunswick	Port Everglades
Cincinnati	Port Jefferson
Duluth-Superior	Port Manatee*
Freeport	Portland
Galveston	San Diego
Hilo*	San Francisco
Honolulu	Savannah
Houston	Seattle
Hueneme	Skagway
Huntington	South Louisiana
Juneau	St. Louis
Kauai*	Stockton
Los Angeles	Tacoma
Martinez	Tampa Bay*
Maui	Two Harbors
Miami	Vancouver
Mobile*	Virginia
New Haven	Wilmington
New York/New Jersey	

* = A facility tour was not conducted, but either a phone conversation or in-person interview took place.

Our interviews covered 164 facilities at the 45 port areas shown in Figure A.1. Facilities ranged in size from a couple of employees to thousands of employees and contractors accessing the facility on a daily basis and from a low volume of maritime traffic (e.g., a couple of vessels per year) to high maritime traffic (e.g., several vessel calls per day). Facility types include barging, launch services and provisions, general cargo and break-bulk, bulk solid (including hazmat), bulk liquid (including hazmat), RORO, petrochemical refineries, chemical manufacturers, OCS facilities, passenger terminals (cruise and ferry), containers, and mixed-use facilities (often a combination of container, general cargo or break-bulk, and RORO). For ease of comparison, we consolidated facility types into the same categories used in the USCG 2015 regulatory analysis, as well as our reconstruction of the break-even analysis in Chapter 8: break-bulk and solids, bulk liquids, container, mixed use, cruise passenger, and ferry passenger. In the figures and tables that follow, we show summary data that describe our sample.

Figure A.2 shows the mix of risk group A facilities (those subject to the final TWIC-reader rule) and non–risk group A facilities (those not subject to the rule). Our sample consists of 34 percent risk group A facilities and 66 percent non–risk group A facilities. Figure A.3 shows the mix of facilities by geographic setting: urban inland (7 percent), rural inland (9 percent), OCS (13 percent), rural coastal (17 percent), and urban coastal (55 percent). Figure A.4 shows the mix of facilities by ownership type: hybrid[458] (4 percent), port authority owner or operator

---

[458] The port authority owns and operates some terminals but also leases land or terminals to other operators.

(21 percent), port authority landlord–tenant (21 percent), and private owner or operator (54 percent).

Figure A.2. Mix of Risk Group A and Non–Risk Group A Facilities Covered in the Sample

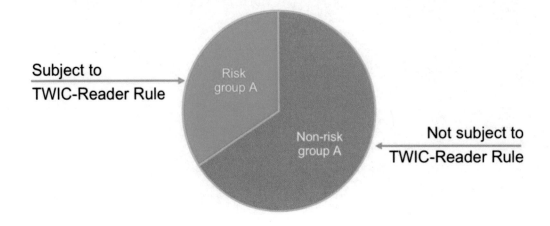

Figure A.3. Mix of Facilities, by Geographic Setting

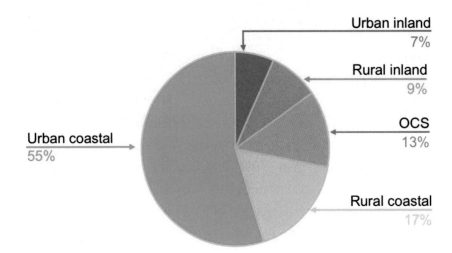

Figure A.4. Mix of Facilities, by Ownership Type

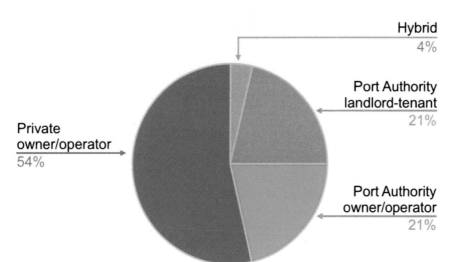

The next series of tables shows the following:

- Table A.3 shows the number of facilities in our sample by USCG district and facility type.
- Table A.4 shows the number of facilities in our sample by facility type and risk group.
- Table A.5 shows the number and percentages of facilities in our sample by access control method.
- Table A.6 shows the number of facilities in our sample by access control method and facility type.
- Table A.7 shows the number of facilities in our sample by access control method and risk group.

Table A.3. Facilities, by USCG District and Facility Type

USCG District[a]	Break-Bulk and Solids	Bulk Liquids	Container	Mixed Use	Passenger Cruise	Ferry	Total
1	1	10	3	—	4	5	23
5	2	7	2	4	—	—	15
7	1	2	2	3	3	—	11
8	2	44	2	4	2	—	54
9	3	1	—	1		—	5
11	2	7	5	4	6	—	24
13	6	—	1	6	2	1	16
14	1	2	—	3	2	—	8
17	—	1	1	—	5	1	8
Total	18	74	16	25	24	7	164

[a] The USCG is organized into nine districts, not consecutive in number.

Table A.4. Facilities, by Facility Type and Risk Group

Facility Type	Risk Group A	Non–Risk Group A	Total
Break-bulk and solids	—	18	18
Bulk liquids	26	48	74
Container	—	16	16
Mixed use	3	22	25
Passenger			
Cruise	23	1	24
Ferry	4	3	7
Total	56	108	164

Table A.5. Facilities, by Access Control Method

Access Control Method	Number of Facilities	Percentage of Sample
Biometrics	13	8
Electronic reader or PACS		
With the CCL	15	9
Without the CCL	51	31
Portable readers	3	2
Visual inspection	82	50

Table A.6. Facilities by Access Control and Facility Type

Access Control Method	Break-Bulk and Solids	Bulk Liquids	Container	Mixed Use	Passenger Cruise	Passenger Ferry
Biometrics	1	3	4	3	2	—
Electronic reader or PACS						
With the CCL	1	10	3	1	—	—
Without the CCL	3	36	3	3	3	3
Portable readers	—	1	—	2	—	—
Visual inspection	13	24	6	16	19	4

Table A.7. Facilities by Access Control Method and Risk Group

Access Control Method	Risk Group A	Non–Risk Group A
Biometrics	3	10
Electronic readers or PACS		
With the CCL	4	11
Without the CCL	22	29
Portable readers	1	2
Visual inspection	26	56

Interview Discussion Guide

Our project team iteratively developed an interview discussion guide that contained the main questions we wanted to ask during site visits. We first identified the key topical areas that were most vital to addressing our project tasks and goals; then we created interview questions to assess these areas. A qualitative researcher assisted in refining the questions to ensure that they were unbiased, nonleading, and open ended so that conversations naturally occurred between our interviewers and participants.

The list of discussion topics included the following:

- background and TWIC implementation

    - description of the participant's roles and responsibilities
    - how the TWIC card is implemented or integrated into security access control programs
    - how other credentials (if any) are used in addition to the TWIC card (e.g., company badge, union membership card)
    - escorting policies for non–TWIC holders

- electronic readers

    - how electronic readers are or will be used at the port or facility
    - types of reader
    - security value of and alternatives to biometrics
    - technological challenges
    - compliance costs

- vetting standards and background checks

    - company background checks
    - opinion of TWIC vetting standards

- security risks and threats

    - port and facility security risks and threats of most concern
    - TWIC's role in mitigating maritime security risks
    - examples of crime or other threats (such as a bomb) and whether the TWIC program played or could have played a risk-mitigation role

189

- the most-common TWIC-related security incidents (e.g., canceled card, fraudulent card)
- overall assessment of the TWIC program
  - the most-frequent complaints about the TWIC program
  - opinion of the key strengths and weaknesses of the TWIC program
  - opinion on how the TWIC program might be improved.

Interview Coding Methodology

Formally coding interview data provides a means of credibly conveying and quantifying, when feasible, the findings of qualitative interview data. Coding breaks down the text into smaller units that can be synthesized into a narrative that reflects research insights gathered from the interviews and site visits. Public Law 114-278 outlines specific aspects of the TWIC program that this assessment must address, some of which relate to the practical use of TWIC at facilities. Therefore, we opted to initially use a deductive approach to coding, which relies on developing a codebook in advance of the formal coding exercise to guide the team through the process, with an inductive approach then used to add and refine codes as coders became more knowledgeable about the content of the interviews.

Before coding commenced, interview notes were formatted in a consistent way, scrubbed for any PII and sensitive security information, and uploaded the notes to Dedoose, a software platform that supports analysis of qualitative and mixed-methods research[459] to aid in organization and theme extraction. The coding team consisted of three primary coders and three reviewers. At the start of the process, we checked intercoder reliability by having the coders review and code the same four interviews. Overlap in coders' use of codes indicated that intercoder reliability was high and that all the coders were applying the codebook in a similar way. Then the team performed line-by-line coding of the remaining interviews. The coding team also held several sessions throughout the process to evaluate line-by-line coding, revisit and review the codebook (adding or modifying codes as necessary), and discuss themes that emerged from the interview coding.

---

[459] The team followed strict data protection procedures. To protect identities, transcripts were hosted on an internal SharePoint site behind a firewall, separate from an interview tracker file that linked an interview number to the people in each of the interviews.

Appendix B. Permanent and Interim Disqualifying Criminal Offenses for TWIC

Table B.1. Disqualifying Criminal Offenses for TWIC

Category	Criminal Offenses
Permanently disqualifying	1. Espionage or conspiracy to commit espionage 2. Sedition or conspiracy to commit sedition 3. Treason or conspiracy to commit treason 4. A federal crime of terrorism as defined in 18 U.S.C. § 2332b(g) or comparable state law or a conspiracy to commit such a crime 5. A crime involving a TSI 6. Improper transportation of a hazmat under 49 U.S.C. § 5124 or a comparable state law 7. Unlawful possession, use, sale, distribution, manufacture, purchase, receipt, transfer, shipping, transporting, import, export, storage of, or dealing in an explosive or explosive device. *Explosive or explosive device* includes an explosive or explosive material, as defined in U.S. Code, Title 18, Crimes and Criminal Procedure; Part I, Crimes; Chapter 12, Civil Disorders; Section 232, Definitions; Paragraph (5); U.S. Code, Title 18, Crimes and Criminal Procedure; Part I, Crimes; Chapter 40, Importation, Manufacture, Distribution and Storage of Explosive Materials; Section 841, Definitions; Paragraphs 841(c) through 841(f); and U.S. Code, Title 18, Crimes and Criminal Procedure; Part I, Crimes; Chapter 40, Importation, Manufacture, Distribution and Storage of Explosive Materials; Section 844, Penalties; Paragraph (j), and a destructive device, as defined in U.S. Code, Title 18, Crimes and Criminal Procedure; Part I, Crimes; Chapter 44, Firearms; Section 921, Definitions; Paragraph (a)(4), and U.S. Code, Title 26, Internal Revenue Code; Subtitle E, Alcohol, Tobacco, and Certain Other Excise Taxes; Chapter 53, Machine Guns, Destructive Devices, and Certain Other Firearms; Subchapter B, General Provisions and Exemptions; Part I, General Provisions; Section 5845, Definitions 8. Murder 9. Threatening to or maliciously conveying false information, knowing it to be false, concerning the deliverance, placement, or detonation of an explosive or other lethal device in or against a place of public use, a state or government facility, a public transportation system, or an infrastructure facility 10. Violations of the Racketeer Influenced and Corrupt Organizations Act, U.S. Code, Title 18, Crimes and Criminal Procedure; Part I, Crimes; Chapter 96, Racketeer Influenced and Corrupt Organizations; Section 1961, Definitions; et seq. or a comparable state law in which one of the predicate acts found by a jury or admitted by the defendant includes one of the permanently disqualifying crimes 11. Attempting to commit any of the crimes in items 1–4 12. Conspiracy or attempt to commit any of the crimes in items 5–10

Category	Criminal Offenses
Interim disqualifying	1. Unlawful possession, use, sale, manufacture, purchase, distribution, receipt, transfer, shipping, transporting, delivery, import, export of, or dealing in a firearm or other weapon. *Firearm or other weapon* includes firearms as defined in 18 U.S.C. § 921(a)(3) and 26 U.S.C. § 5845(a) and items contained on the U.S. Munitions Import List at Code of Federal Regulations, Title 27, Alcohol, Tobacco Products, and Firearms; Chapter II, Bureau of Alcohol, Tobacco, Firearms, and Explosives, Department of Justice; Subchapter B, Firearms and Ammunition; Part 447, Importation of Arms, Ammunition and Implements of War; Subpart C, The U.S. Munitions Import List; Section 447.21, The U.S. Munitions Import List. 2. Extortion 3. Dishonesty, fraud, or misrepresentation, including identity fraud and money laundering, in which the money laundering is related to a crime listed here (except welfare fraud or passing bad checks) 4. Bribery 5. Smuggling 6. Immigration violation 7. Distribution, possession with intent to distribute, or importation of a controlled substance 8. Arson 9. Kidnapping or hostage taking 10. Rape or aggravated sexual abuse 11. Assault with intent to kill 12. Robbery 13. Fraudulent entry into a seaport as described in U.S. Code, Title 18, Crimes and Criminal Procedure; Part I, Crimes; Chapter 47, Fraud and False Statements; Section 1036, Entry by False Pretenses to Any Real Property, Vessel, or Aircraft of the United States or Secure Area of Any Airport or Seaport or a comparable state law 14. Violations of the Racketeer Influenced and Corrupt Organizations Act under 18 U.S.C. § 1961 et seq. or a comparable state law other than any permanently disqualifying offense 15. Voluntary manslaughter 16. Conspiracy or attempt to commit any of the crimes in this section
Under want, warrant, or indictment	A person will be disqualified if he or she is wanted or under indictment in any civilian or military jurisdiction for a felony listed here until the want or warrant is released or the indictment is dismissed.

Appendix C. MSRAM in Relation to the TWIC Program

MSRAM is a comprehensive tool for estimating the risk of an adversarial attack on a maritime target. The tool and associated elicitation process were developed by ABS Consulting for the USCG.[460] Following the classical definition adopted by DHS,[461] MSRAM defines *risk* as the product of threat, vulnerability, and consequence. MSRAM assesses the risk for thousands of scenarios, where each scenario concerns an attack mode (e.g., truck bomb) coupled with a target (e.g., chemical facility). As shown by the black box outline in Figure C.1, when calculating risk, MSRAM focuses mainly on a timeline beginning with the penetration of the target facility's defenses just prior to an attack and ending with primary effects of the attack. In MSRAM's risk construct, the relative scenario threat, derived from intelligence sources external to the USCG, encompasses the adversary's intent, capabilities, and skill.

Figure C.1. A Timeline Bounding the MSRAM Risk Assessment

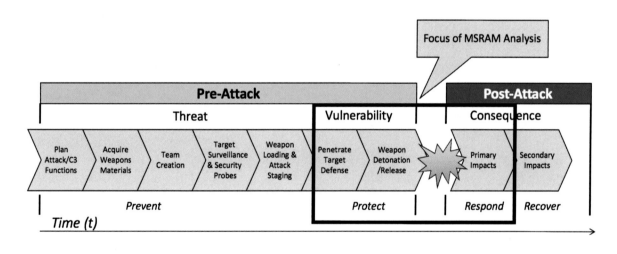

SOURCE: USCG, 2018a.

NOTE: C3 = command, control, and communications.

The deterrence value associated with access control generally and TWIC in particular falls outside the scope of MSRAM's risk calculation, rendering it insensitive to changes in vetting processes that might affect the level of threat. On the far-right "consequence" side of the

---

[460] USCG, 2018a.

[461] National Research Council, *Review of the Department of Homeland Security's Approach to Risk Analysis*, Washington, D.C.: National Academies Press, 2010; Henry H. Willis, Andrew R. Morral, Terrence Kelly, and Jamison Jo Medby, *Estimating Terrorism Risk*, Santa Monica, Calif.: RAND Corporation, MG-388-RC, 2005.

MSRAM timeline in Figure C.1, TWIC and other access control measures are assumed to have no effect on the consequences of any attack, whether the attack rises to the level of a TSI or not. The number of "exposed" individuals and the value of the port facility's surrounding assets are considered independently of access control measures.[462] However, it is conceivable that changes in the TWIC program would affect the vulnerability in MSRAM's risk calculation, albeit with some challenges, as described below.

An MSRAM attack scenario is a combination of attack mode and target. Because attack mode mixes weapon and method of entry, it is somewhat difficult to use attack mode in a way that would enable us to isolate TWIC's relevance. The USCG reader rule analysis, discussed in Chapter 8, considered TWIC to be relevant for only three attack modes out of the dozens listed in MSRAM: passenger or passerby explosive or IED, truck bomb, and terrorist assault team. In our analysis described below, we considered these three attack modes plus sabotage as TWIC-relevant.

Within MSRAM, a facility's capability to stop an attack depends on access control; the training, armaments, and skill of its security team; response time of local law enforcement and the USCG; and other facets of the facility's security architecture. To estimate the probability of attack success, the MSRAM tool elicits responses from the PSS or other knowledgeable security officials about the factors attributed to the facility's owner or operator, the USCG, and local law-enforcement agency that might lead to failure to interdict an attack. These factors, taken together, contribute to a facility's vulnerability. In this step of the elicitation, the effectiveness of a facility's system security is scored in MSRAM as one of several measures intended to reduce the facility's vulnerability and thus reduce the probability of attack success. TWIC and access control are not explicitly modeled in MSRAM, so we assumed that TWIC was incorporated into the system security parameter of MSRAM's vulnerability module.

MSRAM users choose one of three system security options related to the level of cooperation and coordination among the three main stakeholders: owner or operator, local law enforcement, and the USCG. The calculation of the system security parameter in MSRAM's vulnerability module differs by option.[463] Option 1 assumes independence among the three stakeholders, where a single system security category is used to assess each stakeholder's capability to interdict an attack. Option 2 also assumes independence among the three stakeholders but

---

[462] A strong argument has been made in the context of airport security (Donald Stevens, Terry L. Schell, Thomas Hamilton, Richard Mesic, Michael Scott Brown, Edward W. Chan, Mel Eisman, Eric V. Larson, Marvin Schaffer, Bruce Newsome, John Gibson, and Elwyn Harris, *Near-Term Options for Improving Security at Los Angeles International Airport*, Santa Monica, Calif.: RAND Corporation, DB-468-1-LAWA, 2004) that access control can, in fact, influence consequences (injury and death) if its operational inefficiencies lead to long lines and high concentrations of people in unsecured areas. Such is the case when TSA and air carriers attempt to reduce congestion at unsecured ticket counters and security checkpoints by accepting the extra costs of staffing during peak hours. The same could apply to access control measures at maritime facilities if trucks, workers, or passengers are stuck in long lines in unsecure areas while credentials are checked (Stevens et al., 2004).

[463] USCG, 2018a.

assesses each stakeholder's contribution to system security according to the stakeholder's ability to detect, decide, engage, and defeat an attack. So, option 2 requires more user inputs than option 1 does. Option 3 requires the same user inputs as option 2 but assumes collaboration among the three stakeholders. According to the data that the USCG provided, the numbers of facility scenarios for options 1, 2, and 3 in the MSRAM database are 1,788, 798, and 391, respectively, for the four attack modes of passenger/passerby IED, truck bomb, terrorist assault team, and sabotage.

In Table C.1, we illustrate MSRAM's calculation for option 1, which accounts for 60 percent of the scenarios considered. The user selects one of seven categories of system security, each representing a range of the probability of interdicting an attack. For example, category 7 mean 0- to 5-percent probability of interdicting an attack. The middle point of this probability range is 2.5 percent, which then translates to a vulnerability score of 0.975 (i.e., 100 percent minus 2.5 percent).

Table C.1. MSRAM Categories of System Security Under Option 1

Category	Percentage Probability of Interdicting	Assigned Value of Vulnerability
1	95–100	0.025
2	85–95	0.1
3	65–85	0.25
4	35–65	0.5
5	15–35	0.75
6	5–15	0.9
7	0–5	0.975

NOTE: Assigned value of vulnerability is 1 – the midpoint probability of interdicting.

In the absence of a TWIC parameter in MSRAM, we assumed that the hardening of access control measures via changes in the TWIC program could be simulated by, at most, one "downshift" in the category for system security for the owner or operator. (System security for the USCG and local law enforcement is assumed unaffected by TWIC.) This downward shift in category (e.g., from category 7 to category 6) represents a maximum expected change, rather than the expected change in MSRAM due to the TWIC program. Table C.2 summarizes the calculation that simply uses the midpoint values from the rightmost column of Table C.1. This simple conclusion results from the multiplicative nature of the vulnerability calculation for option 1, in which the initial designated system security category for the owner or operator for a given scenario dictates how much the vulnerability might change if the category were to move down by one level toward "hardening."

Table C.2. Expected Changes in Vulnerability for Option 1 Facilities

The Impact of Shifting from Category . . .	to Category . . .	Is That the Vulnerability (and Thus RIN) Will Be Multiplied by . . .
7	6	$0.9 \div 0.975 = 0.92$
6	5	$0.75 \div 0.9 = 0.83$
5	4	$0.5 \div 0.75 = 0.67$
4	3	$0.25 \div 0.5 = 0.50$
3	2	$0.1 \div 0.25 = 0.40$
2	1	$0.025 \div 0.1 = 0.25$

As mentioned, for options 2 and 3, MSRAM requires additional user inputs on each stakeholder's ability to detect, decide, engage, and defeat an attack. For option 2, because of stakeholder independence (like in option 1), only information about the owner or operator is required to determine how the vulnerability might change. We further assumed that TWIC affected only the detection capability and that the hardening due to TWIC is similarly achieved by downshifting the detection capability by one category. However, as described below, the actual change in the vulnerability also depends on the existing categories of the owner or operator's capability to decide, engage, and defeat an attack.

Assume that the probabilities that the owner or operator (noted by the subscript OO in the expressions below) can detect, decide, engage, and defeat an attack are $P_{1,OO}$, $P_{2,OO}$, $P_{3,OO}$, and $P_{4,OO}$, respectively. The system security attributed to the owner or operator is the product of those four probabilities ($P_{1,OO} \times P_{2,OO} \times P_{3,OO} \times P_{4,OO}$), and the corresponding vulnerability V is proportional to $1 - (P_{1,OO} \times P_{2,OO} \times P_{3,OO} \times P_{4,OO})$. Now, suppose that hardening through the TWIC program results in an increase in the probability of detection from $P_{1,OO}$ to $P_{1N,OO}$ and that the new vulnerability V_N is proportional to $1 - (P_{1N,OO} \times P_{2,OO} \times P_{3,OO} \times P_{4,OO})$. Thus, the new (reduced) vulnerability (and thus RIN) due to hardening equals the original vulnerability multiplied by V_N/V, a ratio that appropriately captures the increase in the probability of detection (from $P_{1,OO}$ to $P_{1N,OO}$) as calculated in MSRAM.

For option 3, due to stakeholder collaboration in system security, MSRAM prompts the user for information about all three stakeholders—owner or operator, the USCG (noted by the subscript CG in the expressions below), and local law enforcement (noted by the subscript LE)—to determine how the vulnerability might change. Assume that the probabilities that the USCG can detect, decide, engage, and defeat an attack are $P_{1,CG}$, $P_{2,CG}$, $P_{3,CG}$, and $P_{4,CG}$, respectively. Assume that the probabilities that local law enforcement can detect, decide, engage, and defeat an attack are $P_{1,LE}$, $P_{2,LE}$, $P_{3,LE}$, and $P_{4,LE}$, respectively. As a consequence of stakeholder collaboration and the relevance of the probability of detection (noted by the subscript D), the corresponding vulnerability V is given by a more complicated formula and is proportional to

$1 - (1 - P_D) \times \left(1 - P_{I,OO} \times P_{I,CG} \times P_{I,LE}\right)$, where $P_D = \left(1 - P_{1,OO}\right) \times \left(1 - P_{1,CG}\right) \times \left(1 - P_{1,LE}\right)$, $P_{I,OO} = 1 - P_{2,OO} \times P_{3,OO} \times P_{4,OO}$, $P_{I,CG} = 1 - P_{2,CG} \times P_{3,CG} \times P_{4,CG}$, and $P_{I,LE} = 1 - P_{2,LE} \times P_{3,LE} \times P_{4,LE}$. Like for option 2, suppose that hardening through the TWIC program results in an increase in the probability of detection $P_{1,OO}$ to $P_{1N,OO}$ for the owner or operator but no change in the capabilities of the USCG or local law enforcement. The new vulnerability V_N can be similarly calculated with the above expressions, yielding the ratio of V_N/V.

Appendix D. The Status of GAO and OIG Recommendations

In this appendix, we provide additional information on past GAO and OIG reports on TWIC, published prior to the passage of Public Law 114-278. Table D.1 provides the number of recommendations in each report and their current status. The subsequent text provides additional detail on these recommendations, as provided on the product page for each report. For open recommendations, we have included GAO's comments in full; for the closed recommendations, we have paraphrased or condensed the comment language to highlight GAO's reasons for its determination.

Table D.1. The Status of GAO and OIG Recommendations

Report	Citation	Open	Closed Implemented	Closed Not Implemented
Port Security: Better Planning Needed to Develop and Operate Maritime Worker Identification Card Program	GAO, 2004		2	
Transportation Security: DHS Should Address Key Challenges Before Implementing the Transportation Worker Identification Credential Program	GAO, 2006		2	
Transportation Security: DHS Efforts to Eliminate Redundant Background Check Investigations	GAO, 2007		3	
Transportation Worker Identification Credential: Progress Made in Enrolling Workers and Activating Credentials but Evaluation Plan Needed to Help Inform the Implementation of Card Readers	GAO, 2009		1	3
Transportation Worker Identification Credential: Internal Control Weaknesses Need to Be Corrected to Help Achieve Security Objectives	GAO, 2011a	3		1
Transportation Security: Actions Needed to Address Limitations in TSA's Transportation Worker Security Threat Assessments and Growing Workload	GAO, 2011b		4	
Transportation Worker Identification Credential: Card Reader Pilot Results Are Unreliable; Security Benefits Need to Be Reassessed	GAO, 2013a		1	
Transportation Security: Action Needed to Strengthen TSA's Security Threat Assessment Process	GAO, 2013b		5	
TWIC Background Checks Are Not as Reliable as They Could Be	OIG, 2016		5	

Specific Report Recommendations

Port Security: Better Planning Needed to Develop and Operate Maritime Worker Identification Card Program (GAO, 2004)

Recommendation: To help ensure that TSA meets the challenges it is facing in developing and operating its maritime worker identification card program, the Secretary of Homeland Security should direct the TSA Administrator to employ industry best practices for project planning and management by developing a comprehensive project plan for managing the remaining life of the project.
Status: Closed—Implemented

Recommendation: To help ensure that TSA meets the challenges it is facing in developing and operating its maritime worker identification card program, the Secretary of Homeland Security should direct the TSA Administrator to employ industry best practices for project planning and management by developing specific, detailed plans for risk mitigation and cost–benefit and alternatives analyses.
Status: Closed—Implemented

Transportation Security: DHS Should Address Key Challenges Before Implementing the Transportation Worker Identification Credential Program (GAO, 2006)

Recommendation: To help ensure that the TWIC program can be implemented as efficiently and effectively as possible, the Secretary of Homeland Security [should] direct the Assistant Secretary of Homeland Security for the Transportation Security Administration, in close coordination with the Commandant of the U.S. Coast Guard, to, before TWIC is implemented in the maritime sector, develop and test solutions to the problems identified during TWIC program testing, and raised by stakeholders in commenting on the TWIC proposed rule, to ensure that all key components of the TWIC program work effectively. In developing and testing these solutions, TSA should ensure that the TWIC program will be able to efficiently enroll and issue TWIC cards to large numbers of workers, the technology necessary to operate the TWIC program will be readily available to industry stakeholders and will function effectively in the maritime sector, including biometric card readers and the capability to link facility access control systems with the national TWIC database, ensure that the TWIC program balances the added security it provides with the potential effect that the program could have on the flow of maritime commerce, and closely coordinate with maritime industry stakeholders—particularly those that are currently implementing or using biometric access control systems—to learn from their experiences.
Status: Closed—Implemented

Recommendation: To help ensure that the TWIC program can be implemented as efficiently and effectively as possible, the Secretary of Homeland Security [should] direct the Assistant Secretary of Homeland Security for the Transportation Security Administration, in close coordination with the Commandant of the U.S. Coast Guard, to strengthen contract planning and oversight practices before awarding the contract to implement the TWIC program to ensure that the contract to implement the TWIC program contains

comprehensive and clearly defined requirements, resources are available and measures are in place to provide effective government oversight of the contractor's performance, and a communication and coordination plan is established to capture and address the views and concerns of maritime industry stakeholders during implementation.
Status: Closed—Implemented

Transportation Security Administration: DHS Efforts to Eliminate Redundant Background Check Investigations (GAO, 2007)

Recommendation: To help prevent redundancies and inefficiencies, the Secretary of Homeland Security should ensure that the plan being developed by DHS for coordinating its background check programs include, at a minimum, the steps the agency will take to align its screening and credentialing activities and include specific time frames and budget requirements for implementation. In addition, the plan should describe how and when DHS will establish and apply a common set of design and comparability standards for DHS's background check programs.
Status: Closed—Implemented

Recommendation: To help prevent redundancies and inefficiencies, the Secretary of Homeland Security should ensure that the plan being developed by DHS for coordinating its background check programs include, at a minimum, a discussion of the potential costs/benefits associated with the number of redundant background checks that would be eliminated through harmonization.
Status: Closed—Implemented

Recommendation: To help prevent redundancies and inefficiencies and because of DHS's responsibility for a large number of background check programs, the Secretary of Homeland Security should explore with other federal agencies options for harmonizing background check programs within DHS and other federal agencies.
Status: Closed—Implemented

Transportation Worker Identification Credential: Progress Made in Enrolling Workers and Activating Credentials but Evaluation Plan Needed to Help Inform the Implementation of Card Readers (GAO, 2009)

Recommendation: To minimize the effects of any potential losses resulting from TWIC system failures, and to ensure that adequate processes and capabilities are in place to minimize the effects of TWIC system interruptions, the Assistant Secretary for the Transportation Security Administration should direct the TWIC program office to develop an information technology contingency plan for TWIC systems, including the development and implementation of a disaster recovery plan and supporting systems, as required, as soon as possible.
Status: Closed—Implemented

Recommendation: To help ensure that the TWIC pilot schedule can be reliably used to guide the pilot and identify the pilot's completion date, the Assistant Secretary for the Transportation Security Administration should direct the TWIC program office, in concert with pilot participants to fully incorporate best practices for program scheduling in the pilot schedule to help ensure that (1) all pilot activities are captured; (2) sufficient resources are assigned to all activities; (3) the duration of all activities are established and agreed upon by all stakeholders; (4) a schedule risk analysis is conducted to determine a level of confidence in meeting the planned completion date and impact of not achieving planned activities within scheduled deadlines; and (5) the schedule is correctly updated on a periodic basis.

Status: Closed—Not Implemented

Comments: . . . While TSA made improvements to the TWIC pilot schedule, TSA did not fully implemented [sic] the practices that we recommended and the schedule remained unreliable for managing stakeholder participation and projecting the pilot's completion date. According to TSA, the pilot was completed on May 31, 2011. . . .

Recommendation: To ensure that the information needed to assess the technical, business, and operational impacts of deploying TWIC biometric card readers at Maritime Transportation Security Act (MTSA)–regulated facilities and vessels is acquired prior to the development of the card reader rule, the Assistant Secretary for the Transportation Security Administration and Commandant of the U.S. Coast Guard should direct their respective TWIC program offices to develop an evaluation plan to guide the remainder of the pilot that includes performance standards, a clearly articulated evaluation methodology—including the unit of analysis and criteria—and a data analysis plan.

Status: Closed—Not Implemented

Comments: . . . [W]hile TSA developed a data analysis plan, TSA and USCG reported that they did not develop an evaluation plan with an evaluation methodology or performance standards, as we recommended. . . . According to officials from the independent test agent, they started to use the data analysis plan but stopped using the plan because they were experiencing difficulty in collecting the required data and TSA directed them to change the reporting approach. TSA officials stated that they directed the independent test agent to change its collection and reporting approach because of TSA's inability to require or control data collection to the extent required to execute the data analysis plan. We are therefore closing this recommendation as not implemented.

Recommendation: To ensure that the information needed to assess the technical, business, and operational impacts of deploying TWIC biometric card readers at MTSA-regulated facilities and vessels is acquired prior to the development of the card reader rule, the Assistant Secretary for the Transportation Security Administration and Commandant of the U.S. Coast Guard should direct their respective TWIC program offices to identify how they will compensate for areas where the TWIC reader pilot will not provide the necessary information needed to report to Congress and implement the card reader rule. The information to [be] collected and approach for obtaining and evaluating information obtained through this effort should be documented as part of an evaluation plan. At a minimum, areas for further review include the potential requirements identified in the TWIC Reader Advanced Notice of Proposed Rulemaking but not addressed by the pilot. Sources of information to consider include investigating the possibility of using information resulting from the deployment of TWIC readers at non-pilot port facilities to help inform the development of the card reader rule.

Status: Closed—Not Implemented

Comments: . . . In April 2013, Coast Guard further reported that it augmented

TWIC pilot data by conducting additional studies regarding physical access control systems and congestion delays, as well as other analyses, which it used to complete the TWIC reader Notice of Proposed Rulemaking published in March of 2013. As we reported in May 2013, the studies did not compensate for all of the challenges we identified in our November 2009 report. We are therefore closing this recommendation as not implemented.

Transportation Worker Identification Credential: Internal Control Weaknesses Need to Be Corrected to Help Achieve Security Objectives (GAO, 2011a)

Recommendation: To identify effective and cost-efficient methods for meeting TWIC program objectives, and assist in determining whether the benefits of continuing to implement and operate the TWIC program in its present form and planned use with readers surpass the costs, the Secretary of Homeland Security should perform an internal control assessment of the TWIC program by (1) analyzing existing controls, (2) identifying related weaknesses and risks, and (3) determining cost-effective actions needed to correct or compensate for those weaknesses so that reasonable assurance of meeting TWIC program objectives can be achieved. This assessment should consider weaknesses we identified in this report among other things, and include: (1) strengthening the TWIC program's controls for preventing and detecting identity fraud, such as requiring certain biographic information from applicants and confirming the information to the extent needed to positively identify the individual, or implementing alternative mechanisms to positively identify individuals; (2) defining the term extensive criminal history for use in the adjudication process and ensuring that adjudicators follow a clearly defined and consistently applied process, with clear criteria, in considering the approval or denial of a TWIC for individuals with extensive criminal convictions not defined as permanent or interim disqualifying offenses; and (3) identifying mechanisms for detecting whether TWIC holders continue to meet TWIC disqualifying criminal offense and immigration-related eligibility requirements after TWIC issuance to prevent unqualified individuals from retaining and using authentic TWICs.
Status: Open
Comments: We reported that internal control weaknesses governing the enrollment, background checking, and use of TWIC potentially limit the program's ability to provide reasonable assurance that access to secure areas of MTSA-regulated facilities is restricted to qualified individuals. We further reported that TSA did not assess the internal controls designed and in place to determine whether they provided reasonable assurance that the program could meet defined mission needs for limiting access to only qualified individuals, and that internal control weaknesses in TWIC enrollment, background checking, and use could have contributed to the breach of selected MTSA-regulated facilities during covert tests conducted by our investigators. We recommended that DHS perform an internal control assessment of the TWIC program by (1) analyzing existing controls, (2) identifying related weaknesses and risks, and (3) determining cost-effective actions needed to correct or compensate for those weaknesses so that reasonable assurance of meeting TWIC program objectives can be achieved. In December 2017, a third party contracted by TSA reported on the results of its internal control assessment of the TWIC program, including the TWIC program's internal controls of the enrollment, background checking, and credential issuance processes. We believe that this is a positive step towards

addressing our recommendation. However, the assessment did not include an evaluation of the use of TWIC, including Coast Guard's role in TWIC enforcement. In February 2018, TSA, with assistance from DHS's Science and Technology Directorate, initiated a study with a Homeland Security Operational Analysis Center to conduct an assessment of the TWIC program's security effectiveness in the maritime environment. The study plan sets forth methods for assessing the TWIC program's planned use with card readers. However, the study will not assess information systems controls and related risks for reasonably assuring that use of TWIC with readers and associated systems used for access control decisions are reliable and not surreptitiously altered by cyber intrusions or attack. Absent an assessment of controls for ensuring the reliable use of TWIC with readers, the study will fall short in meeting our recommendation and the deficiencies identified in our report. We continue to believe that the internal control assessment inclusive of TWIC use and the interrelationship between acquiring a TWIC and using it in the maritime environment is needed. For the reasons noted above, as of January 2019, this recommendation remains open.

Recommendation: To identify effective and cost-efficient methods for meeting TWIC program objectives, and assist in determining whether the benefits of continuing to implement and operate the TWIC program in its present form and planned use with readers surpass the costs, the Secretary of Homeland Security should conduct an effectiveness assessment that includes addressing internal control weaknesses and, at a minimum, evaluates whether use of TWIC in its present form and planned use with readers would enhance the posture of security beyond efforts already in place given costs and program risks.

Status: Open

Priority recommendation

Comments: We reported that DHS had not assessed the program's effectiveness at enhancing security. We recommended that DHS conduct an effectiveness assessment that includes addressing internal control weaknesses and, at a minimum, evaluates whether use of TWIC in its present form and planned use with readers would enhance the posture of security beyond efforts already in place given costs and program risks. DHS, through TSA, has taken steps to address this recommendation by having an internal controls assessment conducted of the TWIC program's enrollment, background checking, credential issuance, and continued eligibility review. In February 2018, TSA, with assistance from DHS's Science and Technology Directorate, initiated a study with a Homeland Security Operational Analysis Center to conduct an assessment of the TWIC program's security effectiveness in the maritime environment. The study plan sets forth methods for assessing the TWIC program's planned use with card readers. However, the study will not assess information systems controls and related risks for reasonably [ensuring] that use of TWIC with readers and associated systems used for access control decisions are reliable and not surreptitiously altered by cyber intrusions or attack. Moreover, the assessment does not include an assessment of the federally managed single credential approach in contrast to federally regulated decentralized options, such as the SIDA airport credentialing model, the Hazardous Materials endorsement for truck drivers (wherein an endorsement is added to a driver's license), the federal government's own agency-specific credentialing model which relies on organizational sponsorship and credentials with agency-specific security features, or any combination thereof. Absent an assessment of controls for ensuring the reliable use of TWIC with readers and the above-noted types of credentialing approaches, the study will fall short in meeting our recommendation and the deficiencies identified in our report. With consideration of the above noted shortfalls, DHS should proceed to conduct an assessment of the TWIC program's effectiveness to determine whether the benefits of continuing to implement and operate the program in its present form and planned use with readers surpass the costs. Absent an effectiveness assessment that meets the intent of our recommendation, as of January 2019, this recommendation remains open.

Recommendation: To identify effective and cost-efficient methods for meeting TWIC program objectives, and assist in determining whether the benefits of continuing to implement and operate the TWIC program in its present form and planned use with readers surpass the costs, the Secretary of Homeland Security should use the information from the internal control and effectiveness assessments as the basis for evaluating the costs, benefits, security risks, and corrective actions needed to implement the TWIC program in a manner that will meet stated mission needs and mitigate existing security risks as part of conducting the regulatory analysis on implementing a new regulation on the use of TWIC with biometric card readers.

Status: Open

Comments: We reported that prior to issuing the regulation on implementing the use of TWIC as a flashpass, DHS conducted a regulatory analysis, which asserted that TWIC would increase security. The analysis included an evaluation of the costs and benefits related to implementing TWIC. We further reported that as a proposed regulation on the use of TWIC with biometric card readers is under development, DHS is to issue a new regulatory analysis. Conducting a regulatory analysis using the information from the internal control and effectiveness assessments as the basis for evaluating the costs, benefits, security risks, and needed corrective actions could better inform and enhance the reliability of the new regulatory analysis. Moreover, these actions could help DHS identify and assess the full costs and benefits of implementing the TWIC program in a manner that will meet stated mission needs and mitigate existing security risks, and help ensure that the TWIC program is more effective and cost-efficient than existing measures or alternatives at enhancing maritime security. We therefore recommended that DHS use the information from the internal control and effectiveness assessments we recommended as the basis for evaluating the costs, benefits, security risks, and corrective actions needed to implement the TWIC program in a manner that will meet stated mission needs and mitigate existing security risks as part of conducting the regulatory analysis on implementing a new regulation on the use of TWIC with biometric card readers. In March 2012, DHS reported that upon completion of the internal control and effectiveness assessments, DHS will evaluate the results to determine any subsequent actions, and that any applicable data or risks will be communicated to the Coast Guard for consideration during their regulatory analysis. However, DHS has not implemented the internal control assessment we recommended, which is to be the basis for the effectiveness assessment and addressing this recommendation. Further, the January 15, 2016 effectiveness assessment titled "Security Assessment of the Transportation Worker Identification Credential and Readers" did not substantively address the risk concerns identified in our report. Given shortfalls that remain in addressing our internal control assessment and effectiveness assessment recommendations, this recommendation remains open pending DHS taking corrective actions. As of January 2019, no further action has been taken.

Recommendation: To identify effective and cost-efficient methods for meeting TWIC program objectives, and assist in determining whether the benefits of continuing to implement and operate the TWIC program in its present form and planned use with readers surpass the costs, the Secretary of Homeland Security should direct the Commandant of the Coast Guard to design effective methods for collecting, cataloguing, and querying TWIC-related compliance issues to provide the Coast Guard with the enforcement information needed to assess trends in compliance with the TWIC program and identify associated vulnerabilities.
Status: Closed—Not Implemented
Comments: . . . As of May 2016, Coast Guard reported that it has made updates to its MISLE system to address our recommendation. For example, Coast Guard can now query TWIC compliance reports by district. Coast Guard officials also report that they have requested additional adjustments to the system in order to better query and produce reports from its MISLE system but can provide no timetable for completion. Coast Guard officials, however, report that they will not be implementing certain reporting features highlighted in our report, such as the ability to query TWIC-related compliance issues that occur by the type of facility. Specifically, Coast Guard officials reported that they see no value in building a capability to sort TWIC data by the type of facility. They further reported that data showing that a given type of facility had a given rate of TWIC compliance would have no significance as it would represent many different companies in different locations. . . .

Transportation Security: Actions Needed to Address Limitations in TSA's Transportation Worker Security Threat Assessments and Growing Workload (GAO, 2011b)

Recommendation: The Secretary of Homeland Security should direct the TSA Administrator, and the Attorney General of the United States should direct the Director of the FBI, to jointly assess the extent to which a security risk may exist with respect to the level of access to criminal history records information currently received by TSA to complete Security Threat Assessments, identify alternatives to address any risks, and assess the costs and benefits of pursuing each alternative.
Status: Closed—Implemented

Recommendation: The Secretary of Homeland Secretary should direct the TSA Administrator to conduct an assessment of the risks associated with not utilizing some state-provided criminal history information, as well as an analysis of the costs and benefits of integrating the information into the current adjudication process.
Status: Closed—Implemented

Recommendation: The Secretary of Homeland Secretary should direct the TSA Administrator to develop a workforce staffing plan with timelines articulating how the Transportation Threat Assessment and Credentialing (TTAC) Adjudication Center will effectively and efficiently meet its current and emerging workload requirements, and incorporate the results of TSA's study examining the

appropriateness and costs and benefits of using contractors.
Status: Closed—Implemented

Transportation Worker Identification Credential: Card Reader Pilot Results Are Unreliable; Security Benefits Needed to Be Reassessed (GAO, 2013a)

Matter: Given that the results of the pilot are unreliable for informing the TWIC card reader rule on the technology and operational impacts of using TWICs with readers, Congress should consider repealing the requirement that the Secretary of Homeland Security promulgate final regulations that require the deployment of card readers that are consistent with the findings of the pilot program. Instead, Congress should require that the Secretary of Homeland Security first complete an assessment that evaluates the effectiveness of using TWIC with readers for enhancing port security, as we recommended in our May 2011 report, and then use the results of this assessment to promulgate a final regulation as appropriate. Given DHS's challenges in implementing TWIC over the past decade, at a minimum, the assessment should include a comprehensive comparison of alternative credentialing approaches, which might include a more decentralized approach, for achieving TWIC program goals.
Status: Closed—Implemented

Transportation Security: Action Needed to Strengthen TSA's Security Threat Assessment Process (GAO, 2013b)

Recommendation: To ensure that the Adjudication Center accuracy rate effectively captures the center's accuracy in completing security threat assessments, the Secretary of Homeland Security should direct the TSA Administrator to take the following action. The Adjudication Center should develop an accuracy rate measure that includes accuracy data for cases where adjudicators both approved and disqualified applicants, document this methodology, and implement the process.
Status: Closed—Implemented

Recommendation: To ensure continuity of case reporting, the Secretary of Homeland Security should direct the TSA Administrator to document its case reporting performance management processes.
Status: Closed—Implemented

Recommendation: The Secretary of Homeland Security should direct the TSA Administrator to ensure workforce planning is based on accurate workload projections, establish a mechanism for TSA's Office of Intelligence and Analysis (OIA) Program Management Division and Office of Law Enforcement/Federal Air Marshal Service (OLE/FAMS) Adjudication Center to share and reconcile information included in the Adjudication Center's staffing plan updates, such as timelines for anticipated workload growth.
Status: Closed—Implemented

Recommendation: To advance efforts to address risks identified in the Adjudication Center Balanced Workforce Strategy (BWS) assessment, the Secretary of Homeland Security should direct the TSA Administrator to update and document its Adjudication Center insourcing conversion plan to reflect

revised schedule timeframes, cost and hiring level information.
Status: Closed—Implemented

Recommendation: To advance efforts to address risks identified in the Adjudication Center BWS assessment, the Secretary of Homeland Security should direct the TSA Administrator to review the updated Adjudication Center insourcing conversion plan, and provide it to TSA and DHS leadership for review and implementation approval.
Status: Closed—Implemented

TWIC Background Checks Are Not as Reliable as They Could Be (OIG, 2016)

Recommendation: We recommended that the Assistant Administrator, Office of Intelligence and Analysis, Transportation Security Administration identify a cross-functional coordinating entity with authority, responsibility, and accountability to provide regular guidance and leadership across all Security Threat Assessment processes and supporting offices.
Status: Resolved and Closed

Recommendation: We recommend that the Assistant Administrator, Office of Intelligence and Analysis, Transportation Security Administration conduct a comprehensive risk analysis of the Security Threat Assessment processes to identify areas needing additional internal controls and quality assurance procedures; and develop and implement those procedures, including periodic reviews to evaluate their effectiveness.
Status: Resolved and Closed

Recommendation: We recommend that the Assistant Administrator, Office of Intelligence and Analysis, Transportation Security Administration improve Transportation Worker Identification Credential program–level performance metrics to ensure that they align with the program's core objectives, and direct management officials to use these metrics for all the supporting offices.
Status: Resolved and Closed

Recommendation: We recommend that the Assistant Administrator, Office of Intelligence and Analysis, Transportation Security Administration review current Transportation Worker Identification Credential Security Threat Assessment guidance to ensure it provides adjudicators the necessary information and authority to complete Security Threat Assessments.
Status: Resolved and Closed

Recommendation: We recommend that the Assistant Administrator, Office of Intelligence and Analysis, Transportation Security Administration establish measurable and comparable criteria to use in evaluating and selecting the best criminal and immigration recurrent vetting option.
Status: Resolved and Closed

Appendix E. A Detailed Analysis of TWIC User Fees

This appendix provides a more detailed analysis of the TWIC program's revenue and cost history with a focus on the most-recent three FYs for which data were available: 2016, 2017, and 2018. We broke the program's revenue history down into two parts—fees and enrollments—and reviewed them separately. We reviewed costs in a single section but broke them down into four categories: enrollment, personnel, IT, and other.

Data Used

TSA provided summary revenue and cost data for each FY. It reported fee revenue and total obligations for FYs 2013 through 2018. We computed annual surpluses as the difference between fee revenue and total obligations within a given FY. TSA reported cumulative surpluses, or *carryovers*, directly.

TSA also provided monthly enrollment counts for October 2013 through September 2018. The counts were broken down by enrollment category: standard enrollment, renewal, comparable enrollment, Extended Expiration Date (EED) renewal, and replacement card. TSA also provided monthly counts of expiring cards.[464]

TSA reported personnel costs at a high level of granularity. It provided biweekly compensation and benefit data for every TWIC employee for October 2014 through September 2018. It also broke out overtime pay. The data include each employee's job title, as well as the associated U.S. Office of Personnel Management (OPM) occupational series code. TSA also provided three snapshots detailing authorized positions: August 31, 2015; April 15, 2016; and September 22, 2017. The data files indicate whether each authorized position was filled or vacant.

All other program costs were detailed in transaction-level data files covering FYs 2015 through 2018. The files include transactions related to contracts, interagency agreements, purchases, travel, and training. For each transaction, the data files indicate the vendor name, funding amount, and effective date. Each entry also included a TSA object class code denoting the type of good or service for which the funds were expended.

We collected additional information by reviewing documents and conducting semistructured discussions with SMEs. The documents included *Federal Register* notices and life-cycle cost estimates. The SMEs were employed by or associated with the TWIC program and TSA's

---

[464] Comparable enrollment is available to an applicant with an active HME on a commercial driver's license. *EED renewal* refers to a one-time, three-year STA extension option intended to provide convenience to cardholders in advance of the deployment of TWIC readers. EED renewals were last offered in December 2014. A replacement card is available for a fee when an enrollee's TWIC card is lost, stolen, or damaged.

Business Management Office. We designed the discussions to elicit information about the program's fee and usage history, policies and procedures, spending and investment plans, and demand drivers. They also provided an opportunity to pose specific questions about patterns and anomalies in the administrative data.

Fee History

Each TWIC enrollment falls into one of four categories: standard enrollment, renewal, comparable enrollment, and replacement card.[465] The program charges a fee of $125.25 for a standard enrollment or a renewal. Comparable enrollment is available at the reduced rate of $105.25 to an applicant with an active HME on a commercial driver's license. A replacement card can be obtained for $60.00. The fees are designed to recover not only the initial enrollment, vetting, and credentialing costs but also the cost of maintaining the TWIC over the five-year term.

TSA breaks the user fee into five parts: an Enrollment Segment, a Full Card Production/STA Segment, a Reduced Card Production/STA Segment, a Card Replacement Segment, and an FBI Segment.[466] The Enrollment Segment covers costs associated with the collection and transmission of applicant information, including fingerprints, and the issuance of the physical credential. The Full Card Production/STA Segment and Reduced Card Production/STA Segment cover costs associated with performing and adjudicating STAs, administering the appeal and waiver processes, and producing the physical credential. The full segment applies to standard enrollments and renewals, while the reduced segment is for comparable enrollments. The Card Replacement Segment covers the cost of creating a replacement TWIC. The FBI Segment is the amount the FBI charges to perform a CHRC.[467] Table E.1 presents a decomposition of the user fee for each enrollment type.

---

[465] We omitted EED renewals because TSA last offered them in December 2014.

[466] TSA and USCG, "Transportation Worker Identification Credential (TWIC) Implementation in the Maritime Sector; Hazardous Materials Endorsement for a Commercial Driver's License," *Federal Register*, Vol. 72, No. 16, January 25, 2007a, pp. 3491–3604, p. 3506.

[467] TSA and USCG, 2006, p. 29402.

Table E.1. Constituent Parts of the TWIC User Fee, by Enrollment Type, FY 2018, in Dollars

Enrollment Type	Enrollment	Full Card Production/ STA	Reduced Card Production/ STA	Card Replacement	FBI	User Fee
		Segments				
Standard	34.50	80.75	N/A	N/A	10.00	125.25
Renewal	34.50	80.75	N/A	N/A	10.00	125.25
Comparable	34.50	N/A	70.75	N/A	N/A	105.25
Replacement card	N/A	N/A	N/A	60.00	N/A	60.00

SOURCE: Administrative data provided by TSA.
NOTE: The FBI Segment increased to $11.25 in January 2019. As of the time of this writing, the user fees had not changed in response. Hence, in practice, the Full Card Production/STA Segment was reduced to $79.50.

The data reported in Table E.1 are the actual fees collected by the enrollment vendor, TSA, or FBI for FY 2018. These differ from the fees published in the *Federal Register*. TSA set the initial fees on March 20, 2007: $43.25 for the Enrollment Segment, $72.00 for the Full Card Production/STA Segment, $62.00 for the Reduced Card Production/STA Segment, $36.00 for the Card Replacement Segment, and $22.00 for the FBI Segment.[468] Only the Card Replacement and FBI Segments have changed since then. In September 2007, TSA raised the Card Replacement Segment to $60.00, and it remains at that level to date. The FBI Segment has been reduced four times following reductions in the FBI CHRC fee:

- October 2007: from $22.00 to $17.50[469]
- May 2013: from $17.50 to $14.50[470]
- February 2015: from $14.50 to $12.75
- October 2016: from $12.75 to $10.00.[471]

Enrollment History

Figure E.1 shows total TWIC enrollments, including renewals, EED renewals, and replacement cards, by month for October 2014 through September 2018. Enrollments have been fairly stable in recent years: The annual totals for FYs 2015, 2016, 2017, and 2018 were 461,672, 532,054, 511,883, and 487,799, respectively. Enrollment volume has varied with the season. Enrollments tend to increase from December to March, decrease in April, fluctuate between May

---

[468] TSA and USCG, "Transportation Worker Identification Credential (TWIC) Implementation in the Maritime Sector; Hazardous Materials Endorsement for a Commercial Driver's License," *Federal Register*, Vol. 72, No. 188, September 28, 2007b, p. 55043.

[469] TSA and USCG, 2007b, p. 55046.

[470] Sadler, 2013, p. 24355.

[471] TSA, "Revision of Agency Information Collection Activity Under OMB Review: Transportation Worker Identification Credential (TWIC®) Program," *Federal Register*, Vol. 82, No. 53, March 21, 2017b, p. 14522.

and October, and decrease again in November. The distribution of applications across standard enrollments, renewals, comparable enrollments, and replacement cards has been fairly consistent over time.[472] Figure E.2 shows the breakdown for FY 2018. Standard enrollments constituted the largest share, at 48 percent, followed by renewals at 45 percent. Replacement cards and comparable enrollments constituted approximately 6 percent and 1 percent, respectively.

Figure E.1. TWIC Enrollments, by Month, October 2014 Through September 2018

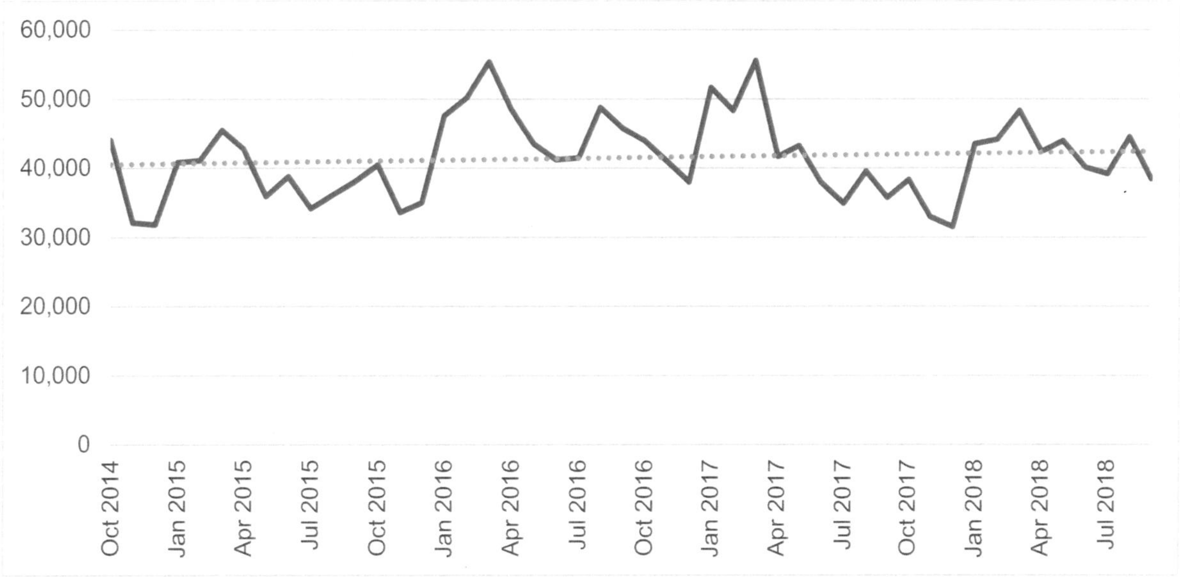

SOURCE: Administrative data provided by TSA.

NOTE: The slope parameter of the trend line (dotted) is not statistically significant (p-value = 0.5093).

---

[472] We omitted EED renewals because TSA last offered them in December 2014.

Figure E.2. TWIC Enrollments, by Type, FY 2018

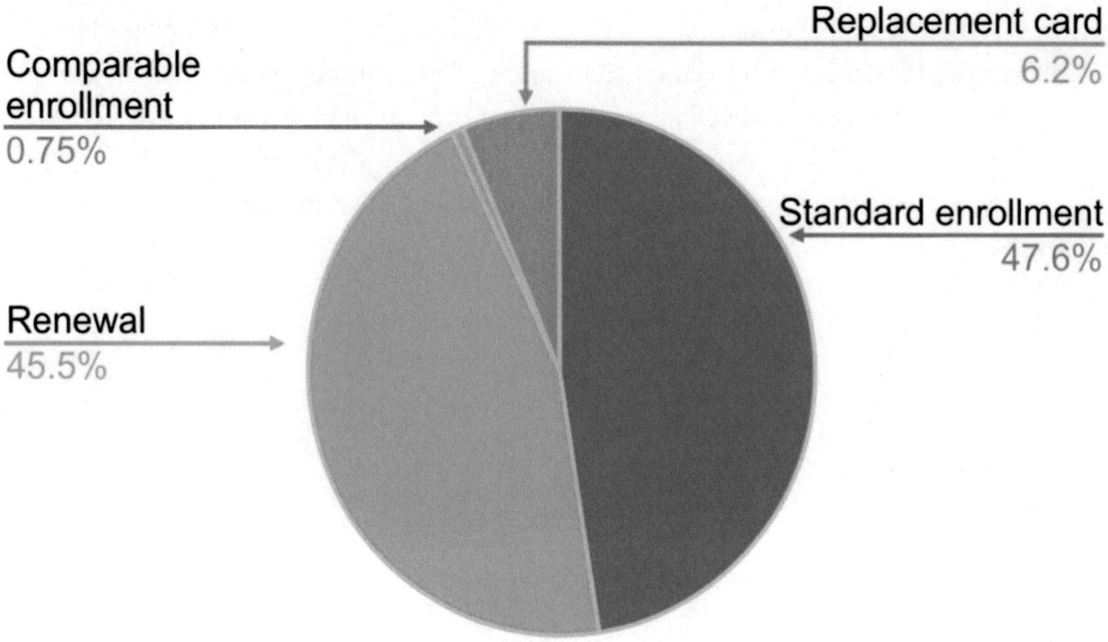

Comparable enrollment
0.75%

Replacement card
6.2%

Standard enrollment
47.6%

Renewal
45.5%

SOURCE: Administrative data provided by TSA.

Cost History

Table E.2 summarizes program costs for FYs 2016, 2017, and 2018. Annual costs are broken down into four categories: enrollment, personnel, IT, and other.

Table E.2. TWIC Costs, by Cost Category, in Dollars

Cost Category	FY 2016	FY 2017	FY 2018
Enrollment			
UES	18,275,121	17,324,524	16,458,284
CHRC	6,537,895	4,849,626	4,597,937
Total	24,813,016	22,174,150	21,056,221
Personnel			
Security specialist	2,294,108	2,905,084	2,783,065
Investigator	776,016	610,009	620,539
Other personnel	2,429,315	2,243,825	2,780,105
Total	5,499,438	5,758,918	6,183,710
IT system			
TIM	6,233,722	6,496,285	9,023,948
TIM CMS	8,028,679	7,224,222	7,827,215
TVS	3,182,734	1,394,760	1,524,553
Total	17,445,134	15,115,266	18,375,716
GPO	7,916,936	6,596,055	7,354,625
ILM Corporation of Virginia	170,604	168,073	177,135
CSOC facility	218,751	126,530	157,509
SAVE	25,200	0	60,000
Other cost	1,633,963	4,827,832	6,896,420
Total	57,723,043	54,766,823	60,261,336

SOURCE: Administrative data provided by TSA.
NOTE: TIM = Technology Infrastructure Modernization. CMS = card management system. GPO = U.S. Government Publishing Office. CSOC = Colorado Springs Operations Center.

Enrollment costs consist of fees paid for UES and CHRCs. *UES* refers to enrollment services that a vendor provides to the TWIC program. These services include "the capture of biometric data (photographs/fingerprints), biographic data, and identity documentation to enroll and register" for the program.[473] The current contract rate for these services is $34.50 per enrollment; a reduced rate of $15.25 applies to a replacement card. The vendor collects the total user fee from the applicant, retains the UES fee, remits the CHRC fee to the FBI, and sends the remainder to TSA. In FYs 2016, 2017, and 2018, enrollment costs accounted for about 40 percent of the TWIC program's total costs. Enrollment costs have roughly tracked enrollment volume, increasing in FY 2016 and decreasing in FYs 2017 and 2018.

Personnel costs have accounted for about 10 percent of program costs historically. Security specialists (OPM occupational series code 0080) review and adjudicate applications. In FYs 2016, 2017, and 2018, they accounted for 42 to 50 percent of total personnel costs.

---

[473] TSA, undated.

Investigators (OPM occupational series codes 1801, 1802, and 1811) perform research to validate potential matches between applicants or cardholders and the consolidated terrorism watch list. Informed by the research, they render decisions as to whether the TWIC program should refuse to issue an applicant a card or revoke the card of an existing cardholder. In the most-recent three FYs, investigators accounted for 10 to 14 percent of total personnel costs. Other personnel include program managers, program analysts, budget analysts, and attorney advisers.

The TWIC program uses two IT systems: TIM for case management and TVS to identify applicants with potential links to terrorism. These systems account for about 30 percent of program costs for FYs 2016, 2017, and 2018. TIM was responsible for the overwhelming majority, accounting for 82 percent of total IT costs in FY 2016, 91 percent in FY 2017, and 92 percent in FY 2018. The TIM costs reported in Table E.2 are broken down into TIM system costs and TIM CMS costs. TIM system costs are shared with other STA programs, but Table E.2 includes only the TWIC program's portion. TIM CMS costs are specific to TWIC; they support the licenses and certificates required for each physical credential. Historically, CMS costs have constituted about half of the TWIC program's total TIM costs in any given year.

Table E.2 identifies four additional costs: card production through GPO, document management by the ILM Corporation of Virginia, facility leases at CSOC, and SAVE checks through U.S. Citizenship and Immigration Services. Among these, GPO costs have been the most significant, accounting for 12 to 14 percent of total program costs for the most-recent three FYs. All remaining costs fall under the heading "other costs." These include expenses related to technology other than TIM and TVS, contract support to the program management office, consulting services, training, and travel.

The Adequacy of Current Revenue Collection

To assess whether fee revenue has been adequate in recent years, HSOAC researchers adopted a simple approach. We tracked annual surpluses and end-of-year carryovers for FYs 2016, 2017, and 2018 and deemed fee revenue adequate if both of the following conditions were true:

- End-of-year carryovers consistently exceeded 25 percent of annual obligations.
- Annual deficits, if any, were small relative to end-of-year carryovers.

The first condition requires that the program hold enough funds in reserve to manage short-term liquidity constraints. SMEs from the TWIC program and TSA's Business Management Office reported that a minimum of 25 percent of annual obligations is required to maintain liquidity from year to year. The 25-percent threshold should be considered a floor on the amount of funds to be held in reserve: A larger reserve could be warranted to cover large, planned investments, such as an IT upgrade. The second condition requires that the program either collect enough fee revenue to cover costs in each FY or hold enough funds in reserve to cover any shortfalls.

Table E.3 summarizes the TWIC program's revenue, cost, and carryover data for FYs 2016, 2017, and 2018. We calculated the carryover percentages by dividing the carryover amounts by the annual cost *net of pass-through costs*—that is, net of UES fees paid to the enrollment vendor and CHRC fees paid to the FBI. The reasonableness of any funds held in reserve to manage short-term liquidity constraints or cover future costs, anticipated or otherwise, should not be determined in relation to costs covered by funds that bypass TSA entirely.

Table E.3. TWIC Revenue, Cost, and End-of-Year Carryover

| FY | Revenue | Cost | | Annual Surplus | End-of-Year Carryover | |
		Total	Net of Pass-Through		Amount	Percentage of Cost
2016	67,787,753	57,723,043	32,910,027	10,064,710	49,819,379	151
2017	62,622,518	54,766,823	32,592,673	7,855,694	59,925,158	184
2018	59,932,641	60,261,336	39,205,115	−328,694	60,617,842	155

SOURCE: Administrative data provided by TSA.
NOTE: All data are in dollars except those in the "Percentage of Cost" column. Percentages were computed by dividing end-of-year carryover by annual cost net of pass-through costs. Annual surpluses do not align with changes in carryover from one FY to the next because the cost data are obligations, rather than expenditures. The change in carryover includes both annual surplus and recoveries (i.e., funds that were obligated but not expended and other billing adjustments).

TWIC revenue exceeded costs in FYs 2016 and 2017 by nearly 15 percent. By the end of FY 2017, carryover was about 1.8 times the annual cost net of pass-through costs. In FY 2018, costs exceeded revenue by about $300,000, but the deficit was covered by the $61 million that the program was holding in carryover. We determined that, with both conditions met, TWIC fee revenue has been adequate in recent years.

Tables E.4 and E.5 provide an alternative view of the adequacy of fees. To determine whether fees have been set appropriately across enrollment types, we computed per-enrollment costs for each enrollment type and compared these costs with the corresponding user fees. We considered the fee and underlying costs to be well aligned if they were within 25 percent of each other. Table E.4 provides top-line figures for FYs 2016, 2017, and 2018. Table E.5 provides a decomposition for FY 2018 only.

Table E.4. TWIC User Fees and Costs per Enrollment, in Dollars

FY	Fee or Cost	Standard Enrollment	Renewal	Comparable Enrollment	Replacement Card
2016	User fee	128.00	128.00	105.25	60.00
	Cost per enrollment	111.83	111.83	92.42	49.54
2017	User fee	125.25	125.25	105.25	60.00
	Cost per enrollment	110.58	110.58	91.59	48.99
2018	**User fee**	**125.25**	**125.25**	**105.25**	**60.00**
	Cost per enrollment	**128.18**	**128.18**	**108.19**	**55.76**

SOURCE: Administrative data provided by TSA.

Table E.5. TWIC Costs per Enrollment, by Cost Category, FY 2018, in Dollars

Cost Category	Standard Enrollment	Renewal	Comparable Enrollment	Replacement Card
Enrollment				
UES	34.93	34.93	34.93	15.68
CHRC	10.13	10.13	N/A	N/A
Total	45.07	45.07	34.93	15.68
Personnel				
Security specialist	6.13	6.13	N/A	N/A
Investigator	1.36	1.36	1.36	N/A
Other personnel	5.91	5.91	4.99	2.57
Total	13.40	13.40	6.35	2.57
IT system				
TIM	19.72	19.72	19.72	N/A
TIM CMS	16.05	16.05	16.05	16.05
TVS	3.33	3.33	3.33	N/A
Total	39.10	39.10	39.10	16.05
GPO	15.08	15.08	15.08	15.08
ILM Corporation of Virginia	0.39	0.39	N/A	N/A
CSOC facility	0.34	0.34	0.34	N/A
SAVE	0.13	0.13	N/A	N/A
Other costs	14.67	14.67	12.38	6.38
Total cost	128.18	128.18	108.19	55.76

SOURCE: Administrative data provided by TSA.
NOTE: The UES and CHRC costs per enrollment are slightly higher than the contracted rates of $34.50, $15.25, and $10.00. This would be consistent with the enrollment counts including STA approvals only.

In FYs 2016 and 2017, user fees exceeded average cost per enrollment for standard enrollments, renewals, and comparable enrollments by 13 to 15 percent, while the fee for replacement cards exceeded the underlying cost by 21 to 23 percent. In FY 2018, user fees aligned more closely with average cost per enrollment across all four enrollment types. Fees for standard enrollments, renewals, and comparable enrollments fell short of the underlying costs, but the margins were less than 3 percent. The fee for replacement cards continued to exceed per-enrollment cost, but the margin shrank to 8 percent.

Appendix F. Rationale for a Break-Even Analysis

Under Executive Order 12866,[474] as amended by Executive Order 13563,[475] federal agencies are required to assess all the costs and benefits of regulatory alternatives and to select regulatory approaches that maximize net benefits. Generally, a regulation's costs are more straightforward to quantify than its benefits. Break-even analyses have been widely used to assess the cost-effectiveness of various federal regulations. In each case, some or all of the benefits cannot be directly quantified—this can occur because the outcome of interest occurs too infrequently to be observable, the benefits cannot be monetized, or appropriate data are simply unavailable.[476] In the case of terrorism-related regulation, often the first case applies: The frequency of events cannot be observed with precision. Accordingly, break-even analysis is commonly used in such situations. Past examples include regulations pertaining to documentation at the U.S. border,[477] highway rail crossings,[478] restrictions on ammonium nitrate sales,[479] security of aircraft repair stations,[480] airline cargo screening standards,[481] and vessel cargo importer and carrier requirements.[482] The academic literature on terrorism prevention also invokes break-even

---

[474] William Jefferson Clinton, president, "Regulatory Planning and Review: Executive Order 12866 of September 30, 1993," *Federal Register*, Vol. 58, No. 190, October 4, 1993, pp. 51735–51744.

[475] Barack Obama, president, "Improving Regulation and Regulatory Review: Executive Order 13563 of January 18, 2011," *Federal Register*, Vol. 76, No. 14, January 21, 2011, pp. 3821–3823.

[476] For an in-depth justification of break-even analyses, including a review of the circumstances in which benefits might not be quantifiable, see Cass R. Sunstein, "The Limits of Quantification," *California Law Review*, Vol. 102, No. 6, December 2014, pp. 1369–1421. For a similar discussion pertaining to homeland security regulations in particular, see Scott Farrow and Stuart Shapiro, "The Benefit–Cost Analysis of Security Focused Regulations," *Journal of Homeland Security and Emergency Management*, Vol. 6, No. 1, 2009.

[477] U.S. Customs and Border Protection and Bureau of Consular Affairs, U.S. Department of State, "Documents Required for Travelers Departing from or Arriving in the United States at Sea and Land Ports-of-Entry from Within the Western Hemisphere," *Federal Register*, Vol. 73, No. 65, April 3, 2008, pp. 18383–18420.

[478] Federal Railroad Administration, "National Highway–Rail Crossing Inventory Reporting Requirements," *Federal Register*, Vol. 80, No. 3, January 6, 2015, pp. 745–790, § V.

[479] Office of the Secretary, DHS, "Ammonium Nitrate Security Program," *Federal Register*, Vol. 76, No. 149, August 3, 2011, pp. 46907–46957, § IV.

[480] TSA, "Aircraft Repair Station Security," *Federal Register*, Vol. 79, No. 8, January 13, 2014, pp. 2119–2143, § III.B.

[481] U.S. Customs and Border Protection, "Air Cargo Advance Screening (ACAS)," *Federal Register*, Vol. 83, No. 113, June 12, 2018, pp. 27380–27407, § V.

[482] Bureau of Customs and Border Protection, DHS, "Importer Security Filing and Additional Carrier Requirements," *Federal Register*, Vol. 73, No. 228, November 25, 2008, pp. 71729–71785, § X.

analyses to study, for example, the effectiveness of full-body scanners at airports[483] and container inspection policies at seaports.[484]

Terrorism risk is generally defined as having three components: the threat to a target, the target's vulnerability to the threat, and the consequences should the target be successfully attacked:[485]

> The *threats* to a target can be measured as the probability that a specific target is attacked in a specific way during a specified period . . . *Vulnerability* can be measured as the probability that damage occurs, given a threat. Damages [sic] could be fatalities, injuries, property damage, or other consequences; each would have its own vulnerability assessment. *Consequences* are the magnitude and type of damage resulting, given a successful terrorist attack.[486]

Break-even analysis requires only information on the costs of the regulation and the consequence of a successful terrorist attack to estimate a break-even threshold. The benefits of improved security measures can be expressed as the avoided consequences of a terrorist attack, measured in terms of averted losses (e.g., injuries and fatalities, property damage, and other economic impacts) that can be monetized. The USCG's 2015 regulatory analysis relied on estimates of the consequences of attack scenarios in MSRAM—whereby improved access controls could presumably mitigate a potential attack.[487] Further, averted losses are a direct function of the frequency with which terrorist attacks in the maritime environment are likely to occur. Although we have no way of knowing what this frequency is, a break-even analysis can help to make explicit the frequency with which terrorist attacks would need to occur before the benefits of averting them outweigh the costs of investments aimed at doing so.

A break-even analysis still does not "solve" the problem of not knowing the probabilities of threats or vulnerabilities. It is neither an answer in and of itself, nor a replacement for cost–benefit analysis. Rather, it provides useful information about the relationship of costs and benefits that, when supplemented with credible threat or hazard information and overlaid on a decisionmaker's risk propensity, can contribute to risk-informed decisions. The break-even threshold is expressed in terms of a required frequency of averting of successful terrorist attacks (i.e., the number of events that would have to be avoided each year for the benefits of a regulation to equal or offset the costs). In the best possible case, an agency might have a sense of

---

[483] Mark G. Stewart and John Mueller, "Cost–Benefit Analysis of Advanced Imaging Technology Full Body Scanners for Airline Passenger Security Screening," *Journal of Homeland Security and Emergency Management*, Vol. 8, No. 1, 2011, art. S30.

[484] Susan E. Martonosi, David S. Ortiz, and Henry H. Willis, "Evaluating the Viability of 100 Per Cent Container Inspection at America's Ports," in Harry W. Richardson, Peter Gordon, and James E. Moore II, eds., *The Economic Impacts of Terrorist Attacks*, Northampton, Mass.: Edward Elgar, 2005, pp. 218–241.

[485] Willis et al., 2005.

[486] Willis et al., 2005, p. xvi.

[487] Office of Standards Evaluation and Development, 2015.

an upper or lower bound.[488] A lower bound, or floor, can be informed by an expected value given a probability distribution of consequences and notion of the minimum frequency of events. An upper bound, or ceiling, can be defined by the baseline level of risk or the expected number of attempted terrorist attacks each year that could be averted. In the case of the TWIC-reader requirements, neither is known.

To highlight how a break-even analysis outlines a *relationship* between costs and benefits, consider Figure F.1.[489] The figure shows the type of curve that is the result of a break-even analysis. On the horizontal axis are benefits, in the form of costs averted by preventing a terrorist attack. On the vertical axis is the effectiveness in the form of events avoided per year, which we call the avoidance rate. The curve shows the pairs of adverse-event costs and associated avoidance rates for which the regulation in question would "break even." The curve runs from the upper-left corner of the graph to the lower right, highlighting an implicit trade-off between the size of an adverse event and the avoidance rate needed to yield a cost-effective regulation. In particular, a costly event (to the far right on the horizontal axis) would need to be averted with less frequency (lower on the vertical axis) and vice versa. The figure also shows that, for an event with a given cost, if the regulation could avoid the adverse event more often than the break-even threshold, the regulation's costs outweigh its benefits; conversely, if the regulation cannot avert an event of a given size with sufficient frequency, the regulation is not cost-effective.

---

[488] Sunstein, 2014.

[489] For a similar example, see Henry H. Willis and Tom LaTourrette, "Using Probabilistic Terrorism Risk Modeling for Regulatory Benefit–Cost Analysis: Application to the Western Hemisphere Travel Initiative in the Land Environment," *Risk Analysis*, Vol. 28, No. 2, April 2008, Figure 2.

Figure F.1. An Example Break-Even Analysis Curve

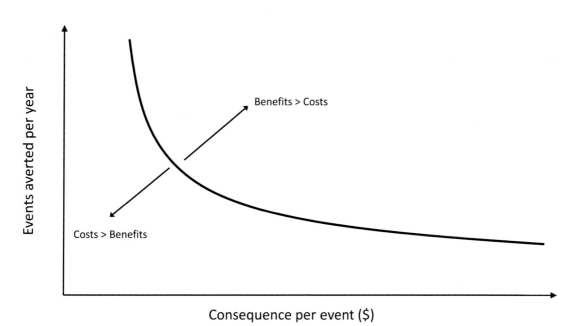

A regulation might also potentially avert multiple types of attacks. In a break-even analysis, such scenarios are typically analyzed separately. It is important to note that a regulation would be cost-effective if it achieved the required avoidance rate for *any* given attack mode. Furthermore, the regulation would also be cost-effective if any combination of improvements in avoidance rates across multiple attack modes were large enough to equal or exceed the break-even threshold (i.e., the quantified annual benefits were to fall in the area above the break-even line in Figure F.1).

Because the required avoidance rate estimated in a break-even analysis can sometimes be small, it can also be helpful to express it in terms of years between avoided events. The two numbers are the inverse of one another, as shown here:

$$years\ between\ avoided\ events = \frac{1}{events\ avoided\ per\ year}.$$

Mathematically, in terms of consequence, avoiding 0.1 events per year is the same as avoiding one event every ten years. We present the break-even threshold both in terms of events avoided per year and years between avoided events. Framing a break-even threshold in terms of years between avoided events can provide an intuitive benchmark for determining whether a regulation is likely to be cost-effective. The break-even threshold implies that an event must occur *at least* as often for the regulation to possibly be cost-effective (i.e., it implies that benefits have a ceiling). An example might help clarify this intuition. Suppose the annual cost of the rule were $1 million across all regulated facilities and vessels—and suppose the benefit of thwarting

221

a single TSI (i.e., the averted losses) were also $1 million.[490] A TSI would therefore need to be averted once a year to "break even." But this means that a TSI would need to *occur* at least once each year in the baseline for it to be feasible to justify the rule (i.e., for the rule to be considered effective) on a cost–benefit basis.[491] If, indeed, a TSI were averted each year because of the regulation, the rule would have zero net costs—hence the sector would break even, spending the same amount on compliance as it benefited in terms of averted losses. Now suppose that the consequence of a TSI were $10 million. In this case, TSIs would need to be averted only once every ten years (for an avoidance rate of 0.1 events per year) to justify the $1 million in annual costs. If the regulation averted more than one TSI every ten years, the rule would be cost-effective because the benefits would exceed the costs. Alternatively, if the consequence of a TSI were $10 million but the regulation averted only one TSI every 50 years, on average (for an avoidance rate of 0.02 events per year), the costs of the rule would be five times the benefits.

Relevance of Break-Even Analysis for Decisionmakers

From a decisionmaker's point of view, a break-even analysis lacks a major piece of information: the real-world likelihood of an event occurring.[492] As noted above, a break-even threshold implies a minimum frequency at which an event must occur for a regulation to be cost-effective. But the threshold cannot help decisionmakers answer whether a given avoidance rate can be achieved. Answering that question requires decisionmakers to have a credible sense of expected value regarding the real-world frequency of an attack.

To illustrate, consider the same example as before: a TSI with a consequence of $10 million. At an annualized cost of $1 million, the break-even threshold for the regulation is avoiding one event every ten years, or 0.1 events each year. Suppose decisionmakers judge that such an event occurs once every five years. Therefore, the break-even threshold implies that, for the regulation's costs to be justified, its measures would need to avert 50 percent of all such events. If, instead, decisionmakers judged that such an event were likely to occur once per year, only 10 percent of all such events would need to be avoided to justify the costs of the rule. In each case, the avoidance rate is 0.1 events per year, but the underlying frequency of the event itself constrains the capacity to achieve that threshold—clearly, it is easier to avoid one in ten attacks than one in two attacks.

---

[490] In this example, for simplicity, we do not specify a time horizon over which costs are incurred or discount future costs. However, the "annual cost" can be interpreted as being an annualized cost accounting for these factors.

[491] If the event itself occurs less than once a year, it is not possible to avert an average of one event each year, so the regulation could not be cost-effective under these conditions.

[492] The consequences of a TSI are also estimated, and some concerns about the adequacy of these estimates are discussed in the main text of Chapter 8. Nevertheless, there are at least some data that can be used to inform consequences; there are virtually no data that can be used to quantitatively estimate the probability of a TSI.

Given that a break-even analysis provides only part of the information necessary to determine whether a regulation is cost-effective, the results of this analysis cannot necessarily lead to a clear decision about desirable options to improve access controls for maritime facilities and vessels. Obviously, improvements that cost less than the current requirements of the TWIC program to use visual inspection, to which we refer as the baseline TWIC program, but perform the same would be desirable. Similarly, improvements that cost about the same as the baseline TWIC program but perform better also would be more desirable. But the choice is less clear for requirements for improved access controls that, for example, reduce the error rate in detecting fraudulent TWIC cards by 10 percent but cost twice as much as the current implementation of the TWIC program. Decisionmakers would need to weigh the public benefits of that option from a security perspective relative to the costs that private interests would absorb along with the inconveniences of the regulation. Break-even analysis could also help decisionmakers understand the trade-offs between cost and performance, even in the absence of knowing the absolute or relative risk of terrorist attacks.

Appendix G. Detailed Estimation of Costs and Benefits

This appendix provides further detail on how we derived inputs for our estimation of costs and benefits detailed in Chapter 8. We further discuss our estimation of costs, including how original USCG estimates were derived and our estimation of costs by category. We then provide additional detail on how we estimated components of the benefits of the TWIC-reader rule.

Detailed Estimation of Costs

In our search for data on the costs of TWIC readers for facilities subject to the final rule, we found that there is no typical facility in terms of security planning—even when comparing two facilities of a similar size and handling the same type of cargo. Many factors influence the various options and configurations available for TWIC implementation, including such factors as the number of access points and the size of the facility's restricted area. Interviewees indicated that certain aspects of pricing and contracting must also be considered when analyzing cost information. Chief among these is that facilities generally work with third-party integrators as vendors and therefore do not typically install readers themselves. The reliance on third-party integrators also means that different facilities might pay different prices even when using the same product if the integrator charges a different rate based on volume or other factors. The list price or manufacturer's suggested retail price (MSRP) of a TWIC reader can serve as a guide, but it is not necessarily the amount that every facility is paying. Further, some vendors do not sell readers outright but instead retain ownership of the hardware and bill an annual license fee for use. We were not able to gather precise information about the costs of annual licenses.

This means that it is often difficult, if not impossible, to itemize the costs attributed to each component of a project: TWIC readers, software, accessories, installation, additional infrastructure, and maintenance. In other cases, we received cost information for an entire port rather than each tenant facility. Where information was available, we could divide the total costs by the number of readers purchased or the number of gates being secured. When that was not feasible, we could contextualize aggregate costs for the collective access control measures at any given facility.

Cost Assumptions from the TWIC-Reader Pilot Program

From 2008 to 2011, TSA conducted the TWIC-reader pilot program, in collaboration with the USCG, under the direction of S&T. This pilot program was intended to help inform analysis about the efficacy and costs—capital and operational—of using electronic readers in the maritime environment. Participants voluntarily agreed to install and use biometric TWIC readers and, in most cases, PACSs capable of reading TWIC cards. DHS provided funds directly to support the pilot program. In addition, the Federal Emergency Management Agency (FEMA) awarded funds to participating ports and individual facility operators to install equipment and infrastructure for the pilot program through the Port Security Grant Program.[493] Seventeen participants completed the pilot program.

Data were collected through direct observation by TSA and independent test agents, documents provided by participants, and direct interviews. The pilot was conducted at MTSA-regulated ports, facilities, and vessel operation sites in these locations:

- the New York/New Jersey port complex
- Annapolis, Maryland
- Norco, Louisiana
- Vicksburg, Mississippi
- Brownsville, Texas
- Los Angeles, California
- Long Beach, California.

The pilot provided one of the first large-scale technology assessments of TWIC readers in a real-world setting. It showed that many options and configurations were available to facility and vessel operators for validating the authenticity of a TWIC card and verifying the identity of a cardholder—and these options came with a wide range of costs. Data collected from the pilot were used to inform key assumptions in the subsequent regulatory analysis of the proposed (and later final) TWIC-reader requirement rulemaking.[494] These assumptions related to the average number of fixed and portable readers, installation costs, and infrastructure costs, including integration with PACSs by facility type. A major concern of facilities, in addition to the capital and upkeep costs of readers, was that the use of readers would lengthen the time it takes to access the facility, potentially creating queues at entry points and generally slowing the flow of commerce. Therefore, entry throughput data (including wait times) were collected at each access point where a TWIC reader was used.

Estimation of Costs, by Component

Where we found additional cost information to be incomplete, or generally anecdotal, we often deferred to the lower cost estimates in the USCG's 2015 regulatory analysis.[495] Thus, this conservative approach builds on the 2015 regulatory analysis in quantifying the effectiveness of the TWIC-reader rule on a cost–benefit basis and supplements the analysis with additional data where available. However, it also means that the costs of the rule could be even higher than presented in this report. Where we draw primarily from the 2015 regulatory analysis, we refer

---

[493] At the time of the pilot program, 35 existing commercial models of TWIC readers were included in TSA's approved reader list, including fixed and portable readers, as well as contact and contactless readers.

[494] USCG, 2016.

[495] Office of Standards Evaluation and Development, 2015.

readers to that report and do not reproduce all of detail here.[496] However, for additional clarity and transparency, at the end of this appendix, we summarize the aggregate costs of the TWIC-reader rule by year, facility type, and cost category.

Capital Costs

In the next sections, we examine each of the capital cost components separately to estimate the implementation costs of the TWIC-reader rule. This starts with an assessment of the number of readers that facilities and vessels require to comply with the rule. However, we assessed that a cost analysis based on the aggregate expenditures of facilities for improved access controls is more appropriate than a bottom-up estimate based on the average number and cost of readers per facility. Given the wide range of options and configurations for acquiring and installing TWIC readers, using the aggregate capital cost of access control improvements rather than per-reader costs might yield a more reliable estimate that is independent of assumptions about the number and type of readers.

In comparison, the 2015 regulatory analysis first estimated the number of readers needed for each facility type: break-bulk terminals, container terminals, large–passenger vessel (cruise) terminals, small–passenger vessel (ferry) terminals, petroleum facilities, and mixed-use facilities.[497] It then estimated a per-reader cost for each component, including equipment, installation, infrastructure, and integration with PACSs. Finally, it multiplied the estimated cost per reader by the estimated number of readers required at that facility type. Hereafter, we refer to the sum of the components as the loaded cost per reader: the cost of the reader itself plus the cost of all supporting accessories, infrastructure, and labor required for installation and PACS integration. Using a loaded cost per reader makes the analytic approach highly sensitive to the key assumption about the number of readers. This could bias cost estimates either up or down when capital costs are not directly related to the number of readers or the number of readers is over- or underestimated. In the 2015 regulatory analysis, the estimated loaded cost per reader was approximately $30,000.[498] Informed by our findings, assuming the same distribution of facility types and fixed versus portable readers, we estimated this figure to be approximately $40,000, or between 1.3 and 1.4 times higher.

---

[496] Office of Standards Evaluation and Development, 2015.

[497] In Chapter 2, we discussed the complexity of maritime facilities, and not every facility would fall obviously into only a single facility type among these categories. (This is true even considering that petroleum facilities include liquid bulk facilities and that USCG added a category for mixed-use facilities.) In addition, data we received from USCG that categorized facilities were, in some cases, inconsistent with the facility operations we observed during our site survey. Therefore, we have additional concerns that existing USCG data do not allow for an easy and entirely accurate categorization of facilities by type.

[498] Individual estimates of the average costs of readers were calculated for each facility type. The weighted average cost is the average cost across all facilities weighted by the proportion of facilities of each facility type.

Estimated Number of Readers for Facilities

We found the 2015 regulatory analysis miscalculated the average number of readers per access point for facilities in the TWIC-reader pilot program. The magnitude of the error varies by facility type and is generally small; however, similar calculation errors led to more-significant underestimation of the average installation and infrastructure costs.[499] The 2015 regulatory analysis also relied on FSPs from a sample of facilities not representative of the regulated universe to estimate the average number of access points per facility.

The 2015 analysis estimates, using the FSP data, that implementation would require an average of 6.2 readers per facility across all facilities subject to the TWIC-reader rule.[500] In comparison, data from the TWIC-reader pilot program would suggest an average of 9.6 readers per facility across all facilities subject to the rule—approximately 55 percent more. The IBIA report also provided an estimate for the number of readers required to comply with the TWIC-reader rule, albeit noting specific limitations with the data.[501] That analysis looked at a small sample of facilities and extrapolated the numbers of readers required to a larger number of MTSA-regulated facilities. The extrapolation was necessarily speculative because the NPRM for the proposed rule had not yet been published, so IBIA did not know what types of facilities or how many facilities would be subject to the TWIC-reader rule.

Informed by a review of 25 ports surveyed by TSA, IBIA calculated that ports with medium to large operations have an average of 170 vehicle and pedestrian access points.[502] We used facilities as the unit of analysis, whereas IBIA used ports; below, we discuss the relevant assumptions to derive comparable estimates. Using information from the Port of Miami, IBIA further assumed that 90 percent of entry points were vehicle gates (the other 10 percent being pedestrian gates) and 22 percent of vehicle gates were multiuse access points requiring two fixed readers (high-mounted readers for container trucks and low-mounted readers for cars).[503] Finally, IBIA estimated that entities subject to the rule would use portable readers at a ratio of about one portable reader for every five fixed readers. This implies that a port with medium to large operations, one containing facilities most likely subject to the TWIC-reader rule, would require about 246 readers or an average of 10.3 readers per facility.[504] IBIA noted that this figure could

---

[499] In the discussion of the estimated installation costs, we provide a more detailed explanation of the calculation error.

[500] The average number of readers per facility is a weighted average across all facilities, weighted by the proportion of facilities of each facility type.

[501] IBIA, "TWIC Reader Acquisition Cost Estimates," June 20, 2011.

[502] IBIA, 2011.

[503] Because IBIA based its assumptions about the configurations and types of access points on those at a single facility—a large container terminal—we question the extent to which the estimates are representative and unbiased.

[504] To convert between ports and facilities, note that TSA and USCG estimated that 3,492 facilities were potentially subject to the regulation (TSA and USCG, 2006). IBIA estimated that the United States had 146 MTSA-regulated ports, which suggests an average of about 24 facilities per port. IBIA estimated that a port with medium to large operations would require 246 readers—an average of 10.3 readers per facility.

be 40 percent lower for ports with average or typical operations for the industry, or about 148 readers per port or an average of 6.2 readers per facility. However, facilities at ports with small operations—which are included in this average—are not likely to be subject to the final rule, so the industry average might not be a reliable benchmark. IBIA further assumed that a vessel would require two fixed readers for crew entry points and that roughly half the vessels would require one portable reader each.

FEMA port security grants provide yet another source of evidence for the number of readers required at each facility. From a sample of FEMA port security grant applications submitted between FY 2017 and FY 2018 where itemized detail was provided, 22 applicants requested a total of 239 readers—an average of 10.9 readers per applicant. Among FSOs who provided us detailed information on the number of readers they purchased, the average was 12.3 readers per facility. This figure, however, oversimplifies findings, given the wide range of options and configurations. For example, approximately half the facilities we visited that provided this information had only one or two readers, while the other half had a dozen or more readers and, in some cases, several dozen. This variation across facilities can result from the different ways in which facilities define their secure areas. For example, if the secure area is the entire facility with only one or two gates, the number of readers will be correspondingly small. Conversely, a facility with multiple, noncontiguous secure areas or large areas with many gates would require more readers.

From all data sources considered, information from the TWIC-reader pilot program falls below the estimate from port security grant applications—the pilot program suggests a weighted average of 9.6 readers per facility for all facilities subject to the TWIC-reader rule.[505] The 2015 regulatory analysis adjusted this prior estimate to account for large ferry terminals requiring significantly more readers than average-sized ferry terminals. Using an analogous adjustment to account for the uneven distribution of readers across facilities, we recalculated a weighted average of 9.9 readers per facility across all facility types. Although our concerns remain that the facilities in the pilot program were not representative of facilities subject to the TWIC-reader rule, using estimates from the pilot program has two advantages: (1) it accounts for differences in the number of readers by facility type, and (2) it is less likely to overrepresent facilities at ports with small operations—which is a concern with the FSP data because they likely underestimate the number of access points and hence the number of readers required. The weighted average of 9.9 readers per facility is generally consistent with data in other sources we found. An alternative approach that would have roughly the same effect would be to increase each estimate of the average number of readers in the 2015 regulatory analysis by about 55 percent for each facility type.

---

[505] Individual estimates of the average number of readers required are calculated for each facility type based on the pilot program data. The weighted average number of readers is based on the proportion of facilities of each facility type and includes all facilities subject to the rule.

Table G.1 reports the total number of readers required to comply with the TWIC-reader rule. Although we were unable to collect information on the exact number of fixed and portable readers for each facility we visited, our findings generally support the estimated distribution readers by reader type and facility type based on the TWIC pilot program. In its report, IBIA estimated a similar ratio of fixed to portable readers for container facilities, but the results were not generalizable to all facility types. Therefore, although we estimated that more readers overall would be required, we assumed the same distribution between fixed and portable readers. We estimated that approximately 5,200 readers would have to be purchased and installed to comply with the rule.

Table G.1. Total Number of Readers Required, by Facility Type

| Facility Type | Number of Facilities | Average Number per Facility | Readers | | | | |
| | | | Fixed | | Portable | | |
			Number	Percentage	Number	Percentage	Total
Bulk liquids	290	10.3	2,517	84	480	16	2,997
Break-bulk and solids	16	8.3	89	67	44	33	133
Container	3	18.0	44	81	10	19	54
Passenger							
Large (cruise)	92	16.0	109	7	1,363	93	1,472
Small (ferry)	63	4.9	0	0	306	100	306
Mixed use	61	4.0	174	71	70	29	244
Total	525	9.9	2,933		2,273		5,206

Estimated Number of Readers for Vessels

The 2015 regulatory analysis estimated that vessels subject to the final rule would need to have two portable readers but would not incur significant installation or infrastructure costs. This might understate actual costs for several reasons. Vendors and other SMEs stated that large vessels and large-vessel terminals (in addition to other large facilities) might choose fixed readers rather than portable readers, or a combination of the two, because they frequently have large numbers of TWIC cardholders arriving at the same time on certain days and are concerned about delays. We also found that vessels would have unique infrastructure needs to utilize readers, further increasing costs even if the average vessel needs fewer readers than the average facility does. This could include installing physical barriers to board crew members and passengers separately to validate worker credentials and fixed equipment, which might require the costly penetration of watertight bulkheads for wiring. We estimated that the total capital costs for vessels subject to the rule are of a similar order of magnitude to those for the average facility, so we did not explicitly break out fixed-reader costs from other capital costs for large passenger vessels. However, to avoid underestimating replacement costs, we continued to assume that vessels would incur costs equivalent to those for replacing two portable readers every five years.

Reader Costs

The 2015 regulatory analysis estimated the cost of TWIC readers to be $5,373 for fixed readers and $7,035 for portable readers, including hardware and software. This information is based on the U.S. General Services Administration schedule for IT (for fixed readers) and information from the TSA's QTL (for portable readers).

Given initial manufacturer pricing for TSA-approved readers, IBIA estimated that the cost of hardware would range from $2,000 to $4,000 for fixed readers—depending in part on indoor/outdoor functionality—and $1,500 to $4,000 for portable readers.[506] IBIA further estimated that software licenses were likely to cost one-third and one-half of the hardware costs for fixed and portable readers, respectively—with the exception of TWIC-to-PACS registration software licenses, which might be required for indoor readers, costing about twice what the reader hardware costs. Thus, the combined hardware and software costs are $4,250 for fixed outdoor readers and portable readers and $8,750 for fixed indoor readers. We note that these prices might be outdated because several reader models represented are no longer commercially available.

From interviews with several vendors of readers capable of reading TWIC cards that use fingerprint verification, we obtained an additional range of reader costs. The MSRP for a single reader ranged from $2,000 to $7,500, which might or might not include accessories that are necessary to operate it. Accessories, such as cables, charging dock, batteries, ethernet adapters, and other pieces that are minimally required for operation, can cost $100 to $500 each. This could add up to $2,500 to the up-front cost of each reader. However, according to invoices that facilities shared with us, the total cost of accessories in addition to a reader typically ranged from $400 to $1,200.

Invoices from facilities show that reader costs vary substantially, similar to the prices quoted by vendors. The cost of fingerprint-reader hardware alone ranged from $1,800 to $10,500 per reader, with most costing between $3,000 and $5,500. In interviews with FSOs, we found reader costs in some cases to be even higher because facilities opted for biometric verification using facial recognition or iris scanning rather than the less-expensive fingerprint verification. These biometric readers cost between $21,000 and $29,000 each, including accessories. Representatives of facilities that invested in this technology said that they had determined that facial recognition was faster or less prone to error (or both) than fingerprint verification.

In other cases, facilities were using electronic, but nonbiometric, readers, including contactless wall switch readers (proximity readers) that allow the user to tap an access card to gain entry. Because these proximity readers lack certain identity validation capabilities of

---

[506] IBIA, 2011.

biometric readers, they would not comply with the TWIC-reader rule. However, they can still electronically verify a TWIC card or a facility-specific credential and are less expensive than biometric readers. Invoices show that contactless readers cost between $250 and $650 each, plus as much as $700 to $1,500 for installation components, such as a wall box to control door access.

The reader cost estimates in the 2015 regulatory analysis were within the range of equipment costs that we found. However, information from vendors and facility invoices indicate that the average cost did not reflect certain components or licensing fees for specific vendors or models. We estimated that these costs could add hundreds of dollars or more per reader. However, we did not observe significantly higher or lower average reader costs. Because it is uncertain which vendors, reader models, and configurations might have higher costs, we relied on the previous cost estimates for reader hardware and software.

Reader Replacement Costs

The 2015 regulatory analysis assumed that readers would have to be replaced every five years, on average. The vendor and facility representatives we interviewed generally agreed with this assessment. In specific cases, interviewees suggested, fixed readers and, specifically, contactless readers had the greatest longevity because they have no moving parts, which can become damaged through general use over time.

Installation Costs

Based on an analysis of data from the TWIC-reader pilot program, the 2015 regulatory analysis estimated that average installation costs per reader range from $3,000 to $33,000, depending on the facility type. Based on the distribution of facilities subject to the final rule, the weighted average installation cost is estimated to be approximately $7,100 per reader. However, we found that the 2015 regulatory analysis miscalculated the average installation cost per reader from the pilot program data. Appendix D (Figure D1) of the 2015 regulatory analysis shows that this calculation failed to account for the number of readers at each facility.[507] For example, for the three petroleum facilities, the arithmetic mean of the final column "cost per reader" shows an installation cost of $6,281 per reader. However, in the two columns immediately to the left, the facilities incurred average installation costs of $75,544 with an average of 10.3 readers per facility, yielding an average installation cost of $7,311 per reader.[508] In this one example, the 2015 analysis underestimated installation costs by 20 percent for petroleum facilities. Across all facility types, the 2015 analysis used data from the pilot to calculate installation costs, underestimating them by approximately 46 percent. When we corrected for these errors, we

---

[507] Because some facilities purchased more readers than others, we use a weighted arithmetic mean to estimate the average cost per reader. The previous regulatory analysis implicitly assigned facilities equal weights regardless of the number of readers purchased and installed.

[508] Multiplying each of the two estimates by the total number of readers validates the second approach: $6,281 × 31 readers = $194,703 and $7,311 × 31 readers = $226,633. The latter figure is equal to the actual total installation costs incurred by these three participants in the pilot program.

found that the weighted average installation cost across all facilities would be approximately $10,100 per reader, or 42 percent more than the estimate in the 2015 analysis.

Although we attempted to validate this estimate of the average installation cost per reader by collecting data from other independent sources, we found relatively few itemized budgets that were generalizable to the entire population of facilities. In most cases, an FSO could provide a total cost for access control improvements but could not break out installation costs. We note that IBIA estimated that installation costs were about $10,000 for fixed outdoor readers, while the estimated installation costs for fixed indoor readers were about $2,000—but also required TWIC-to-PACS software for integration with existing PACSs at an additional cost of $5,000.

Infrastructure and PACS Integration Costs

The 2015 regulatory analysis also miscalculated average infrastructure costs, including PACS integration, on a per-reader basis. Based on the distribution of facilities subject to the final rule, the miscalculated estimate was $17,248 per reader—or 47 percent less than the properly calculated value of $24,629.

We attempted to validate this estimate also by collecting data from other sources. However, the invoice and interview data generally did not distinguish installation from infrastructure and PACS integration costs. We note that IBIA estimated that, for fixed readers, the cost of integration with PACS was of a similar order of magnitude to the cost of the reader hardware itself. Interviews with FSOs and vendors suggested that that this estimate was low and did not account for incompatibility with existing software and other necessary system upgrades, which likely cost tens of thousands of dollars.

TWIC Capital Cost Expenditures, According to Aggregated Facility Data

Past FEMA port security grants for TWIC-related improvements provide an additional source of cost data that are not based on estimated loaded reader costs. Having these data gave us an alternative means to estimate the average up-front capital costs for facilities. According to analysis of 557 FEMA port security grants awarded for between FY 2007 and FY 2018, average TWIC-related expenditures were approximately $440,000 (in 2018 dollars), including the federal share and match contribution.[509] Across all years, the total value of TWIC-related awards accounted for approximately 7.5 percent of the total amount funded by the Port Security Grant

---

[509] In November 2018, the Port Security Grant Program provided us the port security grant award information for TWIC-related improvements. Using facility names and geographic locations, we identified approximately 20 percent of recipients as risk group A facilities. However, because of differences in facility names and awards going to ports with multiple (rather than single) facilities, it was not possible to match all risk group A facilities. Average TWIC-related expenditures for identified risk group A facilities were approximately $400,000, slightly less than for all facilities. A two-sample *t*-test shows that the difference in the average award between the identified risk group A facilities and nonidentified recipients was not statistically significant. Because (1) FEMA generally uses facility risk as an award criterion, (2) it was not possible to match all facilities, and (3) we did not find that being overinclusive would bias our estimates, we did not limit our sample to only identified risk group A facilities.

Program, or approximately $17.3 million per year.[510] In most years, with the exception of FY 2009–FY 2011 awards made under the American Recovery and Reinvestment Act of 2009, the grants had a cost-sharing requirement.[511] Therefore, the total value of TWIC-related improvements generally exceeds the awarded amount. Table G.2 provides a summary of port security grants awarded for TWIC-related improvements between FY 2007 and FY 2018.

Table G.2. Summary of FEMA Port Security Grants for TWIC-Related Improvements

FY	Number of Awards	Federal Award Amount		TWIC-Related Expenditures, Including Matching Contributions	
		Total[a]	Average[b]	Total[a]	Average[b]
2007	89	25,800,000	290,000	34,100,000	380,000
2008	68	22,800,000	330,000	29,900,000	440,000
2009	92	38,700,000	420,000	45,700,000	500,000
2010	63	35,500,000	560,000	35,500,000	560,000
2011	56	26,200,000	470,000	26,200,000	470,000
2012	33	18,000,000	550,000	24,800,000	750,000
2013	31	8,900,000	290,000	11,500,000	370,000
2014	26	6,000,000	230,000	8,000,000	310,000
2015	11	1,900,000	180,000	2,700,000	240,000
2016	39	9,200,000	230,000	11,500,000	290,000
2017	37	11,500,000	310,000	14,300,000	390,000
2018	12	2,700,000	220,000	3,500,000	290,000
Total	**557**	**207,200,000**	**370,000**	**248,000,000**	**440,000**

NOTE: Totals include only grants for TWIC-related improvements, which account for less than 10 percent, on average, of the total funding for all port security grants. Because of rounding, some data do not sum precisely.
[a] In 2018 dollars, rounded to the nearest hundred thousand.
[b] In 2018 dollars, rounded to the nearest ten thousand.

Several port operators and facility operators received multiple awards in the same FY or in different years. When we accounted for multiple awards, we found that average TWIC-related expenditures among approximately 340 entities were $740,000 per recipient.[512] We also note that

---

[510] For the five most recent FYs through FY 2018, the program funded $100 million worth of grants per year. On average, grants for TWIC-related improvements accounted for less than $10 million per year from FY 2014 to FY 2018.

[511] For FY 2007 through FY 2009 and FY 2012 through FY 2014, the cost-sharing requirement was 25 percent for public-sector recipients and 50 percent for private-sector recipients. For FY 2015 through FY 2017, the match requirement was 25 percent for recipients in both sectors. In FY 2018, the match requirement was 25 percent for public-sector recipients and 50 percent for private-sector recipients—except for projects deemed to provide port-wide risk benefit, which need a matching contribution of only 25 percent.

[512] The number of entities is an approximation because recipients were matched by port or facility or by operator name and location. In some cases, different names or variations appeared on applications for the same facility (in the same year or in different years); in other cases, the owner or operator changed. Furthermore, it was not possible to

some recipients had TWIC-related expenditures totaling millions of dollars, including participants in the TWIC-reader pilot program. The wide range of costs reflects, in part, the numerous options and configurations available for TWIC readers.

The grants included improvements that were not necessarily accounted for in the 2015 regulatory analysis. From the FEMA Port Security Grant Program data, it is not always possible to determine whether such improvements were directly related to TWIC. For example, installing an extra gate might be necessary to optimize traffic flows once a reader is installed. Similarly, installing a command and control center might be needed to remotely operate multiple TWIC access gates. The 2015 regulatory analysis did not capture either of these investments specifically, but they might be integral to a facility's TWIC reader implementation plan. In reviewing more-detailed grant applications for FYs 2017 and 2018, we noted that budgets included other items in addition to TWIC readers, installation, and infrastructure, such as cameras, command centers, and guard booths. Such equipment and installations might have been a component of revised security plans and business operations at individual facilities. However, it was not possible to distinguish items required for TWIC-related access control measures from items requested for other security measures.

The facility interviewees noted that TWIC readers alone did not provide benefits without robust access control systems, including fences and gates. Nonetheless, to derive an estimate as close as possible to the direct costs associated with TWIC's implementation, we excluded grants that included investments in specific structures or equipment (e.g., backup generators), on the assumption that not all items were directly TWIC-related—we did not have itemized applications to determine what proportion of costs were directly related to TWIC. Although the average TWIC-related investment in FYs 2017 and 2018 was approximately $360,000, our exclusion of this subset of awards brought the average investment to approximately $300,000—or approximately 20 percent less. The difference in cost might or might not be directly associated with items not explicitly stated in the TWIC-reader requirements.

Recent data show a decrease in the number and dollar amount of TWIC-related Port Security Grant Program awards. In FY 2018, just 12 TWIC-related grants were awarded, totaling $2.7 million, for an average total investment worth approximately $290,000 per facility. Compared with previous years, this reflects a decrease of more than 75 percent in the average number of awards and a decrease of more than 35 percent in the average value of TWIC-related investments. We attribute this decline to the announced delay in the implementation of the TWIC-reader rule.[513] Our estimates are still higher than the costs predicted in the 2015

---

determine whether separate awards were issued for different facilities managed by a single port operator or for different investments at the same facility.

[513] Per our interviews, we know that, in some cases, facilities have recently sought port security grants to update previously purchased readers that had been out of use for several years and were partially obsolete. Given that we did not have specifics of the port security grants, we could not determine whether this could be a reason the average grant amount was lower for FY 2018.

regulatory analysis, whether we include or exclude investments in specific items that might not be directly related to TWIC. This is the case even though the direct TWIC-related portion of FEMA port security grants is likely to be smaller than the total award amount, and recent awards for TWIC requests have been fewer and smaller.

We also conducted interviews at 24 facilities subject to the TWIC-reader rule for which someone was able to provide general cost information, and an additional 11 facilities subject to the rule provided us invoices showing actual expenditures for TWIC-related improvements. This information shows that facilities spent hundreds of thousands of dollars in up-front capital costs, ranging from $150,000 to $1.3 million, to acquire and install TWIC readers. Capital costs were generally significantly lower for portable readers or for facilities where fixed readers integrated easily into existing PACSs. A few facilities adopted facial recognition technology, which tended to be significantly more expensive than fingerprint scanners. The average up-front capital cost for the facilities we visited that provided detailed cost information was approximately $400,000 per facility. Facility interviewees reported that they purchased as few as one and, in some cases, more than 100 readers—they cited various factors that influenced their decisions, including facility type, size, and ownership structure. For example, in some ports, the lessor handled access control for all tenant facilities and purchased readers that lessees borrowed or rented.

Summary of Estimated Capital Costs

In the 2015 regulatory analysis, up-front capital costs—that is, capital costs excluding replacement costs for readers—were estimated to be $99.0 million (about half the total cost of the TWIC-reader rule). This reflects an average up-front capital cost of $190,000 per facility and $14,000 per vessel subject to the final rule.[514]

We found that actual expenditures for TWIC-related investments have generally been higher than the estimates. We estimated that average up-front capital costs had totaled approximately $400,000 (in 2012 dollars) for both facilities and vessels.[515] Although we did not have detailed information on the individual components, we could separately analyze the cost of readers. We could then scale the remaining up-front capital costs by the total number of fixed readers for each facility type to derive the proportion of costs attributable to the combined installation, infrastructure, and PACS integration costs. Table G.3 reports our estimates of the average total and disaggregated up-front capital costs associated with acquiring and installing electronic readers, by facility type. The number of facilities comes from the 2015 regulatory analysis,

---

[514] Again, this is a weighted average based on the distribution of facilities across facility types. We estimated an average capital cost for each facility type.

[515] Using port security grant information, we calculated the average value of TWIC-related improvements as $440,000 in 2018 dollars or approximately $400,000 in 2012 dollars, using the annual GDP implicit price deflator. See Bureau of Economic Analysis, 2019. Similarly, facility and vessel personnel we interviewed estimated that they incurred, on average, approximately $400,000 in TWIC-related capital costs over a similar time period.

paired with our estimates of the average number of readers, average reader and supporting costs, and total average up-front capital costs per facility.

Table G.3. Average Up-Front Capital Costs, by Facility Type

Facility Type	Number of Facilities[a]	Average Number of Readers per Facility	Average Cost per Facility, in 2012 Dollars		
			Reader	Installation, Infrastructure, and PACS Integration	Up-Front Capital
Bulk liquids	290	10.3	58,000	530,000	590,000
Break-bulk and solids	16	8.3	49,000	340,000	390,000
Container	3	18.0	100,000	890,000	990,000
Passenger					
Cruise	92	16.0	110,000	72,000	180,000
Ferry	63	4.9	34,000	0	34,000
Mixed use	61	4.0	23,000	170,000	200,000
Total	**525**	**9.9**	**60,000**	**340,000**	**400,000**

NOTE: Costs are reported in 2012 dollars.
[a] SOURCE: Office of Standards Evaluation and Development, 2015.

Maintenance Costs

In addition to the up-front capital costs, the 2015 regulatory analysis estimated that facilities and vessels would incur maintenance costs equal to 10 percent of reader costs. Interviews with vendors suggest that it is reasonable to estimate an average maintenance cost on a per-reader basis but that those costs were likely to be 50 to 100 percent higher. Vendors provided a range of maintenance costs that were generally 15 to 20 percent of the list price or MSRP. This would put maintenance costs between $800 and $1,400 per reader per year. We also note that we conducted interviews at several facilities that had purchased multiyear warranties with lower average annual costs ranging from $300 to $700 per reader—roughly equivalent to 10 percent of the up-front reader costs. However, other maintenance costs, such as repairs for outdoor-reader housing, would be covered by the facility using its own full-time staff, making total maintenance costs more difficult to determine. Using this information, we estimated that annual maintenance costs would be about 17.5 percent of the up-front reader costs.

Operational Costs

Amending the FSP

In the 2015 regulatory analysis, the estimated costs of amending the FSP were based on the predicted time it would take an FSO to submit an amendment detailing how TWIC readers would be incorporated into their security measures, multiplied by the hourly labor cost of an FSO. This translates to $1,778 per facility. Our interviews with FSOs suggest that updating the FSP could, in some cases, be much more expensive than that. Some facilities indicated that, rather than revise the FSP on their own, they would contract expert security consultants to evaluate a wide range of TWIC-related and other operational impacts. This is because, like plan renewal, an amendment generally involves conducting a new vulnerability assessment. It is not clear what portion of facilities would conduct such an assessment using outside security experts. Although the data were anecdotal, facility personnel provided estimates ranging from $20,000 to $60,000 to submit an FSP amendment. Because we did not have more-specific information, we deferred to the estimates in the 2015 regulatory analysis.

Recordkeeping Systems

The 2015 regulatory analysis estimated that the cost to develop a recordkeeping system to comply with the final rule was equivalent to 40 hours of an FSO's time, plus about six hours per year for ongoing maintenance. Using information from site visits and interviews, we agreed with the assessment that most PACS, as well as software systems for several readers, now in place had this capability. Therefore, we believe that these estimates are reasonable.

Updating the CCL

The 2015 regulatory analysis estimated that some facilities and vessels subject to the rule would have to manually download CCL updates, which takes, on average, 30 minutes per week per facility. Informed by interviews with personnel from vendors and facilities, we found that most electronic reader systems in place automatically update the CCL every 24 hours (or some other user-specified interval) or have the capability to do so. Therefore, the 2015 analysis might have overestimated the number of facilities that would rely on a manual process. As indicated in public comments in response to the NPRM, updating the CCL automatically would not likely be a significant cost burden of the rule. Therefore, we estimated that this cost would be negligible and did not include it in our break-even analysis.

Personnel Training

In the 2015 regulatory analysis, the estimated costs of personnel training included the time for an FSO or vessel security officer and additional security personnel to undergo training on electronically inspecting TWICs. As indicated in the analysis, existing regulations require all security personnel to be familiarized with the TWIC program and the relevant provisions of the FSP; therefore, the cost of the rule includes only the incremental cost of familiarization with electronic TWIC inspection. The 2015 regulatory analysis did not specify whether external trainers would be required to help familiarize security personnel with electronic TWIC inspections. Vendor interviewees indicated that their installers or third-party integrators could provide a technical overview of the reader equipment to the FSO or vessel security officer or to their dedicated security staff and that this cost would be included in the overall package. To the extent that additional outside security experts would be needed to provide training, these costs should also have been included. However, the personnel training cost estimates in the 2015 regulatory analysis seem reasonable.

Additional Costs

Delay Costs Due to Reader Failures

The 2015 regulatory analysis estimated that electronic TWIC inspections would result in delay costs if a reader could not validate a TWIC card or a cardholder's identity, thereby increasing the need for secondary screening procedures. Data from the TWIC pilot program showed that there was an 82.9-percent validation rate for electronic TWIC inspections. Reasons for inspections to be considered invalid included biometric failure; reader failure; user error; unreadable cards; and invalid, expired, or canceled cards. Although not all of these are actual failures, because the readers were presumably identifying invalid, expired, or canceled TWIC cards as they were intended to do, all invalid inspections would likely result in delays that might not have occurred if the facility or vessel personnel conducted only visual inspections. We used the 2015 regulatory analysis estimates for the amount of time required for secondary screening measures, which range from 6 seconds (for an additional visual inspection) to 120 seconds (for security personnel to travel to an unmanned access point, conduct a visual inspection, and grant or deny access). We were not able to independently verify these estimates.

In interviews, SMEs noted that delay costs varied based on the type of biometric verification being conducted. This is one reason certain facilities opted for facial recognition, iris scanning, or vascular (i.e., back-of-hand) scanning technology. They found such methods to be preferable to fingerprint scanning for either (or both) of two reasons: (1) faster validation and (2) fewer errors due to failures to read. Facility personnel estimated that these technologies saved 2 to 3 seconds per person over fingerprint scanners. Because we did not have data to validate these assumptions, we relied on the estimates in the 2015 regulatory analysis.

Additional Costs Due to TWIC Failures

Finally, the 2015 regulatory analysis estimated that TWIC cardholders would incur costs to replace damaged or defective TWIC cards that readers failed to read. We note that the analysis of failure modes was not backed by performance data from the TWIC-reader pilot program or other information. Therefore, the number of cards that would need to be replaced each year is still uncertain.

For the past several years, TSA has offered TWIC cardholders the option to request that replacement cards be sent to them by mail. Therefore, we estimated that the cost burden of replacing a TWIC card would be substantially less than estimated in the 2015 regulatory analysis because many workers could rely on this option rather than driving to TWIC enrollment centers—which could result in commuting costs and potential lost wages from missed work. In this case, workers would incur only the $60 cost of a replacement TWIC card. This reduced the estimated cost of replacement TWIC cards by nearly $1.7 million per year relative to the 2015 regulatory analysis.

The 2015 regulatory analysis did not include license fees or security personnel requirements, but facility personnel identified those costs as potential considerations when planning for reader installation. Although we acknowledge these potential costs or cost savings, we did not explicitly incorporate them in our analysis:

- **license fees:** Several FSOs and vendor interviewees indicated that some facilities paid license fees on readers. Most vendors reported that their software had one-time, rather than annual, fees. IBIA also estimated that some facilities would pay license fees on software for TWIC readers, up to a few thousand dollars per reader. As described in the discussion of the cost of readers, IBIA estimated that software licenses were likely to cost one-third to one-half of the hardware costs for fixed and portable readers, respectively. IBIA also estimated that TWIC-to-PACS registration software licenses, which might be required for indoor readers, cost about twice the cost of the reader hardware. License fees could be included in the bundled cost of reader hardware and software. For this reason, it was not feasible to separate them out from the limited data we collected.

- **security personnel:** Both vendor and facility interviewees indicated that, in some cases, TWIC readers could reduce labor costs. For example, fixed readers can eliminate the need to have a security guard at every entry gate. Instead, several gates with electronic readers could be manned by a single guard who—in person or remotely at a command center—can troubleshoot problems as they arise. Therefore, a facility might be able to save hundreds of thousands of dollars in annual costs if it could substitute readers for guards at multiple gates. These cost savings are most likely to be generated at facilities with large numbers of fixed readers, such as container terminals. For other facilities, TWIC readers can increase the need for security personnel. This is particularly true for mobile readers because a human must be present to operate them. Some facilities reported the need to hire additional personnel as escorts or to drive passenger vans that escort non–TWIC holders out of the restricted (secure) area once they disembarked from ships. Other facilities indicated that they would need to staff additional gates to reduce congestion once they started electronically authenticating TWIC cards. Vessel operators might also need to hire additional security officers to separately screen workers. These security officers would have to remain with the vessel for boarding and disembarkation at each port, so they would also require accommodation aboard the vessel. Because only one vessel would be subject to the rule, we did not account for these costs; they would not materially affect the overall cost estimate. However, should additional vessels become subject to the TWIC-reader rule, this represents a nontrivial cost that should be accounted for.

Government Costs

The 2015 regulatory analysis estimated that the primary cost to the government of the TWIC-reader rule would be to review amendments to security plans submitted by facilities and vessels. The USCG estimated that it would take its personnel four hours to review an amended FSP or three hours to review an amended vessel security plan. The USCG anticipated that it would review 526 amended security plans during the first two years after implementation of the rule, for a total of approximately 2,100 hours. We defer to the USCG's judgment on the costs to the government.

Summary of Industry Costs

Table G.4 summarizes the average costs of TWIC-reader rule, building on the basic framework in the 2015 regulatory analysis and supported with additional cost data collected during the course of this project, for each facility and vessel type. The USCG anticipated a two-year implementation period and estimated that the up-front costs (e.g., capital costs) would be split evenly over the first two years after implementation of the rule. The USCG also estimated that recurring costs (e.g., maintenance) would be incurred each year following the initial capital cost expenditure. As described in the 2015 regulatory analysis report, *additional costs* includes delay costs due to reader failures and card replacement costs due to TWIC failures.

Table G.4. Average Ten-Year Costs of the TWIC-Reader Rule, per Facility or Vessel, by Type

Facility or Vessel Type	Cost, in 2012 Dollars					
	Capital	Maintenance	Operational	Additional	Total 10-Year	Annualized
Bulk liquid	640,000	87,000	12,000	48,000	790,000	95,000
Break-bulk and solids	440,000	73,000	12,000	32,000	550,000	66,000
Container	1,100,000	150,000	12,000	2,000,000	3,300,000	350,000
Passenger						
Large	290,000	160,000	12,000	35,000	500,000	54,000
Small	68,000	51,000	12,000	15,000	150,000	15,000
Mixed use	220,000	35,000	12,000	15,000	280,000	34,000
Vessel	410,000	22,000	13,000	0	450,000	58,000

NOTE: We do not show discounted costs. We calculated annualized costs using a 7-percent discount rate. We rounded dollar amounts to two significant digits.

Tables G.5 through G.11 provide additional detail on the total costs by year, facility or vessel type, and cost component.

Table G.5. Total Costs for 290 Bulk Liquid Facilities, in 2012 Dollars, Undiscounted

Year	Capital			Operational					Additional	Total
	TWIC Readers	Installation, Infrastructure, and PACS Integration	Maintenance	Update FSP	Recordkeeping	Update CCL	Training	Delay	Card Replacement	
1	8,450,000	76,500,000	0	258,000	412,000	0	157,000	1,170,000	204,000	87,100,000
2	8,450,000	76,500,000	1,480,000	258,000	474,000	0	196,000	1,170,000	204,000	88,700,000
3	0	0	2,960,000	0	124,000	0	78,400	1,170,000	204,000	4,540,000
4	0	0	2,960,000	0	124,000	0	78,400	1,170,000	204,000	4,540,000
5	0	0	2,960,000	0	124,000	0	78,400	1,170,000	204,000	4,540,000
6	8,450,000	0	2,960,000	0	124,000	0	78,400	1,170,000	204,000	13,000,000
7	8,450,000	0	2,960,000	0	124,000	0	78,400	1,170,000	204,000	13,000,000
8	0	0	2,960,000	0	124,000	0	78,400	1,170,000	204,000	4,540,000
9	0	0	2,960,000	0	124,000	0	78,400	1,170,000	204,000	4,540,000
10	0	0	2,960,000	0	124,000	0	78,400	1,170,000	204,000	4,540,000
Total	33,800,000	153,000,000	25,100,000	516,000	1,880,000	0	980,000	11,700,000	2,040,000	229,000,000
Annualized	3,730,000	19,700,000	2,380,000	66,400	206,000	0	103,000	1,170,000	204,000	27,500,000

NOTE: We do not show discounted costs by year. We calculated annualized costs using a 7-percent discount rate. We rounded dollar amounts to three significant digits or the nearest hundred dollars.

241

Table G.6. Total Costs for 16 Break-Bulk and Solid Facilities, in 2012 Dollars, Undiscounted

Year	Capital			Operational					Additional	Total
	TWIC Readers	Installation, Infrastructure, and PACS Integration	Maintenance	Update FSP	Recordkeeping	Update CCL	Training	Delay	Card Replacement	
1	397,000	2,700,000	0	14,200	22,800	0	8,700	44,200	7,700	3,200,000
2	391,000	2,700,000	69,400	14,200	26,200	0	10,800	44,200	7,700	3,270,000
3	0	0	138,000	0	6,800	0	4,300	44,200	7,700	201,000
4	0	0	138,000	0	6,800	0	4,300	44,200	7,700	201,000
5	0	0	138,000	0	6,800	0	4,300	44,200	7,700	201,000
6	397,000	0	138,000	0	6,800	0	4,300	44,200	7,700	597,000
7	391,000	0	138,000	0	6,800	0	4,300	44,200	7,700	592,000
8	0	0	138,000	0	6,800	0	4,300	44,200	7,700	201,000
9	0	0	138,000	0	6,800	0	4,300	44,200	7,700	201,000
10	0	0	138,000	0	6,800	0	4,300	44,200	7,700	201,000
Total	1,580,000	5,410,000	1,170,000	28,400	104,000	0	54,100	442,000	76,800	8,860,000
Annualized	174,000	696,000	111,000	3,700	11,400	0	5,700	44,200	7,700	1,050,000

NOTE: We do not show discounted costs by year. We calculated annualized costs using a 7-percent discount rate. We rounded dollar amounts to three significant digits or the nearest hundred dollars.

Table G.7. Total Costs for Three Container Facilities, in 2012 Dollars, Undiscounted

Year	Capital			Operational					Additional	Total
	TWIC Readers	Installation, Infrastructure, and PACS Integration	Maintenance	Update FSP	Recordkeeping	Update CCL	Training	Delay	Card Replacement	
1	153,000	1,340,000	0	3,600	4,300	0	1,600	513,000	89,100	2,100,000
2	153,000	1,340,000	26,800	1,800	4,900	0	2,000	513,000	89,100	2,130,000
3	0	0	53,700	0	1,300	0	800	513,000	89,100	658,000
4	0	0	53,700	0	1,300	0	800	513,000	89,100	658,000
5	0	0	53,700	0	1,300	0	800	513,000	89,100	658,000
6	153,000	0	53,700	0	1,300	0	800	513,000	89,100	812,000
7	153,000	0	53,700	0	1,300	0	800	513,000	89,100	812,000
8	0	0	53,700	0	1,300	0	800	513,000	89,100	658,000
9	0	0	53,700	0	1,300	0	800	513,000	89,100	658,000
10	0	0	53,700	0	1,300	0	800	513,000	89,100	658,000
Total	614,000	2,670,000	456,000	5,300	19,400	0	10,100	5,130,000	891,000	9,800,000
Annualized	67,600	344,000	43,200	700	2,100	0	1,100	513,000	89,100	1,060,000

NOTE: We do not show discounted costs by year. We calculated annualized costs using a 7-percent discount rate. We rounded dollar amounts to three significant digits or the nearest hundred dollars.

Table G.8. Total Costs for 92 Large–Passenger Vessel Facilities, in 2012 Dollars, Undiscounted

Year	Capital		Operational						Additional	Total
	TWIC Readers	Installation, Infrastructure, and PACS Integration	Maintenance	Update FSP	Recordkeeping	Update CCL	Training	Delay	Card Replacement	
1	5,090,000	3,310,000	0	81,800	131,000	0	49,700	277,000	48,100	8,990,000
2	5,080,000	3,310,000	891,000	81,800	150,000	0	62,200	277,000	48,100	9,900,000
3	0	0	1,780,000	0	39,300	0	24,900	277,000	48,100	2,170,000
4	0	0	1,780,000	0	39,300	0	24,900	277,000	48,100	2,170,000
5	0	0	1,780,000	0	39,300	0	24,900	277,000	48,100	2,170,000
6	5,090,000	0	1,780,000	0	39,300	0	24,900	277,000	48,100	7,260,000
7	5,080,000	0	1,780,000	0	39,300	0	24,900	277,000	48,100	7,250,000
8	0	0	1,780,000	0	39,300	0	24,900	277,000	48,100	2,170,000
9	0	0	1,780,000	0	39,300	0	24,900	277,000	48,100	2,170,000
10	0	0	1,780,000	0	39,300	0	24,900	277,000	48,100	2,170,000
Total	20,300,000	6,620,000	15,100,000	164,000	595,000	0	311,000	2,770,000	481,000	46,400,000
Annualized	2,240,000	853,000	1,430,000	21,100	65,300	0	32,800	277,000	48,100	4,970,000

NOTE: We do not show discounted costs by year. We calculated annualized costs using a 7-percent discount rate. We rounded dollar amounts to three significant digits or the nearest hundred dollars.

244

Table G.9. Total Costs for 63 Small–Passenger Vessel Facilities, in 2012 Dollars, Undiscounted

Year	Capital			Operational					Additional	Total
	TWIC Readers	Installation, Infrastructure, and PACS Integration	Maintenance	Update FSP	Recordkeeping	Update CCL	Training	Delay	Card Replacement	
1	1,080,000	0	0	56,900	89,600	0	34,100	81,700	14,200	1,350,000
2	1,080,000	0	188,000	55,100	103,000	0	42,600	81,700	14,200	1,560,000
3	0	0	377,000	0	26,900	0	17,000	81,700	14,200	517,000
4	0	0	377,000	0	26,900	0	17,000	81,700	14,200	517,000
5	0	0	377,000	0	26,900	0	17,000	81,700	14,200	517,000
6	1,080,000	0	377,000	0	26,900	0	17,000	81,700	14,200	1,590,000
7	1,080,000	0	377,000	0	26,900	0	17,000	81,700	14,200	1,590,000
8	0	0	377,000	0	26,900	0	17,000	81,700	14,200	517,000
9	0	0	377,000	0	26,900	0	17,000	81,700	14,200	517,000
10	0	0	377,000	0	26,900	0	17,000	81,700	14,200	517,000
Total	4,310,000	0	3,200,000	112,000	408,000	0	213,000	817,000	142,000	9,200,000
Annualized	475,000	0	303,000	14,400	44,700	0	22,500	81,700	14,200	955,000

NOTE: We do not show discounted costs by year. We calculated annualized costs using a 7-percent discount rate. We rounded dollar amounts to three significant digits or the nearest hundred dollars.

Table G.10. Total Costs for 61 Mixed-Use Facilities, in 2012 Dollars, Undiscounted

Year	Capital			Operational					Additional	Total
	TWIC Readers	Installation, Infrastructure, and PACS Integration	Maintenance	Update FSP	Recordkeeping	Update CCL	Training	Delay	Card Replacement	
1	714,000	5,290,000	0	55,100	88,200	0	33,000	79,100	13,700	6,270,000
2	714,000	5,290,000	125,000	53,300	98,600	0	41,200	79,100	13,700	6,410,000
3	0	0	250,000	0	26,000	0	16,500	79,100	13,700	385,000
4	0	0	250,000	0	26,000	0	16,500	79,100	13,700	385,000
5	0	0	250,000	0	26,000	0	16,500	79,100	13,700	385,000
6	714,000	0	250,000	0	26,000	0	16,500	79,100	13,700	1,100,000
7	714,000	0	250,000	0	26,000	0	16,500	79,100	13,700	1,100,000
8	0	0	250,000	0	26,000	0	16,500	79,100	13,700	385,000
9	0	0	250,000	0	26,000	0	16,500	79,100	13,700	385,000
10	0	0	250,000	0	26,000	0	16,500	79,100	13,700	385,000
Total	2,850,000	10,600,000	2,120,000	108,000	395,000	0	206,000	791,000	137,000	17,200,000
Annualized	315,000	1,360,000	201,000	14,000	43,300	0	21,800	79,100	13,700	2,050,000

NOTE: We do not show discounted costs by year. We calculated annualized costs using a 7-percent discount rate. We rounded dollar amounts to three significant digits or the nearest hundred dollars.

246

Table G.11. Total Costs for One Vessel, in 2012 Dollars, Undiscounted

| | Capital | | Operational | | | | | Additional | | |
Year	TWIC Readers	Installation, Infrastructure, and PACS Integration	Maintenance	Update FSP	Recordkeeping	Update CCL	Training	Delay	Card Replacement	Total
1	14,100	386,000	0	1,300	2,100	0	2,000	0	0	406,000
2	0	0	2,500	0	300	0	500	0	0	3,300
3	0	0	2,500	0	300	0	500	0	0	3,300
4	0	0	2,500	0	300	0	500	0	0	3,300
5	0	0	2,500	0	300	0	500	0	0	3,300
6	14,100	0	2,500	0	300	0	500	0	0	17,400
7	0	0	2,500	0	300	0	500	0	0	3,300
8	0	0	2,500	0	300	0	500	0	0	3,300
9	0	0	2,500	0	300	0	500	0	0	3,300
10	0	0	2,500	0	300	0	500	0	0	3,300
Total	28,100	386,000	22,200	1,300	5,000	0	6,600	0	0	449,000
Annualized	3,200	51,400	2,100	200	600	0	700	0	0	58,100

NOTE: We do not show discounted costs by year. We calculated annualized costs using a 7-percent discount rate. We rounded dollar amounts to three significant digits or the nearest hundred dollars.

Regulatory Reform and Accounting Methods

Executive Order 13771 mandates new accounting methods to ensure consistent and comparable accounting of costs and cost savings for different regulatory actions.[516] However, it does not replace the previous guidance under Executive Order 12866.[517] OMB's Office of Information and Regulatory Affairs provides guidance on the new accounting methods.[518]

The assessment of the USCG's 2015 regulatory analysis described in this report followed the guidance in Executive Order 12866. For direct comparison with the USCG's analysis, we report the costs and benefits of the rule in 2012 dollars. Classification requirements on aggregate MSRAM data limited our use of MSRAM to estimate benefits. Because of these classification restrictions, the USCG was unable to provide more-detailed consequence data or information for more-recent years.

However, to support the USCG's regulatory planning and analysis, we report the revised costs of the TWIC-reader rule under the accounting methods in Executive Order 13771. This involves primarily three adjustments: (1) reporting costs in 2016 dollars, (2) calculating the present value of costs as of 2016, and (3) estimating costs over a perpetual time horizon.[519] We note that the USCG's NPRM for the delay of the effective date for the TWIC-reader rule would also postpone the requirements for two categories of facilities (122 total facilities) for three years until August 23, 2021.[520] This would affect the timing of costs (and benefits) but would not otherwise materially change the analysis. The NPRM includes a discussion of the impact of the delay and a preliminary monetary estimate.[521]

Table G.12 reports the total costs of the TWIC-reader rule for compliance with OMB's revised accounting methods.

---

[516] Donald J. Trump, president, "Reducing Regulation and Controlling Regulatory Costs: Executive Order 13771 of January 30, 2017," *Federal Register*, Vol. 82, No. 22, February 3, 2017, pp. 9339–9341.

[517] Clinton, 1993.

[518] Dominic J. Mancini, acting administrator, Office of Information and Regulatory Affairs, Office of Management and Budget, "Guidance Implementing Executive Order 13771, Titled 'Reducing Regulation and Controlling Regulatory Costs,'" memorandum for regulatory policy officers at executive departments and agencies and managing and executive directors of certain agencies and commissions, April 5, 2017.

[519] To estimate costs in 2016 dollars, we used the GDP implicit price deflator from Bureau of Economic Analysis, 2019. The final rule was anticipated to go into effect on August 23, 2018, so we also discounted costs to a present-value base year of 2016. To estimate costs over a perpetual time horizon, we divided the annualized cost by the discount rate.

[520] USCG, 2018b.

[521] USCG, 2018b.

Table G.12. Total Costs of the TWIC-Reader Rule, by Year, Under the Accounting Methods Required by Executive Order 13771, in Millions of 2016 Dollars

Year	Facility	Vessel	Additional	Government	Undiscounted	Total 7% Discount Rate	3% Discount Rate
1	112.86	0.43	2.70	0.05	116.0	101.4	109.4
2	115.91	0.00	2.70	0.05	118.7	96.9	108.6
3	6.27	0.00	2.70	0.00	9.0	6.8	8.0
4	6.27	0.00	2.70	0.00	9.0	6.4	7.7
5	6.27	0.00	2.70	0.00	9.0	6.0	7.5
6	23.10	0.02	2.70	0.00	25.8	16.1	21.0
7	23.08	0.00	2.70	0.00	25.8	15.0	20.4
8	6.27	0.00	2.70	0.00	9.0	4.9	6.9
9	6.27	0.00	2.70	0.00	9.0	4.6	6.7
10	6.27	0.00	2.70	0.00	9.0	4.3	6.5
10-year cost	312.60	0.48	26.98	0.11	340.2	262.2	302.6
Total[a]	N/A	N/A	N/A	N/A	N/A	533.4	1,182.5
Annualized	N/A	N/A	N/A	N/A	N/A	37.3	35.5

[a] Estimated over a perpetual time horizon using discount rates of 3% and 7%.

Detailed Estimation of Benefits

Alternative Methods of Estimating the Value of a Fatality

We conducted a literature review to identify alternative sources of data on the consequences of terrorist attacks in the maritime environment. The goal of this was not to use other estimates instead of MSRAM data but to inform the extent to which excluding other categories of economic impacts might affect consequence scores. Regulatory analyses generally use a VSL estimate to represent the monetary value of society's willingness to pay for an incremental reduction in the probability of fatality.[522] As of 2016, DOT, which sets a benchmark that many federal agencies use for conducting regulatory analyses, used a VSL estimate of $9.6 million (using a 2015 base year).[523] In the early 2000s, DOT commissioned several studies on the potential economic impact of terrorist attacks at ports. In separate reports, Abt Associates analysts estimated the direct and indirect impacts of two scenarios: a nuclear weapon being smuggled undetected into the United States in a container vessel and detonated in a port or

---

[522] For a discussion of VSL estimates, see Moran and Monje, 2016.

[523] Moran and Monje, 2016.

nearby major city center[524] and a biological agent being smuggled undetected in the United States in a container vessel and released in a port or nearby major city center.[525] These scenarios were later utilized in a break-even analysis to support U.S. Customs and Border Protection's regulatory analysis of the Importer Security Filing and Additional Carrier Requirements interim final rule.[526] Across several scenarios, including different ports and attack modes, the monetary value of fatalities accounted for between half and more than 90 percent of the total direct and indirect damage. In another report for DHS, Charles Meade and Roger Molander estimated the monetary impact of a terrorist-detonated nuclear explosion at the Port of Long Beach.[527] However, they did not use a VSL estimate for fatalities, so the estimated monetary value of fatalities was significantly smaller as a proportion of the overall consequences. In general, the monetary value of fatalities based on VSL estimates tend to be one of the largest components of the consequence of a terrorist attack, but they are not the only economic impact that should be considered.

---

[524] Clark C. Abt, "The Economic Impact of Nuclear Terrorist Attacks on Freight Transport Systems in an Age of Seaport Vulnerability: Executive Summary," prepared for U.S. Department of Transportation, Volpe National Transportation Systems Center, Cambridge, Mass., April 30, 2003.

[525] Clark C. Abt, William Rhodes, Rocco Casagrande, and Gary Gaumer, "The Economic Impacts of Bioterrorist Attacks on Freight Transport Systems in an Age of Seaport Vulnerability: Executive Summary," prepared for U.S. Department of Transportation, Volpe National Transportation Systems Center, Cambridge, Mass., May 9, 2003.

[526] Industrial Economics, *Regulatory Analysis and Final Regulatory Flexibility Analysis for the Interim Final Rule: Importer Security Filing and Additional Carrier Requirements—Cost, Benefit, and Feasibility Study as Required by Section 203(c) of the SAFE Port Act*, Cambridge, Mass., prepared for U.S. Customs and Border Protection and the U.S. Department of Homeland Security, November 2008.

[527] Charles Meade and Roger C. Molander, *Considering the Effects of a Catastrophic Terrorist Attack*, Santa Monica, Calif.: RAND Corporation, TR-391-CTRMP, 2006. Instead of VSL, the authors used the average life insurance payment for deaths from 9/11 as a proxy for the cost of a single fatality, which resulted in a smaller monetary estimate for each fatality. The total direct costs exceeded $1 trillion, but the monetary value of anticipated life insurance and workers' compensation claims accounted for just 10 percent of the total.

Bibliography

Abt, Clark C., "The Economic Impact of Nuclear Terrorist Attacks on Freight Transport Systems in an Age of Seaport Vulnerability: Executive Summary," prepared for U.S. Department of Transportation, Volpe National Transportation Systems Center, Cambridge, Mass., April 30, 2003. As of July 31, 2019:
https://www.abtassociates.com/sites/default/files/migrated_files/d294e2d2-13f0-40b6-bc93-fbf4c5831e8e.pdf

Abt, Clark C., William Rhodes, Rocco Casagrande, and Gary Gaumer, "The Economic Impacts of Bioterrorist Attacks on Freight Transport Systems in an Age of Seaport Vulnerability: Executive Summary," prepared for U.S. Department of Transportation, Volpe National Transportation Systems Center, Cambridge, Mass., May 9, 2003. As of July 31, 2019:
https://www.abtassociates.com/insights/publications/report/economic-impacts-of-bioterrorist-attacks-on-freight-transport-systems

Adelman, Robert, Lesley Williams Reid, Gail Markle, Saskia Weiss, and Charles Jaret, "Urban Crime Rates and the Changing Face of Immigration: Evidence Across Four Decades," *Journal of Ethnicity in Criminal Justice*, Vol. 15, No. 1, 2017, pp. 52–77.

Akbar, Amna, "Policing 'Radicalization,'" *UC Irvine Law Review*, Vol. 3, No. 4, December 2013, pp. 809–884.

Alden, Edward, "National Security and U.S. Immigration Policy," *Journal of International and Comparative Law*, Vol. 1, No. 1, Fall 2010, Art. 3. As of June 30, 2019:
https://scholarship.law.stjohns.edu/cgi/viewcontent.cgi?article=1003&context=jicl

Al-Ightiyal, "Qualities of an Urban Assassin," *Inspire*, Vol. 9, Special Dispatch 4693, May 2, 2012.

Al-Shami, Abu Muhammad al-`Adnani, spokesperson, Islamic State of Iraq and Syria, "Indeed Your Lord Is Ever Watchful," statement, September 9, 2014. As of June 28, 2019:
http://hdl.handle.net/10066/16495

American Association of Port Authorities, "Port Industry Statistics," undated. As of July 6, 2019:
https://www.aapa-ports.org/unifying/content.aspx?ItemNumber=21048

Andre, Virginie, and Shandon Harris-Hogan, "Mohamed Merah: From Petty Criminal to Neojihadist," *Politics, Religion, and Ideology*, Vol. 14, No. 2, 2013, pp. 307–319.

Apps, Peter, "Have Hired Guns Finally Scuppered Somali Pirates?" Reuters, February 23, 2013. As of June 22, 2019:
https://www.reuters.com/article/us-somalia-piracy/have-hired-guns-finally-scuppered-somali-pirates-idUSBRE91B19Y20130212

Ashford, Nicholas A., "The Legacy of the Precautionary Principle in US Law: The Rise of Cost–Benefit Analysis and Risk Assessment as Undermining Factors in Health, Safety and Environmental Protection," in Nicolas de Sadeleer, ed., *Implementing the Precautionary Principle: Approaches from the Nordic Countries, EU and USA*, Sterling, Va.: Earthscan, 2007, pp. 352–378.

Assistant Commandant for Prevention Policy, U.S. Coast Guard, "Reporting Suspicious Activity and Breaches of Security," Policy Letter 08-16, December 14, 2016. As of July 1, 2019:
https://homeport.uscg.mil/Lists/Content/DispForm.aspx?ID=2676&Source=/Lists/Content/DispForm.aspx?ID=2676

"Australian Terror Plan to Hide Plane Bomb in Barbie Revealed," BBC, August 21, 2017. As of June 28, 2019:
https://www.bbc.com/news/world-australia-41006835

"Background Check Company Comparisons," *The Best Background Check Companies of 2019*, last modified January 30, 2018. As of July 1, 2019:
https://www.business.com/categories/background-check-companies/

Baker, Bryan, "Estimates of the Illegal Alien Population Residing in the United States: January 2015," Washington, D.C.: U.S. Department of Homeland Security, Office of Immigration Statistics, Office of Strategy, Policy and Plans, December 2018. As of June 30, 2019:
https://www.dhs.gov/sites/default/files/publications/18_1214_PLCY_pops-est-report.pdf

———, "Estimates of the Lawful Permanent Resident Population in the United States: January 2015," Washington, D.C.: U.S. Department of Homeland Security, Office of Immigration Statistics, Office of Strategy, Policy and Plans, May 2019. As of June 30, 2019:
https://www.dhs.gov/sites/default/files/publications/lpr_population_estimates_january_2015.pdf

Barrett, Devlin, "Arrests in Domestic Terror Probes Outpace Those Inspired by Islamic Extremists," *Washington Post*, March 9, 2019.

Basra, Rajan, and Peter R. Neumann, "Criminal Pasts, Terrorist Futures: European Jihadists and the New Crime–Terror Nexus," *Perspectives on Terrorism*, Vol. 10, No. 6, 2016, pp. 25–40. As of June 22, 2019:
http://www.terrorismanalysts.com/pt/index.php/pot/article/view/554

Batalova, Jeanne, Sarah Hooker, and Randy Capps, *DACA at the Two-Year Mark: A National and State Profile of Youth Eligible and Applying for Deferred Action*, Washington, D.C.: Migration Policy Institute, August 2014. As of June 30, 2019: https://www.migrationpolicy.org/research/daca-two-year-mark-national-and-state-profile-youth-eligible-and-applying-deferred-action

Batalova, Jeanne, Andriy Shymonyak, and Michelle Mittelstadt, *Immigration Data Matters*, Washington, D.C.: Migration Policy Institute, March 2018. As of June 30, 2019: https://www.migrationpolicy.org/research/immigration-data-matters

Beadle, Andrew, "Ashdod Attack a Wake-Up Call for U.S. Ports, Says ILWU Official," *JOC*, March 29, 2004.

Bearak, Max, "Falling Oil Prices Spark a Rise in Kidnappings by West African Pirates," *Washington Post*, May 10, 2016. As of February 21, 2019: https://www.washingtonpost.com/news/worldviews/wp/2016/05/10/falling-oil-prices-spark-a-rise-in-kidnappings-by-west-african-pirates/

Belli, Roberta, Joshua D. Freilich, Steven M. Chermak, and Katharine A. Boyd, "Exploring the Crime–Terror Nexus in the United States: A Social Network Analysis of a Hezbollah Network Involved in Trade Diversion," *Dynamics of Asymmetric Conflict*, Vol. 8, No. 3, 2015, pp. 263–281.

Bergen, Peter, and David Sterman, "The Real Terrorist Threat in America: It's No Longer Jihadist Groups," *Foreign Affairs*, October 30, 2018.

Bindemann, Markus, Meri Avetisyan, and Tim Rakow, "Who Can Recognize Unfamiliar Faces? Individual Differences and Observer Consistency in Person Identification," *Journal of Experimental Psychology: Applied*, Vol. 18, No. 3, September 2012, pp. 277–291.

Bjelopera, Jerome P., *Domestic Terrorism: An Overview*, Washington, D.C.: Congressional Research Service, R44921, August 21, 2017. As of June 22, 2019: https://www.hsdl.org/?abstract&did=803523

Bjelopera, Jerome P., Bart Elias, and Alison Siskin, *The Terrorist Screening Database and Preventing Terrorist Travel*, Washington, D.C.: Congressional Research Service, R44678, November 7, 2016. As of March 6, 2019: https://fas.org/sgp/crs/terror/R44678.pdf

Bonelli, Laurent, "The Guys from the Ghetto," *Le Monde Diplomatique*, February 2015. As of June 22, 2019: https://mondediplo.com/2015/02/04radicalisation

Bonneau, Joseph, Cormac Herley, Paul C. van Oorschot, and Frank Stajano, "The Quest to Replace Passwords: A Framework for Comparative Evaluation of Web Authentication Schemes," *2012 IEEE Symposium on Security and Privacy*, Institute of Electrical and Electronics Engineers, 2012, pp. 553–567.

Bureau of Customs and Border Protection, U.S. Department of Homeland Security, "Importer Security Filing and Additional Carrier Requirements," *Federal Register*, Vol. 73, No. 228, November 25, 2008, pp. 71729–71785. As of July 3, 2019:
https://www.govinfo.gov/app/details/FR-2008-11-25/E8-27048

Bureau of Economic Analysis, U.S. Department of Commerce, "Implicit Price Deflators for Gross Domestic Product," National Income and Product Accounts, Table 1.1.9, updated May 30, 2019.

Bureau of Transportation Statistics, U.S. Department of Transportation, "Port Profiles," undated. As of July 6, 2019:
https://www.bts.gov/content/port-performance-profiles

———, "Freight Facts and Figures 2017, Chapter 2: Freight Moved in Domestic and International Trade," updated November 5, 2017. As of June 26, 2019:
https://www.bts.gov/bts-publications/freight-facts-and-figures/freight-facts-figures-2017-chapter-2-freight-moved

Burke, Jason, "The Age of Selfie Jihad: How Evolving Media Technology Is Changing Terrorism," *CTC Sentinel*, Vol. 9, No. 11, November–December 2016, pp. 16–22. As of June 28, 2019:
https://ctc.usma.edu/the-age-of-selfie-jihad-how-evolving-media-technology-is-changing-terrorism/

Butcher, Kristin F., and Anne Morrison Piehl, *Why Are Immigrants' Incarceration Rates So Low? Evidence on Selective Immigration, Deterrence, and Deportation*, Cambridge, Mass.: National Bureau of Economic Research, Working Paper 13229, July 2007. As of June 30, 2019:
https://www.nber.org/papers/w13229

California Department of Transportation, "Freight Planning Fact Sheet: Port of Los Angeles," January 2014.

Caltrans—*See* California Department of Transportation.

Carafano, James Jay, "Small Boats, Big Worries: Thwarting Terrorist Attacks from the Sea," Washington, D.C.: Heritage Foundation, Backgrounder 2041, June 11, 2007. As of February 21, 2019:
https://www.heritage.org/homeland-security/report/small-boats-big-worries-thwarting-terrorist-attacks-the-sea

Carroll, Rory, Paul Lewis, Peter Walker, Nadia Khomami, and Tom Dart, "San Bernardino Shooting Suspects Raised Few Red Flags Before 'Horrendous' Crime," *The Guardian*, December 3, 2015. As of March 6, 2019:
https://www.theguardian.com/us-news/2015/dec/03/san-bernadino-shooting-suspects-syed-rizwan-farook-tashfeen-malik

Chambers, Matthew, Michael J. Sprung, Alisa Fine, Daniel Friedman, Lydia Rainville, Daniel Hackett, Daniel S. Smith, Katherine Chambers, Patricia Dijoseph, Marin Kress, Kenneth Ned Mitchell, and Amy Tujague, *Port Performance Freight Statistics Program: Annual Report to Congress 2018*, U.S. Department of Transportation, Bureau of Transportation Statistics, April 1, 2019. As of July 27, 2019:
https://rosap.ntl.bts.gov/view/dot/39609

Cilluffo, Frank J., Sharon L. Cardash, and Andrew J. Whitehead, "Radicalization: Behind Bars and Beyond Borders," *Brown Journal of World Affairs*, Vol. 13, No. 2, Spring–Summer 2007, pp. 113–122.

Cilluffo, Frank J., and G. Saathoff, *Out of the Shadows: Getting Ahead of Prisoner Radicalization—A Special Report*, Washington, D.C.: George Washington University Homeland Security Policy Institute and University of Virginia Critical Incident Analysis Group, 2006.

Clear, Todd R., Bruce D. Stout, Harry R. Dammer, Linda Kelly, Patricia L. Hardyman, and Carol Shapiro, "Does Involvement in Religion Help Prisoners Adjust to Prison?" *NCCD Focus*, San Francisco, Calif.: National Council on Crime and Delinquency, November 1992. As of June 30, 2019:
http://www.nccdglobal.org/sites/default/files/publication_pdf/religion-and-prisoners.pdf

Clinch, Matt, Arjun Kharpal, and Michael Sheetz, "Las Vegas Massacre Suspect Stephen Paddock Committed Suicide, Police Say," CNBC, October 2, 2017. As of February 21, 2019:
https://www.cnbc.com/2017/10/02/las-vegas-gunman-suspect-is-stephen-paddock-64-of-mesquite.html

Clinton, William Jefferson, president, "Regulatory Planning and Review: Executive Order 12866 of September 30, 1993," *Federal Register*, Vol. 58, No. 190, October 4, 1993, pp. 51735–51744. As of July 6, 2019:
https://www.govinfo.gov/app/details/FR-1993-10-04

Coats, Daniel R., director of national intelligence, *Statement for the Record: Worldwide Threat Assessment of the US Intelligence Community*, *Office of the Director of National Intelligence*, submitted to the U.S. Senate Select Committee on Intelligence, January 29, 2019. As of June 22, 2019:
https://www.odni.gov/index.php/newsroom/congressional-testimonies/item/1947-statement-for-the-record-worldwide-threat-assessment-of-the-us-intelligence-community

Code of Federal Regulations, Title 27, Alcohol, Tobacco Products, and Firearms; Chapter II, Bureau of Alcohol, Tobacco, Firearms, and Explosives, Department of Justice; Subchapter B, Firearms and Ammunition; Part 447, Importation of Arms, Ammunition and Implements of War; Subpart C, The U.S. Munitions Import List; Section 447.21, The U.S. Munitions Import List. As of July 6, 2019:
https://www.govinfo.gov/app/details/CFR-2019-title27-vol3/CFR-2019-title27-vol3-sec447-21

Code of Federal Regulations, Title 33, Navigation and Navigable Waters; Chapter I, Coast Guard, Department of Homeland Security (Continued); Subchapter H, Maritime Security; Part 101, Maritime Security: General; Subpart A, General; Section 101.105, Definitions. As of June 25, 2019:
https://www.govinfo.gov/app/details/CFR-2018-title33-vol1/CFR-2018-title33-vol1-sec101-105

Code of Federal Regulations, Title 33, Navigation and Navigable Waters; Chapter I, Coast Guard, Department of Homeland Security; Subchapter H, Maritime Security; Part 101, Maritime Security: General; Subpart C, Communication (Port–Facility–Vessel); Section 101.305, Reporting. As of July 1, 2019:
https://www.govinfo.gov/app/details/CFR-2015-title33-vol1/CFR-2015-title33-vol1-sec101-305

Code of Federal Regulations, Title 33, Navigation and Navigable Waters; Chapter I, Coast Guard, Department of Homeland Security (Continued); Subchapter H, Maritime Security; Part 104, Maritime Security: Vessels; Subpart D, Vessel Security Plan (VSP); Section 104.405, Format of the Vessel Security Plan (VSP). As of June 26, 2019:
https://www.govinfo.gov/app/details/CFR-2010-title33-vol1/CFR-2010-title33-vol1-sec104-405

Code of Federal Regulations, Title 33, Navigation and Navigable Waters; Chapter I, Coast Guard, Department of Homeland Security (Continued); Subchapter H, Maritime Security; Part 105, Maritime Security: Facilities. As of July 2, 2019:
https://www.govinfo.gov/app/details/CFR-2010-title33-vol1/CFR-2010-title33-vol1-part105

Code of Federal Regulations, Title 33, Navigation and Navigable Waters; Chapter I, Coast Guard, Department of Homeland Security; Subchapter K, Security of Vessels; Part 120, Security of Passenger Vessels; Subpart C, Plans and Procedures for Vessel Security; Section 120.300, What Is Required to Be in a Vessel Security Plan? As of June 26, 2019: https://www.govinfo.gov/app/details/CFR-2009-title33-vol1/CFR-2009-title33-vol1-sec120-300

Code of Federal Regulations, Title 33, Navigation and Navigable Waters; Chapter I, Coast Guard, Department of Homeland Security; Subchapter K, Security of Vessels; Part 120, Security of Passenger Vessels; Subpart C, Plans and Procedures for Vessel Security; Section 120.305, What Is the Procedure for Examination? As of June 26, 2019: https://www.govinfo.gov/app/details/CFR-2009-title33-vol1/CFR-2009-title33-vol1-sec120-305

Code of Federal Regulations, Title 33, Navigation and Navigable Waters; Chapter I, Coast Guard, Department of Homeland Security (Continued); Subchapter P, Ports and Waterways Safety; Part 160, Ports and Waterways Safety—General; Subpart C, Notification of Arrival, Hazardous Conditions, and Certain Dangerous Cargoes; Section 160.202, Definitions. As of June 25, 2019: https://www.govinfo.gov/app/details/CFR-2018-title33-vol2/CFR-2018-title33-vol2-sec160-202

Code of Federal Regulations, Title 46, Shipping; Chapter I, Coast Guard, Department of Homeland Security (Continued); Subchapter O, Certain Bulk Dangerous Cargoes; Part 151, Barges Carrying Bulk Liquid Hazardous Material Cargoes; Subpart 151.50, Special Requirements; Section 151.50-31, Chlorine. As of August 1, 2019: https://www.govinfo.gov/app/details/CFR-2018-title46-vol5/CFR-2018-title46-vol5-sec151-50-31

Code of Federal Regulations, Title 46, Shipping; Chapter I, Coast Guard, Department of Homeland Security (Continued); Subchapter O, Certain Bulk Dangerous Cargoes; Part 154, Safety Standards for Self-Propelled Vessels Carrying Bulk Liquefied Gases; Subpart A, General; Section 154.7, Definitions, Acronyms, and Terms. As of August 1, 2019: https://www.govinfo.gov/app/details/CFR-2018-title46-vol5/CFR-2018-title46-vol5-sec154-7

Code of Federal Regulations, Title 49, Transportation; Subtitle B, Other Regulations Relating to Transportation (Continued); Chapter I, Pipeline and Hazardous Materials Safety Administration, Department of Transportation; Subchapter C, Hazardous Materials Regulations; Part 171, General Information, Regulations, and Definitions; Subpart A, Applicability, General Requirements, and North American Shipments; Section 171.8, Definitions and Abbreviations. As of August 1, 2019: https://www.govinfo.gov/app/details/CFR-2018-title49-vol2/CFR-2018-title49-vol2-sec171-8

Code of Federal Regulations, Title 49, Transportation; Subtitle B, Other Regulations Relating to Transportation (Continued); Chapter I, Pipeline and Hazardous Materials Safety Administration, Department of Transportation; Subchapter C, Hazardous Materials Regulations; Part 172, Hazardous Materials Table, Special Provisions, Hazardous Materials Communications, Emergency Response Information, Training Requirements, and Security Plans; Subpart B, Table of Hazardous Materials and Special Provisions; Section 172.101, Purpose and Use of Hazardous Materials Table. As of August 1, 2019: https://www.govinfo.gov/app/details/CFR-2018-title49-vol2/CFR-2018-title49-vol2-sec172-101

Code of Federal Regulations, Title 49, Transportation, Subtitle B, Other Regulations Relating to Transportation (Continued); Chapter I, Pipeline and Hazardous Materials Safety Administration, Department of Transportation; Subchapter C, Hazardous Materials Regulations; Part 173, Shippers: General Requirements for Shipments and Packagings; Subpart C, Definitions, Classification and Packaging for Class 1; Section 173.50, Class 1: Definitions. As of August 1, 2019: https://www.govinfo.gov/app/details/CFR-1996-title49-vol2/CFR-1996-title49-vol2-sec173-50

Code of Federal Regulations, Title 49, Transportation; Subtitle B, Other Regulations Relating to Transportation (Continued); Chapter I, Pipeline and Hazardous Materials Safety Administration, Department of Transportation; Subchapter C, Hazardous Materials Regulations; Part 173, Shippers: General Requirements for Shipments and Packagings; Subpart I, Class 7 (Radioactive) Materials; Section 173.403, Definitions. As of August 1, 2019: https://www.govinfo.gov/app/details/CFR-2018-title49-vol2/CFR-2018-title49-vol2-sec173-403

Code of Federal Regulations, Title 49, Transportation; Subtitle B, Other Regulations Pertaining to Transportation (Continued); Chapter I, Pipeline and Hazardous Materials Safety Administration, Department of Transportation; Subchapter C, Hazardous Materials Regulations; Part 176, Carriage by Vessel; Subpart J, Detailed Requirements for Class 4 (Flammable Solids), Class 5 (Oxidizers and Organic Peroxides), and Division 1.5 Materials; Section 176.415, Permit Requirements for Division 1.5, Ammonium Nitrates, and Certain Ammonium Nitrate Fertilizers. As of August 1, 2019: https://www.govinfo.gov/app/details/CFR-2018-title49-vol2/CFR-2018-title49-vol2-sec176-415

Code of Federal Regulations, Title 49, Transportation; Subtitle B, Other Regulations Pertaining to Transportation (Continued); Chapter XII, Transportation Security Administration, Department of Homeland Security; Subchapter A, Administrative and Procedural Rules; Part 1515, Appeal and Waiver Procedures for Security Threat Assessments for Individuals; Section 1515.7, Procedures for Waiver of Criminal Offenses, Immigration Status, or Mental Capacity Standards. As of June 25, 2019: https://www.govinfo.gov/app/details/CFR-2018-title49-vol9/CFR-2018-title49-vol9-sec1515-7

Code of Federal Regulations, Title 49, Transportation; Subtitle B, Other Regulations Relating to Transportation (Continued); Chapter XII, Transportation Security Administration, Department of Homeland Security; Subchapter C, Civil Aviation Security; Part 1542, Airport Security. As of July 4, 2019: https://www.govinfo.gov/app/details/CFR-2018-title49-vol9/CFR-2018-title49-vol9-part1542

Code of Federal Regulations, Title 49, Transportation; Subtitle B, Other Regulations Relating to Transportation (Continued); Chapter XII, Transportation Security Administration, Department of Homeland Security; Subchapter D, Maritime and Land Transportation Security; Part 1570, General Rules. As of June 24, 2019: https://www.govinfo.gov/app/details/CFR-2018-title49-vol9/CFR-2018-title49-vol9-part1570

Code of Federal Regulations, Title 49, Transportation; Subtitle B, Other Regulations Relating to Transportation (Continued); Chapter XII, Transportation Security Administration, Department of Homeland Security; Subchapter D, Maritime and Land Transportation Security; Part 1572, Credentialing and Security Threat Assessments. As of June 24, 2019: https://www.govinfo.gov/app/details/CFR-2018-title49-vol9/CFR-2018-title49-vol9-part1572

Collier, Kit, and John Sifton, *Lives Destroyed: Attacks Against Civilians in the Philippines*, Washington, D.C.: Human Rights Watch, July 2007. As of June 22, 2019: https://www.hrw.org/reports/2007/philippines0707/

Commandant, U.S. Coast Guard, *Guidance for the Implementation of the Transportation Worker Identification Credential (TWIC) Program in the Maritime Sector*, Washington, D.C., Navigation and Vessel Inspection Circular 03-07, July 2, 2007. As of June 23, 2019: https://homeport.uscg.mil/Lists/Content/DispForm.aspx?ID=2764&Source=/Lists/Content/DispForm.aspx?ID=2764

———, *CH-2 to 03-03, Implementation Guidance for the Regulations Mandated by the Maritime Transportation Security Act of 2002 (MTSA) for Facilities*, Washington, D.C., Commandant Publication P16700.4, Navigation and Vessel Inspection Circular 03-03, Change 2, February 28, 2009. As of August 1, 2019: https://www.dco.uscg.mil/Portals/9/DCO%20Documents/5p/5ps/NVIC/2003/NVIC_03-03_CHANGE_2.pdf

Commandant, USCG—*See* Commandant, U.S. Coast Guard.

Committee on Homeland Security, U.S. House of Representatives, *Homeland Security Failures: TWIC Examined*, Serial No. 110-81, October 31, 2007. As of June 23, 2019: https://www.hsdl.org/?abstract&did=31819

Conrad, Richard, program manager, Aviation Program Management Division, Office of Intelligence and Analysis, Transportation Security Administration, "TSA Rap Back Overview Brief," presented at Transportation Security Administration/Federal Bureau of Investigation Rap Back Workshop, March 28, 2017.

Cormier, Anthony, "Orlando Shooter Omar Mateen Had a Juvenile Arrest Record," *Tampa Bay Times*, June 16, 2016. As of February 21, 2019: https://www.tampabay.com/news/orlando-shooter-omar-mateen-had-a-juvenile-arrest-record/2282020

Cruickshank, Paul, "A View from the CT Foxhole: An Interview with Alain Grignard, Brussels Federal Police," *CTC Sentinel*, Vol. 8, No. 8, August 2015. As of June 22, 2019: https://ctc.usma.edu/a-view-from-the-ct-foxhole-an-interview-with-alain-grignard-brussels-federal-police/

———, "A View from the CT Foxhole: Nicholas Rasmussen, Former Director, National Counterterrorism Center," *CTC Sentinel*, Vol. 11, No. 1, January 2018. As of February 21, 2019: https://ctc.usma.edu/view-ct-foxhole-nicholas-rasmussen-former-director-national-counterterrorism-center/

Curtis, Glenn E., and Tara Karacan, *The Nexus Among Terrorists, Narcotics Traffickers, Weapons Proliferators, and Organized Crime Networks in Western Europe*, Washington, D.C.: Federal Research Division, Library of Congress, December 2002. As of June 22, 2019: https://www.loc.gov/rr/frd/pdf-files/WestEurope_NEXUS.pdf

Cuthbertson, Ian M., "Prisons and the Education of Terrorists," *World Policy Journal*, Vol. 21, No. 3, Fall 2004, pp. 15–22.

Davenport, Christian, and Drew Harwell, "Orlando Shooter's Firm Ran Two Background Checks on Him, It Said, and Found Nothing," *Washington Post*, June 13, 2016. As of February 21, 2019: https://www.washingtonpost.com/news/wonk/wp/2016/06/13/orlando-shooters-firm-ran-two-background-checks-on-him-it-said-and-found-nothing/?utm_term=.8264e28e19ed

De Luce, Dan, "Why Is It So Hard to Stop West Africa's Vicious Pirates?" *Foreign Policy*, September 23, 2016. As of June 22, 2019: https://foreignpolicy.com/2016/09/23/the-world-beat-somali-pirates-why-cant-it-stop-west-african-piracy/

DeBacco, Dennis, and Richard Schauffler, "State Progress in Record Reporting for Firearm-Related Background Checks: Fugitives from Justice," Washington, D.C.: Bureau of Justice Statistics, National Center for State Courts, and National Consortium for Justice Information and Statistics, February 2017. As of July 1, 2019: https://www.ncjrs.gov/App/Publications/abstract.aspx?ID=272699

Decker, Scott, and David C. Pyrooz, "'I'm Down for a Jihad': How 100 Years of Gang Research Can Inform the Study of Terrorism, Radicalization and Extremism," *Perspectives on Terrorism*, Vol. 9, February 2014, pp. 104–112. As of June 29, 2019: http://www.terrorismanalysts.com/pt/index.php/pot/article/view/405

DeWitt, Samuel E., Shawn D. Bushway, Garima Siwach, and Megan C. Kurlychek, "Redeemed Compared to Whom? Comparing the Distributional Properties of Arrest Risk Across Populations of Provisional Employees with and Without a Criminal Record," *Criminology and Public Policy*, Vol. 16, No. 3, August 2017, pp. 963–997.

DHS—*See* U.S. Department of Homeland Security.

Dishman, Chris, "Terrorism, Crime, and Transformation," *Studies in Conflict and Terrorism*, Vol. 24, No. 1, 2001, pp. 43–58.

Duane, Marina, Nancy G. La Vigne, Emily Reimal, and Mathew Lynch, *Criminal Background Checks: Impact on Employment and Recidivism*, Washington, D.C.: Urban Institute, March 1, 2017. As of July 1, 2019: https://www.urban.org/research/publication/criminal-background-checks-impact-employment-and-recidivism

Duchaine, Brad, "Individual Differences in Face Recognition Ability: Impacts on Law Enforcement, Criminal Justice and National Security," *Psychological Science Agenda*, June 2015. As of July 1, 2019:
https://www.apa.org/science/about/psa/2015/06/face-recognition

European Union External Action, homepage, undated. As of June 28, 2019:
https://eeas.europa.eu/headquarters/headquarters-homepage_en

Farber, Daniel A., "Breaking Bad? The Uneasy Case for Regulatory Breakeven Analysis," *California Law Review*, Vol. 102, No. 6, December 2014, pp. 1469–1493.

Farrow, Scott, and Stuart Shapiro, "The Benefit–Cost Analysis of Security Focused Regulations," *Journal of Homeland Security and Emergency Management*, Vol. 6, No. 1, 2009.

FBI—*See* Federal Bureau of Investigation.

Federal Bureau of Investigation, "Key Findings of the Behavioral Analysis Unit's Las Vegas Review Panel (LVRP)," undated a. As of June 19, 2019:
https://www.hsdl.org/?abstract&did=820782

———, "National Crime Information Center (NCIC)," undated b. As of July 1, 2019:
https://www.fbi.gov/services/cjis/ncic

Federal Railroad Administration, "National Highway–Rail Crossing Inventory Reporting Requirements," *Federal Register*, Vol. 80, No. 3, January 6, 2015, pp. 745–790. As of July 3, 2019:
https://www.govinfo.gov/app/details/FR-2015-01-06/2014-30279

Forbes, Jami, "Does al-Qa'ida's Increasing Media Outreach Signal Revitalization?" *CTC Sentinel*, Vol. 12, No. 1, January 2019, pp. 25–28. As of June 28, 2019:
https://ctc.usma.edu/al-qaidas-increasing-media-outreach-signal-revitalization/

Friedman, Matthew, "Just Facts: As Many Americans Have Criminal Records as College Diplomas," New York: Brennan Center for Justice, November 17, 2015. As of June 29, 2019:
https://www.brennancenter.org/blog/just-facts-many-americans-have-criminal-records-college-diplomas

GAO—*See* U.S. Government Accountability Office.

Gill, Paul, John Horgan, and Paige Deckert, "Bombing Alone: Tracing the Motivations and Antecedent Behaviors of Lone-Actor Terrorists," *Journal of Forensic Sciences*, Vol. 59, No. 2, March 2014, pp. 425–435.

Goel, Vindu, "That Fingerprint Sensor on Your Phone Is Not as Safe as You Think," *New York Times*, April 10, 2017. As of July 1, 2019:
https://www.nytimes.com/2017/04/10/technology/fingerprint-security-smartphones-apple-google-samsung.html

Goggins, Becki R., and Dennis A. DeBacco, *Survey of State Criminal History Information Systems, 2014*, Washington, D.C.: U.S. Department of Justice, Office of Justice Programs, Bureau of Justice Statistics, December 2015. As of June 22, 2019:
https://www.ncjrs.gov/pdffiles1/bjs/grants/249799.pdf

Goldman, Adam, Mark Berman, and Joel Achenbach, "FBI Says San Bernardino Attacks Considered Act of Terrorism; Shooter Pledged Allegiance to Islamic State Leader," *Washington Post*, December 4, 2015. As of February 12, 2019:
https://www.washingtonpost.com/news/post-nation/wp/2015/12/04/san-bernardino-attackers-tried-to-cover-their-tracks-official-says/

Gonzales, Alberto R., U.S. Attorney General, "Stopping Terrorists Before They Strike: The Justice Department's Power of Prevention," prepared remarks, World Affairs Council of Pittsburgh, Pittsburgh, Pennsylvania, August 16, 2006. As of June 29, 2019:
https://www.justice.gov/archive/ag/speeches/2006/ag_speech_060816.html

Grassi, Paul A., James L. Fenton, Naomi B. Lefkovitz, Jamie M. Danker, Yee-Yin Choong, Kristen K. Greene, and Mary F. Theofanos, *Digital Identity Guidelines: Enrollment and Identity Proofing Requirements*, Gaithersburg, Md.: National Institute of Standards and Technology, U.S. Department of Commerce, Special Publication 800-63A, June 2017. As of March 21, 2019:
https://pages.nist.gov/800-63-3/sp800-63a.html

"Greece: 1988 Overview," MIPT Terrorism Knowledge Base, last updated October 31, 2005. As of January 28, 2019:
https://web.archive.org/web/20051201121302/http://www.tkb.org/MorePatterns.jsp?countryCd=GR&year=1988

Green, David, "The Trump Hypothesis: Testing Immigrant Populations as a Determinant of Violent and Drug-Related Crime in the United States," *Social Science Quarterly*, Vol. 97, No. 3, September 2016, pp. 506–524.

Greenberg, Andy, "Hackers Say They've Broken Face ID a Week After iPhone X Release," *Wired*, November 12, 2017. As of July 1, 2019:
https://www.wired.com/story/hackers-say-broke-face-id-security/

———, "The Untold Story of NotPetya, the Most Devastating Cyberattack in History," *Wired*, August 22, 2018. As of January 29, 2019:
https://www.wired.com/story/notpetya-cyberattack-ukraine-russia-code-crashed-the-world/

Guest, Greg, Arwen Bunce, and Laura Johnson, "How Many Interviews Are Enough? An Experiment with Data Saturation and Variability," *Field Methods*, Vol. 18, No. 1, February 2006, pp. 59–82.

Hamm, Mark S., *Terrorist Recruitment in American Correctional Institutions: An Exploratory Study of Non-Traditional Faith Groups—Final Report*, Rockville, Md.: National Institute of Justice, December 2007. As of June 29, 2019:
https://www.ncjrs.gov/App/Publications/abstract.aspx?ID=242801

———, "Prisoner Radicalization: Assessing the Threat in U.S. Correctional Institutions," *NIJ Journal*, No. 261, October 2008. As of June 29, 2019:
https://www.nij.gov/journals/261/pages/prisoner-radicalization.aspx

Hamm, Mark, and Ramon Spaaj, *Lone Wolf Terrorism in America: Using Knowledge of Radicalization Pathways to Forge Prevention Strategies*, Washington, D.C.: National Institute of Justice, February 2015. As of June 29, 2019:
https://www.ncjrs.gov/App/Publications/abstract.aspx?ID=270795

Hannah, Greg, Lindsay Clutterbuck, and Jennifer Rubin, *Radicalization or Rehabilitation: Understanding the Challenge of Extremist and Radicalized Prisoners*, Santa Monica, Calif.: RAND Corporation, TR-571-RC, 2008. As of June 30, 2019:
https://www.rand.org/pubs/technical_reports/TR571.html

Harris, Dan, and Dan Lieberman, "Pirate Attacks Down as Private Maritime Security Business Booms," ABC News, September 27, 2012. As of June 22, 2019:
https://abcnews.go.com/Blotter/pirate-attacks-private-maritime-security-business-booms/story?id=16352840

Hoffman, Bruce, "The Global Terror Threat and Counterterrorism Challenges Facing the Next Administration," *CTC Sentinel*, Vol. 9, No. 11, November–December 2016, pp. 1–7. As of June 28, 2019:
https://ctc.usma.edu/november-december-2016/

———, "Al-Qaeda's Resurrection," Council on Foreign Relations, expert brief, March 6, 2018. As of June 28, 2019:
https://www.cfr.org/expert brief/al-qacdas-rcsurrcction

Holder, Eric, Janet Napolitano, and James Clapper, "We're Safer Post-9/11," *USA Today*, op-ed, September 8, 2011. As of January 28, 2019:
https://www.dni.gov/index.php/newsroom/press-releases/press-releases-2011/item/336-holder-napolitano-clapper-we-re-safer-post-9-11-usa-today-op-ed

Horgan, John G., Paul Gill, Noemie Bouhana, James Silver, and Emily Corner, *Across the Universe? A Comparative Analysis of Violent Radicalization Across Three Offender Types with Implications for Criminal Justice Training and Education*, Washington, D.C.: National Institute of Justice, June 2016. As of June 29, 2019:
https://www.ncjrs.gov/App/Publications/abstract.aspx?ID=272097

Howard, Russell O., and Colleen Traughber, *The Nexus of Extremism and Trafficking: Scourge of the World or So Much Hype?* MacDill Air Force Base, Fla.: Joint Special Operations University, October 2013. As of June 22, 2019:
https://apps.dtic.mil/docs/citations/ADA591814

Howard, Ryan, "Cost of a Background Check: How Much Should You Pay?" *VeriFirst*, June 2, 2017. As of July 1, 2019:
https://blog.verifirst.com/blog/bid/305407/cost-of-a-background-check-how-much-should-you-pay

Hutchinson, Steven, and Pat O'Malley, "A Crime–Terror Nexus? Thinking on Some of the Links Between Terrorism and Criminality," *Studies in Conflict and Terrorism*, Vol. 30, No. 12, 2007, pp. 1095–1107.

IBIA—*See* International Biometrics and Identification Association.

Ilardi, Gaetano Joe, Victoria Police, adjunct research associate, Global Terrorism Research Centre, "Prison Radicalisation: The Devil Is in the Detail," paper presented at the Australian Research Council Linkage Project on Radicalisation Conference, Understanding Terrorism from an Australian Perspective: Radicalisation, De-Radicalisation and Counter Radicalisation, Monash University, Australia, November 8, 2010. As of June 29, 2019:
http://artsonline.monash.edu.au/radicalisation/files/2013/03/conference-2010-prison-radicalisation-gji.pdf

Industrial Economics, *Regulatory Analysis and Final Regulatory Flexibility Analysis for the Interim Final Rule: Importer Security Filing and Additional Carrier Requirements—Cost, Benefit, and Feasibility Study as Required by Section 203(c) of the SAFE Port Act*, Cambridge, Mass., prepared for U.S. Customs and Border Protection and the U.S. Department of Homeland Security, November 2008. As of August 1, 2019:
https://www.regulations.gov/document?D=USCBP-2007-0077-0200

Institute for Water Resources, "NDC: Navigation and Civil Works Decision Support," undated. As of July 6, 2019:
https://www.iwr.usace.army.mil/About/Technical-Centers/NDC-Navigation-and-Civil-Works-Decision-Support/

Interagency Commission on Crime and Security in U.S. Seaports, *Report of the Interagency Commission on Crime and Security in U.S. Seaports*, Fall 2000. As of June 28, 2019: https://www.hsdl.org/?abstract&did=437742

International Biometrics and Identification Association, "TWIC Reader Acquisition Cost Estimates," June 20, 2011. As of January 28, 2019: https://www.ibia.org/download/datasets/1009/IBIA%20TWIC%20Reader%20Acquisition%20Cost%20Estimates%20(final).pdf

"Investigators Look for Missed Signals in Fort Hood Probe," CNN, November 10, 2009. As of February 21, 2019: http://www.cnn.com/2009/CRIME/11/09/fort.hood.shootings/index.html

Jackson, Brian A., Peter Chalk, Kim Cragin, Bruce Newsome, John V. Parachini, William Rosenau, Erin M. Simpson, Melanie W. Sisson, and Donald Temple, *Breaching the Fortress Wall: Understanding Terrorist Efforts to Overcome Defensive Technologies*, Santa Monica, Calif.: RAND Corporation, MG-481-DHS, 2007. As of July 1, 2019: https://www.rand.org/pubs/monographs/MG481.html

Jackson, Brian A., Edward W. Chan, and Tom LaTourrette, "Assessing the Security Benefits of a Trusted Traveler Program in the Presence of Attempted Attacker Exploitation and Compromise," *Journal of Transportation Security*, Vol. 5, No. 1, March 2012, pp. 1–34.

Jackson, Brian A., Ashley L. Rhoades, Jordan R. Reimer, Natasha Lander, Katherine Costello, and Sina Beaghley, *Practical Terrorism Prevention: Reexamining U.S. National Approaches to Addressing the Threat of Ideologically Motivated Violence*, Santa Monica, Calif.: RAND Corporation, RR-2647-DHS, 2019. As of June 29, 2019: https://www.rand.org/pubs/research_reports/RR2647.html

Jacobs, James B., *The Eternal Criminal Records*, Harvard University Press, 2015.

"Japan Researchers Warn of Fingerprint Theft from 'Peace' Sign," *Phys.org*, January 11, 2017. As of July 1, 2019: https://phys.org/news/2017-01-japan-fingerprint-theft-peace.html

Jenkins, Brian Michael, *The Origins of America's Jihadists*, Santa Monica, Calif.: RAND Corporation, PE-251-RC, 2017. As of June 30, 2019: https://www.rand.org/pubs/perspectives/PE251.html

"Just Terror," *Dābiq*, No. 12, November 2015, p. 3.

King, Peter, representative, U.S. House of Representatives, comments made during a debate about the Security and Accountability for Every Port Act, *Congressional Record*, Vol. 152, No. 52, May 4, 2006, pp. H2107–H2153. As of August 1, 2019: https://www.govinfo.gov/app/details/CREC-2006-05-04/CREC-2006-05-04-pt1-PgH2107-2

Kissel, Richard, ed., *Glossary of Key Information Security Terms*, Washington, D.C.: National Institute of Standards and Technology, U.S. Department of Commerce, NISTIR 7298, revision 2, May 2013. As of June 25, 2019:
https://www.nist.gov/publications/glossary-key-information-security-terms-1

Kredo, Adam, "Al Qaeda Publishes Blueprint for Attacks on Key U.S. Transportation Systems," *Washington Free Beacon*, August 15, 2017. As of June 22, 2019:
https://freebeacon.com/national-security/al-qaeda-publishes-blueprint-attacks-key-u-s-transportation-systems/

Kurley, Megan C., Robert Brame, and Shawn D. Bushway, "Scarlet Letters and Recidivism: Does an Old Criminal Record Predict Future Offending?" *Criminology and Public Policy*, Vol. 5, No. 3, August 2006, pp. 483–504.

———, "Enduring Risk? Old Criminal Records and Predictions of Future Criminal Involvement," *Crime and Delinquency*, Vol. 53, No. 1, January 2007, pp. 64–83.

Kuzel, Anton J., "Sampling in Qualitative Inquiry," in Benjamin F. Crabtree and William L. Miller, ed., *Doing Qualitative Research*, Newbury Park, Calif.: Sage Publications, 1992, pp. 31–44.

LaFree, Gary, Michael E. Jensen, Patrick A. James, and Aaron Safer-Lichtenstein, "Correlates of Violent Political Extremism in the United States," *Criminology*, Vol. 56, No. 2, May 2018, pp. 233–268.

Landgrave, Michelangelo, and Alex Nowrasteh, "Criminal Immigrants: Their Numbers, Demographics, and Countries of Origin," Washington, D.C.: Cato Institute, Immigration Research and Policy Brief 1, March 15, 2017. As of June 30, 2019:
https://www.cato.org/publications/immigration-reform-bulletin/criminal-immigrants-their-numbers-demographics-countries

———, "Criminal Immigrants in 2017: Their Numbers, Demographics, and Countries of Origin," Washington, D.C.: Cato Institute, Immigration Research and Policy Brief 11, March 4, 2019. As of June 30, 2019:
https://www.cato.org/publications/immigration-research-policy-brief/criminal-immigrants-2017-their-numbers-demographics

Las Vegas Metropolitan Police Department, *LVMPD Criminal Investigative Report of the 1 October Mass Casualty Shooting*, August 3, 2018. As of February 12, 2019:
https://www.lvmpd.com/en-us/Documents/1-October-FIT-Criminal-Investigative-Report-FINAL_080318.pdf

LaTourrette, Tom, and Henry H. Willis, *Using Probabilistic Terrorism Risk Modeling for Regulatory Benefit–Cost Analysis: Application to the Western Hemisphere Travel Initiative Implemented in the Land Environment*, Santa Monica, Calif.: RAND Corporation, WR-487-IEC, 2007. As of July 1, 2019:
https://www.rand.org/pubs/working_papers/WR487.html

Lee, Sheila Jackson, representative, U.S. House of Representatives, "Homeland Security Failures: TWIC Examined," remarks before the U.S. House of Representatives Committee on Homeland Security, October 31, 2007.

Lerner, Davide, "It's Not Islam That Drives Young Europeans to Jihad, France's Top Terrorism Expert Explains," *Haaretz*, August 20, 2017. As of June 22, 2019:
https://www.haaretz.com/world-news/europe/it-s-not-islam-that-drives-young-europeans-to-jihad-terrorism-expert-says-1.5477000

Lichtblau, Eric, and Matt Apuzzo, "Orlando Gunman Was on Terror Watchlist, F.B.I. Director Says," *New York Times*, June 13, 2016. As of June 22, 2019:
https://www.nytimes.com/2016/06/14/us/omar-mateen-fbi.html

Light, Michael T., and Ty Miller, "Does Undocumented Immigration Increase Violent Crime?" *Criminology*, Vol. 56, No. 2, 2018, pp. 370–401.

Ljujic, Vanja, Jan Willem van Prooijen, and Frank Weerman, "Beyond the Crime–Terror Nexus: Socio-Economic Status, Violent Crimes and Terrorism," *Journal of Criminological Research, Policy and Practice*, Vol. 3, No. 3, 2017, pp. 158–172.

"Maersk's Cargo Operations Hit Hard by Cyberattack," *Maritime Executive*, June 28, 2017. As of June 28, 2017:
https://www.maritime-executive.com/article/maersks-cargo-operations-hit-hard-by-cyberattack

Makarenko, Tamara, "The Crime–Terror Continuum: Tracing the Interplay Between Transnational Organised Crime and Terrorism," *Global Crime*, Vol. 6, No. 1, February 2004, pp. 129–145.

Makarenko, Tamara, and Michael Mesquita, "Categorising the Crime–Terror Nexus in the European Union," *Global Crime*, Vol. 15, No. 3–4, 2014, pp. 259–274.

Mancini, Dominic J., acting administrator, Office of Information and Regulatory Affairs, Office of Management and Budget, "Guidance Implementing Executive Order 13771, Titled 'Reducing Regulation and Controlling Regulatory Costs,'" memorandum for regulatory policy officers at executive departments and agencies and managing and executive directors of certain agencies and commissions, April 5, 2017. As of July 3, 2019:
https://www.whitehouse.gov/sites/whitehouse.gov/files/omb/memoranda/2017/M-17-21-OMB.pdf

Martin Associates, "The 2014 National Economic Impact of the U.S. Coastal Port System," prepared for the American Association of Port Authorities, Lancaster, Pa., March 2015. As of February 6, 2019:
http://aapa.files.cms-plus.com/SeminarPresentations/2015Seminars/2015Spring/US%20Coastal%20Ports%20Impact%20Report%202014%20methodology%20-%20Martin%20Associates%204-21-2015.pdf

Martonosi, Susan E., David S. Ortiz, and Henry H. Willis, "Evaluating the Viability of 100 Per Cent Container Inspection at America's Ports," in Harry W. Richardson, Peter Gordon, and James E. Moore II, eds., *The Economic Impacts of Terrorist Attacks*, Northampton, Mass.: Edward Elgar, 2005, pp. 218–241.

McNeill, Jena Baker, James Jay Carafano, and Jessica Zuckerman, "30 Terrorist Plots Foiled: How the System Worked," Washington, D.C.: Heritage Foundation, Backgrounder 2405, April 29, 2010. As of June 30, 2019:
https://www.heritage.org/terrorism/report/30-terrorist-plots-foiled-how-the-system-worked

Meade, Charles, and Roger C. Molander, *Considering the Effects of a Catastrophic Terrorist Attack*, Santa Monica, Calif.: RAND Corporation, TR-391-CTRMP, 2006. As of July 3, 2019:
https://www.rand.org/pubs/technical_reports/TR391.html

Meierrieks, Daniel, and Friedrich Schneider, "The Short- and Long-Run Relationship Between the Illicit Drug Business and Terrorism," *Applied Economics Letters*, Vol. 23, No. 18, 2016, pp. 1274–1277.

Midgett, Amy, "Latest Developments Regarding TWIC Reader Final Rule," *Coast Guard Maritime Commons: The Coast Guard Blog for Maritime Professionals*, August 3, 2018. As of June 25, 2019:
https://mariners.coastguard.dodlive.mil/2018/08/03/8-3-2018-latest-developments-regarding-twic-reader-final-rule/

Monaco, Kristen, and Lindy Olsson, *Labor at the Ports: A Comparison of the ILA and ILWU*, 2005. As of February 6, 2019:
https://www.metrans.org/sites/default/files/research-project/AR%2004-02_final_draft_0_0.pdf

Monahan, J., "The Individual Risk Assessment of Terrorism," *Psychology, Public Policy, and Law*, Vol. 18, No. 2, 2012, pp. 167–205.

Monks, Kieron, "Piracy Threat Returns to African Waters," CNN, January 3, 2018. As of January 2019:
https://www.cnn.com/2017/05/25/africa/piracy-resurgence-somalia/index.html

Moran, Molly J., acting General Counsel, U.S. Department of Transportation, and Carlos Monje, Assistant Secretary for Transportation Policy, U.S. Department of Transportation, "Guidance on Treatment of the Economic Value of a Statistical Life (VSL) in U.S. Department of Transportation Analyses: 2016 Adjustment," memorandum to secretarial officers and modal administrators, Washington, D.C., August 8, 2016. As of July 1, 2019:
https://www.transportation.gov/office-policy/transportation-policy/revised-departmental-guidance-on-valuation-of-a-statistical-life-in-economic-analysis

Moreau, Ron, "India–Pakistan Tensions Grow in Wake of Attacks," *Newsweek*, November 26, 2008. As of January 29, 2019:
https://www.newsweek.com/india-pakistan-tensions-grow-wake-attacks-85313

Morral, Andrew R., and Brian A. Jackson, *Understanding the Role of Deterrence in Counterterrorism Security*, Santa Monica, Calif.: RAND Corporation, OP-281-RC, 2009. As of June 23, 2019:
https://www.rand.org/pubs/occasional_papers/OP281.html

"Mumbai Terror Attacks Fast Facts," CNN, updated November 12, 2018. As of February 19, 2019:
https://www.cnn.com/2013/09/18/world/asia/mumbai-terror-attacks/index.html

Nash, Kim S., Sara Castellanos, and Adam Janofsky, "One Year After NotPetya Cyberattack, Firms Wrestle with Recovery Costs," *Wall Street Journal*, June 27, 2018. As of January 28, 2019:
https://www.wsj.com/articles/one-year-after-notpetya-companies-still-wrestle-with-financial-impacts-1530095906

National Consortium for Justice Information and Statistics, *Improving the National Instant Background Screening System for Firearms Purchases: Recommendations by SEARCH*, version 2, February 2013. As of July 1, 2019:
http://www.search.org/files/pdf/Improving%20NICS%20for%20Firearms%20Purchases.pdf

National Counterterrorism Center, "Terrorist Identities Datamart Environment (TIDE)," 2017. As of June 23, 2019:
https://www.dni.gov/index.php/nctc-newsroom/nctc-resources/item/1718-terrorist-identities-datamart-environment-tide-fact-sheet-current-as-of-30-june-2016

National Institute of Standards and Technology, *Personal Identity Verification (PIV) of Federal Employees and Contractors*, Federal Information Processing Standards Publication 201-2, August 2013. As of July 23, 2019:
https://csrc.nist.gov/publications/detail/fips/201/2/final

National Memorial Institute for the Prevention of Terrorism, *The MIPT Terrorism Annual: 2006*, Oklahoma City, 2006.

National Research Council, *Review of the Department of Homeland Security's Approach to Risk Analysis*, Washington, D.C.: National Academies Press, 2010. As of July 2, 2019:
https://www.nap.edu/catalog/12972/review-of-the-department-of-homeland-securitys-approach-to-risk-analysis

NCTC—*See* National Counterterrorism Center.

Nero, Mark Edward, "Long Beach Port Terminal Hit by Ransomware Attack," *Press-Telegram* (Long Beach, Calif.), July 24, 2018. As of June 23, 2019:
https://www.presstelegram.com/2018/07/24/long-beach-port-terminal-hit-by-ransomware-attack/

New America, "Terrorism in America After 9/11," undated. As of July 26, 2019:
https://www.newamerica.org/in-depth/terrorism-in-america/

———, "What Is the Threat to the United States?" *Terrorism in America After 9/11*, Washington, D.C., c. 2017. As of June 28, 2019:
https://www.newamerica.org/in-depth/terrorism-in-america/what-threat-united-states-today/

NIST—*See* National Institute of Standards and Technology.

Nowrasteh, Alex, *Terrorism and Immigration: A Risk Analysis*, Washington, D.C.: Cato Institute, Policy Analysis 798, September 13, 2016. As of June 30, 2019:
https://www.cato.org/publications/policy-analysis/terrorism-immigration-risk-analysis

———, *Terrorists by Immigration Status and Nationality: A Risk Analysis, 1975–2017*, Washington, D.C.: Cato Institute, Policy Analysis 866, May 7, 2019. As of June 30, 2019:
https://www.cato.org/publications/policy-analysis/terrorists-immigration-status-nationality-risk-analysis-1975-2017

Obama, Barack, president, "Improving Regulation and Regulatory Review: Executive Order 13563 of January 18, 2011," *Federal Register*, Vol. 76, No. 14, January 21, 2011, pp. 3821–3823. As of July 6, 2019:
https://www.govinfo.gov/app/details/FR-2011-01-21/2011-1385

O'Brien, McKenzie, "Fluctuations Between Crime and Terror: The Case of Abu Sayyaf's Kidnapping Activities," *Terrorism and Political Violence*, Vol. 24, No. 2, 2012, pp. 320–336.

Office of Inspector General, U.S. Department of Homeland Security, *TWIC Background Checks Are Not as Reliable as They Could Be*, OIG-16-128, September 1, 2016. As of June 26, 2019:
https://www.oig.dhs.gov/sites/default/files/assets/Mgmt/2016/OIG-16-128-Sep16.pdf

———, *Review of Coast Guard's Oversight of the TWIC Program*, OIG-18-88, September 28, 2018a. As of January 24, 2019:
https://www.oig.dhs.gov/sites/default/files/assets/2018-10/OIG-18-88-Sep18.pdf

———, *DHS' and TSA's Compliance with Public Law 114-278, Transportation Security Card Program Assessment*, OIG-19-16, December 14, 2018b. As of June 26, 2019:
https://www.oig.dhs.gov/sites/default/files/assets/2018-12/OIG-19-16-Dec18.pdf

Office of Management and Budget, "Regulatory Analysis," Washington, D.C., Circular A-4, September 17, 2003. As of July 1, 2019:
https://obamawhitehouse.archives.gov/omb/circulars_a004_a-4/

Office of Port and Facility Compliance, U.S. Coast Guard, *Policy Advisory Council (PAC) Document Registry*, CG-FAC-2018, February 2018. As of June 23, 2019:
https://homeport.uscg.mil/Lists/Content/DispForm.aspx?ID=2711&Source=/Lists/Content/DispForm.aspx?ID=2711

Office of Standards Evaluation and Development, Standards Evaluation and Analysis Division, U.S. Coast Guard, *Transportation Worker Identification Credential (TWIC)–Reader Requirements: Notice of Proposed Rulemaking—Preliminary Regulatory Analysis and Initial Regulatory Flexibility Analysis*, Washington, D.C., USCG-2007-28915, February 2013. As of August 1, 2019:
https://www.regulations.gov/document?D=USCG-2007-28915-0120

———, *Transportation Worker Identification Credential (TWIC)–Reader Requirements: Final Rule—Regulatory Analysis and Final Regulatory Flexibility Analysis*, Washington, D.C., USCG-2007-28915, November 2015. As of July 28, 2019:
https://www.regulations.gov/document?D=USCG-2007-28915-0231

Office of the Inspector General, U.S. Department of Justice, *Audit of the Federal Bureau of Investigation's Management of Maritime Terrorism Threats*, Audit Division 19-18, March 2019, redacted for public release. As of June 28, 2019:
https://www.oversight.gov/report/doj/audit-federal-bureau-investigations-management-maritime-terrorism-threats

Office of the Secretary, U.S. Department of Homeland Security, "Ammonium Nitrate Security Program," *Federal Register*, Vol. 76, No. 149, August 3, 2011, pp. 46907–46957. As of July 3, 2019:
https://www.govinfo.gov/app/details/FR-2011-08-03/2011-19313

OIG—*See* Office of Inspector General.

Olivier, Roy, *Jihad and Death: The Global Appeal of the Islamic State*, Cynthia Schoch, trans., New York: Oxford University Press, 2017.

OMB—*See* Office of Management and Budget.

"Oregon Gunman Chris Harper Mercer Discharged from US Army," BBC, October 2, 2015. As of January 28, 2019:
https://www.bbc.com/news/world-us-canada-34423534

O'Toole, Alice J., "Psychological and Neural Perspectives on Human Face Recognition," in Stan Z. Li and Anil Jain, eds., *Handbook of Face Recognition*, New York: Springer, 2005, pp. 349–369.

Ousey, Graham C., and Charis E. Kubrin, "Immigration and Crime: Assessing a Contentious Issue," *Annual Review of Criminology*, Vol. 1, 2018, pp. 63–84.

Passel, Jeffrey S., and D'Vera Cohn, "U.S. Unauthorized Immigrant Total Dips to Lowest Level in a Decade," Pew Research Center, November 27, 2018. As of June 30, 2019:
https://www.pewhispanic.org/2018/11/27/u-s-unauthorized-immigrant-total-dips-to-lowest-level-in-a-decade/

Pigeon, Maisie, Emina Sadic, Sean Duncan, Chuck Ridgway, and Kelsey Soeth, *The State of Maritime Piracy 2017: Assessing the Economic and Human Cost*, Broomfield, Colo.: One Earth Future, May 23, 2018. As of June 23, 2019:
http://oceansbeyondpiracy.org/reports/sop

Port Houston, about page, undated. As of June 26, 2019:
https://porthouston.com/about-us/

Port of Los Angeles, "2018 Facts and Figures," c. 2019. As of July 2, 2019:
https://www.portoflosangeles.org/business/statistics/facts-and-figures

Port of San Diego, "Port of San Diego Releases Additional Information on Cybersecurity Incident," press release, September 27, 2018. As of February 12, 2019:
https://www.portofsandiego.org/press-releases/general-press-releases/port-san-diego-releases-additional-information-cybersecurity

Port of South Louisiana, "Overview," undated. As of June 26, 2019:
http://portsl.com/overview/

"Port Security: TWIC Cards Aren't the Answer," *The Dispatcher*, Vol. 67, No. 5, May 2009, pp. 1, 7, 8. As of February 6, 2019:
http://archive.ilwu.org/wp-content/uploads/2015/04/Dispatcher-MAY-09-FINAL-lo-res-Job58364.pdf

Press Secretary, White House, "Statement from the Press Secretary," February 16, 2008. As of June 28, 2019:
https://www.whitehouse.gov/briefings-statements/statement-press-secretary-25/

Public Law 107-56, Uniting and Strengthening America by Providing Appropriate Tools Required to Intercept and Obstruct Terrorism Act of 2001, October 26, 2001. As of June 29, 2019:
https://www.govinfo.gov/app/details/PLAW-107publ56

Public Law 107-71, Aviation and Transportation Security Act, November 19, 2001. As of June 25, 2019:
https://www.govinfo.gov/app/details/PLAW-107publ71

Public Law 107-295, Maritime Transportation Security Act of 2002, November 25, 2002. As of June 23, 2019:
https://www.govinfo.gov/app/details/PLAW-107publ295

Public Law 107-296, Homeland Security Act of 2002, November 25, 2002. As of May 12, 2019:
https://www.govinfo.gov/app/details/PLAW-107publ296

Public Law 109-347, Security and Accountability for Every Port Act of 2006, or the SAFE Port Act, October 13, 2006. As of June 24, 2019:
https://www.govinfo.gov/app/details/PLAW-109publ347

Public Law 110-53, Implementing Recommendations of the 9/11 Commission Act of 2007, August 3, 2007. As of June 29, 2019:
https://www.govinfo.gov/app/details/PLAW-110publ53

Public Law 111-5, American Recovery and Reinvestment Act of 2009, February 17, 2009. As of July 3, 2019:
https://www.govinfo.gov/app/details/PLAW-111publ5

Public Law 114-278, an act to require the Secretary of Homeland Security to prepare a comprehensive security assessment of the transportation security card program and for other purposes, December 16, 2016. As of June 24, 2019:
https://www.govinfo.gov/app/details/PLAW-114publ278

Public Law 115-230, Transportation Worker Identification Credential Accountability Act of 2018, August 2, 2018. As of June 25, 2019:
https://www.govinfo.gov/app/details/PLAW-115publ230

Pyrooz, David C., Gary LaFree, Scott H. Decker, and Patrick A. James, "Cut from the Same Cloth? A Comparative Study of Domestic Extremists and Gang Members in the United States," *Justice Quarterly*, Vol. 35, No. 1, 2018, pp. 1–32.

Rabasa, Angel, Robert D. Blackwill, Peter Chalk, Kim Cragin, C. Christine Fair, Brian A. Jackson, Brian Michael Jenkins, Seth G. Jones, Nathaniel Shestak, and Ashley J. Tellis, *The Lessons of Mumbai*, Santa Monica, Calif.: RAND Corporation, OP-249-RC, 2009. As of June 23, 2019:
https://www.rand.org/pubs/occasional_papers/OP249.html

Rasmussen, Nicholas J., director, National Counterterrorism Center, Office of the Director of National Intelligence, "World Wide Threats: Keeping America Secure in the New Age of Terror," testimony before the U.S. House of Representatives Committee on Homeland Security, November 30, 2017. As of June 28, 2019:
https://docs.house.gov/meetings/HM/HM00/20171130/106651/HHRG-115-HM00-Wstate-RasmussenN-20171130.pdf

Rath, Saroj Kumar, *Fragile Frontiers: The Secret History of Mumbai Terror Attacks*, New Delhi: Routledge, 2014.

Romney, A. Kimball, Susan C. Weller, and William H. Batchelder, "Culture as Consensus: A Theory of Culture and Informant Accuracy," *American Anthropologist*, Vol. 88, No. 2, June 1986, pp. 313–338.

Sadler, Steve, assistant administrator, Transportation Security Administration, U.S. Department of Homeland Security, "TSA's Role in the Transportation Worker Identification Credential (TWIC) Program," statement before the U.S. House of Representatives, Committee on Homeland Security, Subcommittee on Border and Maritime Security, June 18, 2013. As of January 24, 2019:
https://www.tsa.gov/news/testimony/2013/06/18/tsas-role-transportation-worker-identification-credential-twic-program

Sanderson, Thomas M., "Transnational Terror and Organized Crime: Blurring the Lines," *SAIS Review of International Affairs*, Vol. 24, No. 1, Winter–Spring 2004, pp. 49–61.

Saul, Jonathan, "Boat That Attacked Gas Tanker Off Yemen Carried Explosives: Shipowner," Reuters, November 3, 2016. As of January 6, 2019:
https://www.reuters.com/article/us-yemen-shipping-attack/boat-that-attacked-gas-tanker-off-yemen-carried-explosives-shipowner-idUSKBN12Y2L3

———, "Global Shipping Feels Fallout from Maersk Cyber Attack," Reuters, June 29, 2017. As of March 6, 2019:
https://www.reuters.com/article/us-cyber-attack-maersk-idUSKBN19K2LE

Science for Environment Policy, *The Precautionary Principle: Decision-Making Under Uncertainty*, prepared for the Directorate-General of the European Union for Environment and the Science Communication Unit at the University of the West of England, Future Brief 18, 2017. As of July 1, 2019: https://publications.europa.eu/en/publication-detail/-/publication/1c737cfe-beb8-11e7-a7f8-01aa75ed71a1

SEARCH—*See* National Consortium for Justice Information and Statistics.

Secure Technology Alliance, *TWIC® Card/Reader Use with Physical Access Control Systems: A Field Troubleshooting Guide*, version 1.0, May 2018. As of June 23, 2019: https://www.securetechalliance.org/twic-card-reader-challenges-with-physical-access-control-systems-a-field-troubleshooting-guide/

Shannon, Sarah K. S., Christopher Uggen, Jason Schnittker, Melissa Thompson, Sara Wakefield, and Michael Massoglia, "The Growth, Scope, and Spatial Distribution of People with Felony Records in the United States, 1948–2010," *Demography*, Vol. 54, No. 5, October 2017, pp. 1795–1818.

Sharif, Mahmood, Sruti Bhagavatula, Lujo Bauer, and Michael K. Reiter, "Accessorize to a Crime: Real and Stealthy Attacks on State-of-the-Art Face Recognition," *CCS '16: Proceedings of the 2016 ACM SIGSAC Conference on Computer and Communications Security*, 2016, pp. 1528–1540.

Shelley, Louise I., and John T. Picarelli, "Methods and Motives: Exploring Links Between Transnational Organized Crime and International Terrorism," *Trends in Organized Crime*, Vol. 9, No. 2, December 2005, pp. 52–67.

Sieff, Kevin, "Everyone Thought the Somali Pirate Threat Had Ended. Then a Tanker Was Attacked," *Washington Post*, March 15, 2017. As of March 6, 2019: https://www.washingtonpost.com/news/worldviews/wp/2017/03/15/everyone-thought-the-somali-pirate-threat-had-ended-then-a-tanker-was-attacked/

Simon, Jeffrey, *The Implications of the Achille Lauro Hijacking for the Maritime Community*, Santa Monica, Calif.: RAND Corporation, P-7250, 1986. As of June 28, 2019: https://www.rand.org/pubs/papers/P7250.html

Smith, Allison G., *Risk Factors and Indicators Associated with Radicalization to Terrorism in the United States: What Research Sponsored by the National Institute of Justice Tells Us*, Washington, D.C.: U.S. Department of Justice, National Institute of Justice, NCJ 251789, June 2018. As of June 29, 2019: https://www.hsdl.org/?abstract&did=812672

Smith, Meagan, and Sean M. Zeigler, "Terrorism Before and After 9/11: A More Dangerous World?" *Research and Politics*, October–December 2017, pp. 1–8.

Soothill, Keith, and Brian Francis, "When Do Ex-Offenders Become Like Non-Offenders?" *Howard Journal of Criminal Justice*, Vol. 48, No. 4, September 2009, pp. 373–387.

Spalek, Basia, and Salah el-Hassan, "Muslim Converts in Prison," *Howard Journal of Criminal Justice*, Vol. 46, No. 2, May 2007, pp. 99–114.

Stevens, Donald, Terry L. Schell, Thomas Hamilton, Richard Mesic, Michael Scott Brown, Edward W. Chan, Mel Eisman, Eric V. Larson, Marvin Schaffer, Bruce Newsome, John Gibson, and Elwyn Harris, *Near-Term Options for Improving Security at Los Angeles International Airport*, Santa Monica, Calif.: RAND Corporation, DB-468-1-LAWA, 2004. As of July 2, 2019:
https://www.rand.org/pubs/documented_briefings/DB468-1.html

Stewart, Mark G., and John Mueller, "Cost–Benefit Analysis of Advanced Imaging Technology Full Body Scanners for Airline Passenger Security Screening," *Journal of Homeland Security and Emergency Management*, Vol. 8, No. 1, 2011, art. S30.

Stimson Study Group on Counterterrorism Spending, *Protecting America While Promoting Efficiencies and Accountability*," Washington, D.C.: Stimson Center, May 16, 2018. As of June 23, 2019:
https://www.stimson.org/content/counterterrorism-spending-protecting-america-while-promoting-efficiencies-and-accountability

Subcommittee on Border and Maritime Security, Committee on Homeland Security, U.S. House of Representatives, *Threat, Risk, and Vulnerability: The Future of the TWIC Program*, hearing, Serial No. 113-23, June 18, 2013. As of June 23, 2019:
https://www.hsdl.org/?abstract&did=739349

Sunstein, Cass R., "The Limits of Quantification," *California Law Review*, Vol. 102, No. 6, December 2014, pp. 1369–1421.

Terrorist Screening Center, "Frequently Asked Questions," January 2017. As of June 23, 2019:
https://www.fbi.gov/file-repository/terrorist-screening-center-frequently-asked-questions.pdf

"The Rāfidah: From Ibn Saba' to the Dajjāl," *Dābiq*, No. 12, January 2016, p. 3.

"They Plot and Allah Plots," *Dābiq*, No. 9, May 2015, p. 3.

Transportation Security Administration, "TWIC®," undated. As of June 25, 2019:
https://www.tsa.gov/for-industry/twic

———, "Security Threat Assessment for Individuals Applying for a Hazardous Materials Endorsement for a Commercial Driver's License," interim final rule and request for comments, *Federal Register*, Vol. 69, No. 226, November 24, 2004, pp. 68719–68749. As of June 28, 2019:
https://www.govinfo.gov/app/details/FR-2004-11-24/04-26066

———, "Provisions for Fees Related to Hazardous Materials Endorsements and Transportation Worker Identification Credentials," *Federal Register*, Vol. 78, No. 80, April 25, 2013, pp. 24353–24360. As of June 23, 2019:
https://www.govinfo.gov/app/details/FR-2013-04-25/2013-09732

———, "Aircraft Repair Station Security," *Federal Register*, Vol. 79, No. 8, January 13, 2014, pp. 2119–2143. As of July 3, 2019:
https://www.govinfo.gov/app/details/FR-2014-01-13/2014-00415

———, business year 2018 Transportation Worker Identification Credential business case provided to the authors, August 15, 2016a.

———, "TWIC® Factsheet," October 2016b.

———, Transportation Worker Identification Credential program brief, October 31, 2016c.

———, "Transportation Worker Identification Credential (TWIC® Program)," briefing to the Delaware Bay Joint Area Committee/Area Maritime Security Committee, February 15, 2017a.

———, "Revision of Agency Information Collection Activity Under OMB Review: Transportation Worker Identification Credential (TWIC®) Program," *Federal Register*, Vol. 82, No. 53, March 21, 2017b, p. 14521–14522. As of June 23, 2019:
https://www.govinfo.gov/app/details/FR-2017-03-21/2017-05534

———, *Transportation Worker Identification Credential Appeal Timelines Fiscal Year 2019 Report to Congress*, February 1, 2019.

Transportation Security Administration and U.S. Coast Guard, "Transportation Worker Identification Credential (TWIC) Implementation in the Maritime Sector; Hazardous Materials Endorsement for a Commercial Driver's License," *Federal Register*, Vol. 71, No. 98, May 22, 2006, p. 29395–29462. As of June 23, 2019:
https://www.govinfo.gov/app/details/FR-2006-05-22/06-4508

———, "Transportation Worker Identification Credential (TWIC) Implementation in the Maritime Sector; Hazardous Materials Endorsement for a Commercial Driver's License," *Federal Register*, Vol. 72, No. 16, January 25, 2007a, pp. 3491–3604. As of August 1, 2019:
https://www.govinfo.gov/app/details/FR-2007-01-25/07-19

———, "Transportation Worker Identification Credential (TWIC) Implementation in the Maritime Sector; Hazardous Materials Endorsement for a Commercial Driver's License," *Federal Register*, Vol. 72, No. 188, September 28, 2007b, pp. 55043–55049. As of August 1, 2019:
https://www.govinfo.gov/app/details/FR-2007-09-28/07-4750

Transportation Worker Identification Credential/Maritime Transportation Security Act Policy Advisory Council, U.S. Coast Guard, "Redefining Secure Areas and Acceptable Access Control," Policy 01-08, January 7, 2008.

———, "Incorporating TWIC into Existing Physical Access Control Systems," Policy Letter 08-09, July 15, 2009.

Trump, Donald J., president, "Reducing Regulation and Controlling Regulatory Costs: Executive Order 13771 of January 30, 2017," *Federal Register*, Vol. 82, No. 22, February 3, 2017, pp. 9339–9341. As of July 7, 2019:
https://www.govinfo.gov/app/details/FR-2017-02-03/2017-02451

TSA—*See* Transportation Security Administration.

"TWIC Flunks Latest Test," *The Dispatcher*, Vol. 71, No. 6, June 2013, pp. 1,6. As of February 6, 2019:
http://archive.ilwu.org/wp-content/uploads/2015/04/DispatcherJUNE2013lores.pdf

TWIC/MTSA Policy Advisory Council—*See* Transportation Worker Identification Credential/Maritime Transportation Security Act Policy Advisory Council.

Universal Enroll, "About," undated a. As of November 4, 2018:
https://universalenroll.dhs.gov/about

———, "TWIC Canceled Card Lists," undated b (updated daily). As of June 26, 2019:
https://universalenroll.dhs.gov/canceled-card-lists

Unnithan, Sandeep, "Why India Didn't Strike Pakistan After 26/11," *Yahoo! News*, October 20, 2015. As of January 28, 2019:
https://in.news.yahoo.com/why-india-didnt-strike-pakistan-221055284.html

U.S. Census Bureau, 2010 Census of Population, P94-171 redistricting data file, undated. As of July 1, 2018:
https://www.census.gov/quickfacts/fact/table/US/PST045218

———, "Foreign Trade," last revised June 11, 2019. As of February 6, 2019:
https://www.census.gov/foreign-trade/reference/products/catalog/usatradeonline.html

U.S. Coast Guard, "U.S. Coast Guard Maritime Security (MARSEC) Levels," undated. As of June 26, 2019:
https://www.uscg.mil/what-is-marsec/

———, "Transportation Worker Identification Credential (TWIC) Implementation in the Maritime Sector; Hazardous Materials Endorsement for a Commercial Driver's License," final rule and request for comments, *Federal Register*, Vol. 72, No. 16, January 25, 2007, pp. 3491–3604. As of June 23, 2019:
https://www.govinfo.gov/app/details/FR-2007-01-25/07-19

———, "Privacy Impact Assessment for the Marine Information for Safety and Law Enforcement (MISLE)," DHS/USCG/PIA-008, September 3, 2009. As of June 23, 2019:
https://www.dhs.gov/publication/dhsuscgpia-008-marine-information-safety-and-law-enforcement-misle

———, "Transportation Worker Identification Credential (TWIC)–Reader Requirements," *Federal Register*, Vol. 78, No. 56, March 22, 2013, pp. 17781–17833. As of July 1, 2019:
https://www.govinfo.gov/app/details/FR-2013-03-22/2013-06182

———, "Transportation Worker Identification Credential (TWIC)–Reader Requirements," *Federal Register*, Vol. 81, No. 163, August 23, 2016, pp. 57652–57713. As of June 23, 2019:
https://www.govinfo.gov/app/details/FR-2016-08-23/2016-19383

———, *MSRAM 2018 User Manual*, c. 2018a, Not available to the general public.

———, "TWIC-Reader Requirements; Delay of Effective Date," *Federal Register*, Vol. 23, No. 121, June 22, 2018b, pp. 29067–29081. As of June 23, 2019:
https://www.govinfo.gov/app/details/FR-2018-06-22/2018-13345

U.S. Coast Guard and Transportation Security Administration, "Transportation Worker Identification Credential Program (TWIC) Implementation in the Maritime Sector; Hazardous Materials Endorsement for a Commercial Driver's License," *Federal Register*, Vol. 72, No. 188, September 28, 2007, pp. 55043–55049. As of June 23, 2019:
https://www.govinfo.gov/app/details/FR-2007-09-28/07-4750

———, "Transportation Worker Identification Credential (TWIC) Implementation in the Maritime Sector; Hazardous Materials Endorsement for a Commercial Driver's License," *Federal Register*, Vol. 73, No. 89, May 7, 2008, pp. 25562–25566. As of June 25, 2019:
https://www.govinfo.gov/app/details/FR-2008-05-07/E8-10232

U.S. Code, Title 6, Domestic Security; Chapter 1, Homeland Security Organization; Subchapter III, Science and Technology in Support of Homeland Security; Section 185, Federally Funded Research and Development Centers. As of May 12, 2019:
https://www.govinfo.gov/app/details/USCODE-2017-title6/USCODE-2017-title6-chap1-subchapIII-sec185

———, Title 6, Domestic Security; Chapter 1, Homeland Security Organization; Subchapter VIII, Coordination with Non-Federal Entities, Inspector General, United States Secret Service, Coast Guard, General Provisions; Part H, Miscellaneous Provisions; Section 469, Fees for Credentialing and Background Investigations in Transportation. As of February 1, 2019: https://www.govinfo.gov/app/details/USCODE-2017-title6/USCODE-2017-title6-chap1-subchapVIII-partH-sec469

———, Title 18, Crimes and Criminal Procedure; Part I, Crimes; Chapter 12, Civil Disorders; Section 232, Definitions. As of July 6, 2019: https://www.govinfo.gov/app/details/USCODE-2017-title18/USCODE-2017-title18-partI-chap12-sec232

———, Title 18, Crimes and Criminal Procedure; Part I, Crimes; Chapter 40, Importation, Manufacture, Distribution and Storage of Explosive Materials; Section 841, Definitions. As of July 6, 2019: https://www.govinfo.gov/app/details/USCODE-2017-title18/USCODE-2017-title18-partI-chap40-sec841

———, Title 18, Crimes and Criminal Procedure; Part I, Crimes; Chapter 40, Importation, Manufacture, Distribution and Storage of Explosive Materials; Section 844, Penalties. As of July 6, 2019: https://www.govinfo.gov/app/details/USCODE-2017-title18/USCODE-2017-title18-partI-chap40-sec844

———, Title 18, Crimes and Criminal Procedure; Part I, Crimes; Chapter 44, Firearms; Section 921, Definitions. As of July 6, 2019: https://www.govinfo.gov/app/details/USCODE-2017-title18/USCODE-2017-title18-partI-chap44-sec921

———, Title 18, Crimes and Criminal Procedure; Part I, Crimes; Chapter 47, Fraud and False Statements; Section 1036, Entry by False Pretenses to Any Real Property, Vessel, or Aircraft of the United States or Secure Area of Any Airport or Seaport. As of July 6, 2019: https://www.govinfo.gov/app/details/USCODE-2017-title18/USCODE-2017-title18-partI-chap47-sec1036

———, Title 18, Crimes and Criminal Procedure; Part I, Crimes; Chapter 96, Racketeer Influenced and Corrupt Organizations; Section 1961, Definitions. As of July 6, 2019: https://www.govinfo.gov/app/details/USCODE-2017-title18/USCODE-2017-title18-partI-chap96-sec1961

————, Title 18, Crimes and Criminal Procedure; Part I, Crimes; Chapter 113B, Terrorism; Section 2332b, Acts of Terrorism Transcending National Boundaries. As of June 29, 2019: https://www.govinfo.gov/app/details/USCODE-2017-title18/USCODE-2017-title18-partI-chap113B-sec2332b

————, Title 26, Internal Revenue Code; Subtitle E, Alcohol, Tobacco, and Certain Other Excise Taxes; Chapter 53, Machine Guns, Destructive Devices, and Certain Other Firearms; Subchapter B, General Provisions and Exemptions; Part I, General Provisions; Section 5845, Definitions. As of July 6, 2019: https://www.govinfo.gov/app/details/USCODE-2017-title26/USCODE-2017-title26-subtitleE-chap53-subchapB-partI-sec5845

————, Title 46, Shipping; Subtitle VII, Security and Drug Enforcement; Chapter 701, Port Security; Subchapter I, General; Section 70101, Definitions. As of June 24, 2019: https://www.govinfo.gov/app/details/USCODE-2017-title46/USCODE-2017-title46-subtitleVII-chap701-subchapI-sec70101

————, Title 46, Shipping; Subtitle VII, Security and Drug Enforcement; Chapter 701, Port Security; Subchapter I, General; Section 70105, Transportation Security Cards. As of June 24, 2019: https://www.govinfo.gov/app/details/USCODE-2017-title46/USCODE-2017-title46-subtitleVII-chap701-subchapI-sec70105

————, Title 49, Transportation; Subtitle III, General and Intermodal Programs; Chapter 51, Transportation of Hazardous Material; Section 5124, Criminal Penalty. As of July 6, 2019: https://www.govinfo.gov/app/details/USCODE-2017-title49/USCODE-2017-title49-subtitleIII-chap51-sec5124

————, Title 49, Transportation; Subtitle VII, Aviation Programs; Part A, Air Commerce and Safety; Subpart iii, Safety; Chapter 449, Security; Subchapter II, Administration and Personnel; Section 44936, Employment Investigations and Restrictions. As of July 26, 2019: https://www.govinfo.gov/app/details/USCODE-2009-title49/USCODE-2009-title49-subtitleVII-partA-subpartiii-chap449-subchapII-sec44936

U.S. Customs and Border Protection, "Air Cargo Advance Screening (ACAS)," *Federal Register*, Vol. 83, No. 113, June 12, 2018, pp. 27380–27407. As of July 3, 2019: https://www.govinfo.gov/app/details/FR-2018-06-12/2018-12315

U.S. Customs and Border Protection and Bureau of Consular Affairs, U.S. Department of State, "Documents Required for Travelers Departing from or Arriving in the United States at Sea and Land Ports-of-Entry from Within the Western Hemisphere," *Federal Register*, Vol. 73, No. 65, April 3, 2008, pp. 18383–18420. As of July 2, 2019: https://www.govinfo.gov/app/details/FR-2008-04-03/E8-6725

U.S. Department of Homeland Security, *The National Security Strategy for Maritime Security*, Washington, D.C., September 2005. As of June 23, 2019:
http://purl.access.gpo.gov/GPO/LPS119037

———, *Small Vessel Security Strategy*, DHS 20080307, revision 1.4, April 2008. As of June 23, 2019:
https://www.dhs.gov/publication/small-vessel-security-strategy

———, *DHS Lexicon Terms and Definitions*, Instruction Manual 262-12-001-01, October 16, 2017. As of June 23, 2019:
https://www.hsdl.org/?abstract&did=820128

U.S. Department of the Treasury, "Specially Designated Nationals and Blocked Persons List (SDN) Human Readable Lists," last updated June 28, 2019. As of June 29, 2019:
https://www.treasury.gov/resource-center/sanctions/sdn-list/pages/default.aspx

U.S. Government Accountability Office, *Port Security: Better Planning Needed to Develop and Operate Maritime Worker Identification Card Program*, Washington, D.C., GAO-05-106, December 10, 2004. As of June 23, 2019:
https://www.gao.gov/products/GAO-05-106

———, *Transportation Security: DHS Should Address Key Challenges Before Implementing the Transportation Worker Identification Credential Program*, Washington, D.C., GAO-06-982, September 29, 2006. As of June 23, 2019:
https://www.gao.gov/products/GAO-06-982

———, *Transportation Security: DHS Efforts to Eliminate Redundant Background Check Investigations*, Washington, D.C., GAO-07-756, April 26, 2007. As of June 23, 2019:
https://www.gao.gov/products/GAO-07-756

———, *Transportation Worker Identification Credential: Progress Made in Enrolling Workers and Activating Credentials but Evaluation Plan Needed to Help Inform the Implementation of Card Readers*, Washington, D.C., GAO-10-43, November 18, 2009. As of June 23, 2019:
https://www.gao.gov/products/GAO-10-43

———, *Transportation Worker Identification Credential: Internal Control Weaknesses Need to Be Corrected to Help Achieve Security Objectives*, Washington, D.C., GAO-11-657, May 10, 2011a. As of July 27, 2019:
https://www.gao.gov/products/GAO-11-657

———, *Transportation Security: Actions Needed to Address Limitations in TSA's Transportation Worker Security Threat Assessments and Growing Workload*, Washington, D.C., GAO-12-60, December 8, 2011b. As of June 23, 2019:
https://www.gao.gov/products/GAO-12-60

―――, *Transportation Worker Identification Credential: Card Reader Pilot Results Are Unreliable; Security Benefits Need to Be Reassessed*, Washington, D.C., GAO-13-198, May 8, 2013a. As of July 3, 2019:
https://www.gao.gov/products/GAO-13-198

―――, *Transportation Security: Action Needed to Strengthen TSA's Security Threat Assessment Process*, Washington, D.C., GAO-13-629, July 19, 2013b. As of June 23, 2019:
https://www.gao.gov/products/GAO-13-629

―――, *Standards for Internal Control in the Federal Government*, Washington, D.C., GAO-14-704G, September 10, 2014. As of June 26, 2019:
https://www.gao.gov/products/GAO-14-704G

―――, *Criminal History Records: Additional Actions Could Enhance the Completeness of Records Used for Employment-Related Background Checks*, Washington, D.C., GAO-15-162, February 12, 2015. As of June 30, 2019:
https://www.gao.gov/products/GAO-15-162

U.S. House of Representatives, *Aviation and Transportation Security Act*, Washington, D.C., House Report 107-296, November 16, 2001. As of June 25, 2019:
https://www.govinfo.gov/app/details/CRPT-107hrpt296/CRPT-107hrpt296

U.S. Senate, "Maritime Transportation Security Act of 2002: Conference Report," *Congressional Record*, Vol. 148, No. 147, November 14, 2002, pp. S10973–S11032. As of July 26, 2019:
https://www.congress.gov/congressional-record/2002/11/14

―――, "Improving America's Security Act of 2007," *Congressional Record*, Vol. 153, Part 4, February 28, 2007, pp. 4862–4920. As of July 26, 2019:
https://www.govinfo.gov/app/details/CRECB-2007-pt4/CRECB-2007-pt4-Pg4862-2

―――, TSA Modernization Act, Bill 1872, 115th Congress, placed on legislative calendar under general orders, June 6, 2018. As of July 4, 2019:
https://www.congress.gov/bill/115th-congress/senate-bill/1872

USA Trade, "USA Trade Online," undated. As of July 6, 2019:
https://usatrade.census.gov/

USCG—*See* U.S. Coast Guard.

USCG and TSA—*See* U.S. Coast Guard and Transportation Security Administration.

Useem, Bert, "U.S. Prisons and the Myth of Islamic Terrorism," *Contexts*, Vol. 11, No. 2, 2012, pp. 34–39.

Useem, Bert, and Obie Clayton, "Radicalization of U.S. Prisoners," *Criminology and Public Policy*, Vol. 8, No. 3, August 2009, pp. 561–592.

Vidino, Lorenzo, Francesco Marone, and Eva Entenmann, *Fear Thy Neighbor: Radicalization and Jihadist Attacks in the West*, the Hague: International Centre for Counter-Terrorism, June 14, 2017. As of June 28, 2019:
https://icct.nl/publication/fear-thy-neighbor-radicalization-and-jihadist-attacks-in-the-west/

White, David, Richard I. Kemp, Rob Jenkins, Michael Matheson, and A. Mike Burton, "Passport Officers' Errors in Face Matching," *PLoS ONE*, Vol. 9, No. 8, 2014, e103510.

Wiener, Jonathan B., and Michael D. Rogers, "Comparing Precaution in the United States and Europe," *Journal of Risk Research*, Vol. 5, No. 4, 2002, pp. 317–349. As of July 1, 2019:
https://scholarship.law.duke.edu/faculty_scholarship/1191/

Williams, Heather J., Nathan Chandler, and Eric Robinson, *Trends in the Draw of Americans to Foreign Terrorist Organizations from 9/11 to Today*, Santa Monica, Calif.: RAND Corporation, RR-2545-OSD, 2018. As of June 28, 2019:
https://www.rand.org/pubs/research_reports/RR2545.html

Williams, Jacqueline, "Australia Details 'Sophisticated' Plot by ISIS to Take Down Plane," *New York Times*, August 4, 2017. As of June 28, 2019:
https://www.nytimes.com/2017/08/04/world/australia/sydney-airport-terror-plot-isis.html

Willis, Henry H., and Tom LaTourrette, "Using Probabilistic Terrorism Risk Modeling for Regulatory Benefit–Cost Analysis: Application to the Western Hemisphere Travel Initiative in the Land Environment," *Risk Analysis*, Vol. 28, No. 2, April 2008, pp. 325–339.

Willis, Henry H., Andrew R. Morral, Terrence Kelly, and Jamison Jo Medby, *Estimating Terrorism Risk*, Santa Monica, Calif.: RAND Corporation, MG-388-RC, 2005. As of July 2, 2019:
https://www.rand.org/pubs/monographs/MG388.html

Wood, Graeme, "The American Climbing the Ranks of ISIS," *The Atlantic*, March 2017. As of June 29, 2019:
https://www.theatlantic.com/magazine/archive/2017/03/the-american-leader-in-the-islamic-state/510872/

Zong, Jie, Jeanne Batalova, and Micayla Burrows, "Frequently Requested Statistics on Immigrants and Immigration in the United States," Washington, D.C.: Migration Policy Institute, March 14, 2019. As of June 30, 2019:
https://www.migrationpolicy.org/article/frequently-requested-statistics-immigrants-and-immigration-united-states